Arthur John Maclean

East Syrian Daily Offices

Arthur John Maclean

East Syrian Daily Offices

ISBN/EAN: 9783743393882

Manufactured in Europe, USA, Canada, Australia, Japa

Cover: Foto ©Lupo / pixelio.de

Manufactured and distributed by brebook publishing software (www.brebook.com)

Arthur John Maclean

East Syrian Daily Offices

Publications of the Eastern Church Association

Crown 8vo. 8s. 6d.

1. **EAST SYRIAN DAILY OFFICES**

A. J. MACLEAN, M.A., Dean of Argyll and the Isles

In Preparation

2. **RUSSIA AND THE ENGLISH CHURCH DURING THE LAST FIFTY YEARS**

W. J. BIRKBECK, Magdalen College, Oxford

In Preparation

REPORT FOR 1893

LONDON: RIVINGTON, PERCIVAL & CO.

East Syrian Daily Offices

TRANSLATED FROM THE SYRIAC
WITH INTRODUCTION, NOTES, AND INDICES
AND AN APPENDIX
CONTAINING THE LECTIONARY AND GLOSSARY

BY

ARTHUR JOHN MACLEAN, M.A.

DEAN OF ARGYLL AND THE ISLES
JOINT-AUTHOR OF
'THE CATHOLICOS OF THE EAST AND HIS PEOPLE'

PUBLISHED FOR THE
EASTERN CHURCH ASSOCIATION

RIVINGTON, PERCIVAL & CO.
KING STREET, COVENT GARDEN
LONDON
1894

DEDICATED TO

MY FORMER FELLOW-WORKERS

AT URMI

PREFACE

IN presenting the first publication of the revived Eastern Church Association to its members, a few words are, perhaps, necessary to explain the object in view. The aim of the Association is to disseminate as accurate information as is possible about the Eastern Churches, whether concerning their history and formal teaching or their actual condition. The time is gone by when it is wise to be satisfied with half-truths or incorrect and one-sided information. There are no books which show more accurately the historical and doctrinal position of a Church than its Liturgies and other services. It is hoped, therefore, that the publication of this work will help to give a clear idea of the formal and professed teaching of what is by no means the least interesting of the separated Churches of the East—one, too, which the Archbishop of Canterbury's Mission has made familiar to many English Churchmen.

If these prayers can in any way add to the body of modern devotional literature any fresh element which may correct some popular tendencies, it will be a further gain to the Church.

Our best thanks are due to the Dean of Argyll and the Isles for putting at the disposal of the Association his translation of these offices, and for the care he has taken to render them into dignified and stately English.

A. C. HEADLAM,
Secretary of the Eastern Church Association.

February 1st, 1894.

CONTENTS

	PAGE
INTRODUCTION,	vii
FERIAL EVENING SERVICE, WEEK 'BEFORE,' WITH THE MARTYRS' ANTHEMS,	1
FERIAL EVENING SERVICE, WEEK 'AFTER,'	55
FESTIVAL EVENING SERVICE,	68
FERIAL NIGHT SERVICE,	85
FERIAL MORNING SERVICE,	103
Martyrs' Anthems for Week-day Mornings,	109
MOTWA FOR WEDNESDAYS AT THE NIGHT SERVICE,	130
FESTIVAL NIGHT SERVICE,	151
Feasts of our Lord,	152
Sundays,	155
Memorials of Saints,	163
FESTIVAL MORNING SERVICE,	165
Martyrs' Anthem for Sunday Mornings,	172
COMPLINE,	185
THE SERVICES IN THE FAST—	
Sundays,	205
Weeks of the mysteries,	211
Ordinary weeks,	220
Prayer at noon,	224

An Occasional Karuzutha,	225
Rogation of the Ninevites,	226
Blessing of the Months,	229
Farcings of the Psalms,	236
Prayers on various occasions,	249
Indices to the Psalms,	259
Appendix—	
The Kalendar and Lectionary.	264
Index to the Lectionary,	284
Glossary,	291

INTRODUCTION

THE present work is a translation of the daily offices of the Eastern Syrians, who are also known as Nestorians. Their liturgies, baptismal office, and ordination service have long been given to the Western reader in the translations of Renaudot, Badger, and Denzinger. But as far as the writer of these pages knows, the daily offices have never been translated; and he desires, therefore, to present an English version of the complete non-liturgical services as far as they are contained in the East Syrian Psalter, and in the books known as *Qdhamuwathar* ('Before and after') and *Ṭakhsa* ('Order'), a description of which is appended to this Introduction. These books contain, with very few exceptions, the whole of the ferial offices, and also the Sunday and festival offices, as far as they do not vary with the season or the day. The parts of the service proper to seasons and holy days are contained in the books known as *Khudhra* ('Cycle'), *Geza* or *Gaza* ('Treasury'), and *Kashkul* ('containing all'), three immense volumes, which it is impossible to translate if the limits proposed in this book are to be adhered to. But what is here given will be enough to show the nature of the daily services.

It must be borne in mind that Eastern office books differ greatly from Western in having no 'Order of

Morning and Evening Prayer.' There is no arrangement, there are very few rubricks; the different parts of the service have to be sought for in different books, and the best-known parts of the service are traditional. The office books printed by the Archbishop of Canterbury's Mission at Urmi and by that of the Lazarists, which are described below, remedy this defect to a certain extent by giving the traditional arrangement. This translation follows these authorities, noting the points where they differ; and where they fail to be explicit (as happens not unfrequently), recourse has been had to information obtained from personal inquiries during a sojourn among the East Syrians. But the indulgence of all who remember the complication of the subject, the difference of usages, the chaotic state of the manuscripts, and the inherent dislike of being cross-examined which exists in every Oriental mind, is asked for this attempt to put before the European reader an orderly view of the East Syrian services.

The *Sunhadus*, or Book of Canon Law, orders four[1] services in the day for all men—the Evening Service, Compline, the Night Service, and the Morning Service. The first and last it recognises as having the greatest authority, and their length, it says, is not to be added to or taken from; but the other two are to be 'according to the rule of the monastery,' and there is no limit as to their length or shortness for laymen (v. § 2).

---

[1] There are also relics of Terce and Sext in the Fast (pages 219, 224). The *Sunhadus* orders seven hours of prayer for monks and for 'good priests and laymen' (Book vi. § 1).

Compline is now almost obsolete, except on certain days of the year, when it is usually joined on to the Evening Service.

The following is the structure of each of the three principal services :—

Evening Service.

Glory be to God, etc. Kiss of peace. Lord's prayer, farced.

Evening collect, different for (*a*) Sundays and festivals of our Lord ('feasts'); (*b*) saints' days ('memorials') and ferias.

First Marmitha[1] (psalms), different for (*a*) the various days of the week, one for each; (*b*) for memorials falling on Fridays; (*c*) for other memorials; (*d*) for feasts and Sundays, Advent to Epiphany; (*e*) for other feasts and Sundays.

Second Marmitha, ferias only, varying with the day of the week.

Collect, (*a*) Sundays and feasts; (*b*) memorials [not ferias].[2]

Prayer of incense, said by all, farced [not ferias;[2] on feasts five times, on Sun. and mem. thrice].

Collect of the censer [not ferias].[2]

Lakhumara (ascription of praise, said by all), farced, with collect preceding and following.

First Shuraya (short psalm), varies (*a*) on ferias with the day of the week, and according as the week is 'before' or 'after';[3] and (*b*) with the number of the Sunday in each Shawu'a (division of the year) [not feasts and memorials].

First Anthem, (*a*) varies on ferias as first Shuraya; (*b*) is fixed for Sundays [not said in the fast[4]].

---

[1] See Glossary for technical terms. It has seemed better to transliterate these into English than to borrow parallel technical terms from the Greek or other rituals.

[2] In practice these three are in some places used daily.

[3] See below, page xvi.

[4] The services in the fast partake of the nature both of the ferial and of the festival offices. For their structure see page 205.

Fixed collect, four invariable psalms, and another fixed collect.

Second Shuraya, varies as the first.

Second Anthem, varies as the first.

Karuzutha (Litany) in two parts, said by the deacon, with special suffrages on Sundays, feasts, and memorials.

Fixed collect. Deacon's interjection. Holy God, said by all, farced with Gloria. Collect, (*a*) Sundays and feasts; (*b*) memorials and ferias. Deacon's interjection, etc.

Suyakhi (additional psalms), with two collects, feasts and memorials only.

Collect, (*a*) feasts; (*b*) Sundays and ferias.

Royal Anthem (Sundays, feasts, memorials), proper for the day, the last two verses being the same for each Sunday of a Shawu'a; or *Evening Anthem* (ferias), varying according to season, or only according to the day of the week.

Collect, (*a*) on ferias fixed, but distinct ones for Wed. and Fri.; (*b*) on Sundays, etc., proper to season or day.

Letter psalm (portion of cxix.) (M., T., Th., Sa.), or *Third Shuraya* (Sun., W., F., feasts, mem.), varying according to day of week on ferias, and according as week is 'before' or 'after'; otherwise according to season.

Lord's Prayer, farced. Two fixed collects.

Suba'a (Compline), on memorials and in the fast,[1] with one collect preceding and two following.

Martyrs' Anthem [in practice, ferias only], one for each day of the week, and two collects.

One or more fixed collects for help, according to the number of priests present, one for each; three fixed collects; Blessing, Kiss of peace, and Nicene Creed.

Night Service.

Glory be to God, etc. Kiss of peace. Lord's prayer, farced. Deacon's interjection.

---

[1] See Note 4, preceding page. By this term the great fast is always meant.

Collect, (a) Sundays and feasts; (b) ferias and memorials, and two fixed collects, with response after each of the three.

The Psalms (one-third of the psalter on ferias and Sundays, one-seventh on memorials, the whole on feasts), with appropriate collects. On feasts the psalms are said in three portions, with parts of the Motwa between, and a proper Canon, Tishbukhta, and Karuzutha, with collects and Madrasha (doctrinal hymn).

Qaltha (short psalm), on days when the liturgy is to be said, preceded by fixed collect (but not feasts and memorials).

Collect, (a) Sundays; (b) feasts and memorials; (c) ferias.

The Motwa (anthem sung sitting) varies with the season and day, except on Wednesdays, when special anthems are said, one for weeks 'before,' one for weeks 'after,' but the ending is the same for both weeks. On other ferias the last verse is invariable.

Proper *collect, Canon, Tishbukhta* on memorials; on Sundays, *collect of the season*, three fixed *Tishbukhyatha*.

Proper *Karuzutha* and *Madrasha*, with collects (Sun., mem.).

Suyakhi (two additional hulali), on Sundays, with collects.

Qali d'Shahra, an additional hulala on Sundays, feasts, and memorials (as noted in Geza), with collects prefixed to each Marmitha.

Night Anthem, with collects (Sun., feasts, mem.) proper for day, the two last verses on Sundays being invariable.

Collect and Shubakha (short psalm, proper for the day), on Sundays only; *collect and Canon* (proper for the day), on feasts and memorials; *collect and Shubakha*, on ferias, one for each week-day.

Tishbukhta, on Sundays fixed; on feasts proper; on memorials as on ferial Fridays; on ferias, one for each week-day.

Karuzutha, (a) Sun., feasts, mem., and in the fast in the 'weeks of the mysteries'; (b) ferias. On some days a special Karuzutha is appointed.

Morning Service.

Two collects, (*a*) Sun., feasts, mem. ; (*b*) ferias.

Nine fixed psalms, with three collects, two of which are different on ferias and Sundays, feasts, memorials. The psalms are farced more simply on ferias than on other days.

Collect and *Morning Anthem* proper for day, with last verses invariable [Sun., feasts, mem.] ; collect and *Lakhumara* [ferias].

Collect and Ps. li. 1-18 [ferias].

Collect and fixed *Tishbukhta,* (*a*) Sun., mem., feasts ; (*b*) ferias. No collect on ferias.

Another *Tishbukhta* [Sun., feasts, mem.].

Benedicite [Sun., feasts, mem.].

Collect and *Gloria in Excelsis* [Sun., feasts], or collect of the season and proper *Tishbukhta* [mem.].

Collect, (*a*) Sundays and feasts ; (*b*) memorials ; (*c*) ferias.

Deacon's interjection, and Holy God, said by all (farced) ; Lord's prayer (farced). Kiss of peace (not ferias ?).

Two collects, (*a*) Sundays and feasts ; (*b*) memorials and ferias, with an extra collect on Sundays when the Martyrs' Anthem is said.

The *Martyrs' Anthem,* one for each morning of the week [in practice, ferias only].

Two fixed *Morning Anthems* [ferias].

Two collects when the Martyrs' Anthem has been said.

One or more fixed collects for help, and the rest as at the Evening Service.

The special feature of the Evening Service is that it has different forms for different weeks. Each week is called either 'before' or 'after,'[1] according as the first or second choir begins the service, and there is a different

---

[1] Or 'first' and 'last.' If the first choir begins one anthem, psalm, or hymn, the second choir begins the next, and so on alternately.

Evening Service for each day of each of these two weeks. The Morning Service, on the other hand, is in the main invariable throughout the year, although the festival and ferial services differ. The special feature of the Night Service, which is a very long one, and (if said at all) is joined on to the Morning Service, is the recitation of the psalter. Although several psalms are said at the other services, yet at the Night Service the psalter is recited complete, one-third on each week-day, so that the whole is said in full twice a week; on feasts of our Lord it is said complete; on Sundays and other holy days selections are made. It has been pointed out that this is approximately the Lenten arrangement of the Holy Eastern Church, which at other times of the year recites the psalter once only in the week.[1] The division of the psalter into twenty *hulali* (to which a twenty-first is added, made up of certain Old Testament canticles) also recalls the twenty καθίσματα of the Greeks. Two beautiful features in the East Syrian recitation of the psalms are the appropriate collects before each subdivision of the *hulali*, gathering up the thoughts of the psalms, and the *giyuri*, or 'farcings,' of each psalm, clauses introduced after the first or the first and second clauses, and at the end of the psalm, usually giving it a Christian application. In practice the psalms are said on week-days in monotone and antiphonally, one person on each side, not necessarily a priest or deacon, taking each clause. They are recited very rapidly. On Sundays and festivals several psalms are sung.

We must specially notice the anthems, of which

---

[1] W. J. B. in the *Guardian*, Nov. 4th, 1891, pp. 1783-4.

there are a large number at the various services. These are in metre, and are divided into verses or stanzas, each with the same number of lines—in some cases as few as two, in some as many as fourteen; and these lines roughly scan and occasionally rhyme. Before each verse or collection of verses is placed a clause, usually from the psalter, which is sung in monotone, and which gives it its keynote; this seems to be an unique feature. The two choirs sing the verses alternately to a chant. In this book the places where the choirs change are noted by an asterisk, and the lines of the verses are marked by full stops. The chants to which these anthems are sung are purely traditional, and are not written down. In the books we find names of tunes, but these are not more than names; and we also find a few passages in the manuscripts marked with lines in red ink, one, two, or three, which are said to be musical directions. These anthems are sung by all persons who can read Old Syriac —that is, generally speaking, by all who can read at all; for the people have a great idea of congregational worship, although the musical effect is not all that might be desired. Those who cannot read cannot, of course, join in the singing; but there are certain portions of the service, such as the Lord's Prayer, the *Lakhumara*, Holy God, and Nicene Creed, which all can say. The collects and 'conclusions,' or blessings, can be said by priests only; and if none are present, they are entirely omitted. Those who cannot join in the anthems give expression to their devotion by frequent prostrations and ejaculations. In the congregational character of their services, therefore, the East Syrians resemble the

Russians rather than the Greeks, amongst whom the people remain silent. On the subject of these anthems it may be remarked that of all parts of the daily offices they are the most Eastern in tone. They are expressed in poetry, and are as different as possible from the logical and somewhat prosaic formularies of our own Communion and of the Church of Rome. They must be judged, therefore, as poetry, and not by the strict laws of logic; nor should we press every phrase home, and see superstition where no superstition is intended. When, for instance, in one of the beautiful 'Martyrs' Anthems' we read, 'We take refuge in the strength of your bones,' we may reflect that this method of speech to an Oriental conveys a very different sense from what it would convey to the more logical Western. This caution has not always been borne in mind by those who have criticised Greek devotions to the Blessed Virgin. At the same time, it may be remarked that the exuberance of poetical fancy which is found in many of the Greek offices is not a feature of the East Syrian. Their addresses to St. Mary (in devotion to whom they yield to none) and their invocations of saints are remarkably staid, and most carefully make a difference between *Ora pro nobis* and prayers which may be addressed to God alone. The invocations take three forms: we find prayers to God that the saints may pray for us; indirect wishes that they may pray for us; and direct invocations asking them to pray for us. The East Syrian says, 'Mary, pray for us; in thy prayers we take refuge,' but he never says, 'Mary, grant our request.'

An interesting question arises which it is not always easy to answer. When we find that these offices have certain features in common with the Greek, the West Syrian (Jacobite), or the Armenian offices, can we argue that these features are older than the schism which separated the East Syrians from these bodies? This question has often been answered in the affirmative, on the ground that after the various schisms none of these bodies would have borrowed from the others. Mr. Hammond, in the introduction to his *Liturgies Eastern and Western*, uses this argument to prove the antiquity of the so-called Liturgy of Nestorius (III. § 9); and so Dr. Salmon uses it to show the antiquity of books venerated by both Catholicks and Valentinians (*Introduction to the New Testament*, v.). But although it may and does apply in some cases—(and on other grounds it is probable that the 'Liturgy of Nestorius' dates from before 431 A.D.)—it is not a rule that we can always use with certainty. It is quite possible for one of these separated Churches to adopt a feature of one of its rivals in a spirit of emulation. Thus it is hard to believe that all the festivals in the East Syrian kalendar which are common to it and the Greek or other kalendars, are more ancient than the schism. Let us take the festivals of the Blessed Virgin. That which falls just before the Epiphany is probably purely East Syrian: it is movable, in the peculiar East Syrian manner. But the festival on August 15th would seem to have come to them from without, probably from the Greeks; for it was only founded about 600 A.D. by the Emperor Maurice.[1] Similarly, the festival of the Nativity of the Virgin, which we find in this kalendar, is said to have been founded by Pope Sergius I. in the year 695 A.D.[1] Perhaps the East Syrian festival on May 15th is the Latin Sancta Maria ad Martyres of May 13th, a festival founded to commemorate the dedication of the Pantheon at the beginning of the seventh century.[2] We may notice in this connection that the East Syrians have no festivals of the Purification, Annunciation, Conception, or Visitation. The last two are of late and Western institution. We can draw no certain deduction from the fact that the East Syrians, unlike their neighbours, the Armenians, celebrate Christmas on December 25th, as a distinct festival from the Epiphany on January 6th; since the Greeks in the time of St. Chrysostom had already made the distinction, and it is possible that the East Syrians may have borrowed it before the schism. But (in view of the Armenian use) it is at least possible that they may have continued to join the two festivals till after that date, and that they may have copied the Greeks later. If this reasoning is correct, it follows that we cannot assert features of the East Syrian service books, which are also found in those of other Christian bodies, to be necessarily of an earlier date than the Council of Ephesus.

We may notice a few among many resemblances between the East Syrian and Greek services. The

---

[1] Smith and Cheetham, *Dict. Chr. Antiquities*, s.v. Festivals of Mary the Virgin.

[2] The writer is indebted for this suggestion to the Rev. W. C. Bishop, M.A.

so-called Liturgy of Nestorius, while retaining the East Syrian structure, has a large number of phrases apparently borrowed from Constantinople, and its reputed authorship is probably due to this fact. It would seem to be the work of some East Syrian father, who had the Constantinople service books before him. This hypothesis is far more probable than that Nestorius, the Patriarch of Constantinople, should have written a liturgy on a model with which he was not familiar, for a people with whom he had no personal connection.[1] Again, if we turn to the general *karuzutha*, or litany, or to the other litanies used on various occasions, we cannot fail to see the great similarity between them and the Greek ectenes. The use of the general litany at almost all services, liturgical and non-liturgical, is one point of resemblance; the structure of the litanies is another. We may see this by comparing the general litany given below (page 6) with the following extracts[2] from Dr. Littledale's *Offices of the Holy Eastern Church* (page 123) :—

Priest or Deacon. In peace let us beseech thee, Lord. *Ans.* Lord, have mercy.

For the peace of the whole world, for the prosperity of the holy Churches of God, and for the unity of all, let us beseech the Lord, etc.

Deacon. Further we beseech thee for our Archbishop N, and for all our brotherhood in Christ. *Ans.* Lord, have mercy (thrice).

Let us ask of the Lord for the angel of peace, a faithful guide and guardian of our souls and bodies. *Ans.* Grant, O Lord.

---

[1] The same may be said of the so-called 'Liturgy of Theodore the Interpreter.' [2] Also given in Shann's *Euchology*, p. 2.

Let us ask of the Lord for pardon and remission of our sins and offences.

Let us ask of the Lord for what is good and profitable to our souls, and for peace to the world.

Another resemblance we find in the ending of the collects. These frequently end among the Greeks, as among the East Syrians they almost always end, with the words, 'Father, Son, and Holy Ghost, for ever,' without pleading the merits of our Saviour. Again, the invariable evening and morning psalms are the same in both rites, save only that in the evening the Greeks say 141, 142, 130, 117, when the East Syrians say 141, 142, 119 (one portion), 117; both say 148, 149, 150 in the morning.[1] Among minor points we may notice that the name, *Motwa*, of an anthem at the Night Service, sung sitting, corresponds exactly to the Greek κάθισμα, one meaning of which is 'an anthem sung while the people sit.' How great is the number of ecclesiastical words taken direct from the Greek may be seen by a reference to the Glossary.

The reader will notice several curious points in these daily services. One is the absence of any kind of lections. This defect is in theory partly remedied by the large number of lections in the liturgy, although in practice these also, except the Gospel, are generally omitted, owing to the extreme scarcity of lectionaries, or books containing the lections written in full, and to the difficulty of finding the lections when only the

---

[1] Several of the Greek daily offices are translated in Mr. G. V. Shann's *Euchology* (Kidderminster, 1891) and in Lady Lechmere's *Synopsis* (Gilbert and Rivington).

first and last few words are given, with the number of the ancient *shahkha*, or section, as in the Khudhra. Another point is the love of tautology, especially in the collects. The same epithet is repeated again and again where we should have chosen a distinct one.[1] Exuberance of epithets and synonyms is a common characteristic of all Eastern offices, and occasions no little difficulty to the English translator. The arrangement of the kalendar and lectionary also presents several remarkable features. Almost all the saints' days ('memorials') which have special services, fall on Fridays, chiefly between Christmas and Lent, and not on fixed days of the month. We notice also the division of the year into *shawu'i*, or periods of about seven weeks each; the length (fifty days) of the Fast; the selection of three weeks of the Fast as 'weeks of the mysteries,' each day of which, except the Saturday, has special lections; the distinction between 'feasts of our Lord' and 'memorials of saints'; the fast of Advent or 'Annunciation' beginning on December 1st; the four rogations[2] of three days each in the spring; the grouping together of the saints' days, as the Four Evangelists, the Twelve Apostles, the Seventy Apostles, the Greek Doctors, the Syrian Doctors, and the like; the name 'Passover,' *Pisḳha*, for Maundy

---

[1] In the same way we notice how the psalms are repeated. Those said at the Night Service are said again, either at the same service or in the course of the day. Part of Ps. xii. is said twice on First Monday Evening; Ps. lxv. and lxvi. twice on certain Sunday evenings; Ps. cxvii. is said twice daily; Ps. xxviii. twice on Tuesdays; Ps. cl. five times on Saturdays (three times at the same service, that of the Night).

[2] The Syriac name *ba'utha* exactly corresponds to 'rogation.'

Thursday, while the Greek πάσχα is Easter Day; and the name of the last *shawu‘a* of the ecclesiastical year—that before Advent—viz. the Hallowing of the Church. During this period the lections deal specially with the Church, in both senses of the word; and perhaps the dedication of some great church, such as the Patriarchal Church at Seleucia-Ctesiphon, is commemorated. But the tradition of this is lost.

The infrequent occurrence of Nestorian language will perhaps surprise the reader. If we put aside the mention of the names of Nestorius, Theodore the Interpreter, and Diodorus of Tarsus, and a very few passages (almost all of which are capable of an orthodox interpretation), we shall find no trace of heterodoxy in the following pages. In some of the anthems in the Khudhra proper to festivals, which do not fall within the scope of this book, more doubtful language is occasionally used. On the other hand, we find much that is quite inconsistent with true Nestorianism.

The texts used for this translation are as follows:—

1. (A.) A manuscript of the Qdhamuwathar[1] ('Before and after'), written A.D. 1738 in the village of Huwasan, in the district of Arni of the Pinyanshayi, in Kurdistan, and now in the possession of Mr. Athelstan Riley. Its contents are:—psalms at Evening Service in full; evening Shurayi, anthems, and Letter psalms for weeks 'before' and weeks 'after'; morning Shubakhi and Tishbukhyatha for each week-day; Shurayi for Sunday evenings, two for each Sunday of the shawu‘a; the last

---

[1] For the meaning of all these technical terms see Glossary.

verses of the Royal Anthem for Sunday evenings, one for each shawu'a throughout the year; Tishbukhyatha for Sunday night and morning service (among which are the Benedicite and Gloria in excelsis); the Martyrs' Anthems, one for the morning and one for the evening of each week-day; anthems in place of the Motwa at the night service on Wednesdays, one for the week 'before' and one for the week 'after'; the psalms of the Qaltha at Sunday night service; Canons for feasts and memorials. This book does not contain, as many copies do, the anthems for the blessing of the months, and the Martyrs' Anthems for Sundays, which are not now said in most places.

2. (U.) The printed edition of the Qdhamuwathar, issued by the press of the Archbishop of Canterbury's Mission at Urmi, in red and black, in small 4to (1894). It is arranged in a convenient form for use; and in addition to the matter contained in the manuscripts of the Qdhamuwathar, the collects and benedictions are given from the Ṭakhsa, the litanies from the Dawidha (Psalter), the Lakhumara, Holy God, Lord's prayer (as farced), several rubricks (and the whole arrangement) from tradition, and the services for the Fast, festival Litanies, and some anthems from the Khudhra and Abukhalim. The contents are as follows:—

    Lord's prayer, collect, etc., beginning the service.
    Marmyatha (psalms) for the six week-day evenings.
    The rest of the service for first Monday evening in full (Martyrs' Anthem and the karuzutha excepted).
    The service for other week-day evenings where it differs from First Monday.

Ferial Night and Morning Service in full, except the psalms at the former and their prayers[1] and the Motwa.

Evening Service on Sundays, feasts of our Lord, and memorials, excepting the proper anthems, etc., from the Khudhra or Geza.

Night and Morning Service for the same.

The Services of the Great Fast.

Short anthems for the Rogation of the Ninevites.

Anthems for the blessing of the months.

The Martyrs' Anthems, one for each morning and each evening (Sundays included).

The Compline Service.

Karuzwatha (litanies) for general use.

Special karuzwatha and collects for festivals, etc. (these are not given in this translation).

The special anthems for Wednesday Night Service.

In this edition no alteration is made from the texts of the manuscripts, except that a blank is left where the names of Nestorius, Theodore, and Diodorus occur. The present writer is indebted to his former colleagues, the missionaries at Urmi, for an advance copy of this book.[2]

3. (P.) The Psalter, printed by the same press in 1891, in octavo. This contains all the psalms, divided into hulali and marmyatha, and each psalm is divided into clauses as it is said or sung; at the end a twenty-first

---

[1] These are contained in the psalter mentioned below, which is printed so as to be bound with this book.

[2] The missionaries have kindly supplied a list of the manuscripts used:—(1) *Qdhamwwathar.* Copy belonging to Mar Gabriel of Urmi, very full, written A.D. 1840, from a very trustworthy and old Alqosh manuscript; copy written in 1450 by Raban Gabriel of Mansuriya in the district of Diarbekir; copy of Mart Mariam, Urmi, written in 1713; copy without date, but apparently written about 1680, giving the Bohtan text; an Urmi copy written in 1743. (2) *Khudhra.* Copy of Mart Mariam, Urmi, written about A.D. 1500; copy of Guktapa village, written in 1697 by Mar Yonan of Ada (or Mar Abraham of all Azerbaijan?); another copy by the same, somewhat older, in the posses-

hulala is added from certain Old Testament canticles; and the collects and farcings proper to the various marmyatha and psalms are printed in their proper places. The clauses of the psalms differ greatly from our divisions, and are usually shorter than our half-verses.

4. (T.) The Ṭakhsa, issued by the same press in 1890 and 1892, red and black, large 4to, in two parts. The first part contains the three liturgies, special anthems on festivals, called *Qanun dkhilat*, and the baptismal office. The second part contains the collects and benedictions in the daily offices, and the occasional prayers (and in this translation its text of these is exclusively followed); offices of preparing the elements before the liturgy; of absolution; of renewal of the leaven; of consecration of Churches with and without oil; several long blessings or conclusions, and rules with regard to the Altar service. In the preparation of this edition of the Ṭakhsa several comparatively modern manuscripts, the only ones available, were collated from different districts inhabited by the East Syrians. The oldest of these, written at Alqosh about 1500 A.D., was taken as the basis, and all matter taken from other manuscripts was included in brackets. We must specially notice that these printed books aim rather at representing the present use of the East Syrians than at

---

sion of the Archbishop of Canterbury's Mission at Urmi; copy in the possession of the Rev. Dr. Shedd, written by Qashisha Audishu of Alqosh, about 1730. (3) *Abukhalim*. Copy of Qudshanis, quite modern, but representing a very trustworthy old text; copy belonging to Dr. Shedd, written in the Alqosh district about 1750; a third belonging to Mar Gabriel of Urmi, of the same date. (4) *Dawidha* or Psalter. Copy belonging to the Rev. W. H. Browne, written in Urmi about 1680. The Mart Mariam Khudhra best represents the litanies.

reproducing the most ancient text, and are published for practical rather than antiquarian purposes. It was thought better to err, if at all, on the side of fulness, so that the priests of every district might not miss prayers which they had been accustomed to, whatever they might find in the prints over and above the matter contained in their own copies.

5. (R. C.) The Roman Catholick print of the Psalter and Daily Offices (Paris, 1886), printed in 8vo, red and black, at Leipzig. It contains most of the matter comprised in A., U., and P. (but not the services of the fast, Compline, and Festival Litanies), and also has Thanksgivings after Communion (from the Takhsa), and the service for the three days of the Rogation of the Ninevites from the book called Mimra d'Ba'utha. This print is intended for the use of those of the East Syrians who have conformed to Rome, and who are called the Uniat Chaldeans. The order of the services is indicated as in U. Several alterations from the manuscripts have been made, of which the most prominent is the substitution of other names for those of Diodorus of Tarsus, Nestorius, Theodore the Interpreter, and Narsai; in the Creed the words *he died* and *and from the Son* are added; the Psalms at the night service are greatly shortened; and the name *Mother of God* is often substituted for *Mother of Christ*. These changes,[1] as being devoid of manuscript authority, are not usually noted in the following pages; but where this book apparently follows other manuscript

---

[1] Another change (which is always noted) is where the martyrs are said to be waiting for their full reward till the day of judgment. In these passages R. C. substitutes other words.

readings than those used for U., P., T., the difference is mentioned. This book is not used for the text of the collects and conclusions.

6. (L.) The Lectionary, printed by the Archbishop of Canterbury's Mission at Urmi in 1889, 8vo. This book gives a table of the Lections, Epistle, and Gospel for each day in the year for which they are appointed in the Khudhra, the references being to the chapters and verses in the printed bibles, in classical and vernacular Syriac, now used by the East Syrians. These are issued by the American Bible Society. The compilation of this lectionary was a matter of considerable difficulty, as no manuscript lectionary, giving the lessons in full, was available; in the Khudhra only the first and last few words of each lesson are given, and the ancient *skhakha* or section, chapters and verses not being used. As the number of the section was frequently incorrect in the Khudhras, much searching through the Bible and comparison of different Khudhras in villages at a distance was necessitated. It is to be regretted that, as this was the earliest work printed by the Mission press, and was executed before the workmen had learned their art, there are several misprints in the book; but it is hoped that these have all been corrected in the present translation. There probably remain, however, some errors due to the Khudhras themselves.

7. In the kalendar the Sundays and holy days are given as noted in the Khudhra. A few other days are given from tradition and from a list attached to a copy of the Kashkul, or book of variable ferial anthems, dated May 14, 1443 A.D. These are specially marked.

ABBREVIATIONS

A.   Manuscript of Qdhamuwathar, belonging to Mr. A. Riley.
U.   Urmi edition of Daily Offices (Archbishop of Canterbury's Mission).
P.   Urmi edition of Psalter.
T.   Urmi edition of Ṭakhsa.
R. C.   Roman Catholick edition of Psalter, Daily Offices, etc.
L.   Urmi edition of Lectionary.
Om.   Omits.
Ins.   Inserts.
Syr.   Syriac.
Lit.   Literally.

An asterisk denotes the place where the choirs change.

A full stop in the anthems denotes the end of a line, where the chant is inflected.

In the references the verse last given is not included; in the Psalms the references are to the English Prayer Book version. The letter *a* after the number of a verse denotes the *second* half of the verse.

Transliteration.—Those proper names which are well known, as Joseph, Abraham, and the like, are given in their English form. The rest are transliterated directly from the Syriac. The object of this transliteration is to shew the exact pronunciation of the names as spoken by the East Syrians, and the following points should be noticed:—The two *k* sounds and the two *t* sounds of Syriac are totally different from one another; the two *s* sounds are almost the same; the aspirated kap and the letter kheith are exactly the same (*kh*). The hard *k* sound is represented by *q*; the hard *t* sound by *ṭ*; the sharp *s* sound by *ṣ*; the aspirated *d* (*dh*) is like *th* in *then*; the aspirated *t* (*th*) as in *thin*; *kh* is a hard, *gh* a soft, aspirate; the aspirated *b* becomes *u* or *w*, at the end of a word approaching *v*; and the vowels have their Continental sounds. A rough breathing is used to denote the Syriac letter ‘E (Ayin), which has often the effect of modifying the vowel; this is then sounded further down the throat; when it has not this effect, the breathing is not written. A smooth breathing or apostrophe is used to denote the half-vowel after certain inseparable prepositions, to separate letters which would otherwise coalesce in English, and to mark a silent Alap at the beginning of a word. Otherwise, silent letters are not noted. In the pronunciation of the vowel long zlama, there is a variation between *é* and *í* in different districts and in different words; the latter sound is by far the more common, and it is therefore adopted here, except in words where the former sound is more usual. It may also be noticed that the Syrian short *a* (pthakha) is in some words pronounced like *e* in *pet* or *pert*.

Words in brackets in this translation are not in the Syriac.

ERRATA

PAGE.	LINE.				
2.	4.	*For*	forgive	*read*	have forgiven.
8.	13.	,,	work	,,	will.
8.	22.	,,	Nersai	,,	Narsai. So pp. 47, 122, 125.
8.	32.	,,	thy	,,	his.
28.	12.	,,	Sergis	,,	Sargis. So pp. 34, 39, 116, 119.
111.	12.	,,	Khiusun	,,	Khiuṣun.
125.	24.	,,	Shalita	,,	Shaliṭa. So p. 136.
138.	3.	,,	Kudahwi	,,	Kudhahwai.
139.	Note 2.	,,	Aguniṣṭi	,,	Aghuniṣṭi.
185.	Note.	,,	Ṣubaʻtha	,,	Ṣubaʻtha.
205.	Note 2.	,,	across	,,	entering.
245.	Psalms 114, 115 should be joined together, not psalms 115, 116.				

FERIAL EVENING SERVICE

WEEK 'BEFORE'

MONDAY

[Rule as to weeks 'before' and 'after'[1] :—*The weeks are alternately 'before' and 'after,'[2] as determined by the Khudhra. If Sunday is 'before,' so also are Monday, Wednesday, and Friday, but Tuesday, Thursday, and Saturday are 'after'; and vice versâ.*]

Priest. Glory be to God in the highest, *thrice.* And on earth peace and a good hope to men, at all times and for ever. Amen.[3]

They answer,[4] Bless, O my Lord.

They give the kiss of peace.[5]

Our Father which art in heaven, Hallowed be thy Name. Thy kingdom come.* Holy, holy, holy art thou. Our Father which art in heaven. Heaven and earth are full of the greatness of thy glory. The watchful ones[6] and men cry to thee, Holy, holy, holy art thou.* Our Father which art in

---

[1] Given in R. C.; not U. This is the old rule.

[2] Also called 'first' and 'last.'

[3] So U.; R. C. om. *Amen.*

[4] So R. C.; om. U. These words are addressed to God, not to the priest.

[5] The universal custom, though not mentioned in U. or R. C.

[6] The angels.

A

2   FERIAL EVENING SERVICE

heaven, Hallowed be thy Name. Thy kingdom come. Thy will be done in earth, As it is in heaven. Give us this day the bread of our need. And forgive us our debts. As we forgive our debtors. And lead us not into temptation. But deliver us from the Evil one. For thine is the kingdom, and the power, and the glory, for ever and ever. Amen.* Glory be to the Father, and to the Son, and to the Holy Ghost.* From everlasting to everlasting. Amen.¹ * Our Father which art in heaven, Hallowed be thy Name. Thy kingdom come.* Holy, holy, holy art thou. Our Father which art in heaven. Heaven and earth are full of the greatness of thy glory. The watchful ones and men cry to thee, Holy, holy, holy art thou.

Deacon. Let us pray. Peace be with us.

Evening prayer. Let us confess, O my Lord, thy Godhead, and worship thy Majesty, and lift up perpetual praise without ceasing to thy glorious Trinity, at all times, Lord of all, Father, Son, and Holy Ghost, for ever.² *They answer,* Amen.

FIRST MARMITHA.³ Ps. xi., xii., xiii., xiv. *After the first clause of the first psalm of each Marmitha say,* Hallelujah, Hallelujah, yea Hallelujah, *and repeat the first clause. After each Marmitha,* Glory be to the Father, and to the Son, and to the Holy Ghost. From everlasting to everlasting. Amen.

SECOND MARMITHA. Ps. xv., xvi., xvii. Gloria. *Then,*⁴ Hallelujah, Glory to thee, O God, *thrice.* O Lord, have mercy upon us. *Deacon.* Peace be with us.

*Or,*⁵ Hallelujah, Hallelujah, yea Hallelujah. Let us pray. Peace be with us.

---

¹ R. C. adds *and Amen.*

² So almost all prayers end. R. C. rightly adds that in prayers addressed directly to our Lord the words *Father, Son, and Holy Ghost* must be omitted. Collects may only be said by a priest.

³ If the week is 'before,' the first choir begins; if 'after,' the second choir. So alternately throughout the services. The psalms are not farced on week-days at Evensong.

⁴ So U.   ⁵ So R. C.

Prayer of the Lakhumara.[1] For all thy helps and graces (given) to us, which cannot be repaid, let us confess and glorify thee without ceasing in thy crowned Church, which is full of all helps and all blessings. For thou art the Lord, and[2] Creator of all, Father, Son, and Holy Ghost, for ever. *Amen.*

They all say the Lakhumara. Thee, Lord of all, we confess. And thee, Jesus Christ, we glorify. For thou art the Quickener of our bodies. And thou art the Saviour of our souls. *I was glad when they said unto me, We go into the house of the Lord.*[3] Thee, Lord of all, etc. Glory be, etc. From everlasting, etc. Thee, Lord of all, etc. *They say*, Let us pray. Peace be with us.[4]

Prayer after the Lakhumara. Thou, O my Lord, art in truth the Quickener of our bodies; And thou art the good Saviour of our souls, and the perpetual Keeper of our life. And thee we are bound to confess, worship, and glorify at all times, Lord of all, Father, Son, and Holy Ghost, for ever. *Amen.*

FIRST SHURAYA. Ps. xii. 1-7.[5] Save, Lord, for the godly are come to an end. *Hallelujah, Hallelujah, yea Hallelujah.* Save, Lord, for the godly are come to an end.[6]* And the faithful, etc. Glory be, etc. From everlasting, etc. Hallelujah, Hallelujah, yea Hallelujah.

FIRST ANTHEM: *to the tune* Lo, he hath led me captive.[7]

---

[1] U. inserts before this the prayer of incense as on festivals (see below, page 69).

[2] Om. *and*, U.

[3] *In a private house say,* In every place art thou, O God. Receive our petition, U.

[4] R. C. om. this last response.

[5] All psalms on ferias are said in practice by one voice on each side, clause by clause alternately (the clauses being usually rather shorter than our half verses), and in monotone.

[6] Thus all Shurayi begin and end.

[7] These tunes are mostly forgotten; all the tunes known are quite traditional, and are not written down.

Save, Lord, for the godly are come to an end. Lo, the godly are come to an end, and the faithful is minished, and the just is destroyed. And there is none good among men. With a double heart every man speaketh, and with dissembling lips. Each man with his neighbour. Of envy and guile and slander. Is our whole humanity[1] full. Love, the chief of the commandments. Is rooted out from our thoughts.[2] There is great fear lest we all be destroyed in thy anger. For thy justice is silent with us. And hath given place to thy lovingkindness.[3] O our Lord, have pity on us.

Ps. xii. 1.

The Lord is faithful in his words. Our Saviour gave the promise of life to those that desire his love. And made them rich in his knowledge. And filled them with the wisdom of his power. And taught them to pray at all times. Our Father which art in heaven, hallowed be thy Name. And[4] thy kingdom come to us. And[4] thy will be done on earth, as it is in heaven. Give us the bread of our need. And lead us not into temptation. But deliver us from the Evil one. For thine is the kingdom. And the power and the glory.

Ps. cxlv. 13, Syr.

Glory be to the Father, and to the Son, and to the Holy Ghost. O Mary, who didst bear the medicine of life to the children of Adam. In thy petition we will take refuge. And in the confident hope of the prayers of St.[5] John. We will conquer the Evil one and his host. And by the prayer of the prophets, apostles, and martyrs. And fathers and teachers. And by the prayer of our holy father.[6] And of the confessors, and of St. George. And the great power of the Cross. And the

---

[1] *Lit.* son of man.
[2] *Lit.* thought.
[3] *i.e.* All we have is of God's mercy.
[4] R. C., U., om. *And.*
[5] Syr. *Mar* (so throughout). See Glossary.
[6] The Patron Saint. Or this may be taken as a proper name *Awa,* and so throughout. If the church is dedicated to St. Mary, this is taken as referring to any great martyr.

hallowing of the holy Church. We will beseech Christ to have mercy and compassion. Upon our souls.

They say,[1] Let us pray. Peace be with us.

Prayer. Thy mercy, O our Lord and our God, and the care of thy good will towards us are we bound to confess, worship, and glorify at all times, Lord of all, Father, Son, and Holy Ghost, for ever. *Amen.*

PSALMS cxli., cxlii., cxix. 105-113, cxvii. Lord, I have called upon thee, answer thou me. *Hearken to my words and receive my prayer.* Lord, I have called upon thee, answer thou me.* Hearken to my words and receive.* My prayer as the incense before thee, etc.[2]* *At the end of* Ps. cxvii. *say the Gloria. Then,*[3] Lord, I have called upon thee, answer thou me. *Hearken to my words and receive my prayer.*

They say,[4] Let us pray. Peace be with us.

Prayer. Hear, O our Lord and our God, the prayer of thy servants in thy compassion, and receive the petition of thy worshippers in thy mercy; and have compassion on our sinfulness in thy lovingkindness[5] and mercies, O Physician of our bodies, and good Hope of our souls, Lord of all, Father, Son, and Holy Ghost, for ever. *Amen.*

SECOND SHURAYA. Ps. xv. 1-5.

SECOND ANTHEM: *to the tune*[6] He knoweth the thoughts.

He that is before the worlds. O compassionate Father and merciful Son. And pitiful Spirit, the Sanctifier of the unclean. Sanctify our bodies and our souls, and have mercy upon us.   Ps. lv. 20.

---

[1] Om. R. C.

[2] The rest without farcing.

[3] R. C. om. these two clauses.   [4] Om. R. C.

[5] The Syriac word 'ṭaibutha' is in this book rendered either by *lovingkindness* or *grace*. It appears to mean *goodness in its outward aspect*; if the word is used with special reference to God, the giver, it is most appropriately rendered *lovingkindness*; if with special reference to man, the recipient, it is *grace*.

[6] So A., U.; R. C.: *to its own tune.*

Holy and terrible is his Name. May the praises[1] and singing of Hallelujahs of the heavenly hosts. And[2] the petition of the Son on the right hand of the Father. Beseech for us of thy righteousness, and do thou have mercy upon us.

Ps. cxi. 9.

Glory be to the Father, and to the Son, and to the Holy Ghost. O Mary, Mother of the King, the King of kings. Beseech Christ, who shone forth from thy bosom. That he may pity us in his lovingkindness, and make us worthy of his kingdom.

From everlasting to everlasting. O Christ our Saviour, by the prayer of thy saints. The prophets and apostles and martyrs, and all the just. Keep the company of thy worshippers from all harm.

Let all the people say Amen and Amen. Our holy father,[3] be a guide to us. In good deeds which propitiate thy Lord. That by thy prayers we may be helped, and with thee have joy.

Ps. cvi. 46.

The Karuzutha.

The deacon puts on stole and girdle, and standing just below the bema,[4] says the Karuzutha.[5] Let us all stand up, as is right, in sorrow and care. Let us make request and say, O our Lord, have mercy upon us. *The people answer,* O our Lord, have mercy upon us.

He proceeds. Father of mercies and God of all comfort, we make request. *Answer.* O our Lord, have mercy upon us. *And so after each clause.*

O our Saviour, who carest for us and suppliest all things, we, etc.

For the peace, safety, and security of all the world and all the Churches, we, etc.

---

[1] *Lit.* singing 'Holy.'
[2] So A., U.; R. C.: *By.*
[3] Or *Awa,* as above.
[4] The raised place between sanctuary and nave.
[5] This 'litany' is also said in the Liturgy and at Baptism. Except at the litany, no vestments are ordinarily used in the daily offices.

For (this) our land and all lands, and those who live therein in faith, we, etc.

For a moderate climate and a rich year, the fruits and produce (of the earth), and the prosperity of all the world, we, etc.

For the welfare of our holy fathers NN,[1] and all those who serve under them, we, etc.

O merciful God, who in mercy governest all, we, etc.

O thou who art rich in mercies, and overflowing with compassion, we, etc.

O thou who art by nature good, and the giver of all good things, we, etc.

O thou who art glorified in heaven, and worshipped on earth, we, etc.

O thou who by nature hast immortality, and dwellest in the excellent light, we, etc.

Save us all, O Christ our Lord, in thy lovingkindness; and increase in us thy peace and tranquillity, and have mercy upon us.

ANOTHER.[2] Let us pray. Peace be with us. Let us pray and make request of God the Lord of all. *They answer.* Amen (*so for every clause*). That he may hear the voice of our prayer, and receive our petition, and have mercy upon us.

And[3] for the holy catholick Church here and in every place, let us pray, etc. That his peace and tranquillity may abide in it until the end of the world.

For our fathers the bishops, let us pray, etc. That they may stand at the head of their dioceses without blame or stain all the days of their life.

And[3] especially for the welfare of our holy fathers NN,[1] let us pray, etc. That he may keep and raise them at the head of all their dioceses; that they may feed, and serve, and

---

[1] Patriarch, Metropolitan, and Bishop of the diocese.
[2] Often omitted—except the conclusion, from 'Pray and make request.'
[3] R. C. om. *and.*

make ready for the Lord, a perfect people zealous of good and beautiful works.

For presbyters [1] and deacons who are in this service of the truth, let us pray, etc. That with a good heart and pure thoughts they may serve before him.

For all the discreet and holy congregation, children of the holy catholick Church, let us pray, etc. That they may accomplish their good and holy course, and receive from the Lord a good [2] hope and promise in the land of life.

For the memorial of blessed St. Mary [3] the holy Virgin, Mother of Christ [4] our Saviour and Lifegiver, let us pray, etc. That the Holy Ghost who dwelt in her may sanctify us in his lovingkindness, and perfect his work in us, and seal in us his truth all the days of our life.

For the memorial of the prophets and apostles, martyrs and confessors, let us pray, etc. That by their prayers and sufferings he may give us with them a good hope and salvation, and make us worthy of their blessed memorial and their living and true promise in the kingdom of heaven.

For the memorial of our holy fathers, Mar Diodorus, Mar Theodorus, Mar Nestorius, bishops and teachers of the truth, and Mar Ephraim, Mar Nersai, and Mar Abraham, and all the holy, ancient, and true teachers, let us pray, etc. That by their prayers and petitions the pure truth of the doctrine of their religion and of their faith may be kept in all the holy catholick Church till the end of the world.

For the memorial of our fathers and brothers, faithful and true, who have departed and gone from this world in the [5] true faith and orthodox religion, let us pray, etc. That he may loose and forgive their transgressions and offences, and make them worthy to have joy with the just and righteous who were approved by thy will.

---

[1] The Syriac word *kahna* is in this book rendered *priest*, and *qashisha* is rendered *presbyter*.   [2] R. C. om. *good*.

[3] Syr. Mart Mariam. For Mar, Mart, see Glossary.

[4] R. C.: *Jesus*.   [5] R. C.: *this*.

For this country and its inhabitants, for this house and those who care for it,[1] for this village and those that dwell in it,[1] and especially for this congregation, let us pray, etc. That he may take away from us in his lovingkindness, the sword, captivity, robbery, earthquakes, hail,[2] famine, pestilence, and all evil plagues which are against the body.

For those who err from this true faith and are held in the snares of Satan, let us pray, etc. That he may turn the hardness of their hearts and make them to know that God is one, the Father of truth, and his Son Jesus Christ our Lord.

For those who are grievously sick and tempted by evil spirits, let us pray, etc. That our Lord and our God[3] may send to them his Angel of mercy and healing, to visit, cure, heal, help, and comfort them in the multitude of his lovingkindness and mercies.

For the poor and afflicted, orphans and widows, the harassed, troubled, and grieved in spirit in this world, let us pray, etc. That he may give them what they need in his lovingkindness, supply them in his mercy, comfort them in his compassion, and deliver them from him who despitefully useth them.

PRAY and make request to God the Lord of all. That ye may be to him a kingdom, holy priests, and people. Cry to the mighty Lord God with all your heart and all your soul. For he is God the Father of compassion, merciful and pitiful, who willeth not that those whom he hath fashioned should perish, but repent and live before him. And especially must we pray to, confess, worship, glorify, honour, and exalt the one God, the adorable Father, Lord of all, who by his Christ gave a good hope and salvation to our souls, that he may fulfil in us his lovingkindness, mercies, and compassion until the end. *They answer*, Amen.

---

[1] R. C. inverts these clauses and reads *for this town* [or *this village*].
[2] R. C. om. *hail*. [3] R. C. om. *Our Lord and our God*.

He proceeds. With request and beseeching we ask for the Angel of peace and mercy. *Answer.* From thee, O Lord.

Night and day, throughout our life, we ask for continual peace for thy Church, and life without sin. *Answer.* From thee, O Lord.

We ask continual love, which is the bond of perfectness, with the confirmation of the Holy Ghost. *Answer.* From thee, O Lord.

We ask for forgiveness of sins, and those things which help our lives and please thy Godhead. *Answer.* From thee, O Lord.

We ask the mercy and compassion of the Lord continually and at all times. *Answer.* From thee, O Lord.

Let us commit our own souls, and one another's souls, to the Father, Son, and Holy Ghost.[1]

Prayer. To thee, O Lord, mighty God, we entrust our bodies and souls; and of thee, O our Lord and our God, we ask forgiveness of trespasses and sins. Give us this in thy lovingkindness and mercies, as thou art wont, at all times, Lord of all, Father, Son, and Holy Ghost, for ever. *Amen.*

Deacon.[2] Lift up your voices and glorify the living God, all ye people.

They all say, Holy God, Holy Mighty, Holy Immortal, have mercy upon us. Glory be. Holy God. From everlasting. Holy God. *They add,* Let us pray. Peace be with us.

Prayer. Holy and glorious, mighty and immortal, who dwellest in the saints, and whose will is pleased with them, we beseech thee, turn, O my Lord, and pity us, and have mercy upon us, as thou art wont, at all times, Lord of all, etc. *Amen.*

---

[1] R. C. adds answer: To thee, O Lord our God.

[2] Om. U. But apparently by error, as it is referred to in the first service (see below).

Deacon. Bless, O my Lord. Bow your heads for the laying on of hands and receive a blessing.

Priest. May Christ make thy service glorious in the kingdom of heaven.

Prayer. May our souls be perfected in the one complete faith of thy glorious Trinity, and may we all in one union of love be worthy to raise to thee glory and honour, confession and worship, at all times, Lord of all, etc. *Amen.*

EVENING ANTHEM. [Varies according to the season: these anthems are contained in the Kashkul.]¹

Or this invariable anthem:² *to the tune* Blessed martyrs.

I waited patiently for the Lord. The body of Christ and his precious blood. Are on the holy altar. In fear and love. Let us all approach to it. And with the angels chant to him. Holy, holy, holy, Lord God.   Ps. xl. 1.

The poor shall eat and be satisfied. The body of Christ, etc., *as above.*   Ps. xxii. 26.

Glory be to the Father, and to the Son, and to the Holy Ghost. Christ the refuge and true hope of the afflicted. Be, O my Lord, a wall to thy worshippers. And keep them from the Evil one. And heal and salve their pains. In the compassion of thy Godhead. O Merciful one and Forgiver of sins.

Prayer. Pity us, O thou Compassionate one, in thy lovingkindness, and turn to us, O thou who art full of mercies, and delay not to look on us and care for us, O my Lord. For in thee is our hope and confident trust at all seasons and times, Lord of all, etc. *Amen.*

LETTER PSALM,³ cxix. 1-17. Glory be. From everlasting. Hallelujah, Hallelujah, yea Hallelujah.

Our Father, *farced as above*, page 1.

---

¹ A., U. do not mention this (so throughout).
² So A., U.; om. R. C.
³ These are said like the Shurayi.

They say,[1] Let us pray. Peace be with us.

Prayer. May thy Name, O our holy Lord and God, be glorified, and thy Godhead worshipped, and thy Majesty honoured, and thy Greatness celebrated, and thy Being exalted. And may the eternal mercies of thy glorious Trinity protect thy people and the sheep of thy pasture at all times, Lord of all, etc. *Amen. Bless, O my Lord.*[1]

Another. In heaven and on earth, O my Lord, thy Godhead is blessed and thy Majesty worshipped. Holy and glorious, and glorified and high and exalted, is the adorable and glorious Name of thy glorious Trinity at all times, Lord of all, etc. *Amen. Bless, O my Lord.*[1]

The Martyrs' Anthem.[2]

Glorify the Lord, O ye righteous. Holy martyrs, pray for peace. That we may celebrate your festivals with joy.
Ps. xxxiii. 1.

For praise becometh well the just. The martyrs who longed to see Christ. Obtained wings through the sword and flew to heaven.
Ib.

Sing lustily with the voice. The martyrs in their love say to Christ. For thee we die daily.
Ps. xxxiii. 3.

Seek the Lord and be strong. O ye martyrs, ask mercy for the world which taketh. True refuge in the strength of your bones.
Ps. cv. 4.

Who called upon the Lord, and he heard them. Let us call on the martyrs and take refuge in them. That they may pray for us.
Ps. xcix. 6.

---

[1] Om. R. C.
[2] The Martyrs' Anthems are said in U. to be all by Mar Marutha, Bishop of Miparqat. The verses immediately preceding the Gloria, which vary much, seem to be of later date than the rest.

As a city surrounded with a wall. Ye fence in the breaches. Before the persecutors in the times of affliction. <small>Ps. cxxii. 3.</small>

From this time forth for evermore. May the prayers of the martyrs be a wall to us. And drive away from us the attacks of the crafty. <small>Ps. cxv. 18.</small>

Offer to Him the sacrifices of praise. O ye martyrs who were sacrifices to the high priests. May your prayer be a wall to our souls. <small>Ps. cvii. 22.</small>

I will alway bless the Lord. Blessed is your contest, O holy martyrs. For by the blood of your necks ye gained the kingdom. <small>Ps. xxxiv. 1.</small>

His praises shall ever be in my mouth. Blessed is Christ, who strengthened his saints. Here on earth and above in heaven. <small>Ib.</small>

They that love the Lord hate the thing which is evil. Ye martyrs of the Son, that love the Only Begotten. Pray that there may be peace in creation. <small>Ps. xcvii. 10.</small>

Look on him and trust in him. The martyrs saw the Son crucified on the tree. And lowered their necks to the sword, and were crowned. <small>Ps. xxxiv. 5.</small>

Bow down thine ear, O Lord, and answer me. The cross of our Lord was stained with blood. The martyrs saw it and lowered their necks. <small>Ps. lxxxvi. 1.</small>

He divided the sea and let them go through. The cross of Christ was a bridge to the martyrs. And the just passed over by it to the country where there is no fear. <small>Ps. lxxviii. 14.</small>

And more to be desired are they than gold, and than precious stones. The martyrs are like pearls. For their images are fixed in the King's crown. <small>Ps. xix. 10.</small>

The King's daughter stood in glory. The faithful Church is a pearl. And the martyrs in it are propitiatory sacrifices. <small>Ps. xlv. 10.</small>

Within the ports of the daughter of Sion. The martyrs saw a pearl in Sion. And ran and bought it with the blood of their necks. <small>Ps. ix. 14.</small>

Fairer to look on than the children of men. The rose in the gardens is beautiful to behold. But more (beautiful) were the martyrs when they were killed.
<small>Ps. xlv. 3.</small>

How good and beautiful. Precious stones and beryls. Are ye, O martyrs, in the crown of the Son of the King.
<small>Ps. cxxxiii. 1.</small>

Sing to the Lord with harps, and with the sound of singing. I heard the voice of the martyrs singing praises. With the harps of David (going) round Paradise.
<small>. xcviii. 6.</small>

His praise is in earth and in heaven. Praise to that voice which said to the martyrs. Mingle your blood with my blood, and my life with your life.
<small>Ps. cxlviii. 12.</small>

O[1] hear ye this, all ye people. The martyrs were ears of corn, and the kings reaped them. And the Lord placed them in the garner of his kingdom.
<small>Ps. xlix. 1.</small>

He doubtless cometh with joy. The holy martyrs and priests go out. To meet our Lord in the day of his coming.
<small>Ps. cxxvi. 7.</small>

The[2] Lord shall give strength unto his people. May the strength which strengthened the martyr St. James. Be with us by night and by day.
<small>Ps. xxix. 10.</small>

And your prayers be on all of us. Holy martyrs, ask mercy for us. That by your prayers we may receive forgiveness.

And[3] I spake of peace. Peace to thee, Mar Pithiun, the chosen of Christ. Who didst bear all sufferings for the truth of thy Lord.
<small>Ps. cxx. 6.</small>

He reproved kings for their sakes.[4] How fitting it is for the boy Cyriac. When for him (God) reproveth the unjust king.
<small>Ps. cv. 14.</small>

---

[1] A. transposes this verse and the following.
[2] A., R. C. om. this verse.   [3] A. om. this verse.
[4] A. : *How good and beautiful* (Ps. cxxxiii. 1).

And[1] *a joyful mother of children.* The faithful Shmuni encourageth her sons. O my beloved sons, depart in peace. <small>Ps. cxiii. 8.</small>

Beg of the Lord and pray before him. Ask for us from thy Lord, O martyr George. Compassion and mercy, and forgiveness of trespasses. <small>Ps. xxxvii. 7.</small>

Kings of the earth and all peoples. All races call blessed. The Virgin Mary, Mother of Christ. <small>Ps. cxlviii. 11.</small>

Glory be to the Father, and to the Son, and to the Holy Ghost. Peace be with you, holy martyrs. Sowers of peace in the four quarters (of the world).

From everlasting to everlasting. Thy memorial, O our father,[2] is on the holy altar. With the just who conquered and the martyrs who were crowned.

Let all the people say Amen and Amen. By thee, O God, whose mercies are great. Let us be corrected, and not by men.* Come, O my Lord, to help <small>Ps. cvi. 46.</small> us and strengthen our weakness. For in thee is our hope by night and by day.* O Christ, who neglectest not any who call on thee. In thy mercy reject not the request of them that worship thee.* For on thee their eyes hang and on thee they look. That thou mayest forgive their trespasses and wipe out their sins.* O our Lord, by thy right hand overthrow Satan. Who inebriateth without wine and causeth to slip without mud.* With the Publican we ask mercy. Pity us and have mercy upon us.* Thy Cross hath saved us, thy Cross doth save us. May thy Cross be a wall to our souls.* May wars be brought to nought, and disputes laid to rest. And may thy[3] peace rule in the four quarters (of the world).* O our Lord, keep us, for we are as sheep. Among serpents who are worse than wolves.* O our Lord, sow thy peace and tranquillity in the world. And take from us the rod of correction.* O our Lord, bless and keep our congregation. And make thy peace and tranquillity to dwell in it.* O our Lord, give peace in the four quarters (of the world). And bring to

---

[1] U. om. *And.* [2] Or *Awa.* [3] A. om. *thy.*

nought the persecutors who oppose (us). O our Lord, shut the mouth of the unjust. That they speak not evil against the sons of the Church.

Prayer. We beseech thee, who dost make thy Church to grow, and crownest those who love thee, and makest thy athletes to triumph, and helpest thy saints in their glorious, holy, life-giving, and divine contests; turn, O my Lord, and pity and have mercy upon us, as thou art wont, at all times, Lord of all, etc. *Amen.*

Another. By the prayer of thy saints, O our Lord and our God, be reconciled to us. And by the request of thy true (disciples) make our sins to pass away and pardon that which is wanting in us; make our enemies peaceful, quicken our departed; and make us worthy of the excellent glory of thy kingdom, with the just and righteous who fulfil thy will in Jerusalem which is above, Lord of all, etc. *Amen.*

Prayer for help.[1] Make, O my Lord, the help of thy mercies, and the great aid of thy lovingkindness, and the hidden and glorious strength of thy glorious Trinity, and thy right hand full of mercies and compassion, to overshadow and be joined with the weakness of thy worshippers, from thy holy house which is full of all helps and all blessings, by the prayer of all the saints who propitiate thee, Lord of all, etc. *Amen.* *Bless, O my Lord.*[2]

Another. With thy blessing, O our Lord and our God, may thy servants be blessed, and by the care of thy good will may thy worshippers be kept; and may the perpetual peace, O my Lord, of thy Godhead, and the long-enduring tranquillity of thy Majesty, rule among thy people and in thy Church, all the days of the world, Lord of all, etc. *Amen.* *Bless, O my Lord.*[2]

Another. May the blessing of him who blesseth all, and the peace of him who maketh all things peaceful, and the

---

[1] Each priest who is present says one of these prayers, and the rest after the first two are omitted, up to the prayer *Of Mary*: U.

[2] R. C. om. the response.

compassion of him who hath compassion on all, and the guardianship of our adorable God, be with us and among us and around us, and keep us from the Evil one and his hosts, at all seasons and times, Lord of all, etc. *Amen. Bless, O my Lord.*[1]

Another. May we be blessed, O our Lord and our God, with thy blessing, and preserved by thy care; and may thy power come to our assistance, and thy help be joined to us, and thy right hand overshadow us, and thy peace rule among us, and thy cross be a high wall and house of refuge to us, and under its wings may we be protected from the Evil one and his hosts, at all seasons and times, Lord of all, etc. *Amen. Bless, O my Lord.*[1]

Another. Blessed, O my Lord, are the mercies of thy lovingkindness, and adorable are the promises of thy majesty, which teach us at all times to look to thee and to glory in thee, and not to cease from our hope in thee all the days of our life, Lord of all, etc. *Amen. Bless, O my Lord.*[1]

Another. May thy blessing, O our Lord and our God, rest on thy people, and may thy compassion be continually on us, weak and sinful though we be; O thou that art our good hope and house of refuge, full of mercies, and that forgivest trespasses and sins, Lord of all, etc. *Amen. Bless, O my Lord.*[1]

Another. May the peace of the Father be with us, and the love of the Son among us; and may the Holy Ghost direct us according to his will, and on us be his mercies and compassion, at all seasons and times, Lord of all, etc. *Amen. Bless, O my Lord.*[1]

Another. May thy peace, O my Lord, dwell in us, and thy tranquillity rule in us, and thy love increase among us all the days of our life, Lord of all, etc. *Amen. Bless, O my Lord.*[1]

Another. Keep us, O my Lord, with thy right hand, and protect us beneath thy wings; and may thy help be joined to us all the days of our life, Lord of all, etc. *Amen. Bless, O my Lord.*[1]

Another. Give us, O my Lord, perpetual peace, and love

---

[1] R. C. om. the response.

and desire for instruction, and life and blessings and joys, and unfailing sustenance, all the days of our life, Lord of all, etc. *Amen. Bless, O my Lord.*[1]

Another. Be the guardian who doth not sleep to the stronghold where thy sheep dwell, that they be not hurt by wolves that thirst for the blood of thy flock, for thou art an inexhaustible sea, Lord of all, etc. *Amen. Bless, O my Lord.*[1]

Another. Bless us with thy blessing, O our Lord, and surround us with the wall of thy care; deprive us not of good things, and make us to lie down in the bridechamber of light, Lord of all, etc. *Amen. Bless, O my Lord.*[1]

Another. Come, O my Lord, to our assistance in thy compassion, and reveal thyself for our salvation in thy mercy, and cause us to walk in the ways of righteousness all the days of our life, Lord of all, etc. *Amen. Bless, O my Lord.*[1]

Another. O my Lord, may thy lovingkindness shine forth on us when thy justice judgeth us, and may thy mercies come to our assistance in the day when thy greatness shineth forth, Lord of all, etc. *Amen. Bless, O my Lord.*[1]

Another. Make thy blessing and lovingkindness, and thy right hand full of mercies and compassion, to overshadow and be joined to the company of thy worshippers who call on thee and beseech thee, at all seasons and times, Lord of all, etc. *Amen. Bless, O my Lord.*[1]

Another. Bless, O my Lord, in thy lovingkindness, and keep in thy mercy, the company of the faithful who trust in thee, and call on thy holy Name, and beseech thee, at all times, Lord of all, etc. *Amen. Bless, O my Lord.*[1]

Another. Be with us, O my Lord, in thy mercies continually, and direct us according to the will of thy Godhead, all the days of our life, Lord of all, etc. *Amen. Bless, O my Lord.*[1]

Another. May the blessing of mercies, O my Lord, be sent from the treasury of mercies, by the angel of mercies, from the presence of God who aboundeth in mercies, and overflow on the companies of those who ever glorify thee, and call on

---

[1] R. C. om. the response.

thy holy Name, and look and wait for mercies and for salvation, which is from thee, Lord of all. *Amen. Bless, O my Lord.*[1]

Of Mary.[2] May the prayer, O my Lord, of the holy Virgin, and the request of the blessed Mother, and the beseeching and entreating of her who is full of grace, St. Mary the blessed, and the great power of the conquering cross and divine help, and the request of St. John the Baptist, be with us continually, at all seasons and times, Lord of all, etc. *Amen. Bless, O my Lord.*[1]

Of the Apostles. May the prayer, O my Lord, of the holy apostles, and the request of the true preachers, and the beseeching and entreating of the illustrious athletes, the proclaimers of righteousness, sowers of peace in creation, be with us continually, at all seasons and times, Lord of all, etc. *Amen. Bless, O my Lord.*[1]

Of our father.[3] May the prayer and request, and beseeching and entreating of our famous and holy father Mar Awa, Catholicos, and St. Stephen the firstborn of the martyrs, and of the giant of strength, St. George the illustrious martyr, and of Mar N.,[4] and of all the martyrs and saints of our Lord, be with us continually, a high wall and strong house of refuge, to save, deliver, rescue, and guard our bodies and souls from the Evil one and his hosts, at all seasons and times, Lord of all, etc. *Amen. Bless, O my Lord.*[1]

---

[1] R. C. om. the response.

[2] The following three prayers are always said. In U. (but not in T. and R. C.) they are joined together as follows:—May the prayer, O my Lord, of the holy Virgin, and the request of the blessed Mother, and the beseeching and entreating of her who is full of grace, St. Mary the blessed, and the great power of the conquering cross and divine help, and the request of St. John the Baptist, and of the blessed apostles and illustrious fathers, the proclaimers of righteousness, and sowers of peace in creation; and of our famous and holy father Mar Awa, Catholicos, and St. Stephen the firstborn of the martyrs, and of the giant of strength, St. George the illustrious martyr, and of Mar N. and of Mar Augin the blessed, and of all his spiritual company, and of Shmuni and her sons, and of all the martyrs and saints of our Lord, be with us continually, etc.

[3] Or *Awa* (the patron saint).   [4] The patron saint.

The priest takes the cross in his hand, and turning to the people says,[1] Bless, O my Lord. By your command.[2] *They answer,* By the command of Christ, and glory to his holy Name. *And they bow their heads.*[3]

Conclusion.

Glory to thee, Jesus our conquering King, the brightness of the eternal Father, begotten without beginning, before all times and things which came into being; we have no hope and expectation unless it be thou, the Creator. By the prayer of the just and elect who have been approved by thee from the beginning, pardon our sins and forgive our offences, deliver us from our afflictions, answer our requests and bring us to the excellent light, and deliver us by thy living sign from all harm, hidden and open, Christ the hope of our nature, now ✠ and at all times, and for ever and ever. *Amen. He makes the sign of the cross over the people. They answer,*[4] May Christ hear thy prayers. May Christ make thy priesthood famous in the kingdom of heaven.

Another.[5] May the prayer of thy feeble servants, O our Lord and our God, be received before the throne of thy Godhead; and may this our assembling together be for the pleasing of the will of thy majesty; that we may receive from thee in (thy) lovingkindness good health for the body and safe keeping for the soul; increase of fair weather; perpetual peace, O my Lord, and long-enduring tranquillity; continuance of love which passeth not away and departeth not from among us, in every age of this world, Christ the hope of our nature, now, etc.

Another. Blessed is God for ever, and glorified is his holy Name to all eternity. To him we make request, and of the overflowing sea of his mercy we beseech, that he will make us worthy of the excellent glory of his kingdom, and of joy

---

[1] R. C. om. this versicle and response.
[2] *Sc.* I will give the blessing.
[3] They beat their breasts during the blessing.
[4] R. C. om. the response.   [5] These are alternatives.

with his holy angels, and of confidence[1] before him, and of standing at his right hand in Jerusalem which is above, in his lovingkindness and mercies, Christ the hope, etc.

Another. May God the Lord of all, in whose house we have assembled, and before whose majesty we have prayed, in the great hope of his mercy, hear our prayer in his compassion, and receive our request in his pity; and may he wash and cleanse the filth of our trespasses and sins in the overflowing hyssop of his pitifulness, and give rest to the souls of the departed in the glorious mansions of his kingdom. May he sprinkle us all with the dew of his sweetness, and may the right hand of his care overshadow us and all creatures in his lovingkindness and mercies, Christ the hope, etc.

Another. May God the Lord of all, who hath entrusted his praises (to be sung) by our mouth, his songs by our tongue, his canticles by our throats, his religion by our lips, his faith by our hearts, hear our prayers and receive our requests, and be appeased by our beseechings, and return answer to our petitions if they be good and innocent; and from the great treasury of his mercy pour forth his mercies and compassion on us and on all the whole world, Christ the hope, etc.

Another. May the Name of God the Lord of all, who ordereth times and seasons, be glorified among us; and may the right hand of the care of his mercy overshadow us who are feeble and sinful, and all the whole world; the holy Church and its children; our fathers and masters and teachers; our departed who have been separated from us and have gone from among us, and all our brotherhood in Christ, Christ the hope, etc.

Another. To God be glory; to the angels honour; to Satan confusion; to the cross reverence; to the Church exaltation; to the departed quickening; to the penitent acceptance; to prisoners release; to the sick and infirm recovery and healing; and to the four quarters of the world great peace and tranquillity. And also on us who are weak and sinful may the compassion and mercies of our adorable God come,

---

[1] *Lit.* openness of face.

and may they overshadow us, and be poured forth, and remain firm and reign continually, Christ the hope, etc.

Another. By the right hand of thy majesty, our Father which art in heaven, bless us all, O my Lord; keep us all; help us all; assist and protect us all; quicken the departed of us all; let thy right hand overshadow us all, and thy mercies and compassion be poured forth on us all; and may continual praise, honour, confession, worship, and thanksgiving ascend to thee from the mouth of us all, Christ the hope, etc.

Another.[1] May God the Lord of all bless our congregation in his lovingkindness, and keep us from falling in the overflowing multitude of his mercy; answer our petitions from his treasury; and on all the whole world, and on the holy Church and its children, and on this country and its inhabitants, and on this habitation and them that dwell in it, and on us all and every one of us together, may the compassion and mercies of our good God come and be poured forth continually, Christ the hope, etc.

They give the kiss of peace[2] *and say the Nicene Creed.*

We believe in one God the Father Almighty, Maker of all things visible and invisible. And in one Lord Jesus Christ, the Son of God, the only begotten, the firstborn of all creatures. Begotten of his Father before all worlds and not made. Very God of very God. Son of the nature of his Father. By whose hands the worlds were fashioned and everything was created. Who for us sons of men and for our salvation came down from heaven, and was incarnate by the Holy Ghost, and became son of man, and was conceived and born of the Virgin Mary. He suffered and was crucified in the days of Pontius Pilate. And he was buried, and the third day he rose again, as it is written, and ascended unto heaven, and sat down on the right hand of his Father. And furthermore, he is ready to come to judge the dead and the quick. And in one Holy Ghost,

---

[1] This seems to be for use in a monastery or in a private house.

[2] This appears to be the universal custom, but R. C., U. do not mention it; R. C. does not mention the Nicene Creed here.

the Spirit of truth, who proceedeth from the Father, the life-giving Spirit. And in one holy Apostolick and Catholick Church. And we confess one baptism for the forgiveness of sins, and the resurrection of our bodies, and the life for ever and ever. Amen.[1]

FIRST TUESDAY

All as on Monday except the following:—
FIRST MARMITHA. Ps. xxv., xxvi., xxvii.
SECOND MARMITHA. Ps. xxviii., xxix., xxx.
FIRST SHURAYA. Ps. xvii. 1-6 *to* hear me.
FIRST ANTHEM: *to the tune* Light and the Son of light.

Hear, O God, and have mercy upon me. O thou that hearest and delayest not. And answerest, and savest, and rescuest. Hear, O my Lord, our request. And return an answer in thy mercies to our petitions.   Ps. xxx. 11.

Faithful is the Lord in his words. O our Lord, thou hast said. For every one that knocketh at the door of my majesty. The door is opened. And his petitions are[2] answered.   Ps. cxlv. 13, Syr.

Glory be, etc. May the prayer of the Virgin. Mary the Mother of Christ. Be a wall to us. And keep us from the Evil one.

From everlasting to everlasting. O prophets and apostles. And martyrs and priests and teachers. May your prayer be to us. A wall by night and by day.

And let all the people say Amen and Amen. Our holy father.[3] The friend of the heavenly bridegroom. Beg for us mercies. From thy Lord whose love thou didst desire.   Ps. cvi. 46.

---

[1] The R. C. creed ins. *he died* after *Pontius Pilate*; also *and the Son* after *proceedeth from the Father*; and has *the bodies* for *our bodies*. It is not known if the first and third of these are modern alterations like the second.

[2] So A., U.; *shall be*, R. C.   [3] Or *Awa*.

FERIAL EVENING SERVICE

SECOND SHURAYA. Ps. xxi. 1-5.
SECOND ANTHEM: *to the tune* Now is the night.

Hear my prayer, O Lord. We make request to thee, O our Lord. And we beseech thy majesty. As thou hast created me [1] in thy compassion. Give us life by thy coming. For thou hast compassion on sinners. And mercy on them that repent. And causest the multitude of sins to pass away. In the mercies of thy lovingkindness.

<small>Ps. cii. 1.</small>

Hearken to my words and receive [them]. O God, who didst accept the lamb. Of Abel, a perfect lamb. And the offering of righteous Noah. And of faithful Abraham. Receive, O our Lord, our request. And return an answer in thy mercies to our petitions. And make thy peace to dwell among us. All our days.

<small>Ps. cxli. 1.</small>

Glory be, etc. O Mary, the holy Virgin. Mother of Jesus our Saviour. May thy prayer be a refuge. To the company of the faithful. And through thee may our prayers be answered. As a help to our feebleness. And with thee may we see Christ. In the day of his revelation.

From everlasting to everlasting. We keep the memorial of the just. And in their prayers we take refuge. And through them we call on thee. O our Lord, pity us. Make firm in us thy love as it is in them. And let our mouth preach their truth. And confirm their faith in us. O Hope of thy true (disciples).

Let all the people say Amen and Amen. How excellent art thou, O blessed one. And desired is the crown of all thy victories. Which by virtuous deeds. Thou didst gain in heaven. Thou didst convict the adversary. Who fought with thee in the contest. And, lo, thy memorial is celebrated. In heaven and earth.

<small>Ps. cvi. 46.</small>

EVENING ANTHEM. [Varies with the season.]
Or this.[2] *Our help is in the Name of the Lord.* Our help is from God. Who by means of his mercies chastiseth us all. For he is the giver of our life. The hope of

<small>Ps. cxxiv. 7.</small>

---

[1] *Sic*: Qu. *us*?   [2] So A., U.; om. R. C.

the salvation of our souls shall never more be cut off. But let us cry and say. Keep us, O my Lord, in thy compassion, and have mercy upon us.

And our helper in times of trouble. Our help, etc., *as above.* Ps. xlvi. 1.

Glory be to the Father, and to the Son, and to the Holy Ghost O Christ, who didst reconcile at thy coming all creation with him who sent thee. Pity thy Church, saved by thy blood. And bring to an end within it strifeful divisions. Which allow the devil to enter. To the wonderful dispensation of thy manhood. And raise up in it[1] priests to preach the sound faith.

LETTER PSALM, cxix. 17-33.

MARTYRS' ANTHEM.

The righteous shall have an everlasting memorial. Stephen trod the way. And the martyrs walked in his footsteps. And with the bridegroom have joy. In the bridechamber of light that passeth not away. Ps. cxii. 6.

He will not be afraid of any evil tidings. Stephen when he was stoned. Saw the glory of his Lord on high. And the Holy Ghost weaving. A crown for the head of the faithful. Ps. cxii. 7.

He asked life of thee and thou gavest it him. Stephen asked for mercy. For the people who drew near to stone him. Pardon, O our Lord, and forgive them. For they know not what they do. Ps. xxi. 4.

Against the unmerciful people. Stephen when he was being killed. Asked mercy for them that killed him. Like his Lord when he was crucified. By the cruel Jews. Ps. xliii. 1.

And sing lustily with your voice. With a loud voice the martyrs cried. Before the judges and said. We will not deny Christ. Who tasted death for us. Ps. xxxiii. 3.

---

[1] So U.; A. om. *in it.*

Help us, O God our Saviour. O Christ, who didst descend among the martyrs. And didst help them in their contest. Be to us an armour that is not conquered. And a high wall that is not overcome.

Ps. lxxix. 9.

There is none like unto thee, O Lord my God; and there is nothing like thy works. There is no distress with which we have been afflicted. (So great) that we should deny and flee from thy worship. For the gods of the heathen come to nought. And thou alone art not moved.

Ps. lxxxvi. 8.

Such as are planted in the house of the Lord. As trees in a garden. The martyrs are placed in the temple.[1] And over them is placed the altar. And the Holy Ghost ministereth to them.

Ps. xcii. 12.

Ye servants of his that do his pleasure. The watchful ones[2] descend from their place. And sing glory in their canticles. Over the bones of the faithful. Who have performed the will of their Creator.

Ps. ciii. 21.

Offer unto him the sacrifices of glory. The martyrs who were burnt were incense. And fell like (fragrant) roots in the fire. And the smell of their burning was sweet. As spices in the temple.

Ps. cvii. 22.

Even the cedars of Libanus which thou hast planted. The martyrs are cedars which stood. And bowed not down before the judges. And[3] on their graves kings worshipped. That from their bones they might have help.

Ps. civ. 16.

As a city that is surrounded by a wall. The martyrs are walls that fall not down. And blessed fountains that fail not. By your prayers beg for mercies. For the world from the Compassionate one.

Ps. cxxii. 3.

Bow down thine ear, O Lord, and answer me. Moses prayed, (and) the sea divided. Simon prayed and conquered the Evil one. Our Lord prayed and tasted death. And gave life to Adam who had perished.

Ps. lxxxvi. 1.

---

[1] Referring to the fact that only martyrs may be buried in the churches (Sunhadus v. 12, 25).

[2] Angels.

[3] Om. A.

Who is he in the heaven of heavens that can be compared unto the Lord? The sufferings of (this) time are not to be compared. To the kingdom which is prepared. From the foundation (of the world) for the faithful. Who have walked after thy Name.   Ps. lxxxix. 6.

How good and beautiful. How sweet is the smell of that garden. Which is placed in the temple of Jerusalem. And the martyrs enter and have joy. Under the shadow of its¹ branches. Ps. cxxxiii. 1.

Blessed are those that are blameless in the way. Blessed are the martyrs when they hear. The voice of the Father saying to them. Come, enter, and inherit the kingdom. Which awaiteth you from the foundation (of the world). Ps. cxix. 1.

And walk in the law of the Lord. A great blessing that passeth not away. Hath our Lord Jesus promised. To those who have loved him and believed in him. And have kept all his commandments. Ib.

Come, let us kneel and worship Him. Come, let us be blessed² by the martyrs. Come, let us be blessed by the priests. May the prayer of the martyrs and priests. Be a wall to our souls. Ps. xcv. 6.

O God, who is like unto Thee? The death of the athletes is like. To the death which our Lord died. His (death) was to hang on the cross. And theirs the sword and stoning. Ps. lxxxiii. 1, Syr.

Those that are true of heart. To desired blessings which end not. Are the holy martyrs invited. And instead of the sufferings which they endured here. They inherit the kingdom on high. Ps. cxxv. 4.

He flew on the wings of the wind. The chariot sped and descended. The same which bore Elijah. And in it the saints ascend. To meet our Lord when he cometh. Ps. xviii. 10.

---

¹ R. C., U. : *their.*
² A play on the words *kneel* and *bless*, which have the same root.

How good and beautiful. How beautiful are the companies. Of martyrs who stand in prayer. And sweet is the sound of their songs. When[1] they ask mercy for the world.

Ps. cxxxiii. 1.

Righteous and upright.[2] O glorious and holy martyr. St. Cyriac the illustrious. Beg mercy for us from thy Lord. That we may be worthy of forgiveness of trespasses.

Deut. xxxii. 4.

From[3] *the rising up of the sun unto the going down of the same.* Lo, in all quarters of the world is celebrated with processions. The glorious day of the memorials. Of Mar Sergis and Mar Bakus. May their prayers be a wall to us.

Ps. cxiii. 3.

And[3] *I spake of peace.* Peace to thee, O martyr Mar Pithiun. Athlete of Christ the King. Who didst endure stripes and afflictions. From the hands of the impure Astrologer.

Ps. cxx. 6.

And[4] *thy prayers be on all of us.* Peace to thee, Mar Pithiun the martyr. Spiritual treasurer. Supply wealth to the needy. Who take refuge in thy prayers.

Both small and great. Let us take refuge in St. George. That by the strength of his prayers. Our Lord may make straight our ways. And lighten the weight of our limbs.

Ps. cxv. 13.

And I will speak peace of thee. Peace to thee, full of grace. Said the watchful one to Mary. My Lord be with thee, daughter of mortals. From whom the Saviour doth shine forth.

Ps. cxxii. 8, Syr.

Glory be, etc. Peace with the architects. Who built a citadel that falleth not down. And in the name of Jesus adorned and built. A bridechamber on high that is not moved.

From everlasting to everlasting. A crown of victory in[5] thy

---

[1] *And*, A.
[2] *Seek of the Lord and pray before him* (Ps. xxxvii. 7), A.
[3] R. C., U. om. this verse.   [4] A. om. this verse.   [5] *Lit.* of.

contest. Is laid up on high, O our father.[1] Which at the last day thou wilt[2] take. From the right hand of thy Lord who exalted thee.

And let all the people say Amen and Amen. O thou who dost complete the course of the day. And givest the night for rest. Fulfil in us thy lovingkindness. O Lord, by night and day.* O Christ, who hast kept us by day. And brought us to the evening in thy lovingkindness. Give us a restful night. That we may confess thee for thy lovingkindness.* O our Lord, give peace in our country. And bless all our work. That we may be worthy of mercy and compassion. And confidence in the judgment.* Give by the mercy of thy lovingkindness. A restful night and sleep. To all the sick and afflicted. Who call on thee in their affliction.

Ps. cvi. 46.

FIRST WEDNESDAY

All as on Monday, except the following :—
FIRST MARMITHA. Ps. lxii., lxiii., lxiv.
SECOND MARMITHA. Ps. lxv., lxvi., lxvii.
FIRST SHURAYA. Ps. xxiii. 1-5.
FIRST ANTHEM : *to the tune* Compassionate and full.

Day and night. May the prayer of the Virgin Mary. The Mother of Jesus our Saviour. Be to us continually. A wall by night and day.

Ps. xlii. 3.

At all seasons and times. May the prayer, etc., *as above.*

Glory be, etc. Prophets, pray for peace. Apostles, for tranquillity. And martyrs and priests and teachers. May your prayers be a wall to us.

From everlasting to everlasting. Beg and beseech. O our illustrious father.[1] Of Christ whose love thou didst desire. That the congregation which celebrateth thy memorial. May be helped by thy prayers.

---

[1] Or *Awa*.   [2] R.C.: *woven . . . On the day of thy death thou didst take.*

FERIAL EVENING SERVICE

And let all the people say Amen and Amen. O thou who hearest the prayers of thy servants. Who answerest the petitions of thy worshippers. Hear our prayer and the voice of our request. And return answer to our petitions in thy mercies.

<small>Ps. cvi. 46.</small>

SECOND SHURAYA. Ps. xxiv. 1-6.

SECOND ANTHEM: *to the tune* Every breath.

And the land was filled with it. O Mary, who didst bear the medicine of life to the children of Adam. By thy petition may we find mercies in the day of the quickening.

<small>Ps. lxxx. 9.</small>

And deliver the children from death.[1] O Mary, etc., *as above.*

<small>Ps. cii. 20.</small>

Glory be, etc. A fount of life, O Lord, for us thou didst make. All the true sons of thy mysteries who loved thy Name.

From everlasting to everlasting. Our illustrious and holy father,[2] the friend of the Son. Beg from thy Lord compas- and mercies for our souls.

And let all the people say Amen and Amen. O our Lord, help us, send peace, scatter the evil ones. Keep thy Church, free its children from harm.

<small>Ps. cvi. 46.</small>

EVENING ANTHEM: *to the tune* We are not put to shame.[3]

Holy is the tabernacle of the most Highest. The temple of God the Word.[4] With great glory Mary carried in her bosom. And was mother and handmaid.[5] To Jesus the Saviour of all. And therefore all creatures. Rejoice in the day of her festival. And are bidden to the bridechamber of light. To endless joy. And we all, with all generations. Will call her most blessed. And give glory to him who chose her. As the abode of his glorious brightness.

<small>Ps. xlvi. 4.</small>

---

[1] So A.; but R. C. and U.: *The hills were covered with the shadow of it* (Ps. lxxx. 10).   [2] Or *Awa.*   [3] U. om. name of tune.

[4] R. C.: *The Son, the Word* (modern alteration).

[5] Play on the words *ima* (mother) and *amtha* (handmaid).

I will glorify the Word of God. The temple, etc., *as above.* Ps. lvi. 10, Syr.

Glory be, etc. To goodly pearls. Are the bones of the saints like. Fixed in the crown of the King. And their beauty shineth in creation. Come, let us all with perfect love. Honour the day of their memorial. With songs of the Holy Ghost. From morn until even. And let us beg for mercies from their Lord. That he may make his peace to dwell in creation. And by their prayers. May the Church and its children be kept.

From everlasting to everlasting. Blessed is thy memorial, our illustrious father.[1] For because of the truth thou wast persecuted. And didst endure sufferings and afflictions. That thou mightest be an inheritor of the kingdom. And[2] who can tell. The dispensation of thy spiritual deeds? For thou wast adorned with virtue. With vigil, fast, and prayer. May thy prayer be a refuge. To sinners who take refuge in thee. And may we be worthy to raise. Glory to thy Lord who exalted thee.

And let all the people say Amen and Amen. As the censer which Aaron offered. May the sweet fragrance of our congregation please thee. And like the Ps. cvi. 46. petition of the Ninevites. Receive the prayer of thy servants, O my Lord. And return an answer to our petitions in thy mercies. From thy rich treasury. And as thou didst answer Daniel. From the den of lions. Answer, O my Lord, and help thy worshippers. In these times of affliction. For in thee is our confident hope. O Lord, who dost love thy servants.

Prayer instead of Pity us, O thou Compassionate one (page 11):

Arm us, O our Lord and God, with strong and invincible armour, by the prayers of thy blessed Mother. And give us with her a portion and share in thy heavenly bridechamber, Lord of all, etc.

SHURAYA [*in place of a Letter Psalm*]. Ps. xlv. 14-17.

---

[1] Or *Awa*.   [2] R. C., U. om. *And*.

MARTYRS' ANTHEM.
For thy sake have we been killed every day. O holy martyrs who were killed. For the love of Christ. We beseech you for all of us. Beg mercy of God.
_{Ps. xliv. 22.}

In heaven and in earth. Your deeds conquer, and make us to rejoice. In the commemoration of your contests. For Christ's sake were ye killed. And with him will ye reign on high.
_{Ps. cxxxv. 6.}

Seek the Lord and be strong. O martyrs, beg mercy for the world. Which taketh refuge in your bones. That by your request and prayers. We may find mercy in the day of judgment.
_{Ps. cv. 4.}

How good and beautiful. With peace and tranquillity and concord. Is the country filled where ye dwell. And may we be kept from all harm. By your prayers, O blessed ones.
_{Ps. cxxxiii. 1.}

I will alway bless the Lord. Blessed is he who made you, O blessed ones. True physicians. And your bones pour forth help. To him that taketh refuge in them.
_{Ps. xxxiv. 1.}

The camp of the angels of the Lord. In many companies, enter. The martyrs before their persecutors. Crying and saying, Lord, help. Thy servants in times of affliction.
_{Ps. xxxiv. 7.}

Look to Him and trust in Him. They saw Christ and desired his love. Who tasted death for the sake of his Church. And they ran and gave up their souls. To be with him when he is revealed.
_{Ps. xxxiv. 5.}

Offer to him sacrifices of praise. Propitiatory censers and pure. Offerings were ye, O blessed ones. In whom the Father rejoiced, whom the Son accepted. And the Holy Ghost crowned.
_{Ps. cvii. 22.}

The Lord on high is glorious. Above on high is preserved glory. Which the martyrs put on at the quickening. In the glorious country full of blessings. Where life is high above all danger.
_{Ps. xciii. 5.}

And more to be desired are they than gold and than precious stones. Crowns better than gold. And sardonyx stones and pearls. Christ placeth on your heads. And giveth you joy in his bridechamber.   Ps. xix. 10.

Be strong, and your heart shall be established. O martyrs, ye did not fear the fire. And the terrible swords of the judges. For ye were clothed with the love of Christ. And despised all torments.   Ps. xxxi. 27.

Sing unto him a new song. With a new song doth Christ clothe. The friends whom he hath chosen to himself. And in place of the afflictions which they endured. He maketh them to inherit the bridechamber on high.   Ps. xxxiii. 3.

Open me the gates of righteousness. Open your treasures, O blessed ones. And give help to the needy. Who look and wait for your prayer. That by it they may be protected from the Evil one.   Ps. cxviii. 19.

Blessed are those that are blameless in the way. Blessed are ye, holy martyrs. Friends of the heavenly bridegroom. For lo, ye are invited to the kingdom. And life and blessings without end.   Ps. cxix. 1.

And walk in the law of the Lord. An unending blessing. And an unending and unperishing kingdom. Hath our Saviour promised to his saints. Who have loved him and have kept his commandments.   Ib.

Joseph was sold to be a bondservant. The bones of illustrious[1] Joseph. Made a hedge for the Egyptians. And your bones, O holy martyrs. Brought[2] compassion to all creation.   Ps. cv. 17.

Thou hast set a glorious crown upon his head. A beautiful and honourable crown. Did the Lord of glory place. On the illustrious[1] St. Cyriac.[3] Who bore sufferings for the truth.   Ps. xxi. 3.

---

[1] Or *victorious* (so frequently).   [2] *Lit.* became.
[3] Martyr Hurmizd, R. C.

And[1] *I will speak peace of thee.* Peace to thee, illustrious Mar
Babai. Who didst fill every house with bless-
Ps. cxxii. 8.   ings. And lo, the tears of our eyes[2] flow.
Before thy tomb which hath brought us pardon.

Righteous and upright. May the prayer of the martyr Mar
Sergis,[3] who by his strength. Confounded the
Deut. xxxii. 4.   Evil one and his servants. Keep our congrega-
tion. From the Evil one and his hosts.

Beg[4] *of the Lord and pray before him.* Beseech, illustrious
Mar Ishu. Our God Jesus Christ. That
Ps. xxxvii. 7.   when he raiseth the children of dust. He may
cause us to enter his glorious bridechamber.

And[5] *thy prayers be on all of us.* Peace to thee, illustrious
Mar Pithiun. Who didst endure sufferings and afflictions.
From the persecutors of the truth. For the love of Christ.

The Lord shall give strength unto his people. May the power
which descended to the contest. And gave the
Ps. xxix. 10.   martyr St. George the victory. Be our guardian.
From the Evil one and his hosts.

Choice silver which in the earth is tried. A storehouse of help
to us is. Thy pure body, O Mary. Which by
Ps. xii. 7.   its many helps. Doth make us rich in our need.

Glory be, etc. Glory to the Lord who exalted you. And made you a storehouse of life. For the afflicted and distressed. In you take refuge, by you are saved.

From everlasting to everlasting. O armed and illustrious athlete. Our father,[6] inheritor of the kingdom. Beseech Christ that in his mercies. He may make his peace to dwell in creation.

And let all the people say Amen and Amen. The evening
praise we lift up. To thee, O Lord God. And
Ps. cvi. 46.   ask that we may receive. Forgiveness of trespasses from thee.* Give us life without sin, O my Lord.

---

[1] R. C., U. om. this verse.   [2] Babathan (play on words).
[3] Pithiun, R. C.
[4] Om. R. C.; U. places this verse before *Righteous and upright.*
[5] R. C. om. this verse.   [6] Or *Awa*.

And love and peace and concord. And may all our petitions be answered. As seemeth good to thy Godhead.* Sow in us, O my Lord, a desire for prayer. And may our request ascend to thee. And give us twofold health. The sustenance of body and of spirit.

FIRST THURSDAY

All as on Monday, except the following:—
FIRST MARMITHA. Ps. xcvi., xcvii., xcviii.
SECOND MARMITHA. Ps. xcix., c., ci.
FIRST SHURAYA. Ps. xxv. 1-5.
FIRST ANTHEM: *to the tune* [1] Thou art the Light.
O Lord, thou knowest. More than all thou knowest. Lord, what doth help us. In thy lovingkindness supply our life. And may thy mercies pity our trespasses. May thy compassion be a physician to us. And thy love a master and teacher. To thee be glory, and on us be thy mercies. *Ps. xl. 11.*

Thy mercy, O Lord, endureth for ever. To the overflowing mercies of thy lovingkindness. O King Christ, we call. For assistance to our weakness. Because of the times, which are disturbed. And the world, which is in confusion with its sins. Give us immoveable peace. That having it we may confess thee at all times. *Ps. cxxxviii. 8.*

Glory be, etc. O Mary, the holy Virgin. Mother of Jesus our Saviour. Beseech and beg for mercy. For sinners, that they be not destroyed. For in thy prayers they take refuge. May thy prayer be a wall to us. In this world and in that to come.

From everlasting to everlasting. By the prayer of the just who propitiated thee. And the righteous who were approved before thee. The prophets and apostles and teachers. And

---

[1] A. om. name of tune.

martyrs and priests and monks. Keep the assembly of thy worshippers. *That they may raise to thee a new song.* Father, Son, and Holy Ghost.

And let all the people say Amen and Amen. Let us all diligently honour. The glorious day of the memorial. Of our illustrious and holy father.[1] Who was a vessel full of mercies. Worthy of the service of his Lord. And day by day his lamp shineth. May his prayer be a wall to us.

<small>Ps. cvi. 46.</small>

SECOND SHURAYA. Ps. xxviii. 1-8.

SECOND ANTHEM: *to the tune*[2] They are not oppressed.

Lord, I have called daily upon thee. To thee cry the afflicted, O Compassionate one. And in thee the distressed take refuge, O Friend of men. Be a guardian to their life in thy compassion. And rescue them from the Evil one, for on thee they wait.

<small>Ps. lxxxviii. 9.</small>

In the deep of his heart. Jonah called to thee from within the fish, and thou didst answer him. The company of Ananias in the furnace, and thou didst deliver them. And[3] all creation calls to thee with sighing. Pity it and have mercy on it, as thou art wont.

<small>Ps. lxiv. 6.</small>

Glory be, etc. O Mary, Mother of the King, the King of kings. Offer with us a petition to the Son, who is of thee. That he make his peace and tranquillity to dwell in creation. And that the Church and her children be kept from harm.

From everlasting to everlasting. Peace with your company, O blessed ones. Merchants bearing life to the sons of men. Open the treasury of your prayers to the needy. And keep the country where ye dwelt from harm.

And let all the people say Amen and Amen. Make request for us all to thy Lord. O our illustrious and holy father,[4] the friend of the Son. For by thy prayers shall be helped and saved. All who are afflicted and distressed, and who take refuge in thee.

<small>Ps. cvi. 46.</small>

---

[1] Or *Awa*. [2] Om. A. [3] A. om. *And* [4] Or *Awa*.

FIRST THURSDAY

EVENING ANTHEM. [Varies with the season.]

Or this.[1] *We shall give thee thanks for ever.* We give thee thanks, O our Creator, for thou hast mercy on all creation. Thou hast brought into being[2] both the good and the evil in thy compassion. And copiously givest help to the sons of men. O thou who hast abundant mercy, praise to thee. Ps. lxxix. 14.

For thy loving mercy and for thy truth's sake. We give thee thanks, etc., *as above.* Ps. cxv. 1; and cxxxviii. 2.

Glory be to the Father, and to the Son, and to the Holy Ghost. Open to us, O our Lord, the great treasury of thy mercy. That we may receive mercies and salvation for our poor race. And heal the pains of our sins by the great medicine of thy compassion. That our weak race by thy mercies may receive compassion.

LETTER PSALM, cxix. 49-65.

MARTYRS' ANTHEM.

Ye are the blessed of the Lord. The blessed martyrs counted death. As a great gain. And like honours and gifts.[3] Accepted stripes and torments. And now after their deaths. They bestow on the world benefits. And storehouses full of helps. Ps. cxv. 15.

Yea, they thought scorn of the pleasant land. The martyrs who saw the world passing away. And truth abiding. Left buildings and riches. And possessions, which are vanity. And desired the fear of God. And gave their necks to the sword. And lo, they are about[4] to inherit the kingdom. Ps. cvi. 24.

And sing lustily with the voice. The martyrs say, Our crown is fixed. And our recompense laid up. And Christ the King, whom we have loved. Maketh us to enter his kingdom. And because we have suffered with fire and sword. Christ comforts our afflictions. In Paradise, which is full of joys. Ps. xxxiii. 3.

---

[1] So A., U.; om. R. C.

[2] U.: Thou hast given thy compassion both to . . .

[3] Syr.: *a gift.*   [4] And they were invited, R. C.

Thy kingdom is an everlasting kingdom. The martyrs are
invited. To the kingdom on high, and to life
without end. That which ear hath not heard.
And eye hath not seen, as it is written. And to the heart of
the sons of men. Hath not gone up the blessing in which
abide. The illustrious ones who loved Christ.

Ps. cxlv. 13.

Lay hand upon the shield and buckler, and stand up to help me.
With the shield of the Spirit were the true
martyrs armed. When they went down to the
contest. And young men and boys were assembled. To see
an unaccustomed sight. Men fighting with death. And conquering it though they were killed. A wonder greater than
words can tell.

Ps. xxxv. 2.

Look on him and trust in him. O holy martyrs, ye saw
Christ. In the kingdom which is above. And [1]
(departing) from temporal life. Ye have
reached perfection. And have been counted worthy to
glorify. With the spiritual companies. God the Lord of (all)
creatures.

Ps. xxxiv. 5.

The eyes of the Lord are over the righteous. With the eye of
the Spirit was Christ seen. By the holy
martyrs. Who imitated him by their sufferings. For they heard that voice. Every one that beareth
sufferings for my sake. Here on earth from men. Hath joy
in the bridechamber of the kingdom.

Ps. xxxiv. 15.

He spread out a cloud and overshadowed them. Clouds of
light bear up the saints. In the day of resurrection. When is revealed the greatness. Of
the heavenly King of kings. And above, on high, they have
joy. On the right hand of Christ. All who have loved him
and have kept his commandments.

Ps. cv. 38.

They knew not and understood not. The king bade them cast.
The three children into the furnace. And
Another among them. Sprinkled their faces
with dew. And the more the fire was kindled. The more

Ps. lxxxii. 5.

---

[1] A. om. *And.*

their faces shone. Blessed be the Lord who hath exalted his saints.

In the sight of all the people. The martyrs say, We will not deny. The Son of God. For we are the seed of Abraham. And sons of the inheritance of Isaac. For the God of our fathers. We offer a temporal death. And inherit life without end. Ps. cxvi. 16.

Out of the hand of the unrighteous and evil man.[1] The unrighteous king enraged. With anger and envy. Brought sharp wooden nails. And fixed them in the body of the boy. And Christ helped him and aided[2] him. St. Cyriac the illustrious. May his prayers be a wall to us. Ps. lxxi. 3.

Come,[3] let us rejoice and be glad in it. In the day of thy crowning, O martyr Mar Sergis. The watchful ones[4] and men rejoiced. Angels carried thy soul. Sons of men bore thy body in procession. The crown which the Holy Ghost wove. Our Saviour placed on thy head. Beg mercies for us from thy Lord. Ps. cxviii. 24.

His[5] heart is established and feareth not. The martyr Mar Pithiun stood prepared. Before the heathen Magi. And reproved their arrogance. Worship not idols. But worship the one God. For heaven and earth are his. And his dominion endureth for ever. Ps. cxii. 8.

Against the unmerciful people. Dire sufferings and bitter torments. And many kinds of death. The holy martyr bore. St. George the illustrious. For the love of Christ. Because he loved him more than his life. Blessed is he who crowned the martyr with victory. Ps. xliii. i.

The Lord preserveth them that are faithful. By the prayers of the Virgin Mary. The blessed Mother. May thy worshippers, O my Lord, be kept. From the wiles of the Crafty one. And grant us to fulfil thy Ps. xxxi. 26.

---

[1] *His wickedness shall come upon his own head* (Ps. vii. 17), U.
[2] Strengthened, R. C.
[3] Om. R. C. ; U. inverts the position of this and the following.
[4] Angels. [5] A. om. this verse.

will. Both in words and deeds. And to sing to thee glory at all times.

Glory be, etc. Peace to you, holy martyrs. Friends of Christ. Who conquered and overcame and were crowned. And confounded the Evil one in the contest. Blessed are ye in the day of the Son. When the greatness of his glory shineth forth. And ye enter with him to the bridechamber.

From everlasting to everlasting. A garment of grace woven by the Holy Ghost. Art thou, O our father.[1] A fountain of heavenly blessings. Hast thou caused to flow forth by thy steadfast deeds. And thou hast given the flock of thy pasture[2] to drink. Of the word of heavenly[3] life. And lo, a crown of victory is woven[4] for thee.

And let all the people say Amen and Amen. By sea and by land they call to thee, O our Lord. That thou mayest come to help them. Him that calleth by sea thou answerest. And (him that calleth) by land thou dost not neglect. And to us, O my Lord, who call on thee. Come, and help us, and save us. And deliver us from the Evil one and his host.* O Christ, who didst make peace with thine own blood. Between the height and the depth. Make peace, O my Lord, between priests and kings. And raise up thy Church in thy compassion. And let the one sign of faith. Reign in the whole inhabited world. In thy lovingkindness, O merciful Lord.* By thy lovingkindness, O merciful Lord. Bless and keep. This country and its inhabitants. From devils and evil men. And increase in it moderate weather. And[5] love and peace and concord. And health of body and of soul.* By[6] the angels the house. Of our father Abraham was blessed. And by the Lord of the angels. The house of Zacchæus was blessed. And in the house into which thy worshippers have entered. May the Trinity dwell. And may it be blessed in the generation of the righteous.* Drive away Satan, who is the enemy. Of all righteousness. From

Ps. cvi. 46.

---

[1] Or *Awa.* [2] Or *diocese.* [3] U.: *spiritual.* [4] U.: *preserved.*
[5] R. C., A., om. *And.* [6] R. C. om. this verse.

the house where we dwell. And let him not enter and have dominion in it. And¹ establish, O our Lord, its foundations. On the rock of faith. And increase in us life without end.²

FIRST FRIDAY

All as on Monday, except the following :—
FIRST MARMITHA. Ps. lxxxv., lxxxvi.
SECOND MARMITHA. Ps. lxxxvii., lxxxviii.
FIRST SHURAYA. Ps. lxxv. 1-5.
FIRST ANTHEM : *to the tune*³ The disciples of Christ.⁴

Confess him and bless his Name. Confess, O mortals, the Son who saved us. From the dominion of death. Which held us in our sins. For the whole reason that he descended to Sheol. Was that he might bring the dead from the graves to life.⁵ Who can repay the lovingkindness. Which he hath shewed to the race of mortals? [Ps. c. 3.]

My mouth shall speak of wisdom. Take refuge, O sinners, in repentance. For the time is short. The world flourisheth and passeth away. Blessing to the penitent. And judgment to the wicked who have not worked righteousness. For if thou, O my Lord, judgest justly. Who can overcome in the judgment? [Ps. xlix. 3.]

Glory be to the Father, and to the Son, and to the Holy Ghost. We beseech thy lovingkindness, O Christ the King. Remember not the offences of⁶ thy servants. Who have received the mystery of thy body. And may thy lovingkindness defend them in the day of the quickening. And may they be delivered from Gehenna. And with the watchful ones⁷ may they be brought in to meet thee. With great glory, in the heights of heaven.

---

¹ R. C. om. *And.* ² *And let life without end be increased in it*, A.
³ Om. A. ⁴ So U.; R. C. less fully.
⁵ Or, *He went down in both his natures*, but this seems a forced construction. ⁶ *Against*, A. ⁷ The angels.

SECOND SHURAYA. Ps. lxxxii. 1-5.[1]

SECOND ANTHEM: *to the tune*[2] Remain in peace.

I will alway bless the Lord. Blessed is thy day, O Son of the Lord of all. When thou comest and rendest the bosom of Sheol. Glorious is thy quickening, for which are looking. The generations that have passed away and those that remain.
_{Ps. xxxiv. 1.}

They pass away, but thou endurest. Lo, this world passeth away. And all its desires come to nought. And blessed is he who hath prepared for himself. Provision for the world that passeth not away.
_{Ps. cii. 26.}

Glory be to the Father, and to the Son, and to the Holy Ghost. We have no hope in which we may boast. But thy cross which pardoneth our trespasses. It is a high wall to us. And delivereth us from harm.

EVENING ANTHEM. [Varies with the season.]

Or this,[3] *to the tune* God the Word.

Who can express the noble acts of the Lord?[4] Who is sufficient, O our Maker, to confess thee[5] for thy mercy? Who in the beginning didst form us in thy splendid image. And in the latter times hast clothed thyself with us, and turned us to the knowledge of thee. O thou who exaltest our race, glory to thee.
_{Ps. cvi. 2.}

Who is like unto thee, O Lord?[6] Who is sufficient, etc., *as above.*
_{Ex. xv. 11.}

Glory be to the Father, and to the Son, and to the Holy Ghost. Who is sufficient, etc., *as above.*

Prayer instead of Pity us, O thou Compassionate one (page 11):

Quicken, O my Lord, our departed in thy compassion, and set them at thy right hand. Clothe them with excellent glory

---

[1] A. adds: *They knew not, neither understood they.*   [2] Om. A.

[3] So A., U.; om. R. C.; A. om. name of tune.

[4] U.: *For thy loving mercy, and for thy truth's sake* (Ps. cxv. 1).

[5] U. adds: *on our behalf.*

[6] U. adds: *And who is like thy deeds?* (altered from Ps. lxxxvi. 8?)

in thy kingdom, and join them to the just and righteous who fulfil thy will in Jerusalem which is above, O Lord of our death and of our life, Father, Son, and Holy Ghost, for ever. *Amen.*

SHURAYA *in place of a Letter Psalm (if there is no special one in the Kashkul*[1]*).* Ps. cxvi. 11-13 *to* people.

MARTYRS' ANTHEM.

All these things be come upon us, and we have not wandered from thee. Christ the Saviour of the world. The great King of glory. Did the martyrs love and have faith in. So they confounded the devil. And with the angels rejoice on high. And stand before God. And the Enemy and his host. Have they subdued under their feet. Ps. xliv. 18.

Nor lied against thy covenant. Christ is the Saviour of the world. Who suffered for us in his lovingkindness. And trod the way to the kingdom. And in his steps[2] went the martyrs. And gave their bodies to torments. And burnings and tortures. And gained by the blood of their necks. The promised life without end. Ib.

The voice of glory and salvation is in the dwelling of the righteous. At the voice of the holy martyrs. Who sow peace in creation. The spiritual ones fly and descend. Quickly to the holy place. And companies of the spiritual ones cry. With the martyrs in their song of praise. Holy art thou, O Lord of all. Who hast exalted the race of mortals. Ps. cxviii. 15.

For he hath done a marvellous thing. A great marvel hath been wrought for us. By the illustrious athletes and martyrs. Who saw the swords flashing. And the murderers threatening. And their mind moved not nor flinched. Because of their great love for their Lord. And they accepted death as a gift. And they relaxed not their confession of him. Ps. xcviii. 1.

---

[1] A. om. these words.   [2] *Lit.* heels.

And they spared[1] *not their souls from death.* O murdered ones who loved your Creator. And received death of your own free will. And became propitiatory sacrifices. To Christ the King who crowneth you. Offer with us a petition. In the great day of searching. That we may be rescued from torment. And inherit life without end.

Ps. lxxviii. 51.

Offer to him the sacrifices of praise. O martyrs who are propitiatory sacrifices. Who yourselves propitiated your Lord. And with the blood which your necks poured forth. Gained the kingdom which passeth not away. Beseech and beg of the Lord. For sinners that they perish not. Who in your prayers take refuge. May peace and tranquillity be multiplied to them.

Ps. cvii. 22.

He sent his word and healed them. True physicians. Were the martyrs in creation. And cured and healed souls. Which were defiled with sin. Praise to the Lord who chose you. And made strength to dwell in your bones. That ye might be to the race of mortals. Havens of peace in the world.

Ps. cvii. 20.

He brought them unto the haven where they would be. A desired and advantageous haven. Is the treasure of the bones of the saints. A fountain of mercies and of healing. Hast thy will placed (there), O our Saviour. And may the strength which descendeth from on high. And alway visiteth their bones. Keep the assembly of thy worshippers. From the wiles of the Crafty one.

Ps. cvii. 30.

I will magnify thee, O my Lord the King. The King of the highest with his ministers. Helped the company of the faithful. The command went forth that the just martyrs. Should be killed with the sword. The Chaldeans[2] were astonished, standing. Lifting up their hands,[3] and saying. Great is the God of the faithful. Though he is not seen he saveth them.

Ps. cxlv. 1.

---

[1] The Syriac Psalter has *He spared.*
[2] The Magi.
[3] *Lit.* finger.

A great King above all gods. The King of the highest heights. Built a citadel in heaven. And gave it the name Jerusalem. Of the firstborn written in heaven. He fixed a ladder of life in his Church. And leadeth them of his household, and raiseth them up. To the excellent habitation of heaven. That with the spiritual ones they may have joy.[1]   *Ps. xcv. 3.*

Lay[2] *hand upon the shield and buckler, and stand up to help me.* With the shield of the Holy Ghost. Were the martyrs armed in their conflict. When they bowed their necks. Before the swords of the persecutors. And despised stripes and tortures. For the love of Christ. And inherited by the blood of their necks. The kingdom which is not destroyed.   *Ps. xxxv. 2.*

The King's daughter stood in glory. The Church is like to the ark. And the holy altar to the throne. And the martyrs to the bands of principalities.[3] Who minister to Christ. It[4] is built with jasper stones. And sapphires and crystal. Its architects are Peter and Paul. And Theodore and Nestorius.   *Ps. xlv. 10.*

And I will speak peace of thee. Peace to thee, O martyr Cyriac. Athlete of Christ the King. And peace to thy tomb. Which giveth health to the sick. Peace be to thy limbs. From which flow forth helps. Peace to thee and peace to thy mother. And praise to him who gave thee the victory.   *Ps. cxxii. 8.*

Offer[5] *to him the sacrifices of praise.* Reasonable sacrifices were the martyrs. St. Cyriac and Julitta. In their own sufferings and tortures. For the truth of the love of their Lord. And they endured double afflictions. From the persecutors of the truth. That they might be partakers with him. In that kingdom which passeth not away.   *Ps. cvii. 22.*

---

[1] *That they may be inheritors in the kingdom*, R. C., U.
[2] A. om. this verse.   [3] Col. i. 16.   [4] The Church.
[5] R. C., U. om. this verse.

I[1] will alway bless the Lord. Cyriac kneeled[2] in prayer. And called to his Lord, beseeching him. O our Lord Jesus Christ. For thy sake have I been beaten. Send thy strength from on high. And help[3] thy servant in the contest. Before the false teachers say. The faithful have no God.

Ps. xxxiv. 1.

Beg of the Lord and pray before him. Hail, spiritual merchant. O illustrious martyr Mar Sergis! A pearl without flaw. A light hath shone in thy soul. Thou hast bought it with thy blood, and became rich thereby. And thou hast gained wealth which is not destroyed. Ask for the Church and her children. Love and peace and concord.

Ps. xxxvii. 7.

Gird thee with a sword upon thy thigh, O thou most Mighty.[4] O giant in strength, St. George. Who didst despise death and the sword. And cruel rendings. And blows of every kind. And didst work miracles and wonders. And didst turn all men to the truth. Blessed be he that made the athlete to conquer. Who by his strength will overcome error.

Ps. xlv. 4.

This shall they say among the heathen. Blessed art thou, holy Virgin. Blessed art thou, Mother of Christ. Blessed art thou whom all generations. And races call blessed. Blessed art thou in whom the Father was well pleased. Blessed art thou in whom the Firstborn dwelt. Blessed art thou whose name the Holy Ghost. Made to conquer in creation.

Ps. cxxvi. 3.

Glory be, etc. Glory be to the Father who chose you. Illustrious and holy martyrs. Glory be to the Son for whose sake. Ye stood, by his strength in the contest. Glory be to the Holy Ghost. Who adorned (and) wove your

---

[1] Om. R. C.; U. places it after the next verse, with the heading, *For great is the power of prayer which the righteous man prayeth* (St. James v. 16).

[2] Play on words; *bless* and *kneel* have the same root.

[3] U.: *strengthen.*   [4] Syr.: *Giant.*

crowns. May your prayer be a wall to us. Till the end of the world.

From everlasting to everlasting. O our father,[1] who didst conquer in the contest. Lo, in heaven is thy recompense. Christ, for whom thou didst adorn thyself. Hath exalted thy memorial in his Church. A pure censer was thy love. And thou didst propitiate thy Lord by thy deeds. Beseech him with us when he is revealed. In great glory, that he have mercy upon us.

And let all the people say Amen and Amen. O King of kings, our helper. Art thou, O Christ our Saviour. Pity thy servants who call on thee. Ps. cvi. 46. In these times of affliction. For lo, sorrows surround us. And fears on all sides. Quickly let thy mercies prevent us. And make thy face to shine (on us) and save us.* Thou art compassionate from all eternity. And merciful for ever. What is the wickedness of creation. Compared with the overflowing mercies of thy lovingkindness?[2] Sprinkle the face of our nature. With the dew of mercy and pity. And rescue us from the hand of the Evil one. And from the tares, the sons of error.* May Adam and the camp of the just. Moses and the chain of the prophets. And Peter and the company of the apostles. Stephen and all the martyrs. And[3] Ephraim and Nersai the teachers.[4] And Antony and the hermits. Beseech thee, O our Lord Jesus. That thou have mercy on the world.* The departed, who clothed themselves with thee, O our Lord. In the water of baptism. By thee may their bodies be cleansed. From the defilements of sin. To the departed who have eaten of thy body. And have had joy in thy living blood. Grant, O our Lord, a memorial. In the country where the just abide.

---

[1] Or *Awa*.

[2] *i.e.*, Great as is our wickedness, thy lovingkindness is far greater.   [3] *And* om. A.

[4] *And the company of teachers*, R. C., U.

MIDDLE FRIDAY

All as on First Monday, except the following:—
FIRST MARMITHA. Ps. lxxxv., lxxxvi., *as on First Friday.*
SECOND MARMITHA. Ps. lxxxvii., lxxxviii., *as on First Friday.*
FIRST SHURAYA. Ps. xcv. 1-8.
FIRST ANTHEM: *to the tune*[1] Holy apostles.

O come, let us glorify the Lord. Come, mortals, let us confess and glorify. Him who by his death brought to nought the dominion of death. And promised life and resurrection. To all the race of mortals.
<small>Ps. xcv. 1.</small>

O come, let us kneel and worship him. Thee we worship, O Christ our Saviour. For thou art the Quickener and Saviour of all the departed. Who were baptized in thy Name. And confessed thy cross and thy death.
<small>Ps. xcv. 6.</small>

Glory be to the Father, and to the Son, and to the Holy Ghost. Glory be to thee, who by thy resurrection didst promise. Life and quickening to all the race of mortals. And thee let us confess and glorify. For thou art the Quickener of the departed.

SECOND SHURAYA. Ps. cxxxix. 1-5.
SECOND ANTHEM: *to the tune*[1] Being, who by thy will.

Thou hast fashioned me, and laid thine hand upon me. On Friday in the beginning God fashioned Adam from dust. And breathed into him the Spirit. And made him a reasonable being, that he might sing to him praise.
<small>Ps. cxxxix. 4.</small>

O foolish people and unwise. On Friday the Jews crucified our Lord on the top of Golgotha. And on Friday the Slayer slew death. And raised up our nature.
<small>Deut. xxxii. 6.</small>

Glory be to the Father, and to the Son, and to the Holy Ghost.

---

[1] A. om. name of tune.

Let us make request with entreating, and beseech mercy and ask for forgiveness. From the Compassionate one. Whose door is open to all who turn to him and repent.

EVENING ANTHEM. [Varies with the season.]

Or this.[1] *Royal Anthem: to the tune* We are not confounded.

Who can express the noble acts of the Lord?[2] Who is sufficient to tell thy wonders, O Christ the King, our Saviour? For thou, more glorious than all. Ps. cvi. 2.
Wast revealed in the firstfruits[3] which (thou didst take) from us. For thus thou didst will to save those who believe in thee. And to take the form of a servant. And appear in the world in the flesh.[4]

Who is like unto thee, O Lord?[5] Who is, Ex. xv. 11. etc., *as above.*

Glory[6] *be to the Father, and to the Son, and to the Holy Ghost.* Who is, etc., *as above.*

Prayer. Quicken, O my Lord: *as on First Friday* (page 42).

SHURAYA [*in place of a Letter Psalm*]. Ps. xl. 7-10, *to* me.

MARTYRS' ANTHEM. *As on First Friday.*

FIRST SATURDAY

All as on Monday, except the following:—

FIRST MARMITHA. Ps. cxlv., cxlvi., cxlvii. 1-12.

SECOND MARMITHA. Ps. cxlvii. 12, cxlviii., cxlix., cl.

FIRST SHURAYA. Ps. xxx. 1-5.

FIRST ANTHEM: *to the tune* O Compassionate one, whose (door) is open.

---

[1] Om. R. C.; U. om. the name *Royal Anthem.*
[2] U. inverts the order of this and the following heading.
[3] Human nature.
[4] Syr.: *body.*
[5] U. adds: *And who is like thy deeds* (page 42).
[6] Om. U.

And our heart shall rejoice in him. May the cross, which was to us the cause of blessings. And by which our mortal race was freed. Be to us a strong wall, O my Lord. And by it may we conquer the Evil one and all his wiles.

Ps. xxxiii. 20.

Because we have hoped in his holy Name. May the cross, etc., *as above.*

Ib.

Glory be, etc. Sanctify, O our Saviour, thy Church in thy compassion. And make thy lovingkindness to dwell in the temple which is set apart to thy honour. And set up within it thy noble altar. On which are celebrated thy body and blood, O Lord.

From everlasting to everlasting. O our Lord, who in thy mercies didst promise to thy servants. That whoso asketh shall receive, and whoso seeketh shall find. Of thee we ask strength and help. That we may fulfil the will of thy majesty by our deeds.

SECOND SHURAYA. Ps. liv. 1-5.

SECOND ANTHEM: *to the tune*[1] Peace to the martyrs.

From one end of the earth to the other. The cross, which hath held the four quarters of creation. Hath kept thy worshippers. By the compassion of thy Godhead.

Deut. xxviii. 64 ?

From the rising up of the sun unto the going down thereof. The cross, etc., *as above.*

Ps. l. 1.

Glory be, etc. On the top of Golgotha the Church saw Christ. And knelt and worshipped him. And gave glory to him who sent him.

From everlasting to everlasting. Let not the prayer of thy servants, O my Lord, be in vain. But let it be for reconciliation. And forgiveness of sins.

EVENING ANTHEM. [Varies with the season.]

Or this,[2] *to the tune* The mysteries of Friday.

---

[1] A. om. name of tune.
[2] So A., U.; om. R. C.; A. om. name of tune.

Lord, I have called daily upon thee. To thee we cry. Have mercy upon us, O Christ our Saviour. Ps. lxxxviii. 9.

Unto thee have I cried, O Lord my God; keep not silence with me. To thee we cry, etc., *as above.* Ps. xxviii. 1.

Glory be, etc. Glory and confession. Let us raise to the Son, who hath saved us by his cross.

From everlasting to everlasting. May our prayer, O my Lord. Please thy good will, all our days.

LETTER PSALM, cxix. 65–89.

MARTYRS' ANTHEM.

Their gospel is gone out unto all the earth. The holy martyrs clothed with light. Went out to the four quarters of the world to preach. The glorious Trinity. Father, Son, and Holy Ghost. Ps. xix. 4.

And their words into the ends of the world. The martyrs were like the watchful ones.[1] For, while walking on earth in appearance like all men. In their minds above on high. They were dwelling among the angels. Ib.

O bless the Lord, ye angels of his. Like angels were they. Who despised all earthly things, and kept aloof from them. The martyrs, the friends of Christ. (Who) proclaimed the (Holy) Trinity. Ps. ciii. 20.

Sing to the Lord with harps and with the voice of singing. With songs and holy voices. The martyrs sing Hallelujah before the heavenly bridegroom. And cry to him, Holy, Holy. Holy, who givest victory to thy friends. Ps. xcviii. 6.

They that go down to the sea in ships. Hail, merchants, who with the blood of your necks. Obtained wealth that passeth not away for ever. Beseech and beg of the Lord.[2] That he make his peace to dwell in creation. Ps. cvii. 23.

Ye servants of his that do his pleasure. The watchful ones descend from the land of light. And sing a song of praise over the bones of the saints. Ps. ciii. 21.

---

[1] The angels.   [2] *of Christ*, R. C.

To him who maketh the earthborn worthy. To have joy with the spiritual ones.

And more to be desired are they than gold and than precious stones. Like gold and precious stones. Are the bones of the saints laid in the churches of Christ. And they pour forth and give out help. To him that taketh refuge in them.

Ps. xix. 10.

Unto the godly hath shone forth light in the darkness. Like the sun which shineth forth in the sky. The deeds of the saints shine forth in the Churches of the King's Son. And him that taketh refuge in them. The darkness toucheth not.

Ps. cxii. 4.

Majesty and glory are before him. The blessed martyrs saw thy majesty, O our Lord. At the time when they suffered on the cross for thy Name's sake. And all cried, saying. For thee we die.

Ps. xcvi. 6.

He spread out a cloud over them and overshadowed them. The company of Ananias in the furnace. The three boys quenched the flame. May their prayers be a wall to us. From the wiles of the Crafty one.

Ps. cv. 38.

Blessed are those that are blameless in the way. Blessed are the martyrs who loved Christ. And hated the things that are seen, through the fire of his love. And lo, he that recompenseth them hath come. To pay the wage of their deeds.

Ps. cxix. 1.

And walk in the law of the Lord. Blessed are ye, holy martyrs. Athletes who conquered and overcame in the spiritual contest. And lo, your bodies are in the church. And your spirits among the watchful ones.

Ib.

Come,[1] let us rejoice and be glad in it. Rejoice and be glad, holy martyrs. Who in heaven light your lamps. Before the just Judge. Who knoweth the secrets of all men.

Ps. cxviii. 24.

The Lord shall give strength unto his people. O Christ, who didst so strengthen the boy Cyriac. That he let not the truth slip in the multitude of afflictions.

Ps. xxix. 10.

---

[1] R. C. om. this verse.

Keep our assembly by his prayers.¹ From the Evil one at all times.²

The ³ Lord is the strength of his people. O Christ, who didst strengthen the martyr Mar Pithiun. To oppose the evil of the Magi, the sons of error. Strengthen our assembly that it may prevail. Against sufferings and enticements.   *Ps. xxviii. 9.*

O well is thee, and happy is thy soul. Blessed is thy spirit, O martyr George. Who didst serve thy Lord according to his will in this passing world. And lo, the wage of thy deeds is laid up.⁴ With the saints in the kingdom.   *Ps. cxxviii. 2.*

Let them shout from the top of the mountains. Blessed art thou, O Mary, blessed Mother. Who, according to the manifestation of the prophets and sealing of the apostles. Without a husband didst bear Christ.⁵ By the power of the Holy Ghost.   *Isai. xlii. 11.*

Glory be, etc. Peace to you, holy martyrs. Peace to you who conquered in the spiritual contest. Peace be to you who loved. Christ with a pure heart.

From everlasting to everlasting. To the perfection of all the saints. Came our illustrious father⁶ by the help of thy⁷ lovingkindness. O Christ, who exaltest thy saint. Keep our assembly by his prayer.

And let all the people say Amen and Amen. Answer us, O Lord, answer us, O Hope of thy household. Answer us, O God our Saviour, and hear the voice of our request. And return answer in thy mercies to our petitions. O thou who stayest not thy goodness and mercies.* May thy cross, O our Lord, be a guardian. To the beloved assemblies whom thou didst choose to thyself in thy Catholick Church. That they may be worthy⁸ to do   *Ps. cvi. 46.*

---

¹ *prayer*, R. C.   ² *and his hosts*, U.   ³ A. om. this verse.
⁴ *Thou hast received the wage of thy deeds*, R. C.
⁵ *the Saviour*, R. C.   ⁶ Or *Awa*.   ⁷ A., R. C. om. *thy*.
⁸ U.: *And may they be worthy.*

thy will. As in heaven, so on earth.* O Christ our Saviour, let there enter before thee. The prayer and request which thy worshippers have offered to thy majesty. And may thy lovingkindness help us. To tread down the head of the Apostate.* A lamp and light is doctrine. And [1] David among the prophets beareth witness, and Paul also among the apostles. Come, let us have joy in drinking of it. And walk in the way of its commandments.* Open to us, O our Lord, the treasury of thy mercies. That we may receive mercies and salvation for our defiled souls. Like the robber who loved thee. And to whom thou didst promise the kingdom.* Glory [2] to thee, O our good God. For thou hast made us to rest from the works of the day. Glory to thee from all mouths. Father, Son, and Holy Ghost.

---

[1] Om. *And*, A.   [2] R. C. om. this verse.

WEEK 'AFTER'

MONDAY

All as on First Monday, except the following :—
FIRST SHURAYA. Ps. xlii. 1-5.
FIRST ANTHEM : *to the tune* Blessed martyrs.

Like as the hart crieth for the water brook. Who will give me a fountain of tears and a pure heart. To weep and lament and groan. With loud sighing. For the years of my life which are [1] wasted. In vanities without profit ? And I was at fault in my conduct. Ps. xlii. 1.

Woe is me that my sojourning is prolonged. Woe is me that it hath happened to me that the Evil one hath spread a snare for me and I have fallen in it. Thou, O my Lord, hast made me free.[2] And I have despised thy commandments. And when the Evil one saw that I was careless. He spread a snare for me, and I fell into it. Deliver me, O my Lord, from the Evil one who hath led me captive. Ps. cxx. 4.

Glory be, etc. By the prayers of the Virgin Mary, the blessed Mother. May thy worshippers, O my Lord, be preserved. From the wiles of the Crafty one. And grant us to fulfil thy will. Both in words and deeds. And to sing to thee glory at all times.

From everlasting to everlasting. By the prayer of thy saints who have kept thy commandments, O Christ our Saviour.

---

[1] A., U.   [2] Syr.: *a son of freemen.*

Prophets, apostles, and teachers. And martyrs and priests and monks. Keep the assembly of thy worshippers. From the wiles of the Crafty one. And strengthen us to fulfil thy will.

And let all the people say Amen and Amen. A robe of grace woven by the Holy Ghost art thou, O our father.[1] A fountain of heavenly blessings. Hast thou poured forth by thy steadfast deeds. And hast given the flock of thy pasture to drink. Of the word of spiritual life. And lo, the crown of victory is woven [2] for thee.

Ps. cvi. 46.

SECOND SHURAYA. Ps. cxxiii. 1-3 *to the second* upon us.
SECOND ANTHEM: *to the tune* By peace.
Unto thee lifted I up mine eyes, O thou that dwellest in the heavens. Unto thee lifted I up mine eyes, O thou that dwellest on high. For thou hast brought me [3] into being, and by thy will hast created me.[3] Send thy strength and make whole my sickness. And heal my pains with the medicine of thy compassion. For thou art the true Physician, who curest without price. By thy mercies heal my pains and sicknesses.

Ps. cxxiii. 1.

Let thy mercies quickly prevent us. Let thy mercies, O merciful Lord, quickly prevent us.[4] For lo, our hands are stretched out to thee and our heart to heaven. To make request to thee and to beseech. That thou wouldest forgive our trespasses and pardon our sins. And rescue us from the Evil one who threateneth to destroy us. And that thou wouldest strengthen us to fulfil thy will.

Ps. lxxix. 8.

Glory be, etc. By the prayer of Mary who bore thee, and John who baptized thee. Peter and Paul the preachers, and the four gospellers. And Stephen and the band of teachers. And our illustrious father [1] and all the [5] departed. And the twelve confessors and the martyr George. Keep, O our Lord, our land and them that dwell in it.

---

[1] Or *Awa*.   [2] *kept*, U.   [3] *us*, R. C.
[4] *me*, A.   [5] *our*, R. C.

From everlasting to everlasting. By thy ascension, O our Lord Jesus, thou hast exalted our dust. And hast caused us to sit on the right hand of the Father on high by thy love. By the descent of thy Spirit thou hast made our childhood wise. And by the cross of thy light thou hast illumined our knowledge. By the hallowing of the holy Church[1] thou hast hallowed our nature. Adorable is thy dispensation which was for our salvation.

EVENING ANTHEM. [Varies according to the season.]
Or this,[2] *to its own tune.*

O God, my heart is ready, my heart is ready. Let us be ready in fear and love. For the fear-inspiring gift of the mysteries of Christ. And adorn our souls with deeds. By which we may propitiate the Judge of all. That he may pity us when he judgeth the families of the earth. Ps. cviii. 1.

And we are risen and are ready. Let us be ready, etc., as above. Ps. xx. 8.

Glory be to the Father, and to the Son, and to the Holy Ghost. Of our own free will the sufferings of sin have surrounded us.[3] Do thou in thy goodness open the door[4] to our prayer. Our nature is weak and inclined to sin. Give a hand now, for it is laid low. Peradventure it will understand its nature by the mercies of thy lovingkindness.

LETTER PSALM, cxix. 89-105.

SECOND TUESDAY

All as on First Monday, except the following:—

FIRST MARMITHA. Ps. xxv., xxvi., xxvii., *as on First Tuesday.*

SECOND MARMITHA. Ps. xxviii., xxix., xxx., *as on First Tuesday.*

FIRST SHURAYA. Ps. lxvii. 1-6.

---

[1] Referring to the last Shawu'a. See the Kalendar.
[2] Om. R. C.; U. om. name of tune.   [3] *me,* A.   [4] A. om. *the door.*

FIRST ANTHEM: *to its own tune.*[1]
Show the light of thy countenance, and we shall be saved. O Compassionate one, and full of mercies. Relax not thy watch upon us. And[2] send us from thy treasury. Compassion and mercies and[3] salvation.

Ps. lxxx. 3.

Until thou have mercy upon us. At thy door, O our Lord, we knock. And ask mercies of thee. Open to us, and return answer to our petitions. O thou who stayest not thy goodness and mercies.

Ps. cxxiii. 2.

Glory be, etc. May the prayer of the Virgin Mary. The Mother of Jesus our Saviour. Be to us continually. A wall by night and day.

From everlasting to everlasting. O prophets, pray for peace. O apostles, for tranquillity. O martyrs and priests and teachers. May your prayer be a wall to us.

And let all the people say Amen and Amen. Make request and beseech, O our illustrious father.[4] Christ whose love thou didst desire. That the assembly which hath celebrated thy memorial with processions. May be helped by[5] thy prayers.

Ps. cvi. 46.

SECOND SHURAYA. Ps. xl. 16-20.

SECOND ANTHEM: *to the tune*[1] O Compassionate one, whose (door) is open.

Rescue me, and deliver me from this generation for ever. O God, who didst rescue them of the household of Hezekiah. And didst deliver Jerusalem from the Assyrians. Cause thy right hand to overshadow thy worshippers, and save thou them. And bring not on us, O my Lord, the strong foot.

Ps. xii. 8.

In the deep of his heart. When the son of Jesse called to thee, O Lord, and thou didst answer him. Thou didst ease his afflictions and overthrow his enemies. And when we call to thee, bring to nought our persecutors. And raise Churches to reverence thy cross.

Ps. lxiv. 6.

---

[1] A. om. name of tune.   [2] Om. *And,* R. C., U.   [3] Om. *and,* R. C.
[4] Or *Awa.*   [5] Om. *by,* A. (error).

SECOND TUESDAY

Glory be, etc. A great refuge is the holy Virgin. To the faithful who alway ask her prayers. By the strength of her prayer may our assembly be blessed. And the Church be made fruitful in peace and concord.

From everlasting to everlasting. O prophets and apostles, and martyrs and teachers. Beg mercies of God for the world. For priests concord, for kings reconciliation. For the Church, with her children, forgiveness of trespasses.

And let all the people say Amen and Amen. O our holy father,[1] the friend of Christ. Who didst buy the kingdom by thy virtuous deeds. Beg mercies for us from thy Lord who chose thee. That he may have mercy on us and save our souls.   Ps. cvi. 46.

EVENING ANTHEM. [Varies with the season.]

Or this,[2] *to the tune* God the Word.

Who can express the noble acts of the Lord? Who[3] is sufficient, O our Maker, to confess thee[4] for thy mercy? Who in the beginning didst form us in thy splendid image. And in the latter times hast clothed thyself with us and turned us to the knowledge of thee. O thou who exaltest our race, glory to thee.   Ps. cvi. 2.

Because of thy lovingkindness and truth.[5] Who is sufficient, etc., *as above*.   Ps. cxxxviii. 2.

Glory be to the Father, and to the Son, and to the Holy Ghost. Open[6] to us, O our Lord, the great treasury of thy mercy. That we may receive mercies and salvation for our poor race. And heal the pains of our sins by the great medicine of thy compassion. That our weak race by thy mercies may receive compassion.

LETTER PSALM, cxix. 113-129.

MARTYRS' ANTHEM, *as on First Tuesday.*

---

[1] Or *Awa*.   [2] So A., U.; om. R. C.; A. om. name of tune.
[3] As on First Friday, *q.v.* U. has: *Who is like unto thee, O Lord, and who is like thy deeds?* (page 42).   [4] U. adds: *on our behalf.*
[5] U.: *Who can express the noble acts of the Lord?*
[6] As on First Thursday (page 37).

SECOND WEDNESDAY

All as on First Monday, except the following:—

FIRST MARMITHA. Ps. lxii., lxiii., lxiv., *as on First Wednesday.*

SECOND MARMITHA. Ps. lxv., lxvi., lxvii., *as on First Wednesday.*

FIRST SHURAYA. Ps. lxxii. 1-5.

FIRST ANTHEM: *to the tune*[1] The martyrs of the Son.

There shall I make the horn of David to arise. From the house of David and Abraham the Creator chose a virgin. And made his hidden power to dwell in her. By the power of the Holy Ghost. She conceived and bare Christ.[2] The Judge of the heights and the depths.

Ps. cxxxii. 18.

And hath chosen her to be an habitation for himself. From the house, etc., *as above.*

Ps. cxxxii. 14.

Glory be, etc. How fitting is it that we should glorify this holy house. In which are prophets and apostles. And martyrs and priests and teachers. And in which is set up the holy table. For the pardon of the children of Adam.

From everlasting to everlasting. Blessed is he who traded as thou didst trade, O our father.[3] And who collected spiritual riches. And filled his ship with all blessings. And prospered,[4] and departed to the haven. To the place appointed for all the just.

And let all the people say Amen and Amen. O our Lord, thy kingdom come, and[5] thy will be done on earth. As it is in heaven. And give us the bread of our need. And lead us not into temptation. But deliver us from the Evil one.

Ps. cvi. 46.

SECOND SHURAYA. Ps. ci. 1-10.

SECOND ANTHEM: *to the tune* They are not oppressed.

---

[1] A. om. name of tune. [2] R. C.: *the Saviour.* And.
[3] Or *Awa.*   [4] Or, *directed his way.*   [5] Om. *and,* R. C.

For he is thy Lord, worship thou him. O Mary, Mother of the King, the King of kings, etc., *as above,* page 36. Ps. xlv. 12.

Beg of him and beseech him that he have pity upon us. O Mary, etc., *as above.*

Glory be, etc. Peace to your company, O blessed ones. Merchants bearing life to the sons of men. Open the treasury of your prayers to the needy. And keep the land where ye dwelt from harm.

From everlasting to everlasting. Make request for us all to thy Lord. O our illustrious and holy father,[1] the friend of the Son. That by thy prayers may be helped and saved. All who are afflicted and distressed and take refuge in thee.

And let all the people say Amen and Amen. O God, who didst have pity on the Ninevites, have pity on us. And relax not thy watch over our evil generation. And if thou holdest thy door in the face of us sinners. Let whoso goeth knock at the door, O thou Friend of men. Ps. cvi. 46.

EVENING ANTHEM: *to the tune* Thee, O Judge.

Protect me from the wickedness of the froward. Under the wings of thy prayers, O pure Mary, we alway take shelter. And may they stand before us at all times. And by them may we find. Compassion and mercies in the day of judgment. Ps. lxiv. 2.

Do thou protect me and preserve me from mine enemies. Under the wings, etc., *as above.* Ps. xxxii. 8.

Glory be, etc. By the prayer of the prophets who foretold thy mysteries. And by the prayer of the apostles who preached thy gospel. And by the prayer of the martyrs and priests and teachers. O Christ, keep thy worshippers from harm.

From everlasting to everlasting. O our father,[1] pray that our Lord in his mercy. May make whole all pains. May thy prayer be as the smell of sweet incense. And a censer that propitiateth God on behalf of sinners.

---

[1] Or *Awa.*

And let all the people say Amen and Amen. Hear our request, O Hope of our life. And return answer to the petition of our soul in thy mercies. And give us in (thy) lovingkindness healing for our sicknesses. That we may confess thy holy Name, and have mercy upon us.

Ps. cvi. 46.

Prayer. Arm us, O our Lord: *as on First Wednesday* (p. 31).

SHURAYA [*in place of a Letter Psalm*]. Exod. xv. 20, 21, *to* gloriously.

MARTYRS' ANTHEM, *as on First Wednesday.*

SECOND THURSDAY

All as on First Monday, except the following:—

FIRST MARMITHA. Ps. xcvi., xcvii., xcviii., *as on First Thursday.*

SECOND MARMITHA. Ps. xcix., c., ci., *as on First Thursday.*

FIRST SHURAYA. Ps. cxix. 41-49.

FIRST ANTHEM: *to the tune*[1] Our Father which art in heaven.

Let thy mercies come unto me, O Lord, and thy salvation of which thou didst speak. Let thy mercies come to our help, for they have created us. And let them heal our sickness with the medicine of thy compassion.

Ps. cxix. 41.

Turn thou unto me, and have mercy upon me. Come, O my Lord, to our help, and strengthen our weakness. For in thee is our hope by night and by day.

Ps. xxv. 15.

Glory be, etc. On the holy altar let there be a memorial. Of the Virgin Mary, Mother of Christ.

From everlasting to everlasting. O apostles of the Son, and friends of the Only-begotten. Pray that there may be peace in creation.

And let all the people say Amen and Amen. Thy memorial O our father,[2] is on the holy altar. With the just who conquered and the martyrs who were crowned.

Ps. cvi. 46.

---

[1] R. C., U.: *to the tune* May peace be multiplied to thee.   [2] Or *Awa.*

SECOND SHURAYA. Ps. cxix. 121-129.

SECOND ANTHEM: *to its own tune.*[1]

Righteous[2] *art thou, O Lord, and very true are thy judgments.* The righteous thou didst not call to repentance. But sinners thou didst command to repent. Ps. cxix. 137. Turn us in thy compassion, O Christ our Saviour. And in thy lovingkindness pardon our trespasses and our sins.

Turn thou unto me, and have mercy upon me. Turn, O my Lord, unto the prayer of thy servants. And receive our request, and return answer to our Ps. xxv. 15. petitions. And in thy compassion bring to nought the will of the Crafty one. That he disturb not our assembly with the foulness of his envy.

Glory be, etc. O Mary, Mother of the King, the King of kings. Beseech Christ, who[3] shone forth from thy bosom. That he bring to nought wars in all parts of the earth. And bless the crown of the year in his lovingkindness.

From everlasting to everlasting. By the prayer of thy saints, O Christ our Saviour. The prophets and apostles and martyrs, and all the just. Keep thy worshippers from all harm. That they may raise glory to thee by night and by day.

And let all the people say Amen and Amen. O our father,[4] friend of the heavenly Bridegroom. May thy prayer be to us a wall and house of refuge. Ps. cvi. 46. And in the day when thy Lord shineth forth in glory. Beseech him that with thee we may inherit the kingdom.

EVENING ANTHEM. [Varies with the season.]

Or this,[5] *to the tune* Blessed martyrs.

O hear ye this, all ye people. O nature of mortals, let thy hope increase. For thy Quickener hath come. The mysteries of prophecy have come to an end. Ps. xlix. 1. For light hath been sent to the world. The gospel of peace

---

[1] A. om. name of tune.

[2] R. C. divides each verse of this anthem into three lines only instead of four.   [3] *That he pity our vileness.* And: R. C.

[4] Or *Awa.*   [5] Om. R. C.

have the heavenly ones. Preached among the earthly. Blessed is he who hath turned the nations from error.

The poor shall hear thereof and be glad. O nature, etc., *as above.*
Ps. xxxiv. 2.

Glory be to the Father, and to the Son, and to the Holy Ghost. O[1] Christ, the refuge and true hope. Of the afflicted. Be, O my Lord, a wall to thy worshippers. And keep them from the Evil one. And heal and salve their pains. In the compassion of thy Godhead. O Merciful one, who forgivest trespasses.

LETTER PSALM, cxix. 145-161.

MARTYRS' ANTHEM, *as on First Thursday.*

LAST FRIDAY

All as on First Monday, except the following:—

FIRST MARMITHA. Ps. lxxxv., lxxxvi., *as on First Friday.*

SECOND MARMITHA. Ps. lxxxvii., lxxxviii., *as on First Friday.*

FIRST SHURAYA. Ps. cxlv. 1-7, *to* kindness.

FIRST ANTHEM: *to the tune*[2] Blessed be thy Spirit.
I will magnify thee, O my Lord the King. O Christ the King, our Saviour. In the day of thy coming quicken me. And raise me to thy right hand. In the day when thy majesty shineth forth.
Ps. cxlv. 1.

My God, I have put my trust in thee, O let me not be confounded. We venerate thy cross, O my Lord. By it do we stand upright, and by it are we quickened. And by it are our departed quickened. And their bodies put on glory.
Ps. xxv. 1.

Glory be to the Father, and to the Son, and to the Holy Ghost. O God the Father, give me life. O Christ the Son, quicken me

---

[1] As on First Monday (page 11).
[2] So U.; R. C.: *One is the strength*; A. om. name of tune.

who am dead. O Holy Ghost the Paraclete. Bring me to the land of light.

SECOND SHURAYA. Ps. cxlv. 18—end.

SECOND ANTHEM: *to the tune* [1] Let us be ready in fear.

His salvation is nigh them that fear him. The time of this world which passeth away is nigh. And all its desires are destroyed and come to nought. Ps. lxxxv. 9. Hear, O mortals, and offer repentance. Before the day of remembrance come. And every man is recompensed according as he hath done, in the terrible judgment.

As it were a ramping and a roaring lion. When Death, overtaking every man and devouring him. Came unto me, I was greatly moved and disturbed. Ps. xxii. 13. For I am persuaded of my trespasses that they are not as other men's. But that he saw that I was his portion. Thou art my help, my Saviour, and on thee I wait.

Glory be to the Father, and to the Son, and to the Holy Ghost. Glory to thee, Jesus, our victorious King. Who by thy cross didst save our race from error. May thy great power renew our being. And may death be brought to nought and the quickening reign. And may we be made worthy of mercies by thy will, O King, the Quickener.

EVENING ANTHEM. [Varies with the season.]

Or this.[2] *Royal Anthem: to the tune* The great mystery.

Be telling of his salvation from day to day.[3] The gospel of peace and love in mercy hath been preached to us. By the glorious birth [4] of Christ. And by Ps. xcvi. 2. it have we learnt that the Creator is reconciled to us. And hath restored and given to us his glorious image which we had destroyed. By taking firstfruits [5] of us. And making our nature to partake. With his majesty in honour.

---

[1] A. om. name of tune; R. C. not so full.
[2] Om. R. C.; U. om. the title *Royal Anthem*.
[3] U.: *The hope of all the ends of the earth* (Ps. lxv. 5).
[4] U.: *Epiphany.*   [5] Human nature.

*The hope of all the ends of the earth.*¹ The gospel, etc., *as*
Ps. lxv. 5.   *above.*

*Glory*² *be to the Father, and to the Son, and to the Holy Ghost.* The gospel, etc., *as above.*

Prayer. Quicken, O my Lord, *as on First Friday,* page 42.

SHURAYA, *in place of a Letter Psalm (if there is no special one in the Kashkul*³*).* Ps. xxxi. 21-24.

MARTYRS' ANTHEM, *as on First Friday.*

SECOND SATURDAY

All as on First Monday, except the following :—

FIRST MARMITHA. Ps. cxlv., cxlvi., cxlvii. 1-12, *as on First Saturday.*

SECOND MARMITHA. Ps. cxlvii. 12, cxlviii., cxlix., cl., *as on First Saturday.*

FIRST SHURAYA. Ps. cxxiv. 1-6.

FIRST ANTHEM : *to the tune* O King, the Quickener.⁴

And our heart shall rejoice in him. May thy cross, O our
                Saviour, which made peace between the height
Ps. xxxiii. 20.   and the depth. By its great, adorable, and
glorious power. Make peace in the world, which is disturbed and confused by its sins. And do thou make thy peace to dwell in (its) four quarters.

*Because we have hoped in his holy Name.*⁵ May thy cross,
Ib.   etc., *as above.*

Glory be, etc. Keep thy holy Church from harm. O Lord Christ, who didst come to save us. And make thy worshippers worthy in fear and trembling. To lift up praise to thy Godhead.

From everlasting to everlasting. Give us, O our Lifegiver, that which thou knowest will help us. For we know not

---

¹ U.: *It is thou that savedst us from our enemies* (Ps. xliv. 8).
² U. om. this verse.   ³ A., U. om. these words.
⁴ *to the tune* O fountain of blessings, R. C., U.
⁵ R. C., U.: *He maketh wars to cease in all the world* (Ps. xlvi. 9).

what we ask. But for one thing we make request, that thy will may be fulfilled in us. And that thy mercies may intercede for all of us.

SECOND SHURAYA. Ps. cxxv. 1-3.

SECOND ANTHEM: *to the tune*[1] Every breath.

That he might shew forth his power. O Cross, which didst shew wonderful miracles to the sons of men. Keep harm away from the souls which are signed with thee. <small>Ps. cvi. 8.</small>

Shew thy strength, and come and save us. O Cross, etc., as above. <small>Ps. lxxx. 2.</small>

Glory be, etc. O my Lord, be a wall to the Churches in every land. And make thy truth to be a fence and strong bulwark before them.

From everlasting to everlasting. O our Lord, help (us), send peace, scatter the Evil ones. Keep thy Church, make free her children from harm.

EVENING ANTHEM. [Varies with the season.]

Or this,[2] *to its own tune.*

I will alway bless the Lord. Blessed is the High Priest who hath pardoned our trespasses. By the sacrifice of himself. <small>Ps. xxxiv. 1.</small>

And blessed be the Name of his Majesty for ever. Blessed is, etc., as above. <small>Ps. lxxii. 19.</small>

Glory be, etc. Glory[3] and confession. Let us raise to the Son, who hath saved us by his cross.

From everlasting to everlasting. May[3] our prayer, O my Lord. Please thy good will, all our days.

LETTER PSALM, cxix. 161—end.

MARTYRS' ANTHEM, *as on First Saturday.*

---

[1] A. om. name of tune.
[2] So A., U.; om. R. C.; A. om. name of tune.
[3] As on First Saturday (page 51).

EVENING SERVICE

FOR

SUNDAYS, FEASTS OF OUR LORD, AND

MEMORIALS OF SAINTS

Priest. Glory be to God, etc. *Ans.* Bless, O my Lord. *Kiss of peace.* Our Father. All as on First Monday, but sung (page 2).

Evening prayer for Sundays and Festivals.[1] Let us confess, O my Lord, thy Godhead with spiritual praises, and worship thy Majesty with earthly adorations, and glorify thy secret and hidden nature with pure and undefiled ascriptions of glory, Lord of all, etc.

Evening prayer on Memorials, as on First Monday (page 2).

MARMITHA.[2] (*a*) On Festivals and Sundays from Advent to Epiphany, Ps. lxxxvii., lxxxviii. (*b*) On other Festivals and Sundays, Ps. lxv., lxvi., lxvii. (*c*) On Memorials which fall on Fridays, Ps. lxxxv., lxxxvi. (*d*) On Memorials which fall on other days, Ps. xv., xvi., xvii.

They say the Gloria; then Hallelujah, Hallelujah, yea Hallelujah. *Deacon.* Let us pray.[3] Peace be with us.

---

[1] Of our Lord, and so throughout. U. om. *and Festivals.*

[2] Each psalm is farced on feasts and memorials. This table is from U., which directs the psalms to be sung, not said as on ferias. R. C. merely refers to the Khudhra.

[3] U. om. *Let us pray.*

Prayer. Sundays and Festivals. The great, terrible, holy, blessed, excellent, and incomprehensible Name of thy glorious Trinity, and thy lovingkindness to our race, are we bound to confess, worship, and glorify at all times, Lord of all, etc.

Memorials. Thee, O Good, Kind, Compassionate one, full of mercies, the great King of glory, Being who art from everlasting, we confess, worship, and glorify, at all times, Lord of all, etc.

ON SUNDAYS. *How beloved are thy dwellings, thou Lord of hosts. As the fragrance of sweet incense, and the smell of a pleasant censer, receive, O Christ our Saviour, the request and prayer of thy servants. My soul hath a desire and longing for the courts of the Lord. As the fragrance. Glory be. From everlasting. As the fragrance.* Ps. lxxxiv. 1. Ps. lxxxiv. 2.

ON FESTIVALS. *How beloved. As the fragrance. My soul hath a desire. As the fragrance. My heart and my flesh have glorified the living God. As the fragrance. Glory be. As the fragrance. From everlasting. As the fragrance.* Ib.

ON MEMORIALS. *I will alway bless the Lord. As the fragrance. And his praises shall ever be in my mouth. As the fragrance. Glory be. From everlasting. As the fragrance.*[1] Ps. xxxiv. 1.

Deacon. Peace be with us.

The priest says over the censer.[2] Let us lift up praise to thy glorious Trinity at all times, for ever, Lord of all, etc. *Or this.*[3] O Christ, who didst accept the blood of the martyrs in the day when they were killed, accept this incense from the hands of my feebleness in the lovingkindness of thy compassion, for ever. Amen. *He places incense in the censer*

---

[1] R. C. gives this arrangement less fully, and does not mention the farcing *My heart and my flesh*.

[2] So T., U.; om. R. C.; U. om. *Lord of all*, and adds *Amen*.

[3] So U.; om. T., R. C.

which is held by the deacon, signing it with the cross,[1] and the deacon goes round the church and censes the people.[2]

Prayer of the Lakhumara. For all thy helps, etc., as on First Monday (page 3).

They say the Lakhumara. On Festivals of our Lord it is said five times.[3]

Prayer after the Lakhumara. Thou, O my Lord, as on First Monday.

FIRST SHURAYA. *On Sundays they say here the First Shuraya; but on Festivals and Memorials there is none.*

First Sunday of each Shawu'a, Ps. xlvii. 1-5. And from Ascension to Advent add vv. 5-9.

Second Sunday, Ps. lxv. 1-5 to *earth.*

Third Sunday, Ps. lxxxix. 1-5.

Fourth Sunday, Ps. xciii.

Fifth Sunday, Ps. cxxvi. 1-7.[4]

Sixth Sunday, Ps. xlix. 1-5.

Seventh Sunday, Ps. cxxxvii. 1-4.

When a memorial is made of the departed on Sundays, these anthems are said after the Shurayi.[5]

FIRST ANTHEM.[6]

For Sons of the Church.[7]

Make[8] *glad the soul of thy servant.* With all thy saints. Make, O Christ the King. The spirit of thy servant to rest in peace. Where suffering

Ps. lxxxvi. 4.

---

[1] So U.

[2] This is the custom, but it is not mentioned in U., R. C.

[3] So R. C.; U. does not mention festivals. The usage varies.

[4] A. om. ver. 6.

[5] So U.; om. R. C. These anthems are from some copies of the Khudhra. Memorials of the dead are not made on festivals or memorials of saints. If a memorial of the dead is not made, only the first three verses are said.

[6] A. om. all these anthems. On feasts and memorials the two anthems are special, from the Khudhra.   [7] R. C. om. this line.

[8] So U.; in R. C. this anthem is given thus :—

Make glad, etc. With all thy saints. Make, O Christ the King. The spirit of thy servants, etc., *and the rest as above.*

reigneth not. Neither distress nor sorrow. But the promised life without end.

All ye servants of God. Remember me, my beloved. In prayer in the holy temple. For I am separated from you, and for ever. When he setteth up the seat of judgment. And every man standeth to (give account of) his deeds. May our Lord have compassion on me there in his lovingkindness. Ps. lxvi. 14.

Glory be to the Father, and to the Son, and to the Holy Ghost. O Christ the King, our Saviour. Quicken me in the day of thy coming. And set me on thy right hand. With the just who were approved before thee. And believed and confessed thy majesty. That with them I may inherit life without end.

For Laymen.[1]

Thou hast cast me into the dust of death. Thou hast clothed us with a mortal nature, which (our) trespasses ever painfully oppress. And when we have put off the habitation of tribulations, by a groaning departure. The clothing of our actions defileth us. Have pity on us. Ps. xxii. 15.

It is become the head of the building. Thy coming, O my Lord, to our race. Was to turn sinners to the way of repentance. And me, who am the chiefest of all, let thy lovingkindness pardon. And may it stand before my sinfulness in the judgment. Ps. cxviii. 22.

For men. *Glory be to the Father, and to the Son, and to the Holy Ghost.* The trespasses and sins which I have committed

---

Great is our Lord and exceeding glorious (Ps. cxlv. 3). Our confident hope is in God. Who formed our father Adam. The hope of our death and of our life. The world is nought. And nought are its pleasures. But quicken us and give us life in thy lovingkindness.

Glory be to the Father, and to the Son, and to the Holy Ghost. O Christ the King, our Saviour. Quicken us in the day of thy coming. And set us on thy right hand. With the just who were approved before thee. And believed and confessed thy cross. That with them we may inherit life without end.

[1] A., R. C. om. all this anthem.

make me fear thy terrible judgment. And I know not what excuse in the spirit I shall give before thy terrible tribunal. And therefore I beseech thee, O good Physician. Do thou help my weakness and have mercy on me.

For women. *Glory be, etc.* No lamp of virtuous actions. Hast thou, O my feeble soul. So that thou mayest go out to meet the bridegroom. The wise virgins give not oil to the foolish. For them that were rejected for their deeds. The bridechamber is not opened. Abraham refresheth not those who are tormented with a flame.[1] And the Judge forgiveth not those who have not repented. And therefore take refuge, O my soul, in penitence, and say. I have sinned before thee, O Lord. Have pity and mercy on me.

For Children.[2]

Lighten mine eyes, that I sleep not in death. Light and the Son of Light. Abode in the light and dwell in the light. Make me worthy of that light. Which the darkness comprehendeth not.

Ps. xiii. 3.

And in thy light do we see light. The world saw the light. And rejoiced when it was sad. And lo, it lifteth up glory. With her children whom thou hast saved.

Ps. xxxvi. 9.

Glory be to the Father, and to the Son, and to the Holy Ghost. With the light which (shone) at his Epiphany. Those on high and those below have been illumined. At thy second coming. Join me with thy saints.

Prayer. Thy mercy, O our Lord (page 5).

PSALMS cxli., cxlii., cxix. 105-113, cxvii. *under one Gloria, farced as on page 5. But*[3] *on Feasts of our Lord, between each clause of* Ps. cxli. *is said,* Glory to thee: glorious is thy Nativity, *or* Epiphany, *or* Entrance,[4] *or* Resurrection, *or* Ascension, *or*

---

[1] Lit. *are burnt.*
[2] A., R. C. om. all this anthem.   [3] So U. ; om. R. C.
[4] The Hallowing of the Church, or Palm Sunday? (p. 77).

Descent,[1] *or* Revelation,[2] *or* Cross. *Between each clause of* Ps. cxlii. *is said,* Glorious art thou, and glorious is thy [Nativity]; *of* Ps. cxix. 105-113, Glorious is thy [Nativity], which maketh all to rejoice; *of* Ps. cxvii., Let the nation and nations glorify thee. *Then,* Glory be to the Father, etc. *Add,* By all mouths shalt thou be glorified. *Then,* From everlasting, etc. *Add,* Glory be to thee, O God.

Prayer. Hear, O our Lord (page 5).

SECOND SHURAYA.

First Sunday of each Shawu'a, Ps. xlviii. 1-3.
Second Sunday, Ps. lxvi. 1-4.[3]
Third Sunday, Ps. lxxxix. 5-9 to *thee.*
Fourth Sunday, Ps. cxlviii. 1-7 to *earth.*
Fifth Sunday, Ps. cxxvii. 1-5.
Sixth Sunday, Ps. cxxx.[4]
Seventh Sunday, Ps. cxxxviii. 1-4 to *Lord.*[5]

SECOND ANTHEM.[6]

For Sons of the Church.

Lord, I have loved the service of thy house. Because I have loved thy law. And kept thy commandments. The Evil one hath fought with me. With his wiles, and hath conquered me. And in my trespasses I have turned to dust. Thy voice calleth me and raiseth me up.

Ps. xxvi. 8.

---

[1] Pentecost.   [2] Transfiguration.   [3] So A., R. C.; U. adds verse 4.
[4] So U., R. C.; A. om. last verse.
[5] So U., R. C.; A. to *me* in verse 3.
[6] See rubrick and note on the First Anthem. The text of U. is followed here; A. omits all these anthems; R. C. has two anthems, one for weeks 'before,' which is the first three verses of the following anthem *For Laymen,* and one for weeks 'after,' which is as follows:—

Week 'after.'

For he cometh to judge the earth (Ps. xcvi. 13). The King, the Quickener, shineth forth in glory from on high. And giveth life to the dead, and raiseth them that were buried. And the departed rise from

The fruit which Adam plucked in Eden. Hath condemned me to die in my sins. And the Child of the Virgin Mary hath shone forth. He hath justified me, that I should live in thy lovingkindness. And give life at thy coming, O Christ, to thy servant who is fallen asleep. For thou alone hast compassion on sinners.

Ye that stand in the house of the Lord. My brethren and my beloved. And my friends, my companions. Ps. cxxxv. 2. Forget not my memory at the time of service. Which I and ye rendered. To God in the same temple. The way of (my) bodily feet hath ceased. At the spiritual goal. And (my) mouth, the door of praise, is silent. For Death, the slayer, hath closed it. Pray that I be rescued from the terrible judgment. Which is laid up for all transgressors. And that I may be worthy of the kingdom.

Glory be, etc. For them who are adorned with spiritual deeds. The bridechamber is prepared. Which is not made with hands. But hath been set up from the beginning. And is never destroyed. With excellency and beauty and glory are they clothed. Freedom from corruption do they receive. Happiness which hath not gone up into the heart of man. Do they inherit with the assemblies on high. Crowns of the Holy Ghost. Doth Christ the King in the day of his coming. Weave and set on their heads.

From everlasting to everlasting. The just and righteous are exalted to the heights above. When our Lord is revealed. The source of help. Seraphim cry Holy to him.

---

the grave together. And lift up praise to him who giveth life to the dead.

All ye servants of God (Ps. lxvi. 14). Remove sorrow from your heart, O mortals. For the day of our Lord cometh and giveth us joy. And awaketh us from sleep, when the watchful ones sing praises before him. And the angels rejoice in the day of quickening.

Glory be to the Father, and to the Son, and to the Holy Ghost. Let our dead live, O my Lord, and let their bodies rise. As prophesied the prophet, the son of Amoz. That they that sleep should awake, and they that lie in the dust give glory. For thy dew is the dew of light and of truth.

The watchful ones sing Glory to him. The bodies of just and righteous men. Fly to him in the clouds. The voice of angels and of the sons of men. Thundereth forth a song of praise. Heaven and earth together. Tell the glory of his majesty. And we with them will sing glory to him.

For Laymen.

Bow down thine ear, O Lord, and answer me. O Christ the Son, who didst come for our salvation. To renew the image of Adam which was corrupted. Ps. lxxxvi. 1.
And didst put on¹ our body, and in it didst save our race. And didst grant (us) to trust in the resurrection of the dead. Pardon thy servants in thy lovingkindness. In the day of thy coming.

O God, for thy lovingkindness. In thy lovingkindness thou didst create our race at the beginning. And didst clothe it with excellent glory in Paradise. Ps. xxv. 6.
And because it was rebellious, and sinned, and fell from its glory. Thou didst send thy beloved Son to us. And he gave us in his compassion. The promised life which hath no end.

Glory be to the Father, and to the Son, and to the Holy Ghost. Glory² to thee, Jesus, our victorious King. Who by thy cross didst save our race from error. May thy great power renew our being. And may death be brought to nought, and the quickening reign. And may we be made worthy of mercies by thy will. O King, the Quickener.

From everlasting to everlasting. With the just that were approved before thee, O Compassionate one. Who didst grant them to gain the kingdom as their recompense. Make thy servant who is fallen asleep in thy hope to be a partaker (with them). May he who hath received the sign of thy (cross) be numbered in thy flock. Join him, O my Lord, to the companies of them. That fulfil thy will.

---

¹ R. C.: *take.*   ² As on Last Friday (page 65).

FESTIVAL EVENING SERVICE

For Children.

Glorify the Lord, O ye righteous. The souls of the righteous are in the hands of the Lord. For they loved him, and believed in him, and kept his commandments.

Ps. xxxiii. 1.

Glorify him with a new song of praise. For thou hast pleased Christ, who created thee, by thy deed. That thou mightest go and have joy in the bride-chamber of the kingdom.

Ps. xxxiii.

Glory be to the Father, and to the Son, and to the Holy Ghost. To thee, O my Lord, (all) creatures lift up praise. Jesus our Saviour, for thou art their Quickener.

KARUZUTHA.[1] *Deacon.* Let us all stand up, as is right, with joy and rejoicing. Let us make request and say, O our Lord, have mercy upon us. *Ans.* O our Lord, have mercy upon us.

Father of mercies, etc., *as on First Monday* (page 6).

O our Saviour.

For the peace.

For (this) our land.

For a moderate climate.

For the welfare.

For the kings who have power in this world, we, etc.

O merciful God.

For orthodox presbyters and deacons, and all our brotherhood in Christ, we, etc.

O thou who art rich.

O thou who art before all worlds, and whose power abideth for ever, we, etc.

O thou who art by nature.

O thou who willest not the death of a sinner, but rather that he repent of his wickedness and live, we, etc.

---

[1] The additional clauses are said in some places on Sundays, feasts, and memorials; according to U., however, some say them on all Sundays, some only on Feasts of our Lord and Sundays of the Fast. R. C. prints all the clauses together without distinction.

O thou who art glorified.

O thou who by thy holy Nativity [*or* Epiphany, *or* Fast, *or* Entrance,[1] *or* Resurrection, *or* Ascension, *or* Descent, *or* Cross][2] madest the earth to rejoice, and the heavens to be glad, we, etc.

O thou who by nature.

O Saviour of all men, and especially of them that believe in thee, we, etc.

Save us all.

ANOTHER. Let us pray. Peace be with us. Let us pray and make request, *as on First Monday* (page 7).

Prayer. To thee, O Lord (page 10).

Deacon. Lift up your voices, etc.[3] *They all sing,* Holy God, etc. (as on page 10).

Prayer for Sundays and Festivals. Thee, O Holy one, who art by nature holy, and glorious in thy being, and high and exalted above all in thy Godhead; thee, O holy, adorable, and blessed Nature, who art from everlasting, we confess and worship and glorify, at all times, Lord of all, etc.

For Memorials.[4] Holy and glorious, etc., *as on ferias* (page 10).

Deacon. Bless, O my Lord.[5] Bow your heads for the laying on of hands, and receive a blessing.

Priest. May Christ make thy service glorious in the kingdom of heaven.

Here follow the SUYAKHI[6] *on feasts and memorials.*[7]

Prayer[8] *before the Suyakhi on Feasts of our Lord.* Strengthen, O my Lord, our weakness, and aid and help our feebleness, that we may celebrate with all our heart and soul the great and venerable festival of N,[9] by the power and strength of thy mighty arm, Lord of all, etc.

---

[1] Palm Sunday, or the Hallowing of the Church? (page 72, note).
[2] Whichever last preceded.
[3] Om. U.   [4] Om. T.   [5] U. om. *Bless, O my Lord*.
[6] Lit. *Conclusions*. The meaning is additional psalms.
[7] R. C.: *if there are any*.   [8] Om. T., R. C.
[9] The Nativity, etc.

FESTIVAL EVENING SERVICE

Of[1] *the Second Suyakha.* Thee, who art high in thy being, and exalted in thy Godhead, who hast made the heights to bend down to them that are below, and hast sanctified them by taking the holy firstfruits,[2] which thou hast united to thyself, and by thy revelation in the flesh didst make angels and the sons of men to rejoice, we confess, worship, and glorify, at all times, Lord of all, etc.

ROYAL ANTHEM.

Prayer[3] *before the Royal Anthem on Feasts of our Lord.* May thy lovingkindness, O my Lord, come down to help thy worshippers, and let thy mercies overflow to aid them that call on thy Name. Reveal thyself to us to save thy people, and to rescue all the sheep of thy pasture from all harm, hidden and open, Lord of all, etc.

On Sundays.[4] May our souls, etc. (page 11).

They say the proper Royal Anthem[5] (*from the Khudhra*), *repeating it, and adding the Gloria verse.*

The last verses are as follow, on Sundays,[6] *varying with the season.*

SUNDAYS[6] FROM ADVENT TO EPIPHANY. *From everlasting to everlasting.* God promised and affirmed to Abraham of old. In thy Seed shall be blessed all sinful nations. Who are dead in their sins. And are destroyed by error. For this is he who cleanseth them and healeth their pains. As the prophet foresaw in the ages of old. That he should take our pains and carry our sicknesses.[7] And therefore we cry and say. Glory to thee, O Son, the Lord of all. *The*

---

[1] Om. T., R. C. [2] Human nature.

[3] In T. this prayer is marked *after the Shuraya* (misprint?), but it comes in this place. Om. R. C.

[4] So T.; U., R. C. give it (apparently) for all occasions.

[5] Syr.: *Basaliqi.* This is the name of the evening anthem on Sundays, festivals, and memorials; it is said to be so called because kings then attended church (?).

[6] R. C. om. the word *Sundays.* [7] Isai. liii. 4.

verse, Let all the people say, etc., *is not said from Advent to St. Mary's Day.*[1]

IN THE SHAWU'A OF THE EPIPHANY. *From everlasting to everlasting.* There shone forth and were revealed in creation. Three existent Persons. In the latter days on Jordan. The Father who cried and made his voice to be heard from on high. This is my Son and my beloved. And the Spirit who taught us the true faith.

And let all the people say Amen and Amen. O Mary, the holy Virgin. Mother of Jesus our Saviour. Beseech and beg for mercy. Of the Child who shone forth from thy bosom. That he make to pass from us in his lovingkindness. Times full of tribulations. And settle among us peace and tranquillity. And by thy prayers may the Church and her children be preserved from the Evil one. And in the glorious day when his majesty is revealed. May we be worthy with thee to have joy in the bridechamber of light.

Ps. cvi. 46.

From the Great Fast to Pentecost these concluding verses are not said.

IN THE SHAWU'A OF THE APOSTLES. *From everlasting to everlasting.* O Christ, who didst choose thy apostles. And didst clothe them with the strength of the Spirit. That they might be preachers in the whole world. And reveal thy glory and Godhead in creation. By the mighty deeds (wrought) by their hands. Make glad thy Churches with peace and concord. And lift up the head of them that preach thy Name and keep thy commandments. By thy right hand, O my Lord, may our salvation be preserved. And in[2] the peace which (cometh) from thee, may they preach thy victory.* *And let all the people, etc.* O Mary, the holy Virgin, etc., *as above.*

'IN THE SHAWU'A OF SUMMER AND TILL HOLY CROSS DAY. *From everlasting to everlasting.* Answer thy worshippers, O Christ. And send us from thy treasury. Compassion, mercy, and salvation. And forgiveness of trespasses. And as thou

---

[1] So A., explicitly.   [2] A. om. *in* (error ?).

didst answer Daniel from the lions' den. And the company of Ananias in the furnace of fire. So likewise rescue us, O our Lord, from kings and rulers, and evil men and cruel demons. Who like lions threaten to destroy us. By thy mighty power. Make peace in our confusion. And deliver us from their wickedness. And bring to nought their power. And make us to rejoice in thy salvation, O glorious King.* *And let all the people, etc.* O Mary, the holy Virgin, etc., *as above.*

FROM HOLY CROSS DAY TO THE HALLOWING OF THE CHURCH.[1] *From everlasting to everlasting.* By the great power of the cross. Doth the Church gain[2] confidence. Over death and over Satan. And rejoiceth in her[3] salvation. And celebrateth it with praise. In the sight of the enemies of the truth. For it hath exalted her lowliness. By the mighty deeds which it worked in her; and on the day when it was found, lo, her children laud it with songs of praise. O Great Power who wast the conqueror in her strifes. Keep thy promise to her, the boast of her children, the glory of thy revelation.* *And let all, etc.* O Mary, etc., *as above.*

SUNDAYS OF THE HALLOWING OF THE CHURCH. *From everlasting to everlasting.* Thou hast made, O Lord, this holy house. The foundation of thy throne. O Lord, establish it by thy hands. And in it let the prayers and tears of the distressed be accepted. And from it may all helps and gifts flow. To thy people and the sheep of thy pasture, who are saved by thy cross, and who take refuge in the Name of thy majesty.* *And let all, etc.* O Mary, etc., *as above.*[4]

PRAYER AFTER THE ROYAL ANTHEM.

In Advent, the Shawu'a of the Epiphany, and the Shawu'a of the Resurrection, and all Feasts of our Lord.[5] To thy wonderful

---

[1] *Or* Ma'alta (Entrance), A.   [2] *Hath . . . gained*, R. C.
[3] R. C., U. om. *her.*
[4] R. C. adds that according to tradition the Gospel and Zumara for the day (from the Khudhra) are here read. U. also mentions the reading of the Gospel as a Mosul tradition.
[5] T. om. Feasts of our Lord.

and unspeakable dispensation, O my Lord, which in mercy and compassion was perfected and completed and fulfilled, for the renewal and salvation of our nature, in the firstfruits which were of us,[1] we lift up praise and honour, and confession and worship, at all times, Lord of all, etc.

In the Great Fast, in the Shawu'a of Summer, and of Elijah till Holy Cross Day. Pity us, O thou Compassionate one, *as on ferias* (page 11).

In the Shawu'a of the Apostles. May the prayer, O my Lord, of the holy Apostles, and the request of the true preachers, and the beseeching and entreating of the illustrious athletes, the gospellers of righteousness and sowers of peace in creation, be with us continually, at all seasons and times, Lord of all, etc.

In the Shawu'a of the Cross. Make thy peace to dwell in all regions, and raise thy Church by thy cross, and keep her children in thy lovingkindness, that in her they may lift up to thee praise, honour, confession, and worship, at all times, Lord of all, etc.

In the Shawu'a of the Hallowing of the Church. Make firm, O my Lord, the foundations of thy Church in thy compassion, and strengthen her bars in thy lovingkindness, and make thy glory to dwell in the temple which is set apart to the honour of thy service, in all the days of the world, Lord of all, etc.

On Memorials of St. Mary. May the prayer, O my Lord, of the holy Virgin, and the request of the blessed Mother, and the beseeching and entreating of her who is full of grace, St. Mary the blessed, be with us and among us, at all seasons and times, Lord of all, etc.

On Memorials of our father.[2] May the prayer and request, and beseeching and entreating of our famous and holy father, Mar N the illustrious, and of all his companions, be with us continually, at all seasons and times, Lord of all, etc.

On Memorials of martyrs and confessors. May the prayer, O

---

[1] Human nature.   [2] The patron saint.

my Lord, of thy martyrs, and the request of thy confessors, and the beseeching and entreating of the athletes who fulfilled thy will, pray for us to thy Godhead that thou mayest grant us thy peace and tranquillity, in all the days of the world, Lord of all, etc.

On the Memorial of the Doctors. May the prayer, O my Lord, of the holy priests, and the request of the illustrious doctors, and the beseeching and entreating of the illustrious athletes, the gospellers of righteousness, be with us continually, at all seasons and times, Lord of all, etc.

On the Memorial of St. John the Baptist. May the prayer of the elect Baptist, and the request of the good herald, and the beseeching and entreating of the true preacher, the famous and holy martyr, St. John the illustrious, and of all his companions, be with us continually, at all times, Lord of all, etc.

THIRD SHURAYA. [Varies with the season.] Gloria. Hallelujah, Hallelujah, yea, Hallelujah.

Our Father, etc., farced (page 1).

They[1] give the kiss of peace.

Prayer. May thy Name, etc. (page 12).

Another. In heaven and on earth, etc. (page 12).

Here follows the SUBA'A[2] *on Memorials*[3] *(from the Kudhra).*

Prayer before the Suba'a. Make us worthy, O our Lord and God, of a peaceful evening, and a restful night, and a morning in which good things are proclaimed, and a day of good deeds of righteousness; that thereby we may propitiate thy Godhead, all the days of our life, Lord of all, etc.

They say the Suba'a.

The deacon says the Karuzutha. Let us all stand up, as is right, with joy and rejoicing.[4] Let us make request and say,

---

[1] So U. ; om. R. C.

[2] 'Compline,' added to Evening Service on Memorials (as also in the Great Fast and the Rogation of the Ninevites), but not on Sundays and Festivals of our Lord. For Compline as a separate service, see below.

[3] *If there is one* : R. C.   [4] In the fast, *in sorrow and care.*

O our Lord, have mercy upon us. *Answer*, O our Lord, have mercy upon us.

He proceeds. O mighty Lord, Almighty, God of our fathers, we make request. *Answer*, O our Lord, etc., *and so after each clause.*

O Holy and Glorious one, who dwellest in the saints, and whose will is propitiated (by them), we, etc.

O King of kings and Lord of lords, who dwellest in the excellent light, we, etc.

O thou whom no man hath seen, nor can see, we, etc.

O thou who willest that all men should live and turn to the knowledge of the truth, we, etc.

For the welfare of our holy fathers NN,[1] and all those who serve under them, we, etc.

O merciful God, who in mercies governest all, we, etc.

O thou who art glorified in heaven and worshipped on earth, we, etc.

Make thy peace and tranquillity to dwell in the assembly of thy worshippers, O Christ our Saviour, and have mercy upon us.

They say, Holy God (page 10), *and* Our Father.

Prayers[2] *after the Suba'a.* O thou who openest thy door to them that knock at it, and returnest answer to the petitions of them that ask of thee, open, O our Lord and our God, the door of mercies to our prayer; and receive our request, and return answer in thy mercies to our petitions from thy rich and overflowing treasury, O thou who art good, and stayest not thy mercies and gifts to the needy and afflicted, thy servants who call on thee and beseech thee, at all seasons and times, Lord of all, etc.

Another.[2] O thou who hearest the voice of the just and righteous who propitiate thee continually, and who grantest the wish of them that fear thee, hear, O my Lord, the prayer

---

[1] Patriarch, Metropolitan, and Bishop of the diocese.
[2] Om. T. in this place (see Night Service).

of thy servants in thy compassion, and receive the request of thy worshippers in thy mercy, and have compassion on the afflicted and tormented, thy servants who call on thee and beseech thee, at all seasons and times, Lord of all, etc.

Then follow the prayers for help, one or more for each priest who is present; the prayers Of Mary, Of the Apostles, *and* Of our father; *the Conclusion, Kiss of peace, and Nicene Creed, as on ferias* (page 16).

FERIAL NIGHT SERVICE

Priest. Glory be to God in the highest, *thrice.* And on earth peace and a good hope to men, at all times and for ever. *Answer*, Amen. Bless, O my Lord.[1] *They give the kiss of peace.*[1]

Our Father,[2] *farced* (page 1).

Deacon. Let us arise to prayer. Let us pray. Peace be with us.

Prayer. Let us arise, O my Lord, in thy power, and be confirmed in thy hope, and be lifted up and strengthened by the high arm of thy might; and may we be worthy, by the help of thy lovingkindness, to lift up to thee praise, and honour, and confession, and worship at all times, Lord of all, etc.

They answer,[3] Hallelujah,[4] Glory be to thee, O God, *thrice*. O Lord, have mercy upon us. Let us arise to prayer. Let us pray. Peace be with us.

Prayer.[4] Strengthen, O our Lord and our God, our weakness in thy compassion, and comfort and help the wants of our soul in thy lovingkindness; waken the sleep of our thoughts and lighten the weight of our limbs; wash and cleanse the filth of our trespasses and of our sins. Illumine the darkness of our minds, and stretch forth (thine arm) and

---

[1] Not mentioned in U., but it is the universal practice.

[2] For the Canon which precedes the Lord's Prayer on all Fridays, see below in the service of the Weeks of the Mysteries in the Fast.

[3] So U.; R. O. directs after each Hulala (below) to be said, Hallelujah, *twice*. Glory be, etc., Hallelujah, *twice*. Glory be, etc., Hallelujah, *twice*. O Lord, have mercy upon us. Let us pray; peace be with us.   [4] Om. R. C. in this place.

confirm us, and give us strength and a helping hand, that thereby we may arise and confess thee and glorify thee, without ceasing, all the days of our life, Lord of all, etc.

They say,[1] Hallelujah, etc., *as above.*

Prayer.[1] May the secret strength, O my Lord, of thy Godhead, and the wondrous help of thy Majesty, and the great aid of thy Mercy, strengthen the weakness of our feeble nature to lift up to thee praise and honour, confession and worship, at all times, Lord of all, etc.

They say,[1] Hallelujah, etc., *as above.*

The Hulali.[2]

They say seven Hulali in monotone, as follows, without farcing, but with the Gloria after each Marmitha. Between each Marmitha they kneel down, and between each Hulala they prostrate themselves.

Monday and Thursday,   Hulali 1-7 inclusive.
Tuesday and Friday,   Hulali 8-14 inclusive.
Wednesday and Saturday, Hulali 15-21 inclusive.

Before each Hulala is said its proper prayer, as given below, and after each Hulala they all say, Hallelujah, Glory be, etc., *as above,*[3] *and prostrate themselves.*

Prayers of the Hulali and Marmyatha.[4]

Of Hulala I. *Of Psalms* 1, 2, 3, 4. Make us worthy, O our Lord and God, to go on in virtuous deeds which please

---

[1] Om. R. C. in this place.   [2] Divisions of the Psalms.

[3] In R. C. the rules have been adapted to modern needs; each day three Hulali only are said. After the first two the Gloria, and Hallelujah, etc., as in note above. Before the second Hulala comes the prayer, *Strengthen, O our Lord*; and before the third, *May the secret strength.* After the third, *Hallelujah, Hallelujah. Let us pray, peace be with us.* On Monday, Hulali 1, 2, 3; Tuesday, Hulali 4, 5, 6; Wednesday, Hulali 7, 8, 9; Thursday, Hulali 10, 11, 15; Friday, Hulali 16, 17, 18; Saturday, Hulali 19, 20, 21.

[4] From P., T.; the prayers of the Marmyatha are given here for convenience, that all the Psalter prayers may be together; but they are only used on festivals and memorials. On ferias and Sundays the first prayer in each Hulala alone is said. So U.

and propitiate thy majesty, that our will may be in thy law, and that we may meditate in it day and night, Lord of all, etc.

Of Psalms 5, 6, 7. Hear the words of our prayer, O my Lord, and incline thine ear to the sound of our crying; and turn not thy face from the sound of our beseeching, O thou in whose goodness is our confident hope, at all seasons and times, Lord of all, etc.

Of Psalms 8, 9, 10. Thee, O Lord our Lord, hidden in thy being, who from the mouth of boys and children hast perfected thy praise, are we bound to confess, worship, and glorify, at all seasons and times, Lord of all, etc.

OF HULALA II. *Psalms* 11, 12, 13, 14. Confirm, O my Lord, thy hope in us, and fill our soul with thy help; and may thy lovingkindness pardon our sins, and the eternal mercies of thy glorious Trinity come to the assistance of thy worshippers who call upon thee and beseech thee, at all seasons and times, Lord of all, etc.

Of Psalms 15, 16, 17. Make us worthy, O our Lord and our God, with consciences pure and sanctified by thy truth, to dwell in thy holy tabernacle and walk in thy way blameless, all the days of our life, Lord of all, etc.

Or this. Grant us, O our Lord and our God, with a pure heart and good and beautiful deeds, to dwell in thy holy tabernacle, and to walk (therein); O Being who art from everlasting, we confess, worship, and glorify (thee) at all times, Lord of all, etc.

Of Psalm 18. Thee, O glorious strength of thy servants, and strong hope of thy worshippers, and mighty refuge of them that fear thee, helper and exalter of the horn of their salvation, we are bound to confess, worship, and glorify, at all seasons and times, Lord of all, etc.

Of Psalms 19, 20, 21. Thee, who art hidden from all in thy being, and art revealed and shinest forth in wondrous deeds of thy dispensation, the power of whose might heaven and earth declare, we are bound, etc.

OF HULALA III. *Psalms* 22, 23, 24. Thy glorious Godhead,

full of mercies and compassion, and hope, life, and salvation for all creatures, we are bound, etc.

Of Psalms 25, 26, 27. Lo, on thee, O our Lord and our God, hangeth the eye of our souls; in thee is our hope and confident trust; and of thee we ask forgiveness of our offences. Grant (this) in thy lovingkindness and mercies, as thou art wont, at all times, Lord of all, etc.

Of Psalms 28, 29, 30. Unto thee, O my Lord, do we cry, and in thee we take refuge, and of thee we ask forgiveness of. trespasses and sins. Grant this in thy lovingkindness and mercies, as thou art wont, at all times, Lord of all, etc.

OF HULALA IV. *Of Psalms* 31, 32. We beseech thee, who art our trust and confident hope, our help and our protection, and the great refuge of our weakness, turn, O my Lord, and pity us and have mercy upon us, as thou art wont, at all times, Lord of all, etc.

Of Psalms 33, 34. Thee, who art glorified by the righteous, and worshipped by the upright in heart, and confessed and blessed in heaven and in earth, are we bound to confess, worship, and glorify, at all seasons and times, Lord of all, etc.

Of Psalms 35, 36. We beseech thee, who judgest right judgment, and whose searching is full of justice, whose vengeance is full of mercy and pity, turn, O my Lord, and pity us and have mercy upon us, as thou art wont, at all times, Lord of all, etc.

OF HULALA V. *Of Psalm* 37. Thee, who art good and kind, compassionate and full of mercies, great King of glory, Being who art from everlasting, we confess, worship, and glorify, at all seasons and times, Lord of all, etc.

Of Psalms 38, 39, 40. Chasten us not, O my Lord, in thine anger and wrath. Recompense us not as our offences deserve, but in thy mercies and pity turn, O my Lord, and pity and have mercy upon us, as thou art wont, at all times, Lord of all, etc.

OF HULALA VI. *Of Psalms* 41, 42, 43. Thee, who art rich in thy love and overflowing with thy compassion, kind in thy goodness, unspeakable in thy glory, great King of glory, Being who art from everlasting, we confess, worship, and glorify, at all seasons and times, Lord of all, etc.

Of Psalms 44, 45, 46. Thee, O our Creator, who givest us benefits, and holdest and rulest our souls by the mild purpose of thy will, great King of glory, etc.

Of Psalms 47, 48, 49. Thee, O excellent and glorious King, whose majesty the nations and peoples, clapping their hands, do worship, are we bound to confess, worship, and glorify, at all seasons and times, Lord of all, etc.

OF HULALA VII. *Of Psalms* 50, 51, 52. Thee, O God of gods and Lord of lords, great King of glory, Being who art from eternity, we confess, worship, and glorify, at all seasons and times, Lord of all, etc.

Of Psalms 53, 54, 55. We beseech thee, who destroyest the ungodly, and scatterest the proud, and overthrowest the strong, who ever raisest in (thy) lovingkindness them that fear thy holy Name, turn, O my Lord, and pity and have mercy upon us, as thou art wont, at all times, Lord of all, etc.

Of Psalms 56, 57, 58. Have mercy upon us, O our Lord and our God, and pardon, wipe out, and take away our offences in the overflowing mercies of thy lovingkindness, O thou Merciful one, who forgivest trespasses and sins, Lord of all, etc.

OF HULALA VIII. *Of Psalms* 59, 60, 61. Deliver us, O our Lord and our God, from the wiles and snares of the apostate Enemy by thy great and strong power, and by thy high and invincible arm, O thou who art good, and on whom is placed our confident hope, at all times and seasons, Lord of all, etc.

Of Psalms 62, 63, 64. On thee, O my Lord, our souls wait, and to thy compassion the eyes of our hearts look, and of thee we ask forgiveness of our offences. Grant this in thy lovingkindness and mercies, as thou art wont, at all times, Lord of all, etc.

Of Psalms 65, 66, 67. Thee beseemeth praise in thy chosen Church, and to thee is owed confession in glorious

Zion; thee becometh worship in thine exalted dwelling-place, Lord of all, etc.

OF HULALA IX. *Of Psalm* 68. May the eternal mercies of thy glorious Trinity, O our Lord and our God, protect thy sinful and weak servants, who call on thee and beseech thee, at all times, Lord of all, etc.

Of Psalms 69, 70. Save, O my Lord, thy people from the flood of destruction, and draw our souls out of the tempests of sin. And may thy truth support us, and make us to walk in the paths of righteousness, all the days of our life, Lord of all, etc.

OF HULALA X. *Of Psalms* 71, 72. In thee, O my Lord, do we put our hope, and in thy mercies do we place our confident trust, and of thy lovingkindness we make request; be, O my Lord, a helper to our weakness and a refuge to our confusion, a saviour to our affliction and a pardoner to our sinfulness, a gatherer together of our scattered state and an equipper of our need. And turn not thy face from the sound of our beseeching, O thou who art good, and in whom is placed our confident trust, at all seasons and times, Lord of all, etc.

Of Psalms 73, 74. Thee, who art patient in spirit in thy lovingkindness and a two-fold avenger in thy justice, great King of glory, etc., *as before.*

Or this. Thee, O our good God and King, who art full of mercies, the power of whose majesty reigneth over all, whose mercies and compassion overflow, are we bound, etc.

Of Psalms 75, 76, 77. We confess, O our Lord and our God, the mercy of thy lovingkindness to us, and worship the care of thy goodwill towards us, and lift up to thee praise, and honour, and confession, and worship, at all times, Lord of all, etc.

OF HULALA XI. *Of Psalm* 78. We beseech thee, O wise Ruler and wondrous Governor of thy household, great Treasure who pourest forth all helps and benefits in thy mercy, turn, O my Lord, and pity, etc., *as before.*

Of Psalms 79, 80, 81. Save, O my Lord, thy people, and

bless thine inheritance, and make thy glory to dwell in the temple which is set apart for thy honour, all the days of the world, Lord of all, etc.

OF HULALA XII. *Of Psalms* 82, 83, 84. Thee, O King whom kings worship, and the adorable honour of whose majesty companies and ten thousands of angels and archangels, standing with great fear and trembling, serve and celebrate, we are bound, etc.

Of Psalms 85, 86. Be gracious, O my Lord, to the prayer of thy servants, and be pleased with the service of thy worshippers; pardon the trespasses of them that glorify thee, and take away the heat of thine anger from them of thy household, O thou who art good and carest for our lives, at all seasons and times, Lord of all, etc.

Of Psalms 87, 88. Confirm, O my Lord, the foundations of thy Church in thy compassion, and strengthen her bars in thy lovingkindness, and make thy glory to dwell in the temple which is set apart for the honour of thy service, all the days of the world, Lord of all, etc.

OF HULALA XIII. *Of Psalm* 89. Pour forth on us, O my Lord, thy graces, and multiply thy helps to us, and strengthen us; as thou art wont, to please thee according to thy will, and to walk after thy commandments and propitiate thy Godhead in good deeds of righteousness, all the days of our life, Lord of all, etc.

Of Psalms 90, 91, 92. Thee, who holdest all by the power of thy word, and rulest the worlds and creatures by the mild purpose of thy will, great King of glory, etc., *as before.*

OF HULALA XIV. *Of Psalms* 93, 94, 95. Thee, adorable and glorious, excellent and magnifical, exalted above all in thy being, great King of glory, etc.

Of Psalms 96, 97, 98. A new praise, O my Lord, and exalted confession, suppliant worship, and continual thanksgiving are we bound to lift up to thy glorious Trinity, at all times, Lord of all, etc.

Of Psalms 99, 100, 101. Thee, who sittest on the chariot of the cherubim, and art celebrated by the bands of angels, whose purpose moveth the earth, and whose commandment maketh the whole world to tremble, are we bound, etc.

OF HULALA XV. *Of Psalms* 102, 103. O thou who hast compassion on the trespasses of sins in the multitude of thy longsuffering, have compassion, O our Lord and our God, on the misery, desolation, and error of our feeble nature, in the overflowing mercies of thy lovingkindness, O Merciful one, who forgivest trespasses and sins, Lord of all, etc.

Of Psalm 104. Thee, who art clothed with excellence and splendour and decked with unspeakable light, by whose purpose the worlds were created and created things set fast, are we bound, etc.

Of Psalm 105. Let us confess thee, O our good God, and call on thy Name to help us; and let our lips speak of thy glory, for thou art the Lord who art good to thy worshippers, and hast mercy on all, Lord of all, etc.

OF HULALA XVI. *Of Psalm* 106. Grant us, O my Lord, to confess thy lovingkindness, and make us worthy to relate thy wonders; and strengthen us to confess, worship, and glorify the hidden and glorious strength of thy glorious Trinity, at all times, Lord of all, etc.

Of Psalms 107, 108. Thy lovingkindness, O my Lord, is everlasting, and in it both high and low take refuge. May it stand before our trespasses, and keep us from the Evil one and his hosts, at all seasons and times, Lord of all, etc.

Or this. May thy lovingkindness, O my Lord, hear the words with which we cry in our afflictions; and do thou rescue us from persecutors, and protect us under thy wings from the Evil one and his hosts, at all seasons and times, Lord of all, etc.

Of Psalms 109, 110, 111. O my Lord, save thy people from the wicked, and deliver thy flock from the crafty; rescue thy Church from the haters and enemies of thy Name. For thou art the praise of our strength and the crown of our boasting, Lord of all, etc.

OF HULALA XVII. *Of Psalms* 112, 113, 114, 115. Grant us, O my Lord, to be thine and to fear thee; to be moved by thy word and to dread thy decree, to take heed to thy commandments and to appease thy Godhead with good deeds of righteousness, all the days of our life, Lord of all, etc.

Of Psalms 116, 117, 118. May the overflowing, blessed, and unspeakable mercies of thy glorious Trinity come to the assistance of thy worshippers who call on thee and beseech thee, at all times, Lord of all, etc.

Or this. Have mercy on us, O our Lord and our God, and hear our prayers and receive our request; turn not thy face from the sound of our beseeching, O thou who art good, and on whom rests our confident trust at all seasons and times, Lord of all, etc.

Of Psalm 119 (*vv.* 1-89). We beseech thee, who art good and givest good things to them that are good; who art just and lovest them that are just; who art holy and dwellest in the holy, and whose will is appeased (by them), turn, O my Lord, and pity and have mercy upon us, as thou art wont, at all times, Lord of all, etc.

OF HULALA XVIII. *Of Psalm* 119 (*from v.* 89). Thee, O Being who hast neither beginning nor end, hidden and incomprehensible nature, everlasting and unbounded, Creator, Maker, and Ruler of all, are we bound, etc.

Of Psalms 120, 121, 122, 123, 124, 125. To thee we cry in our afflictions, in thee we take refuge in our distresses, of thee we ask forgiveness of our offences. Grant this in thy lovingkindness and mercies, as thou art wont, at all times, Lord of all, etc.

Of Psalms 126, 127, 128, 129, 130, 131. Turn us towards thee in thy compassion, and receive us into thy household, O good Shepherd, who didst go out to seek us, and didst find us when we were lost, and willest that we should return in thy lovingkindness and mercies, Lord of all, etc.

OF HULALA XIX. *Of Psalms* 132, 133, 134, 135. We beseech thee, who art the hope of the just, the confident trust of the righteous, the great refuge of the distressed, the help of them that call on thy holy Name, turn, O my Lord, and pity us and have mercy upon us, as thou art wont, at all times, Lord of all, etc.

Of Psalms 136, 137, 138. Thee, O our good God and King full of mercies, who didst order lights[1] for the joy of our service, that in their light we might rejoice and have joy all the days of our life, are we bound, etc.

Of Psalms 139, 140, 141. To thee, O Searcher of our thoughts and Investigator of our hearts, who dost know our secrets and dost furnish us with blessings, who dost establish the heights and the depths in thy lovingkindness and mercies, we lift up praise, and honour, and confession, and worship, at all times, Lord of all, etc.

OF HULALA XX. *Of Psalms* 142, 143, 144. To thee, O my Lord, we cry, that thou mayest come to assist us; in thee we take refuge, that thou mayest be found to help us; and of thee we beg that thou mayest aid our weakness, that we may keep thy lifegiving and divine commandments. Grant this in thy lovingkindness and mercies, as thou art wont, at all times, Lord of all, etc.

Of Psalms 145, 146, 147 (*vv.* 1-12). Thee, O King of kings and Lord of lords, the power of whose majesty holdeth and ruleth heaven and earth and all that is in them, are we bound, etc.

Of Psalms 147 (*from v.* 12), 148, 149, 150. O my Lord, answer thy Church, which calleth to thee with contrition, and receive the beseeching of thy flock, which knocketh at the door of thy majesty. Fulfil in her the promise which (thou madest) to her, that the doors of Sheol and its tyrants should not prevail against her for ever. Confirm in her thy only begotten word, (spoken) to Peter, who planted her, in Jerusalem which is above, Lord of all, etc.

OF HULALA XXI. *Of Exodus* xv. 1-22 *and Isaiah* xlii. 10-14, xlv. 8. Thee, O excellent and magnifical, strong and glorious, mighty and warlike, powerful and full of mercies, great King of glory, etc., *as before.*

Of Deut. xxxii. 1-21.[2] Pour into our hearts, O my Lord, the good seed of thy doctrine, and cause to descend on us the dew of thy lovingkindness, that we may grow according to thy

---

[1] Of the firmament.   [2] To *vanities.*

will, and bring forth fruits which please thy majesty, all the days of our life, Lord of all, etc.

Of Deut. xxxii. 21 [1]-44. We beseech thee, O jealous and just one, who in thy jealousy destroyest the wicked, and in thy wrath rootest out the evildoers, and keepest (thy) promise and lovingkindness to them that fear thy holy Name, turn, O my Lord, and pity and have mercy on us, as thou art wont, at all times, Lord of all, etc.

Prayer[2] *for all days when the Eucharist is to be celebrated.* For thy nature, which is hidden and incomprehensible, and unbounded by the thought and folly of all creatures, O my Lord, glory is fitting and the sound of praise is right. Worship is seemly and due from all whom thou hast created and formed in heaven and in earth, Lord of all, etc.

If the Eucharist is celebrated, they add the Qaltha.[3]

QALTHA.[4] *Monday.* The habitation that is apart amidst the woods[5] floateth and passeth by. And the overflowings of water convey it to the mountains of Qardu. Ps. xv., xvi., xvii., under one Gloria. (*Each side says two clauses at a time.*)

Tuesday. O thou who cultivatest the earth and makest the mountains to hang with richness. Cultivate our minds, that they may bear (thy) kindly yoke. Ps. xxv., xxvi., xxvii.

Wednesday. By the prayers of thy Mother, O our Lord, have pity on our lives. And by the request of the just and chaste, answer those who call on thy Name. Ps. xlv.

Thursday. What is this that the nations have left their gods. And swear in the name of a man,[6] who is not as thou sayest ? Ps. xcvi., xcvii., xcviii.

Friday. In the bonds of mortality is man bound. And he

---

[1] From *And I will move.*   [2] Om. R. C.
[3] So U.   [4] From U.
[5] The ark resting on the mountains of Kurdistan ?   [6] Our Lord.

hath not the desire to depart from it even by death. Ps. lxxxviii.

Saturday. Dost thou not know that our iniquity hath hung us on the Cross. And our audacity hath made us to die without remedy? Ps. cxlvii. (from v. 12), cxlviii., cxlix., cl.

Prayer before the Motwa. May the prayer of our feebleness please thee, O our Lord and our God, and may the request of our weakness enter before thee, and may thy mercies greatly intercede for our sinfulness; and from the great treasury of thy compassion may the petitions of our need be answered, at all seasons and times, Lord of all, etc.

THE MOTWA,[1] *an anthem which varies according to the season, except on Wednesdays, when the Special Anthems are said.*[2] *The Motwa (which is found in the Kashkul for ferias) begins on Mondays with the Sunday evening Royal Anthem; on Tuesdays with the Sunday Night Anthem; on Thursdays with the Sunday Morning Anthem; on Saturdays with the Sunday Anthem of the Mysteries, as used at the Liturgy. It ends daily on ferias as follows, except on Wednesdays, and except in the Fast and the Rogation of the Ninevites:*

From[3] everlasting to everlasting. O merciful God, pity thy people. And make not thine inheritance a scorn and mockery to the nations. Look from thine abode and see the oppression. Which we suffer from the enemies. And let thy lovingkindness quickly shine forth upon us. That the nations say not, Where is their God?* O merciful God, keep thy servants. From them that hate (us) without a cause, and wish to seize that which is not their own. Fence us round with thy strong truth. That they which hate us may see and be confounded. Surround us with thy care as with a wall. That we may be protected within it and confess thy lovingkindness.* By the prayer of her who bore thee, O our Lord Jesus. Give peace to all the world, which is disturbed and

---

[1] So called because all here sit until the end of the Tishbukhta.
[2] For these, see below.   [3] Om. A., except the first few words.

confused by its sins. And bring to nought wars and enmities on earth. Make peace between priests and kings. That in concord and love may be celebrated. The memorial of her who bore thee, all (our) days.* May the righteous who pleased thee, O our Lord Jesus. The prophets, apostles, and martyrs. And teachers in every country. Beseech thee for our souls. That thou have mercy on us all. And make us worthy with them to confess thee. In the day when they receive the reward of their deeds.* Blessed art thou, O our famous and holy father.[1] Who didst finish thy course in victory. And didst work in the vineyard of Christ. And didst receive a reward for thy deeds. The penny of the good things of heaven. May thy prayers be on all of us. And may we be worthy to inherit the kingdom with thee.

Deacon. Let us pray, Peace be with us.

Prayer of the Shubakha. To thee be glory from those on high, and confession from those below; and worship and praise and exaltation from all whom thou hast created and fashioned in heaven and earth, Lord of all, etc.

SHUBAKHA.[2]

Monday. Ps. xiii. How long wilt thou forget me, O Lord, for ever? *Glory be to thee, O God* (thrice). How long wilt ... *(to the end)*.* Glory be to the Father, and to the Son, and to the Holy Ghost.* *Glory be to thee, O God* (thrice).[3] From everlasting to everlasting. Amen.* *Glory be to thee, O God* (thrice). How long wilt thou forget me, O Lord, for ever?* *Glory be to thee, O God* (thrice).

Tuesday. Ps. xxviii.
Wednesday. Ps. lxvii.
Thursday. Ps. liv.

---

[1] Or *Awa.*
[2] *i.e.* Psalm of glory.
[3] R. C. om. these words here.

FERIAL NIGHT SERVICE

Friday. Ps. xcv. 1-8¹ (*unless there is a special one in the Kashkul*).

Saturday. Ps. cl. *All farced as above.*

TISHBUKHTA.²

*Monday, by Mar Abraham, Doctor.*³ Turn to the prayer of thy servants, O our Saviour. And receive our request and return answer to our petitions.* Because thou art the refuge and hope of the weak. By thy help may we conquer the wiles of the Evil one.* For lo, he at all times setteth snares for our souls. And wisheth, in his cunning, to defile us with his wickedness.* Send, O my Lord, thy strength, and let it destroy his enticements. That he may not pursue after us, and that we fall not into the gulf of sin.* May the strength of thy lovingkindness strengthen our weakness. That we may⁴ be approved before thee in our deeds, O Compassionate one.* And make us worthy to sing to thee in the day of thy coming. The praise that ceaseth not for ever and ever, Amen.

*Tuesday, by*³ *Mar Awa, Catholicos, or, as some say, by Mar Thomas of Urhai.*⁵ The heights and the depths, and all that is in them, are not sufficient. To confess thine Essence, O Being who fashionest all.* They are too small to tell thy love towards us. And the greatness of thy lovingkindness and thy manifold mercies.* Which thou didst grant to our race, unworthy though we were. O thou who art good and kind, and didst put on⁶ our nature.* And didst save it⁷ from death and raise it⁸ to heaven. And didst make it⁹ higher than every lord and ruler.* And lo, the assemblies of angels worship before thee. And cry without ceasing, all with one accord.* Holy art thou, O Father, Son, and Holy Ghost. To thee be glory from all, for ever and ever. Amen.

---

¹ Om. R. C.
² *i.e.* hymn of praise.
³ So U.; A., R. C. om. name of author.
⁴ R. C.: *and may we*.
⁵ The Apostle.
⁶ R. C.: *take*.
⁷ R. C.: *us*.
⁸ R. C.: *didst ascend*.
⁹ R. C.: *didst sit down*.

Wednesday, by Mar Abimelek.[1] May thy mercies be on our trespasses. O Christ, who lovest the voice of the penitent.* Hear our request (and) heal us, for thou art good. And remove from us the canker of our wickedness.* Because thou knowest the suffering of our race. With thy good medicine heal our wounds.* Bestow thy compassion on our scars. And heal us, O our Lord, as thou art wont.* And with the dew of thy lovingkindness. Let us cleanse our stains according to thy will.* And grant us with one accord to confess thy Name. Father, Son, and Holy Ghost.* Father, Son, and Holy Ghost.[2] For ever and ever, Amen and Amen.

Thursday, by Mar Ephraim.[1] Receive, O our Lord, the request of us all. Who make our offerings to thee with beseeching.* Hear, O God, the voice of thy servants. And the entreaty of them that glorify thee.* For thou art our King, and in thy great Name. We have hope and confidence.* Grant us to gain unanimity. Without doubting, in the faith.* While we confess that by thy will. All things were fashioned from nought.* The nature of thine existence cannot be understood. By creatures, O hidden Being.* Who dwellest in light, and like whom there is none. And whom men cannot approach.* By thy fashionings, O my Lord, is made known. The greatness of thy wealth, to the work of thy hands.* For thou art Lord and Maker. Who art all-powerful and suppliest all.* We earnestly desire forgiveness of trespasses. Bestow (it) on us, as thou art wont.* And grant us from our souls. To apply medicines to our wounds.* We ask for mercies, O Lord of all. Supply thy wealth to our need.* And if any waver and go astray. In the error of the wile of the enemy.* May thy compassion be their guide. And tread out the way for their consciences.* That they may know that it is by thy care. That our captive nature hath gained freedom.* And that with one, perfect, and pure heart. We may serve before thee according to thy will.*

---

[1] So U.; A., R. C. om. name of author. [2] A., R. C. om. this line.

And diligently do at all times. That which pleaseth thy Godhead.* And with one accord raise glory. To Father, Son, and Holy Ghost.* Who saved us by the firstfruits [1] which (were taken) from us. And hath not recompensed us according to our wickedness.* To him be praise from his worshippers. For ever and ever, Amen and Amen.

Friday, by Mar Abraham of Nithpar, or, as some say, by Mar John of Beith-raban.[2] Glory to him who in his goodness and love. Revealed his praise to the sons of men.* He created a dumb nature from dust. And adorned it with a soul endowed with treasures.* He placed praise in a lowly body. That all creation might sing his glory.* Come, ye who can speak, sing glory to him. Before we lie down in the sleep of death.* In the long night let us remember death. Which shutteth our mouth and putteth us to silence.* The just who glorified him by night. Even when dead are alive.* And the wicked who did evil against his great glory. Even while living are dead.* Let us awake our body by prayers. And by Hallelujahs of hidden power.* That we may be companions of the wise. Virgins whom our Lord praised.* And that in the night when he maketh the worlds to tremble. We may be watching and see the Son.* That we be not sunk in (evil) desires. But that we may see his glory in the day when he shineth forth.* And that we may be before him as watchful servants. In the hour when he directeth the children of his bridechamber.* And the wicked remain in torture. And suddenly the door of mercies is shut.* While we live we shall labour somewhat. For after our [3] death is the day of recompense.* The body which giveth itself earnestly to prayers. In the day of the quickening flieth in the air.* And seeth our Lord, without shame. And entereth with him into the house of the kingdom.* The watchful ones [4] and the just love him. They who have kept vigil and

---

[1] Human nature; *i.e.* by the Incarnation.
[2] So U.; A., R. C. om. name of author.   [3] Om. *our*, R. C., U.
[4] The angels.

laboured in prayer.¹ * Blessed is he who hath made us vessels of his glory. And hath placed his praise in the mouth of (creatures of) dust. And glory to his mercies who hath united. Men of clay with the spiritual ones.* That they may sing all the nights. And at all times, Holy to his name.* And let us all give him praise. For ever and ever, Amen and Amen.

*Saturday, by Mar Ephraim.*² Blessed is the Being who hath created us and saved us by his Christ. And brought us to the knowledge of the Trinity.* O God the Word, the Only-begotten of the Father. Thee alone may I please in our manhood which thou didst put on.³ * And may I not stay nor cease, O Christ our Saviour. From confessing thy Name at all times.

The Karuzutha.

They rise up, and the deacon says the Karuzutha. Let us all stand up, as is right, in sorrow and care. Let us make request and say, O our Lord, have mercy upon us. *The people answer.* O our Lord, have mercy upon us.

He proceeds. O mighty Lord, Eternal Being, who dwellest in the highest heights, we make request. *Answer.* O our Lord, etc., *and so after each clause.*

O thou who, in thy great love with which thou didst love us, didst honour⁴ the fashioning of our race by the image of thy glory, we, etc.

O thou who didst promise to faithful Abraham good things to them that love thee, and by the revelation of Christ wast made known to thy Church, we, etc.

O thou who wilt not that our nature should perish, but that it should repent (and turn) from the error of darkness to the knowledge of the truth, we, etc.

O thou who alone art the Maker and Fashioner of created things, and dwellest in the excellent light, we, etc.

---

[1] Syr.: *prayers*. [2] So U.; A., R. C. om. name of author.
[3] *take*, R. C. [4] U.: *in thy great love didst love us, and didst*.

For the welfare of our holy fathers NN,[1] and all those who serve under them, we, etc.

O merciful God, who in mercies governest all, we, etc.

O[2] thou who art glorified in heaven and worshipped on earth, we, etc.

Give us the victory, O Christ our Lord, in thy coming, and give peace to thy Church, saved by thy precious blood, and have mercy upon us.

---

[1] Patriarch, Metropolitan, and Bishop of the diocese.
[2] U. om. this clause here.

FERIAL MORNING SERVICE[1]

Prayer before the Morning Psalms. O Compassionate, Merciful, and Pitiful one, whose door is open to them that repent, and who ever callest sinners to come near to thee in penitence; open, O our Lord and our God, the door of mercies to our prayer; and receive our request, and return an answer in thy mercies to our petitions, from thy rich and overflowing treasury, O thou who art good and who stayest not thy mercies and gifts to the needy and afflicted, thy servants, who call on thee and beseech thee, at all seasons and times, Lord of all, etc.

They answer. Amen. Bless, O my Lord.[2]

Another. O my Lord, all creatures whom thou hast created, who have been fashioned by thy purpose, who by thy will have come into being, the cause of whose being thou art, and the breath and inspiration of our life, hasten to kneel and worship thee, sing and chant Hallelujah to thee, are glad and rejoice in thee, ask and entreat thee, make request and beseech thee, confess and glorify thee, Lord of all, etc.

THE PSALMS. Psalm c., *farced thus.* Glorify the Lord, all the whole earth. *O Giver of light, O Lord, we lift up glory to thee.* Glorify the Lord all the whole earth.* Serve the Lord, etc., *to the end of the Psalm.** Glory be, etc.* From everlasting to everlasting. Amen. Glorify the Lord, all the whole earth.* *O Giver of light, etc.* Let us pray, Peace be with us.

Prayer. To thee, O my Lord, we lift up glory and confession, and continually offer worship and thanksgiving to thy living

---

[1] This follows the Night Service without a break.
[2] R. C. om. the response.

and holy Name, for thou art the Lord and Creator of all, Father, Son, and Holy Ghost, for ever. *Amen.*

Ps. xci. and Gloria, *farced, as before, with* Glorious is thy confident hope, O Christ our Saviour.

Deacon. Let us pray, Peace be with us.

Prayer. Glorious, O my Lord, is the great and confident hope of thy Godhead, and high and exalted is the wondrous refuge of thy Majesty, and all who hope in thee, and trust in thee, and call on thy holy Name, and beseech thee, at all seasons and times, shall not be ashamed, O Lord of all, etc.

Ps. civ. (vv. 1-16 to *full of sap*), *farced with* Glory becometh thee, O God.[1] *No Gloria. Add* Glory becometh, etc.

Ps. cxiii., *farced with* Glory to him who created the light. *No Gloria. Add* Glory to him, etc.[2]

Ps. xciii., cxlviii., cxlix., cl., cxvii., *said without farcing, and all under one Gloria. Add* Glorify the Lord, all the whole earth.[3] * O Giver of light, O Lord, even to thee do we lift up glory.

Deacon. Let us pray, Peace be with us.

Prayer of the Lakhumara. Thee, O my Lord, we are bound, heaven and earth and all that is in them, to confess, worship, and glorify, for all thy helps and graces towards us, the greatness of which cannot be repaid, Lord of all, etc.

They all say the Lakhumara. Thee, Lord of all, we confess. And thee, Jesus Christ, we glorify. For thou art the Quickener of our bodies. And thou art the Saviour of our souls. *My voice shalt thou hear in the morning, O Lord, and in the morning I will be prepared, and will appear before thee.* (Ps. v. 3.) Thee, Lord of all. Glory be. From everlasting. Thee, Lord of all. Let us pray, Peace be with us.

Prayer. Thee, who quickenest our bodies in thy compassion, and answerest (us), and savest our souls by the mild purpose of thy will, great King of glory, Being who art from

---

[1] R. C. : *The glory of the Lord shall be for ever.*
[2] Sometimes said without farcing. R. C. om. the farcing at the end.
[3] *Or,* With every breath let us praise the Lord.

everlasting, we confess, worship, and glorify, at all seasons and times, Lord of all, etc.

Ps. li. (vv. 1-18). Have mercy upon me, O God, after thy goodness. And according to the multitude of thy mercies do away mine offences. *Have mercy upon me, O Lord.* Have mercy upon me, O God, after . . . not despise.* *Have*[1] *mercy upon me, O Lord.*[2] Glory be.* From everlasting. *Have mercy upon me, O Lord.** Have mercy upon me, O God, after thy goodness. And according to the multitude of thy mercies do away mine offences.* *O Christ the King, have mercy upon me. O Christ the King, glory to thy Name.*[3]

TISHBUKHTA[4] *by Mar Ephraim, or, as some say, by Mar Awa, Catholicos.* To thee be glory, O our God. And to thee be praise, O our Maker. We bless thee, who didst form us. O compassionate Lord. O merciful God. Pitiful Creator. O Saviour, who dost preserve us. Who dost help and aid us. We worship thee, O our[5] Lord. For thou art long-suffering, and thy lovingkindness is great. O Merciful one, pity us and have mercy upon us. Turn to us in the multitude of thy mercies. Our confident hope and strong refuge. O Lord our God, make thy face to shine, and we shall be saved. O thou who receivest the penitent in mercy. Receive our prayer and service. O thou who hearest[6] the voice of thy worshippers. Let our request come before thee, and have mercy upon us. O thou who forgivest the trespasses of mortals in thy compassion. Forgive us our trespasses and sins in thy compassion. O thou who pardonest the sins of the sons of men in thy lovingkindness. Pardon our many sins, and have mercy upon us.* O good Hope of the sons of men, give us peace and tranquillity. That we may confess thy Trinity, O Lord of all, for ever. Amen. *Repeat thrice from the asterisk.*

---

[1] In this Psalm each choir says two clauses at a time.
[2] R. C. om. this clause here.   [3] R. C. om. the last clause.
[4] Om. A.; R. C. om. name of author.   [5] R. C. om. *our.*
[6] U.: *hear* (misprint?).

They say, Let us pray, Peace be with us.

Prayer. O Christ, the good Hope of the sons of men, and the peaceful Haven which giveth peace to (all) creatures; do thou, O my Lord, grant us thy peace and tranquillity, that therein we may confess and glorify thee without ceasing, all the days of our life, Lord of all, etc.

Deacon.[1] Lift up your voices, and glorify the living God, all ye people.

They all say, Holy Ghost, Holy Mighty, Holy Immortal, have mercy upon us. Glory be. Holy God. From everlasting. Holy God. Let[1] us pray, Peace be with us.

They say,[2] Our Father, *farced* (page 1).

Prayer before the Martyrs' Anthem. O Compassionate one, whose Name is Holy, who art good and just from everlasting, overflowing with lovingkindness and mercy,[3] pour forth, O our Lord and our God, the compassion of the kindness of thy love on the souls of thy worshippers, who call on thee and beseech thee, at all seasons and times, Lord of all, etc.

Another. Bless, O my Lord, thy servants in thy lovingkindness, and keep thy worshippers from all harm in the overflowing abundance of thy mercy; feed, rule, help, and protect our lives beneath the wings of the care of thy love; save, rescue, and deliver our bodies and our souls from the Evil one and his hosts, at all seasons and times, Lord of all, etc.

THE MARTYRS' ANTHEM. *One for each day in the week (see below, page* 109).

DAILY ANTHEM.[4] At the early dawn of the morning we glorify thee, O Lord. For thou art the Saviour of all creatures. Give us in thy compassion. A day full of peace. And grant us forgiveness of sins.* Cut not off our hope.

---

[1] Om. U.

[2] U. ins. a rubrick directing that if the Martyrs' Anthem be not said, the Lord's Prayer be omitted, and the anthem *At the early dawn* be immediately begun.

[3] *Or,* whose grace and mercy are overflowing from everlasting.

[4] Om. A.

FERIAL MORNING SERVICE

Shut not thy door in our face. Stay not thy care for us. And recompense us not as we deserve, O God. For thou alone knowest our weakness.* Sow, O our Lord, in the whole world. Love, and peace, and concord. And raise up priests, and kings, and judges, and give peace to them of high estate. Heal the sick and preserve the whole. And pardon the trespasses of all the sons of men.* In the way that we walk. Let thy lovingkindness keep us, O my Lord. As (it kept) the boy David from Saul. Give us, in thy compassion, that towards which we make our way. That we may arrive, according to thy will, in peace.* By the lovingkindness which preserved the prophet Moses in the sea. And raised up Daniel from the (lions') den. And by which were rescued. They of the company of Ananias in the furnace. Deliver us, O our Lord, from the Evil one.

Another.[1] At morning time we all arise. And worship the Father. And lift up praise to the Son. And confess the Holy Ghost.* May the lovingkindness of the Father. And the compassion of the Son. And the pity of the Spirit. A threefold mystery, be our help, all our days.* In thee, O our Helper. O our[2] true Physician, have we confident trust. Apply the medicine of thy mercies, and heal our bruises. That we be not utterly destroyed.* Without thy help we are very weak. In keeping thy commandments. O Christ, who aidest those who fulfil thy will. Keep thy worshippers.* [3] With entreaty let us beg and beseech mercy. And ask for forgiveness. From the Compassionate one, whose door is open. To all to (turn) to him and repent.* [3] Day by day I promise thee that to-morrow I will repent. My days have passed and gone. And my trespasses remain. O Christ, pity me and have mercy upon me.[4]

They say, Let us pray, Peace be with us.

Prayer. Of thee, O great[5] and true Hope, for whom the just and the prophets waited in their generations, whom the

---

[1] Om. A.
[2] R. C. om. *our*.
[3] U. ins. *And*.
[4] U. om. *and have mercy upon me*.
[5] So T.; U., R. C. ins. *excellent* after *great*.

righteous pleased by their labours, and the holy martyrs propitiated by the precious blood which poured forth from their necks, we beseech and ask, Grant us, O our Lord and our God, that we may take refuge in the power hidden in their bones, and be helped by their prayers, and with them and among them, and in their companies, and around their tombs, and in the glorious temples set apart for the honour of their service, be made worthy to lift up to thee praise, honour, confession, and worship, at all times, Lord of all, etc.

Another. May the martyrs, O our Lord and our God, who by thy power and help overcame, humiliated, and brought to nought the error of heathenism, and exalted and raised the true faith of thy Name, make request, O my Lord, and beseech for us of thy justice, in the great and glorious day when thy justice is revealed from heaven, O just Judge, full of mercies, who forgivest offences and sins, Lord of all, etc.

Then follow the prayers for help,[1] *one or more for each priest who is present, the prayers* Of Mary, Of the Apostles, *and* Of our father, *with the Conclusion, as at the Evening Service* (page 16).

Conclusion. Bestow, O our Lord and our God, in thy lovingkindness, at this morning time, salvation to the oppressed, release to the prisoners, restoration to the tormented, healing to the sick, return to those who are far away, preservation to those who are near, pardon to sinners, acceptance to the penitent, exaltation to the righteous, supply of their needs to the poor, finding to the lost, bringing back to them that are driven away, a good and acceptable memorial to the departed, mercy and compassion to all that are created and made; and grant to us and all men those things which will help us weak sinners, and please thy majesty, in thy lovingkindness and mercies, Christ the hope of our nature, now ✠ and at all times and for ever and ever. *Amen. He makes the sign of the cross over the people.*

---

[1] These may only be said in a church, U.; in U. only the first two are mentioned, then the prayers *Of Mary*, etc.

Or[1] *any of the Conclusions at the Evening Service may be used* (page 20).

They[2] *answer,* May Christ hear thy prayers, etc., *as at the Evening Service.*

They give the kiss of peace, and say the Nicene Creed (page 22).

THE MORNING MARTYRS' ANTHEMS

Monday Morning.

My voice shalt thou hear in the morning, O Lord. At morning time, when are opened. The doors on high to prayer. Receive, O our Lord, our request. Ps. v. 3. And return answer to our petitions in thy mercies. And grant hope and salvation. To the souls who wait for thee.

And in the morning will I be ready, and will appear before thee. The morning of our Lord hath seen him come. And suddenly our Saviour shineth forth. And Ib. giveth a reward to the just. Blessed is he who hath prospered. And hath worked in the vineyard of Christ. And hath received his reward abundantly.

O let us hear thy lovingkindness in the morning. Make us worthy, O our Lord, of that morning. When heaven and earth rejoice. And[3] the just Ps. cxliii. 8. rejoice in their labours. And the righteous in their recompense. And the martyrs also in their crowns. And the nations in the forgiveness of their trespasses.

And in the morning shall my prayer come before thee. At morning time prayed. Moses the chosen, on the top of the mount. And there God Ps. lxxxviii. 13. answered him. And gave him the staff of help. That he might descend and save Israel. From the subjection of the Egyptians.

---

[1] Om. U.   [2] Om. R. C.   [3] U. om. *And.*

To show thy lovingkindness in the morning. At morning time Moses saw. A terrible vision on the top of the mount. God praised with processions. Cherubim bearing his throne. Seraphim singing Holy in his honour. And angels serving him.

Ps. xcii. 2.

Sing to the Lord with harps and with a voice of singing. At morning time sang. David the boy with his harp. Songs of the Holy Ghost. And the beasts assembled and came. To the sweet sound of his words. When he sang Hallelujah.

Ps. xcviii. 6.

And let us praise him with songs. At morning time the martyrs sang. A new song in the judgment hall. We will not deny Christ. Who for us endured. Suffering and death and the cross. And saved our race from error.

Ps. xcv. 2.

God hath sent forth his lovingkindness and truth. At morning time the dove. Was sent forth by perfect Noah. Because of the waters of the flood. And she turned and came to the ark. Bearing an olive leaf. A sign of peace and tranquillity.

Ps. lvii. 4.

Thou hast given a token for such as fear thee. At morning time a sign. Of peace and tranquillity was seen. The bow of our Lord in the clouds. And the mouth of the Creator sware. I will not cause a flood. Henceforward and for ever.

Ps. lx. 4.

In the sight of all the people. In the morning the martyrs in the judgment hall. Raised and lifted up their voices. We do not worship idols. We worship one God. And confess his Son Jesus. He will deliver[1] us from the fire.

Ps. cxvi. 16.

Be strong, and your heart shall be established. In the morning the martyrs in the judgment hall. Comfort one another and say. The Lord (is) our helper, we will not fear. What man doeth unto us. Whose crown and power come to nought. But the kingdom of the Lord is for ever.

Ps. xxxi. 27

---

[1] Lit. *delivereth.*

O hear ye this, all ye people. At morning time was heard. The voice which said to the athletes. Take up your crosses and come after me. For I am your Lord and your Master. Your God and Strengthener. And ye are my disciples. Ps. xlix. 1.

He executeth judgment for them that suffer wrong. In the morning the faithful Shmuni.[1] Offered prayer to God. O God, execute judgment for me. Against the unrighteous Antiochus. Who killeth my sons as lambs. And threateneth me as a lion. Ps. cxlvi. 6.

And your prayers be on all of us. Gadai and Maccabæus, with Tersai. Hebron and Khiusun, with Bakus. And the seventh son, Jonadab. And their teacher, Eleazar. And their mother, faithful Shmuni. May their[2] prayer be a wall to us.

The camp of the angels of the Lord. At morning time the martyrs went forth. Many a company of saints. From the prison, saying. Hasten, O king, to cut off our heads.[3] That we may depart and go up to heaven. To our Lord who waiteth for us. Ps. xxxiv. 7.

For he hath done a marvellous thing. That which was wrought was a marvel. From one end of the world to the other. In the beloved boy Cyriac. Whom at the age of three years. Grace overshadowed. And he was strengthened in the faith. Ps. xcviii. 1.

Righteous and upright. May[4] thy prayer, O martyr, be to us. A high wall and refuge. That[5] the arrows of the Evil one may go astray. That he pierce us not with his barb. Who hateth our race at all times. And ever wisheth for our destruction. Deut. xxxii. 4.

---

[1] 2 Macc. vii.
[2] *your*, A.
[3] Syr.: *head.*
[4] R. C.: *May the prayer of the martyr George. Be to us a high wall. That*, etc. U.: *May the prayer of the martyr be to us. A high wall and refuge*, etc.
[5] U.: *And may the arrows . . . go.*

Like[1] *as the arrow in the hand of the giant.* How hard was the arrow. With which St. George struck Satan. And moreover (Satan) affirmed within himself. By Jesus and his disciples. I have not been struck as by this arrow. The arrow of Saint George.

Ps. cxxvii. 5.

O come and hearken, and I will tell you. Hearken and wonder, ye discerners. A Virgin hath borne in Bethlehem. The light of the whole world. And lo, her memorial is celebrated with processions. In the four quarters of creation. And in heaven amongst the angels.

Ps. lxvi. 14.

Glory be, etc. Glory to thee at morning time. From high and low. O Son who sittest on the right hand. For with the sound of the horn are awaked. Old men and young men and children. Whom thou hast created for thy glory.

From everlasting to everlasting. Blessed is he who hath traded. As thou, O our father,[2] hast traded. And hath collected spiritual riches. And hath filled his ship with all good things. And hath prospered and come to the haven. To the set place of all just men.

And let all the people say Amen and Amen. O our Lord, thy kingdom come. And thy will be done on earth. As it is in heaven. Give us the bread of our need. And lead us not into temptation. But deliver us from the Evil one.* May the help which followed. Moses, the firstborn of the prophets. And which divided the sea before the people. Follow thy worshippers. Who have come to ask forgiveness. From the treasury of thy kindness.

Ps. cvi. 46.

Tuesday Morning.

Praise the Lord, O ye righteous. O martyrs, ye were merchants. And lo, your storehouse is in heaven. Ye have bought the pearl. With the blood that your necks poured forth.

Ps. xxxiii. 1.

---

[1] So A.; om. R. C., U. This verse is said not to be ancient, and is not received in Kurdistan. It is found in U. in the Martyrs' Anthem for Sunday Mornings 'before' (below).   [2] Or *Awa*.

For it becometh well the upright to give praise. The martyrs who were exalted, and attained. Unto Jerusalem that is in heaven. And bought with the blood of their necks. The country for which they waited.   Ib.

They went from one nation to another. Ye departed from country to country. But departed not from your Lord. And in every country that ye entered.[1] Ye placed a storehouse of life.   Ps. cv. 13.

The Lord will abide in it for ever. In the country where your bones are laid. Dwell peace and tranquillity. And the camp of the watchful ones on high. Keepeth it and its inhabiters.   Ps. lxviii. 16.

Happy are the people that are in such a case. Happy is the country where are laid. Your bones as storehouses. And when the light of the sun is darkened. The light from your bones shineth forth.[2]   Ps. cxliv. 15.

Unto the godly hath shone forth light in the darkness. A light hath shone forth from your bones. And hath made my captive mind (to follow) after you. And I went forth to see your deaths. And wondered in myself at your crowns.   Ps. cxii. 4.

More to be desired are they than gold and than precious stones. Your bones are pearls. And your bodies are the fragrance of incense. The blood which flowed from your necks. Brought favour[3] to all creation.   Ps. xix. 10.

Shall they that are in the graves show thy lovingkindness? Lo, in the Church are your bones. And ye have the keys of the heights. O blessed ones, open your treasures. And give help to the needy.   Ps. lxxxviii. 11.

As a city surrounded with a wall. Like beams in a building. The martyrs girded creation. And when the earth was about to fall. They supported it by the power of their bones.   Ps. cxxii. 3.

---

[1] Or *passed through*.   [2] Syr.: *hath shone forth*.
[3] Syr.: *was compassion*.

I was strengthened and could not attain unto it. The sea cannot make a breach. In the wall which your love surroundeth. And Satan hath no power. In the land where your bones are laid.

Ps. cxxxix. 5.

For thy sake have we been killed daily. The Lord, whose martyrs were killed. For the glory of his majesty. In the day when his cross shineth forth. Placeth them on his right hand.

Ps. xliv. 22.

For there the Lord promised[1] *a blessing and life for evermore.* Where the martyrs were killed. And their limbs cut off. There the Holy Ghost came down. And made peace amidst desolation.

Ps. cxxxiii. 4.

O come, let us kneel and worship him. Before your graves let us reverence.[2] The power hidden in your bones. And we who have seen your deaths on earth. Will see your crowns in heaven.

Ps. xcv. 6.

They that go down to the sea in ships. O martyrs, ye were merchants. And journeyed by sea and land. Ye have brought peace to the sea by (your) tears. And to the land by your prayers.

Ps. cvii. 23.

Out of the deep have I called unto thee, O Lord, and thou hast heard my voice. . Out of the deep did the martyrs cry to thee. And thy lovingkindness answered them. Out of the deep do we call to thee. Come and help us and save us.

Ps. cxxx. 1.

I will alway bless the Lord. Blessed be the Lord, whose servants have fallen asleep. For[3] he exalteth their memorials. They sleep and are in peace and at rest. And from them helps spring forth.

Ps. xxxiv. 1.

How good and beautiful. How excellent is the crown of your heads. Woven by faith. And adorned by the Holy Ghost. With good and precious stones.

Ps. cxxxiii. 1.

---

[1] Syr.: *commanded.* [2] Same word as *worship.*
[3] Syr.: **And.**

As a thirsty and tired land that desireth water. As a land that thirsteth for water. And daily longeth for moisture. So thirsted the martyrs. For the love of their dear Lord. _{Ps. lxiii. 2.}

They are new (gods) which now have been made. Come in peace, O ye new bridegrooms. Sons of the mystery of baptism. Whom grace made to grow. In the name of the Trinity. _{Deut. xxxii. 17.}

And I spake of peace. Peace be to your bones. And rest to your limbs. For ye were like to your Lord. By whose death sinners have obtained life. _{Ps. cxx. 7.}

Confess him and bless his Name. Confess the truth and be not slack. Behold the swords and tremble not. For ye have put on hidden armour. Wrought by the Holy Ghost. _{Ps. c. 3.}

Both small and great. The martyr said to his fellow. Feeling compassion for his companion. Come, let us die for Jesus. And inherit eternal life. _{Ps. cxv. 13.}

The Lord is faithful in his words. The word which our Lord spakè. The martyrs heard, and were strengthened by it. He that dieth for me. Hath everlasting life. _{Ps. cxlv. 13. Syr.}

Their[1] blood have they shed like water on every side of Jerusalem, and there was no man to bury them. Their blood cried out against them that shed it. As Abel against Cain. The souls of the kings who destroyed their bodies. Are tortured in fire. _{Ps. lxxix. 3.}

More to be desired are they than gold and than precious stones. Like chosen stones. And precious pearls. Are the martyrs beloved. Who were killed for Jesus. _{Ps. xix. 10.}

How good and beautiful. How beautiful is that ship. Which bore St. Cyriac. Companies of Cherubim bear it[2] in procession. And Seraphim singing Holy. _{Ps. cxxxiii. 1.}

---

[1] Om. R. C.   [2] *him*, A.

Righteous[1] *and upright.* The true Bar-Khadh-bshaba.[2] The host of Christ. The founder of a holy Church. May his prayer be a wall to us.

Deut. xxxii. 4.

From the rising up of the sun unto the going down thereof. Lo, in all quarters is celebrated with processions. The glorious day of the memorial. Of Raban Hurmizd[3] the victorious. Blessed is he who crowned him with victory.

Ps. l. 1.

Well[4] *is thee and blessing to thy soul.* Well is thee, O martyr Mar Sergis. Thy home is like Paradise thickly planted. Make request to thy Lord and beseech him. For our assembly which flieth to thy prayer.

Ps. cxxviii. 2.

I[5] *will speak peace of thee.* Peace to thee, Mar Pithiun the martyr. Who didst endure all suffering and stripes. At the hand of the abominable Astrologer. And wast given victory by the adorable Jesus.

Ps. cxxii. 8.

He healeth those that are broken in heart, and cureth their pains. Thou wast a healer, St. George. Without medicines and roots. And every one that taketh refuge in thee. Is helped by thy prayers.

Ps. cxlvii. 3.

I will seek to do thee good. Beseech, O thou who art full of grace. The Child who shone forth from thy bosom. That he make his peace and tranquillity to dwell. In his Church, bought by his blood.

Ps. cxxii. 9.

Glory be, etc. Peace to you who have conquered. Peace to you who have been victorious. Peace to you who have become. Partakers in the sufferings of the Son.

From everlasting to everlasting. Thy truth is great, O our father.[6] Thy happiness is exalted and glorious. Make request for us all. That we may share in thy joy.

And let all the people say Amen and Amen. O thou that hearest the prayers of thy servants. And returnest answer to the petitions of thy

Ps. cvi. 46.

---

[1] Om. R. C. [2] Lit. *Son of Sunday.*
[3] *Martyr Hurmizd*, R. C.; *Martyr Bakus*, U.; *Raban* means *Monk.*
[4] Om. R. C.; U. has: *I will speak peace of thee. Peace to thee, O martyr Mar Sergis*, etc.   [5] Om. R. C., U.   [6] Or *Area.*

worshippers. Hear our prayer and the voice of our request. And return answer to our petitions in thy mercies.* O thou whose right hand is stretched out. Whose door is open to the penitent. Open the door to our prayer. And let our request come before thee.* O thou about whose throne stand the fiery ones. And companies of the watchful ones. Take away from us all harm. And rebuke the Evil one and let him be put to silence.* O thou who art true and who liest not. Who hast promised, Knock and[1] I open. Be pleased with the prayer of thy worshippers. And return answer to the petitions of our souls.

WEDNESDAY MORNING.

Let thy servants praise thee, O Lord. O holy martyrs and[2] teachers of faith. Pray that there may be peace in creation. Let wars be brought to nought and contentions cease among us. And may the Church sing praise by the mouth of her children. *Ps. cxlv. 10.*

And thy saints give thanks unto thee. May the holy martyrs who confessed thee in their afflictions. And propitiated thee by the blood which their necks poured forth. Make request for sinners to thee, O our Lord. That in the day of judgment thou mayest forgive their trespasses. *Ib.*

Let them speak of the glory of thy kingdom. The martyrs saw the glory of thy kingdom in their minds. When they were being killed by their persecutors. And they joyfully endured dire tortures in their bodies. And[3] our Lord Jesus received their spirits. *Ps. cxlv. 11.*

Honoured is their blood in his sight. Let us diligently honour with songs of the Holy Ghost. The bones of the martyrs who endured afflictions. That we may find help in the day of the recompense of their labours. From the goodness of the mercies of God. *Ps. lxxii. 14.*

---

[1] Om. *and*, A.   [2] R. C., U. om. *and*.   [3] R. C., A. om. *and*.

The Lord on high is glorious. On high are your crowns, and in the world are your assemblies. O martyrs, preachers of Christ the King. On high and in the deep, lo, your feasts are celebrated. O sowers of peace in the four quarters (of the earth).

<small>Ps. xciii. 5.</small>

Seek the Lord and be strengthened. O martyrs, seek for mercy from the merciful God. That he may make his peace to dwell in the four quarters (of the earth). And when our Lord is revealed and the clouds bear up your bodies. Pray that with you we may inherit the kingdom.

<small>Ps. cv. 4.</small>

My[1] voice shalt thou hear in the morning, O Lord. In the morning the martyrs cried in the judgment hall before the persecutors. We will not deny the heavenly Bridegroom. For he it is who delivereth us from the hands of the ungodly. .And clotheth our bodies with glory in his kingdom.

<small>Ps. v. 3.</small>

And[1] in the morning I will be ready, and will appear before thee. In the morning, when Christ the King, who crowneth you, shineth forth. O prophets, apostles, martyrs, and confessors. And placeth on your heads crowns of glory which fade not. Pray that with you we may inherit the kingdom.

<small>Ib.</small>

Unto the godly hath shone forth light in the darkness. O martyrs, sons of light, who hated the world and its good things. And desired and loved the heavenly Bridegroom. Make request and beseech for us your Lord whom ye desired. That he have pity on us and save our souls.

<small>Ps. cxii. 4.</small>

Blessed are those that are blameless in the way. Blessed are ye martyrs who conquered Satan. And trod under foot the sting of death and of sin. May your prayer be to us a high wall and house of refuge. From the wiles of the Evil one, the Enemy.

<small>Ps. cxix. 1.</small>

---

[1] Om. A.

And walk in the law of the Lord. A blessing that passeth not away, and a kingdom that is not destroyed. Hath our Saviour promised to the friends whom he hath chosen. And instead of afflictions and tortures and lacerations which they endured. They are about[1] to inherit life without end. *Ib.*

Righteous and upright. A tender boy was the illustrious martyr Cyriac. And he astonished with his words the king and his servants. And then received the sword of the cruel king. And by it was crowned for our Saviour's sake. *Deut. xxxii. 4.*

Beg[2] of the Lord and pray before him. Intercessor for all peoples, and herald of all tongues. Thy Lord hath placed thee in his Church, Mar Sergis. That the prayers of the needy may enter before his majesty. That thou mayest receive and cause to come forth helps to man. *Ps. xxxvii. 7.*

Fairer to look at than the children of men. A beautiful shrub, and an olive tree decked with branches. Was St. George, the friend of Christ. Who meekly, in the love he had gained towards his Lord. Stretched forth his shoulder and bore the cross. *Ps. xlv. 3.*

The virgins that be her fellows shall they lead after her. O holy Virgin Mary, the blessed mother. All nations call thee blessed. For thou wast worthy to carry in thy bosom Emmanuel. Whom the prophets described beforehand in their mysteries. *Ps. xlv. 15.*

Glory be, etc. Glory to the power which dwelleth in the bones of the saints. Its voice thundereth in the four quarters (of the world). And they are laid in the churches, and helps well forth from them. And truth is revealed by the power of their words.

From everlasting to everlasting. O thou who didst love purity all the days of thy life. Thou wast chosen blameless by Christ. And because of thy good deeds, in the

---

[1] R. C.: *He hath given them.*   [2] Om. R. C., U.

tabernacle of the saints. Lo, thy soul dwelleth among the angels.

And let all the people say Amen and Amen. Give us, O our Lifegiver, that which thou knowest will help us. For we know not what we ask. But one thing we beg for, that thy will may be accomplished in us. And that thy mercies may intercede for us all.* O Christ, who didst promise, To every one that crieth, I answer. And to him that knocketh at my door, I open. Let not thy mercies and thy lovingkindness be far from thy worshippers. Who take refuge in thee, that they may receive help.*

Ps. cvi. 46.

Thursday Morning.

For he speaketh peace of his people and with his saints. Peace to the martyrs and honour to their bones. And glory to their Lord. And help to us by their prayer.

Ps. lxxxv. 8.

And in thy light do we see light. The martyrs are in the light, and the apostles in the bridechamber of light. And lo, they sing glory. To the Being who dwelleth in the excellent light.

Ps. xxxvi. 9.

And sing lustily with the voice. The martyrs when they enter into the kingdom say. Glory to thee, O our Lord. For we are not confounded, and we trust in thee.

Ps. xxxiii. 3.

Also all they that hope in thee shall not be ashamed. The martyrs say, We have taken refuge in thy cross. O merciful Lord. Slacken not (thy) hold upon us.

Ps. xxv. 2.

He divided the sea, and let them go through. O martyrs, who passed over the bridge of fire to Eden.[1] Pray that we sink not. In the troubled sea of (our) sins.

Ps. lxxviii. 14.

---

[1] *to the high place,* R. C.

Honoured is their blood in his sight. O Christ, who didst receive the blood of the martyrs in the day when they were killed. Receive our petition. And open the door to our prayer. Ps. lxxii. 14.

The Lord on high is glorious. Above on high, and in the boundless treasure. Are laid up the deeds. Of the martyrs, the friends of Christ. Ps. xciii. 5.

From of old hath thy seat been set fast. O Son, the throne of whose kingdom is set fast on high. By the prayer of thy saints. Sustain the earth, which our trespasses have overthrown. Ps. xciii. 3.

Sing to the Lord with harps and with the voice of singing. With the voice of Hallelujahs and songs of the Holy Ghost. The saints sing. And the companies of demons[1] are moved. Ps. xcviii. 6.

My voice shalt thou hear in the morning, O Lord. Every morning the martyrs stand in prayer. And ask for help. For the souls of sinners. Ps. v. 3.

And in the morning I will be ready, and will appear before thee. In the last morning, when the holy martyrs receive. The reward of their deeds. Have compassion on us, O our Lord, in that hour. Ib.

Offer unto him sacrifices of praise. May the prayers of the martyrs, who were pure offerings to their Lord. Be unto us. A wall by night and day. Ps. cvii. 22.

Blessed are those that are blameless in the way. Blessed are the martyrs when they hear that voice. Come, enter, ye blessed of my father. And inherit life without end. Ps. cxix. 1.

And walk in the law of the Lord. Blessed are ye whom your Lord hath placed as a treasury. And on the altar is. Your memorial for ever. Ib.

Do well, O Lord, unto the good. Blessed are the athletes, who pictured to themselves their own beauty. In the habitation of heaven. That it might not remain on earth and be corrupted. Ps. cxxv. 4.

---

[1] Lit. *legions* (St. Mark v. 9).

Unto those that are true of heart. Blessed are the martyrs at that time when are divided. The good from the bad. And they inherit the kingdom.

Ps. cxxv. 4.

The camp of the angels of the Lord. Ye of the company of Diodorus, Theodorus, and Nestorius. Pray that there enter not. Into the Church the darkness of the Egyptians.[1]

Ps. xxxiv. 7.

And your prayers be on all of us. Ye of the company of Mar Ephraim, Mar Nersai, and Mar Abraham. May your prayers be to us. A wall by night and day.

A place where no fear was. In the bridechamber of light, on the right hand of Christ. All the holy martyrs. There have joy.

Ps. liii. 6.

How good and beautiful. How excellent, and how much to be desired, is the glory with which the righteous are clothed. In the day of the resurrection. Through the deeds which they have wrought.

Ps. cxxxiii. 1.

Righteous[2] *and upright.* O illustrious and holy martyr, Mar Cyriac. Beseech Christ. That he cause to pass away the multitude of our evils.

Deut. xxxii. 4.

In heaven and in earth. Thy body is on earth[3] and thy soul is in heaven. O martyr George. Beg for mercies from thy Lord.

Ps. cxxxv. 6.

Unto the godly there hath shone forth light in the darkness. O Christ, who didst shine forth from blessed Mary. By the prayer of her who bore thee. Keep thy Church from harm.

Ps. cxii. 4.

Glory be, etc. Peace to the Church, and tranquillity to all who dwell in her. And glory to the Power. Who strengthened the martyrs in the contest.

From everlasting to everlasting. May the prayer of our father,[4] who was a pure offering to his Lord. Be unto us. A wall by night and day.

---

[1] R. C.: *Of the contentious.* [2] Om. R. C., U.
[3] *Is with us,* R. C. [4] Or *Awa.*

And let all the people say Amen and Amen. Let not, O my Lord, the prayer of thy servants be in vain. But for propitiation. And forgiveness of sins.* I entered into thy house, and worshipped before thy judgment seat.¹ O merciful Lord. Forgive me my trespasses and sins.* This house is a type of heaven. In love without guile. Let us enter into it continually.

Ps. cvi. 46.

Friday Morning.

I will alway bless the Lord. Blessed is the hidden power which dwelt in the bones of the martyrs. For they are laid in their graves. And drive away devils from the world. By their teaching they brought to nought all the error of carved (idols). And they secretly visit creation, and teach (men) to worship thee. For thou art Lord alone.

Ps. xxxiv. 1.

And his praises are ever in my mouth. Blessed is Christ, who clothed his Twelve with strong armour. And they went forth to the four quarters (of the earth). And preached in the world his doctrine. And they destroyed the power of the enemy by the sword of the Spirit. And turned the nations from error. To the truth of their faith.

Ib.

Great is our Lord, and exceeding glorious. Great is the truth of the holy martyrs, which is preached in all regions. Whom neither fire nor sword. Nor the wrath of the heathen king. Nor any other thing did move nor terrify. For God alone did they confess. And despised all tortures.

Ps. cxlv. 3.

Faithful is the Lord in his words. The just martyrs, who conquered and overcame, meditated on the faith. For they know that that word was true. Which our Lord spake. Every one that confesseth me before judges and rulers. I will cause to inherit the

Ps. cxlv. 13.

---

¹ bema (see Glossary).

kingdom on high, which is in heaven. And I will confess him before the Father.

Look to him and trust in him. With the eye of the Spirit, the sons of the right hand looked, and verily saw. The country which is above. Within the veil of the Holy of Holies. And they desired it, and ran towards it by the way of the tortures of their persecutors. And, as by a bridge, they crossed the sea of the world by the cross. To Eden,[1] which is their dwelling.

<small>Ps. xxxiv. 5.</small>

Stretch forth thy right hand upon me. May the right hand of our Lord, which calleth all to the kingdom, bless our assembly. That we may keep vigil on the memorial of the martyrs. And that we also may be helped by their prayers. That they may be to our race a high wall in the last day. When the heights and the depths are amazed.. And[2] the will of the Creator shall reign.

<small>Ps. cxxxviii. 7.</small>

The camp of the angels of the Lord. My mind wondered at the blessed company of athletes, the famous martyrs. How they despised and scorned. This world and its desires. In the glorious brightness of the pearl which is at the head of the cross.[3] With piercing eye they looked and saw it. And desired to seize it.

<small>Ps. xxxiv. 7.</small>

And your prayers be on all of us. By your prayers give help to the needy, O famous martyrs. For ye have filled the earth. With the good seed of your victories. And ye have dug up the thorn-bush which the Evil one sowed with his tares. And ye sowed therein good seed. O athletes, workers of truth.

How good and beautiful. The athletes saw a pearl without flaw on the top of Golgotha. And desired earnestly to attain to it. And bought it with their own blood. And they endured sufferings and dire tortures for it. And lo, the reward of their labours is laid up (for them).[4] Joy without end.

<small>Ps. cxxxiii. 1.</small>

---

[1] *To the high place,* R. C.   [2] Om. *and,* A.   [3] Syr.: *tree.*
[4] *And lo, they have received the reward of their labours,* R. C.

High in all the earth. High and exalted is the glorious and honoured bridechamber which Christ the King. Hath prepared for his athletes. Who loved him, and believed and confessed his Name. And lo, their festivals are celebrated in the four quarters (of the earth). While they cry to him with the voice of Hallelujahs, and say. Blessed is he who hath exalted his saints. Ps. lxxxiii. 18.

He[1] *set my feet upon the rock, and ordered my goings.* On the foundation of the truth of Simon Peter. Built the true Diodorus and Theodorus. With Nestorius and great Ephraim. And Mar Nersai and Mar Bar-Ṣoma, a blessed pair. With Abraham and Job and John. And Michael, heirs of the Church. Ps. xl. 2.

That[1] *it never should move at any time.* On the foundation of the truth of Mar Antony the saints built. Mar Saurishu, and Mar Khnanishu, and Mar John, son of the Seers. And Maran-'amih[2] of Zin, and Mar Shuwkha-l'maran,[3] peace be to him. And Raban[4] Pransi, and Mar Joseph, and Mar Abraham.[5] And Mar Qnuwaya, and Ishu-sauran,[6] and Raban[4] Hurmizd. May their prayer be a wall to us. Ps. civ. 5.

Blessed are those that are blameless in the way. On the foundation of the twelve and the seventy apostles the noble ones built. Mar Augin and Mar Shalita. And Mar Kudhahwai, with Mar Babai.[7] And the pious Mar James of Ṣuwa. And Mar Abraham,[8] and Mar Akha, and Mar John. May their prayer be a wall to us. Ps. cxix. 1.

And[1] *walk in the law of the Lord.* They walked in the footsteps and imitated the deeds. Of those proved ones. Mar Andrew, and Mar Ulugh, and Mar John the Arab. And Raban[4] Salara and his mother, with Mar Micah. And Awa[9]-Yazdadh and Mar Yarith. May their prayer keep our assembly. Ib.

---

[1] Om. R. C.   [2] Lit. *The Lord be with him.*
[3] Lit. *Glory be to our Lord.*   [4] Monk.   [5] U. om. this name.
[6] Lit. *Jesus is our hope.*   [7] *And Mar Milis with Mar Bawni*, R.C.
[8] Om. *And Mar Abraham*, R. C.   [9] Or *Father*.

For[1] *it was founded upon a rock.* On the foundation of the truth of Mar Antony built the saints and fathers. Raban Hurmizd and Mar Abraham. And Raban Simon, and Mar Jozadak, and Mar Aduna, and Ishu-sauran, and Mar John. And Raban Joseph, and Shuwkha-l'ishu[2] and Shuwkha-l'maran. And Mar Gabriel, and Jonah, and Joshua, and Sagi-nuhra.[3] May their prayer be a wall to us.

St. Matt. vii. 25.

I will alway bless the Lord. Blessed is Christ who strengthened the martyr Mar Cyriac in his contest. To stand against the persecutor. And he waxed strong and conquered the kings who contended with him. And by the strength of the Spirit he did valiantly. And endured stripes, and became a sacrifice for his Lord. And received the crown of victory.

Ps. xxxiv. 1.

Rejoice, sing and glorify. With rejoicing the famous martyr Mar George gave up his soul to all afflictions. For he heard Paul saying. That the sufferings of this time are not to be compared. To that glory which the just inherit at the last day. And he who here laboureth and doeth nobly. Even he shall be an inheritor of it.

Ps. xcviii. 5.

The virgins that be her fellows shall they lead after her. O Virgin of the ages, Mary the blessed mother, beseech thy Son. To cause his peace to dwell in this temple. In which the day of thy memorial is celebrated with processions. And to cause the right hand of his mercies to overshadow it as the house of Abram. That all who are afflicted and distressed. From him may receive help.

Ps. xlv. 15.

Glory be, etc. Glory to thee, O good and kind[4] Lord. By whose power the true ones conquered. And by whose help they despised the threats of their persecutors. And destroyed the power of the enemy who boasted. For he saw that the

---

[1] Om. R. C., U.
[2] Lit. *Glory to Jesus.*
[3] Lit. *He hath increased the light.*
[4] Om. *and kind*, A.

martyrs relaxed not their hold. On their true and confident hope.

From everlasting to everlasting. May the prayer of our famous father,[1] who from his childhood, like Samuel, pleased God. And in humility was like Moses, the firstborn of prophecy.[2] In zeal like Elijah. In love of his Lord like Abraham. Be a wall to us. From the wiles of the Crafty one.

And let all the people say Amen and Amen. We offer praise to thy Godhead, O good Lord. For by thy lovingkindness thou dost keep thy worshippers from harm. And thou hast opened, O my Lord, thy door. To them that repent and ask for mercy. And thou stayest not the great treasure of thy gift. From thy flock, O thou who art worshipped by all.   Ps. cvi. 46.

Saturday Morning.

My voice shalt thou hear in the morning, O Lord. In the morning the martyrs were called to be killed. And the right hand of our Lord weaveth their crowns.   Ps. v. 3.

And in the morning will I be ready and will appear before thee. In the morning the martyrs run to the contest. To receive a double reward of their labours.   Ib.

O make me to hear thy lovingkindness in the morning. In the morning our Lord called to the martyrs. Come, take the reward, noble workmen.   Ps. cxliii. 8.

Look to him and trust in him. In the morning the martyrs saw the Holy Ghost. Weaving crowns and placing (them) on their heads.   Ps. xxxiv. 5.

Unto the godly hath shone forth light in the darkness. In the morning the martyrs shine forth like the sun. And go forth to meet the heavenly Bridegroom.   Ps. cxii. 4.

---

[1] Or *Awa*.   [2] The first prophet.

Holy and reverend is his Name. (Ps. cxi. 9.) In the morning the martyrs cry with the watchful ones.[1] Holy, Holy, Holy, God.

They shall bring him offerings. (Ps. lxxii. 10.) In the morning the martyrs make offerings. The prayer of their mouth and the blood of their necks.

The offering of my hands as the evening offering. (Ps. cxli. 2.) In the morning the martyrs offer censers in their hands. And offerings to the King of kings.

As the fragrance of sweet incense,[2] *and an acceptable savour before God.* In the morning the martyrs set forth incense to him. Whose throne is in the fire, which is subject to him.

Be strong, and your heart shall be established. (Ps. xxxi. 27.) In the morning the martyrs encourage one another. Come, let us think scorn of the impious king.

He[3] *reproved kings for their sakes.* (Ps. cv. 14.) In the morning the martyrs stood in the judgment-hall. And reproved kings, and confounded the impious men.

In[3] *the sight of all the people.* (Ps. cxvi. 16.) In the morning the martyrs cry in the judgment-hall. We will not deny the heavenly Bridegroom.

For thy sake have we been killed daily. (Ps. xliv. 22.) Ye who were killed like me, and persecuted for my sake. I and you (go) to Jerusalem that is above.

And[4] *have been counted as sheep appointed to be slain.* (Ib.) The martyrs (went) to death and their Lord to the cross. And the Holy Ghost weaveth their crowns.

From the beginning hath thy seat been prepared. (Ps. xciii. 3.) The throne is prepared and the King's Son sitteth. And the martyrs enter and receive their crowns.

Both small and great. (Ps. cxv. 13.) In the morning the martyrs run to the cross. To drink the wine pressed out by the spear.

---

[1] The angels. [2] *Cf.* the prayer of incense, page 69.
[3] R. C., U. transpose these. [4] U. om. *and.*

The Lord shall give strength unto his people. Grant the strength which strengthened the martyrs in the contest. To the assembly of thy worshippers, O our Lord. *Ps. xxix. 10.*

Open me the gates of righteousness. In the morning the King's Son openeth his treasure. And the martyrs enter in and receive their crowns.[1] *Ps. cxviii. 19.*

That I may go into them and give thanks unto the Lord. In the morning our Lord opened Paradise. And the Robber went in and inherited the kingdom. *Ib.*

When God ariseth to judgment. In the morning our Lord ariseth in the judgment. And calleth to the martyrs, Come, take your crowns. *Ps. lxxvi. 9.*

O[2] sing unto him a new song of praise. In the morning the martyrs lift up a song of praise. To Christ the King, the Peace of all created beings. *Ps. xxxiii. 3.*

How good and beautiful. How fitting is it for the boy Cyriac. When (God) reproveth for him the impious king. *Ps. cxxxiii. 1.*

And a joyful mother of children. In the morning Shmuni encourageth her sons. Fear not him who killeth men. *Ps. cxiii. 8.*

O well is thee, and a blessing to thy soul. O well is thy spirit, O martyr George. Which with the angels dwelleth in heaven. *Ps. cxxviii. 2.*

Let the mount Sion rejoice, and the daughters of Judah be glad. Let the faithful Church rejoice and exult. In the memorial of Mary, the mother of Christ. *Ps. xlviii. 10.*

Glory be, etc. Peace to the martyrs, and glory to their Lord. And to us, by their prayer, mercy and compassion.

From everlasting to everlasting. O our illustrious father,[3] the friend of Christ. Beg of thy Lord mercy for us all.[4]

And let all the people say Amen and Amen. In the morning let us praise, and in the morning let us glorify. The Lord of the morning, the true light.* *Ps. cvi. 46.*

---

[1] U.: *And giveth the reward to the noble labourers.*
[2] Om. A., R. C. [3] Or *Awa*. [4] U.: *for the world.*

In the morning let the prayer of thy worshippers enter. Before thy judgment-seat, O merciful Lord.* At[1] morning time let us praise thy lovingkindness. For thou hast ordered the light for the joy of creation.

MOTWA AT NIGHT SERVICE FOR WEDNESDAY 'BEFORE'[2]

Kings of the earth and all peoples. All nations call blessed.
Ps. cxlviii. 11. The Virgin Mary, Mother of Christ.
Ps. cxxxix. 3, 4. *All things behind and before.* All nations, etc.
O well is thee, and a blessing to thy soul. O well is thee, John, for ever well is thee. When thy[3] Lord
Ps. cxxviii. 2. cometh, whom thou didst love and serve.
Let the righteous be strengthened with honour. Preachers of the Spirit and pillars of light. Were Peter and
Ps. cxlix. 5. Paul in creation.
Their gospel is gone out into all the earth. Matthew and Mark and Luke and John. May your prayer
Ps. xix. 4. be a wall to our souls.
And also I will make him the firstborn. Blessed is the death of the firstborn of the martyrs. Stephen, the
Ps. lxxxix. 28. friend of Christ.
He shall stand before God for ever. Let us diligently celebrate the memorial of the teachers. Who loved
Ps. lxi. 7. Christ and kept his commandments.
As he commanded our forefathers. Let us commemorate the victories of our spiritual fathers. Who laboured
Ps. lxxviii. 5. for us by the love of Christ.
Thy memorial throughout all generations. Thy memorial, O our father,[4] is on the holy altar. With the
Ps. cii. 12. saints who conquered and the martyrs who were crowned.

---

[1] A. om. this last verse.
[2] Both these *Motwi* are from A. and R. C. The sheets of U. have not been received in time for collation. [3] *the*, R. C. [4] Or *Awa*.

Both small and great. Lo, all the [1] departed have lain down in thy hope. That in thy glorious resurrection thou mayest raise them in glory.[2]   Ps. cxv. 13.

Pour out your hearts before him. By fasting and prayer and repentance of the soul. Let us propitiate Christ, and his Father, and his Spirit.   Ps. lxii. 8.

I[3] will alway bless the Lord. Blessed is Christ who condemned Satan. And made our nature to conquer by his holy fast.   Ps. xxxiv. 1.

Look to him and trust in him. With the eye of the Spirit the children looked to thee. When thou wast entering, and they sang praise.   Ps. xxxiv. 5.

Rejoice and sing and give thanks. Thy Passover,[4] O our Saviour, hath gladdened creation. And brought to nought the altars[5] (of the heathen), and set firm the Churches.   Ps. xcviii. 5.

The earth trembled and was moved. The earth was moved when they cried. Crucify, Crucify the King of the Jews.   Ps. lxxvii. 18.

The joy of the whole earth. In the resurrection of the Son created things rejoice. For reconciliation hath been made, and quickening hath reigned.   Ps. xlviii. 2.

Seek the Lord and be strengthened. O martyrs, seek for mercy for the world, which taketh. Refuge in the power of your bones.   Ps. cv. 4.

He asked life of thee, and thou gavest him.[6] Ask for us of thy Lord, O martyr George. Compassion and mercies, and forgiveness of trespasses.   Ps. xxi. 4.

God is gone up in glory, the Lord with the sound of the trump. Blessed is the King who hath gone up, and by his ascension hath made glad. The watchful ones and men, and hath made created things to rejoice.   Ps. xlvii. 5.

---

[1] our, R. C.   [2] in thy glory, R. C.   [3] Om. A.
[4] Piṣkha, derived by the Syrians from root *pṣakh*, whence ethpa'al, *to rejoice*.   [5] A different word, *madhbkha*, is used for the Christian altar.
[6] R. C. : *Seek of the Lord, and pray before him.* Ps. xxxv . 7.

And blessed be the name of his majesty for ever.[1] Blessed is the descent of the Spirit, which made wise his apostles. And gave them victory in the four quarters (of the world).
<small>Ps. lxxii. 19.</small>

And our heart shall rejoice in him. May thy cross, O our Saviour, be to us a weapon. And by it may we conquer the Evil one and all his wiles.
<small>Ps. xxxiii. 20.</small>

With words of praises. Lo, the Church thundereth forth with holy voices. And in her they raise glory to the Lord of created beings.
<small>Ps. cxxxvii. 3, Syr.</small>

VERSES OF PRAYER.[2]

Make me a clean heart, O God. Grant us, O Christ, that with a clean heart. And with good deeds, we may fulfil thy will.
<small>Ps. li. 10.</small>

All the days of my life. Grant us, O Christ, that with openness of face. We may go to meet thee when thou art revealed in the day of thy coming.
<small>Ps. xxiii. 6.</small>

For with him there is mercy. At thy hands, O God, whose mercies are many. Let our correction be, and not at the hands of man.
<small>Ps. cxxx. 7 (?).</small>

Stretch forth thy right hand upon me. O our Lord, with thy right hand overthrow Satan. Who maketh (men) drunken without wine, and causeth them to slip without mud.
<small>Ps. cxxxviii. 7.</small>

Keep me[3] *as the apple of an eye.* O our Lord, keep us who are as lambs. Among serpents[4] that are worse than wolves.
<small>Ps. xvii. 8.</small>

Let thy mercy come unto me, O Lord, even thy salvation, according to thy word. Let thy mercies come to help us, for they have created us. And let them heal our sickness with the medicine of thy compassion.
<small>Ps. cxix. 41.</small>

---

[1] R. C.: *And let us bless the Lord who made us.* Ps. xcv. 6.

[2] R. C. om. all these to the Gloria, but refers to another publication for them. In A., usually only the first words of the headings are given, and there is therefore some uncertainty about them.

[3] So Psalter; A. has *us*. [4] Or *cruel men*.

I have called unto thee with my whole heart, O Lord; answer me, and I will keep thy commandments. To thee we call, O Christ our Saviour. Have mercy on our life, and neglect us not.   Ps. cxix. 145 (?).

O come, let us kneel and worship him. We will confess and worship thee, O Christ our Saviour. For thy door is open to all who turn to thee in penitence.   Ps. xcv. 6.

Thou that liftest me up from the gates of death. O Christ, who didst raise us when we fell, and didst cause us to stand. Rebuke the Evil one, who disturbeth our dwelling.   Ps. ix. 13 (?).

Hide not thy face from us. O Christ, who neglectest not any who cry to thee. In thy mercy reject not the request of thy worshippers.   Ps. xliv. 24 (?).

The Lord of hosts is with us. Our King is with us, and our God is with us. And our helper is the God of Jacob.   Ps. xlvi. 7.

Thou art merciful, O Lord, and righteous. With the publican we ask mercy. Have compassion on us, O God, and have mercy upon us.   Ps. cxvi. 5.

Thy mercy, O Lord, is for ever. We ask mercy and compassion of thee. Keep (them) not from us, thou Friend of men.   Ps. cxxxviii. 8.

Thee, O God, beseemeth praise in Sion. Thee alone beseemeth praise. O God, who governest the worlds by thy will.   Ps. lxv. 1.

Blessed are the people that are in such a case. Blessed are the people that are in such a case. Blessed are the people who have the Lord for their God.   Ps. cxliv. 15.

The Lord will abide in it for ever. Bless and keep our assembly, O our Lord. And make thy peace and tranquillity to dwell in it.   Ps. lxviii. 16.

The Lord preserveth all them that fear him. Keep, O our Lord, the assembly of thy worshippers. From the wiles of the Evil one, the Enemy.   Ps. cxlv. 20.

It is he that hath made us, and not we ourselves. Let us at all times confess the Being who hath made us. Whose lovingkindness our race cannot repay.

Ps. c. 2.

Out of the mouth of young men and children. Glory to the Father, and confession to the Son. And worship and exaltation to the Holy Ghost.

Ps. viii. 2.

Glory be, etc. By the prayer of the Blessed one. May peace reign in creation. And by the request of the Virgin. May the children of the Church be kept.* May the Power which descended from on high. And so[1] hallowed and adorned her for his honour. That[2] she brought forth the true light. And[3] hope and life of (all) created things. Be with us and amongst us. All the days of our life. And[3] heal the sick and infirm. And those who have fallen into temptations. And bring back those who are (absent). On distant journeys. In peace to their homes. That they be not harmed by the Evil one.* And may those who travel by sea. Be rescued from the billows. And those who go on dry land. Be delivered from barbarians. And may those who have been taken captive. Be released from their bonds. And those who have been taken by force. Be comforted in their sorrow by thy compassion. And if any are tormented by the Evil one. May thy great power rebuke him. And if any go on in sins. Pardon and forgive their trespasses. And if any have made offerings. May thy Godhead be pleased with them. And them that have lain down in thy hope. Quicken and bring to life in thy lovingkindness.* And may we who have taken refuge. In the prayer of the Blessed one. Mary the holy Virgin. Mother of Jesus our Saviour. Be kept by it from the Evil one. And overcome all his wiles.* And in that great day of searching. When the dead rise from the graves.[4] When the good are separated from the wicked. May we be worthy with her to have joy. In the bridechamber of the kingdom on high. And to sing a triple song of glory. To Father, Son, and Holy Ghost.

---

[1] A. om. *And so.* [2] A. om. *That.* [3] A. om. *And.*
[4] So T. (in the Preparation of the Oblation). R. C., A. om. this line.

From everlasting to everlasting. The divisions and orders of the spiritual ones. With the priests in the Church, are singing praise. For a memorial of the holy martyr. Mar George, who did brave deeds and conquered, and was crowned.* And he suffered troubles and afflictions. Fire and the sword and stoning. The persecutors inflicted on him. Many and various torments. He put the wicked king to shame. Who persecuted the good servants. And despised the excellency of his power. And the gods which he worshipped. Zeus and Apollo and Artemis. The work of men's hands.* And the giant of strength, Mar George, cried. And said to the nobles of the king. Ye shall not worship idols. Carved and wrought by artificers. For lo, Christ is the King of kings. And Lord of all gods. He giveth an inheritance to all that fear him. A bridechamber, and a blessing that passeth not away. And he clotheth with glory in his kingdom. The illustrious martyrs who have believed in him.* And kneeling in prayer before his Lord, he besought and made request, saying. Take away in thy lovingkindness. From all who keep the commemoration. Of this day of my persecution. Hail and famine and pestilence. And locust and young locust and caterpillar. And the blast that destroyeth the fields. And the terror of the night. And pains and diseases and afflictions.[1] And all evil confusions. And keep all the inhabited world. By the great power of thy Godhead.

And let all the people say Amen and Amen. Among the companies clothed with light. And the bands of angels. The bridechamber is kept[2] for thee in heaven. At the right hand of the King, Christ our Saviour.* O our famous and holy father. Mar Awa Catholicos.[3] Who didst work a work of righteousness. In the Church, the spouse of Christ. And didst love fast and prayer. And perfect and true love.* And lo, from the place where

Ps. cvi. 46.

---

[1] R. C. om. this line.

[2] R. C.: *woven*, in allusion to the marriage ceremony of weaving with osiers a partition in the great room of a house to form the bridechamber.

[3] T. (*ubi supra*), R. C.: *Mar N. the illustrious.*

thy illustrious body is laid up. Well forth helps. And healing to all that are afflicted. And take refuge in thy prayers.* Great is the power by which thou didst conquer the devil. And which brought thee to the land that is full of good things. And now beseech for us all. That with thee we may sing in the kingdom. A new praise which ceaseth not. To Father, Son, and Holy Ghost.

For ever and ever.[1] May he who blessed just Abram. And delivered Isaak, be with us and among us. May God,[2] who looked on pure Jacob. Bless our assembly with his right hand.* May the Lord, who was with Joseph. Be the guardian of our ways. May the Mighty one, who looked on Moses. Accompany us at all times. May he who gave victory to Joshua, the son of Nun. Make his right hand to overshadow us. May he who shepherdeth all, and chose David. Keep us from the Evil one and his host.* May the Lord, who enriched Solomon. Increase the[3] wealth of our fields. May the Highest, who looked on Isaiah. Cause his peace to dwell among us. And may our prayers be accepted. As those of Elijah and Elisha. And[4] may our request be heard. As that of righteous Daniel.* May Jesus, the Lord of the prophets. And the crown of the apostles. Keep us who have believed in his Name. From the Evil one and his hosts.[5] May the glorious Trinity. Be with us for ever.

He gathered them out of all lands. From Cush, and Egypt, and Thebais. The saints went first and came forth. Mar Augin and Mar Shalita. Architects of the holy Church.* With the companies of famous old men. The blessed seventy and two. Just, pure, and virgins. Mighty in fame. Chosen vessels of honour. And desirable temples of purity. Havens of peace and tranquillity. And storehouses of love and concord. Overflowing springs of mercies. And blessed fountains of pity. Seas full of wisdom. Rivers of knowledge. Treasures of fast and

Ps. xlviii. 13.

Ps. cvii. 3.

---

[1] R. C.: *God, even our own God, shall give us his blessing. God shall bless us.* Ps. lxvii. 6, 7.   [2] Syr.: *El.*
[3] A. *his* (error).   [4] A. om. *And.*   [5] R. C. om. this line

of prayer. Famed abodes of the Holy Ghost.* Likeness and type of the prophets. Image and picture of the apostles. Resemblance and effigy of the doctors. Substance and perfection of the priests. Illustrious among the fathers. Noble among the monks. Sons of the yoke of the famous martyrs. And sons of the band of the confessors. Sons of the camp of the anchorets. And sons of the number of the weepers.[1]* Adorable is the Father who chose them. And[2] holy is the Son who gave them victory. Glorious is the Spirit who encouraged them. To persevere in his teaching. Bright is the light wherewith they are clothed. Excellent is the glory in which they have joy.* And strong, and firm, and established, and high. Is the high wall of their prayers. Which surroundeth the assemblies of their sons. Blessed is he in whose love the just are inebriated. Who have preached his truth in creation.

The mountain which God hath chosen to himself to dwell there. In the difficult mountain of Mirda,[3] which is Izla. Which is more inaccessible and difficult Ps. lxviii. 16. and parched than all the mountains in the world. The Divine lovingkindness. Was pleased to make men of fire and spirit.* Giants clothed with truth. And sons of the mighty among angels. First of all is. Mar Augin, of sweet report. His name beareth witness to his victories. Which, being interpreted, is The good man. And spiritual in truth. Who hastened his course thither. And the seventy-two blessed ones. Came with him from Egypt. And after no short time. Holy Mar Andrew. And Mar Ulugh, the renowned old man. And Mar John, the Arab. Of Khirta by race and family. And spiritual in truth. Who did wonderful miracles. And quickened a dead man by his prayer.* And Mar Abraham of Kashkar. Fellow-countryman[4] of great Abram. Far greater than can be expressed. Is the grace which dwelt in him. And[5] Mar Babai, the disciple of the truth. Who walked in the true

---

[1] Monks. [2] R. C. om. *And.* [3] Mardin, in Mesopotamia.
[4] Syr.: *Son of the country of.* [5] A. om. *And.*

way. And was not slack, and was not moved. By the conflict with the power of the Evil one. And he endured heat and cold. From morning till evening.* And ¹ Mar Kudahwi the illustrious. Who went rejoicing in the ranks (of the martyrs). And was lifted up on the wings of the Spirit. To the high ² and glorious country.* And by them was fulfilled that which is written. That ³ from the top of the mountains shall cry. And give praise to the Lord. All generations and tribes. Old men, young men, and children.⁴ Who come to their appointed habitations. That they may receive thence helps. That by their prayers we also. May be worthy with them to have joy.

The hope of all the ends of the earth. O Christ, the hope of thy true ones. Prophets, apostles, and martyrs, and priests and doctors. Keep our souls by their prayers. And grant us to walk in their paths.* Bless, O my Lord, the holy Church wherein are laid up their bones. Bless and keep thy flock. Which was committed to their hands. Bless and keep thine inheritance. Which hath been gained by their labours. Bless and keep the faithful. Who celebrate their festivals with processions. Bless and keep the rich. Who honour their tombs. Bless and keep the poor. Who take refuge in their prayers. Bless and heal the infirm. Who take shelter under the wings of their bones. Bless and keep all who journey. On land or by sea. Bless and keep all conditions (of men). And sustain the weak by thy will. And heal the sick and infirm. And those who fall into temptations.* Bless the crown of the fruits. And make peaceful the temperature of the air. And keep priests and kings. In love and faith.* Bless and keep and save and rescue. All who are afflicted and distressed. And take refuge in the prayer of thy friends. The prophets, apostles, and doctors. And martyrs and priests and monks. Bless and keep in thy lovingkindness. The assembly that celebrateth the day of their memorials with processions.

<small>Ps. lxv. 5.</small>

---

¹ A. om. *And.* ² R. C.: *good.* ³ A. om. *That.* ⁴ R. C.: *boys.*

How[1] *good and beautiful.* Glorious is the day of the memorial. Of the illustrious and holy martyr Mar Pithiun, chosen of Christ. Who against error. Made his truth to shine forth, and gave up his soul for his Lord.* And in joy he endured. Terrible and bitter tortures. And was not moved by afflictions. And was not made slack by sufferings. But boldly rebuked. The madness of Adur-prazd'gard. Who, like a roaring wolf. Was madly desirous that he should be killed. And poured out his wrath without pity. On the two combatants.[2] 'Adur-hurmizd and Anahidh. Sons of the teaching of the athlete.* And confidently Mar Pithiun answered. And said to the officers of the Magi. I am prepared for suffering. And desire to depart. Come near, O men, finish in deed. That which ye are commanded (to do). And he kissed the instruments of iron. By which they cut off his limbs. And he glorified and confessed Christ. That he was counted worthy to suffer for his name.* And in the end of his contest he begged of his Lord in his suffering, and said. Whosoever calleth on thy Name. And taketh refuge in the prayer of thy servant. Hear, O my Lord, the voice of his prayer. And in thy mercies accept his request. And return answer to his petitions. And make us all worthy in thy compassion. To be heirs of thy kingdom.

Ps. cxxxiii. 1.

[*Another, composed by Mar Shimun (Simon), Metropolitan of the city of Amidh.*[3]]

And[1] *their prayers be on all of us.* In the chain of the mountains of the Kurds. Went forth the saints—may their prayer be a wall to us. In the mind of these victorious ones our Lord poured forth his grace.* First, Mar Saurishu. Whose habitation[4] was in the road[5] of the Zab. He brake the yoke of evil demons. And showed his noble deeds in the world. He wrought a spiritual work. And made a bridge to the (country) on high.* And Raban[6] Hurmizd of Persia.[7] In

---

[1] Om. R. C.   [2] Syr.: *Agunisti* (ἀγωνισταί).   [3] Diarbekir.
[4] Monastery.   [5] *Lit.* journey.   [6] Monk.   [7] Syr.: Paris (Fars).

the realm of Assyria. Wrought a quiet work. And departed and went to heaven. Raban Joseph the Seer. Whose monastery is in the Kurdish mountain. Saw exalted revelations. Above the nature of man.* And the great habitation[1] near thereby. Called Kmul, the fountain of love. Hath the fame of the Paradise of Eden. Thus history relateth.* Mar Isaak, glorious among teachers. Made for the monks six books. Showing them the ascents. To heaven amongst the just.* And John the Egyptian. Whose habitation[1] is Ṭur, called the Upper. Who raised a dead man at Nicæa. He and Mar James of Nisibis. And Mar Akha in the above-named mountain, drank no water. For the space of seven years together. He remained in this subjection. And an angel suddenly raised him up. To heaven before the Creator. The Lord gave him ordination. And he received in one moment the degree.* Mar Guria on the top of the mountain. Endured heat and cold. May his prayer be a wall to us. Against Satan the enemy. And Mar James, who against Marṭas. Offered prayers.[2] To God with praises. He is the beloved one, who flew and was wafted away.* May the prayers of these saints keep from evil demons. The faithful in every country. And men, wheresoever they dwell. Glory to the Power who gave them victory. And on us be his mercies by their prayers.

MOTWA AT NIGHT SERVICE FOR WEDNESDAY 'AFTER'

To the tune Lord of all.[3]

For he is thy Lord, worship thou him. Mary the Holy Virgin. Beseech and beg of Christ. That he have mercy on the world. Which taketh refuge in thy prayer. And let the Church rejoice in thy festival.

Ps. xlv. 12.

---

[1] Monastery.   [2] Genuflexions; Syr.: *maṭunyi* (see Glossary).
[3] A. om. name of tune.

And let her children within her. Be kept from harm and the opposition. Of the devil, the apostate.

Seek of him, and beseech him that he have pity on us. Mary the holy, etc.

He hath dispersed abroad and given to the poor. Open the treasure which thy Lord hath given thee. O John the preacher. And give help to the needy. Ps. cxii. 9. Who take refuge in thee, and call on thy name. To him that is sick give healing. To him that is distressed be a comfort. And whomsoever the Evil one vexeth. May thy prayer be a wall to him.

He set my feet upon the rock, and ordered my goings. The apostles, who are a stone that moveth not. Built a building that is not destroyed. By Ps. xl. 2. the power which they received from their Lord. They rooted out heathenism, and built up the Church. Hail, disciples of the truth. Who completed and raised up your building. And[1] adorned (and) built temples of the Spirit. In the souls of the faithful.

Seek the Lord and be strengthened. O chosen and holy Apostles. Pray and seek of the Lord. That there may be peace in creation. And that Ps. cv. 4. wars and contentions may cease. May there be concord among priests. And may agreement be multiplied among kings. And in the four quarters of the world. (May there be) great peace and tranquillity.

Offer to him sacrifices of praise. Chosen Stephen offered up. His body and soul with alacrity. For he saw his Lord bound. Before the judge who should Ps. cvii. 22. beat him. And he also offered as a sacrifice. His body to death by stoning. And received the crown of victory. And was the firstborn of martyrdom.

Thee, O Lord, beseemeth praise in Sion.[2] Praise to thee, O our Saviour. For by thy strength victory was given. To the three wonderful men. Pure Ps. lxv. 1.

---

[1] A. om. *And.*

[2] R. C.: *Out of the mouth of young men and boys.* Ps. viii. 2.

temples of the Holy Ghost. Diodorus, who laboured in argument. And illustrious Theodorus. And holy Nestorius. May their prayer be a wall to us.

And a joyful mother of children. In the memorial of the priests, lo, the Church. Glorious and holy, rejoiceth. For they stood up in her as pillars. That there might be teachers from amongst her sons. In every age their teaching conquereth. And their true faith. For that they reproved kings, and were not overcome. By the threats of their wickedness.

Ps. cxiii. 8.

Thy memorial throughout all generations.[1] O our father,[2] who didst conquer in the contest. Lo, thy recompense is in heaven. Christ, for whom thou didst adorn thyself. Hath exalted thy memorial in his Church. Thy love was a pure censer. And thou didst propitiate thy Lord by thy labours. Beseech with us, that[3] when he is revealed. In great glory, he have mercy upon us.

Ps. cii. 12.

Unto thee shall all flesh come. Unto thee, O my Lord, shall all flesh come. Who gavest forgiveness of trespasses to all. With thy hyssop may the bodies. Which sin hath defiled be made white. Come, mortals, bearing burdens. Lay down the weight of your trespasses. And take from the altar for your pardon. The coal which pardoned the prophet.

Ps. lxv. 2.

And thou saidst,[4] *Repent, ye children of men.* At the preaching of the prophet. Nineveh was saved by fasting. And by intercession and prayer. He stayed the angel of death from it. In suffering and tears of repentance. Let us take refuge in the temple. And call for mercy to help us. Until the light[5] fade.

Ps. xc. 3.

Out of the mouth of young men and boys.[6] (They gave) praise to thee, O our Saviour. When thou wast entering Jerusalem. And boys with olive

Ps. viii. 2.

---

[1] R. C.: *The Lord remember all thy offerings.* Ps. xx. 3.   [2] Or *Awa.*
[3] A. om. *that.*   [4] So A. and Psalter; R. C.: *he said.*   [5] Or *the Sun.*
[6] R. C.: *Thee, O Lord, beseemeth praise in Sion.* Ps. lxv. 1.

branches. Sang glory before thee, saying. Hosanna to thee in the highest. Hosanna to the Son of David. Blessed is thy coming unto us. In the power and glory of thy angels.

He who did eat my bread, in whom I trusted, hath greatly deceived me. Our Saviour broke bread. And gave it to the disciple of guile. And Satan entered into him. And he became a useless vessel. And changed not his mind. But let deceit pass within him. He became a stranger to his calling. And was not helped by his blessing.   Ps. xli. 9.

The Lord declared his salvation. Our Lord set forth himself. And showed how hard was his suffering. And he kept vigil and laboured, that[1] if it were possible. That hour might pass from him. Awake and pray ye, he warned us. That ye enter not into temptation. Our Lord bore witness that suffering is hard. For his sweat was changed to blood.   Ps. xcviii. 3.

It is become the head of the building. Thy resurrection, O our Lord, was life. To the race of men which was destroyed. For they have risen, and have been quickened and gained life. By the great power of the cross. And they rejected and threw down heathenism. And all the error of idols. And they knelt and worshipped the one Being. Who by his living Son saved the world.   Ps. cxviii. 22.

For thy sake have we been killed daily.[2] Ye who were killed, and loved your Creator. And received death of your own free will. And were propitiatory sacrifices. To[3] Christ the King, who crowned you. Offer with us a request. That in the great day of searching. We may be rescued from torment. And inherit life without end.   Ps. xliv. 22.

Gird thee with the sword upon thy thigh, O thou most Mighty. A giant of strength was St. George. Who despised death and the sword. And bitter maimings.   Ps. xlv. 4.

---

[1] A. om. *that.*

[2] R. C.: *They* (Psalter *he*) *spared not their souls from death* (Ps. lxxviii. 51).   [3] A.: *etc.* (and om. the rest of this verse).

And stripes of all kinds. And [1] wrought miracles and wonders. And turned all men to the truth. Blessed is he who gave victory to the athletes. By whose power we will conquer error.

He shall save the children of the poor.[2] The Word of the Father in his love was pleased. To save our race which was destroyed. He took of us the likeness of a servant. And ascended and sat[3] on the right hand. Glorify (him) now, ye mortals. For lo, the Son of our race is in heaven. Praised with processions of the exalted ones. Cherubim, Seraphim, and Angels.

Ps. lxxii. 4.

Glorify the Lord with a new song. It was a new wonder that was wrought. By the apostles in the temple of Jerusalem. When in the name of Jesus they made to walk. Him that was lame from his mother's womb. And the crowds of the Crucifiers[4] marvelled. To see the greatness of the wonderful deed. That in the Name of Jesus whom they had crucified. The lame man was made to walk.

Ps. xcvi. 1.

His lightnings lightened the world. The cross of light which was shown. To Constantine in heaven. Like a mighty one of the Virtues went. At the head of the camp to war. And (then) were moved and astonished, the companies. Of the heathen who worship created things. And they left off the error of heathenism. And venerated[5] and honoured the cross.

Ps lxxvii 18.

The king's daughter stood in glory. O Church, the spouse of Christ. Who saved thee with his blood from error. And promised thee by his resurrection. Life and good things which are not destroyed. Adorn thyself with alacrity. And pay thanksgiving. Confessing without doubt. The true faith.

Ps. xlv. 10.

---

[1] A. om. the rest of this verse.
[2] R. C. : *I will glorify the Word of God.* Ps. lvi. 10.
[3] A. : *made to sit* (error?).   [4] The Jews.   [5] Syr.: *worshipped.*

Verses of Prayer.[1]

With the pleasure of the victory of thy right hand. From thy treasury, O Lord of all. May the petitions of thy servants be answered. For thou art their helper. And in thee is placed their confident hope. Keep them in thy compassion. And aid them in thy lovingkindness. And give them a helping hand. That they may lift up (a song of) praise to thee. Ps. xvi. 12.

The eyes of all hang on thee. On thee, O Christ our Saviour. Lo, the eyes[2] of the distressed hang. And heal thou the pains and sicknesses. Of those who have fallen into temptations. As thou didst promise in thy Gospel. Which is full of life and joys. Whoso diligently knocketh. At the door of my majesty, it is opened to him. Ps. cxlv. 15.

Thou art merciful, O Lord, and righteous. Thou art compassionate from everlasting. And merciful for all generations. How great is the iniquity of creation. In the overflowing mercies of thy lovingkindness. Sprinkle the face of our nature. With the dew of mercy and pity. And rescue us from the hand of the Evil one. And from the tares, the sons of error. Ps. cxvi. 5.

A great King above all gods. O King of kings, our helper. Thou art Christ our Saviour. Pity thy servants who call to thee. In these times of affliction. For lo, sorrows surround us. And terrors on all sides. Let thy mercies quickly prevent us. And make thy face to shine and save us. Ps. xcv. 3.

He sitteth upon the cherubims, let the earth be moved. O thou that sittest on the right hand of the Father. With thy right hand bless our assembly. And with the arm of thy might. Keep them that are bought with thy blood. Let thy light drive out from thy Church. The Ps. xcix. 1.

---

[1] R. C. om. all these to the Gloria, but refers to another publication for them.   [2] Syr.: *look*.

darkness of ignorance. And with the just who were approved before thee. Make us worthy to inherit the kingdom.

The Lord shall give his people the blessing of peace. Bless our assembly, O our Saviour. And make thy grace to dwell in it. And give us strength to glorify thee. The assemblies of them that are above with them that are below. And (grant) us all to love one another. And obtain love and concord. Even as the Spiritual ones obtained. The one wish, to be approved by thee.
Ps. xxix. 11.

We that are thy people and sheep of thy pasture. Keep, O our Lord, in thy compassion. The great assembly of thy flock. That the devil be not puffed up and attack it. As of old time. Send thy power from on high. And let it be a wall to our camp. And let it stand before us, that we be not harmed. And may the sheep of thy pasture be kept safe.
Ps. lxxix. 14.

Great is the power of prayer which a righteous man prayeth. Great is the power of prayer. To which love and peace are joined. And it wipeth out a multitude of sins. (And) bringeth (us) to the knowledge of the Lord. And giveth a reward and recompense. And openness of face to the faithful. In the great day of searching. When the good are separated from the evil.
St. James v. 16.

O let the sighing of the prisoner come before thee. Prayer is the key of creation. It openeth the door of the kingdom. And giveth a reward and recompense. From the treasury which enricheth all. By it, O my Lord, let thy grace open. The door of thy gift to the needy. And pour forth thy mercies on thy servants. Who take refuge in thee and call on thy Name.
Ps. lxxix. 12.

Thus he speaketh in visions with his saints. Thou spakest by the prophets. O Lord of the prophets and apostles. I desire not your deaths. O sinners, turn from your iniquity. Return answer to our petitions, and grant to us. Restoration of our bodies and souls. Seasons bearing joy. Dividing benefits and gifts.
Ps. lxxxix. 20.

In the evening and morning, and at noonday. To work in the spiritual vineyard. Hast thou called us, O our Lord, in thy lovingkindness. Grant us to fulfil thy will. In perfecting the fruits of thy commandments. For thou art the true vine. And thy Father is the vinedresser. And we all are the branches. Receive the fruits of our lips. Ps. lv. 18.

Show thy servant the light of thy countenance, and save me in thy lovingkindness. Show unto our souls, O Father. The light of the brightness of thy Only-begotten. And let our minds ever be illuminated. By the beams of thy lovingkindness. And let the fire of thy love burn in us. And be kindled thereby at all times. And without ceasing let us raise to thee. Glory, O Being who art Lord of all. Ps. xxxi. 18.

I have gone astray like a sheep that is lost; O seek thy servant. From the number of the hundred of thy flock. O good and true shepherd. I alone have gone astray. And by my wickednesses I have provoked thee. O my Lord, neglect not my request. For thou alone hast compassion on all. But seek me in thy compassion. And forgive my trespasses in thy lovingkindness. Ps. cxix. 176.

Holy and reverend is his name. O our Lord, thy kingdom come. Thy will be done on earth. As it is in heaven. Among the Spiritual ones who serve thee. Give us the bread of our need. And lead us not into temptation. But deliver us from the Evil one. For thine is the kingdom. Ps. cxi. 9.

He sitteth on high and beholdeth the depth. O thou that sittest on the right hand of the Father. With thy right hand bless our assembly. And with thy mighty arm. Keep them that are bought with thy blood. Let thy light drive out from thy Church. The darkness of ignorance. With the just who were approved before thee. Make us worthy to inherit the kingdom. Ps. cxiii. 5.

Rescue me and preserve me from this generation for ever. O our Lord, rescue thy worshippers. From evil (men) and enemies. And from cruel devils and demons. And from evil thoughts. And from sinful deeds. And from devastation, and captivity, and robbery. And from pains and sicknesses. And from the searching of thy just judgment.

Ps. xii. 8.

Have mercy upon us, O Lord, have mercy upon us. By the request of the just. And the prayer of the prophets. And the intercession of the apostles. And the beseeching of the martyrs. O Lord, and the entreating. Of all the holy Church. Now have mercy upon us. And at that day[1] lead us not into judgment.

Ps. cxxiii. 3.

Let my prayer be in thy sight as the incense. As the censer which Aaron offered. May the savour of our assembly be pleasing to thee. And as the request of the Ninevites. Receive, O my Lord, the prayer of thy servants. And as thou didst answer Daniel. From the den of lions. Answer, O my Lord, and help thy worshippers. In these times of affliction.

Ps. cxli. 2.

And praise thy name for ever. Glory to thy mercies, O Lord of all. Glory to thy will, O Almighty. Glory to thee from those on high. Glory to thee from those below. Visit the sick with thy compassion. And accept the request of thy worshippers. That their heart may rejoice in thy salvation. And that they may ever say, Glory to thee.

Ps. lxvi. 3 (?).

For thy loving mercy and for thy truth sake. Glory to thy mercies, which have become to us. A road to the door of thy kingdom. Christ, our anointing oil. The free medicine, hath been sent. Come forth at our request, Rabboni.[2] According to thy true promise. The sick need this. Not the true sons of thy mysteries.

Ps. cxv. 1.

Open me the gates of righteousness. Thou art compassionate and full of mercies. Open thy treasury to the needy. And return answer to the petitions of

Ps. cxviii. 19.

---

[1] Lit. *then.*   [2] Syr.: *Rabu li.*

thy worshippers. Who call on thy holy Name. And may
we be aided by thy lovingkindness. To perfect all thy commandments. For thou art a sea of compassion. And forgivest
the trespasses of mortals.

Heal me, O Lord, for my bones are vexed. O Christ, the true
Healer. Heal our vices in thy compassion.
And cleanse and purify our defilements. With Ps. vi. 2.
the medicine of thy kind will. For we have sinned and done
foolishly, and moved thee to anger. And we are not worthy
of thy compassion. With thy hyssop may we be made white.
And worthy of an answer to our petitions.

At all seasons and times. In suffering and tears we beseech
(thee). O good and kind Lord. Open thy treasury to the
needy. Who knock at the door of thy majesty. And give
peace to the world by thy will. And bring to nought all
contentions therein. And by thy commandment let wars
cease. Which disturb creation.

He that is before the worlds. O Being who art from everlasting, and neglectest not. Sinners who call
on thee. Make thy peace to dwell in creation. Ps. lv. 20.
And thy tranquillity in the holy Church. And may priests
and kings be bound together. By perfect love and concord.
That we, a quiet and peaceful habitation. May dwell in
purity of life.

FOR A JOURNEY. *Arise and help us, and deliver us, for thy
mercy's sake.* O Lord, who wast with Jacob.
And didst protect his life from Esau. Be with Ps. xliv. 26.
thy servants, O Compassionate one. In the journey that is
set before them. And keep them without harm. From the
wickedness of the Crafty ones. And bring them back in
peace. And let thy power accompany them and be with
them.

FOR RAIN. *Hear my voice, O God, when I beseech thee.* Hear,
O my Lord, the voice of the husbandmen.
Who see the crops dried up. Send thy dew Ps. lxiv. 1.
for their comfort. And wipe away the tears of their eyes.
And as they have been humbled by correction. Let them

now be encouraged by mercy. And may all conditions (of men) eat and be satisfied. And make offerings to thee.

Hear, O God, and have mercy upon me. Lo, heaven and earth weep. And pour forth tears of sorrow. For they see thy servants afflicted. And there is no helper to rescue (them). Awake, Lord, as one that sleepeth. And as in the times of old. And save and rescue thy worshippers. From the hands of the persecutors.

Ps. xxx. 11.

Glory be, etc. By the prayer of the Blessed one. May peace reign in creation, etc. *And the other verses as on Wednesday 'before'* (page 134).

NIGHT SERVICE

FOR

SUNDAYS, FEASTS OF OUR LORD, AND MEMORIALS OF SAINTS

Priest. Glory be to God, etc. *Ans.* Bless, O my Lord. *Kiss of peace.* Our Father, *farced and sung slowly* (page 1).

Deacon. Let us arise to prayer. Let us pray, Peace be with us. *All as on ferias,* page 85.

Prayer on Sundays and Feasts.[1] Let us arise, O my Lord, in the hidden power of thy Godhead, and let us be confirmed in the wondrous hope of thy majesty, and raised and strengthened by the high arm of thy might; and may we be worthy by the help of thy lovingkindness to lift up to thee praise, and honour, and confession, and worship, at all times, Lord of all, etc.

Prayer on Memorials.[1] Let us arise, O my Lord, in thy power, *as on ferias.*

They[2] *say,* Hallelujah, etc., *page 85.*

Prayer.[2] Strengthen, O our Lord, *page 85.*

They[2] *say,* Hallelujah, etc.

Prayer.[2] May the secret strength, *page 86.*

They[2] *say,* Hallelujah, etc.[3]

---

[1] So T.; R. C. and U. give the first prayer also for memorials.
[2] R. C. om. all these in this place (see below).
[3] U. om. this last response in the festival service (error?).

FEASTS OF OUR LORD

The Hulali[1] and Motwi.

On Feasts of our Lord they recite the Psalter from the beginning, and say eleven Hulali (Ps. i. to lxxxi. incl.), *with farcings and the proper prayers before each Hulala and each Marmitha (see above,* page 86). *But they do not say* Hallelujah *between each Hulala; and each side says two clauses at a time.*[2] *They say* Ps. lxxviii., *farced thus: between each pair of clauses* Hallelu, *four times,* Hallelujah in the Nativity of Christ [*or* Baptism, etc.].[3]

Prayer before the Motwa on Feasts. We beseech thee, O Treasure of helps and Fountain of all benefits, overflowing Sea of compassion and mercy, great Abyss of pardon and pity, turn, O my Lord, and have pity and mercy upon us, as thou art wont, at all times, Lord of all, etc.

They say the First Motwa *as in the Geza.*

At the end of the Motwa they pray. To thy wonderful and unspeakable dispensation, *as at the Evening Service,* page 80.

They say the proper Canon, Tishbukhta, *and* Karuzutha[4] *for the day.*

Prayer. Of thee, who art full of mercies and compassion, and of the great riches of the kindness of thy love, and the overflowing treasure of thy compassion, we ask help and

---

[1] In R. C. the rules for reciting the Psalter have been adapted and simplified thus:—
Feasts of our Lord and Memorials, Hulali 12, 13, 14, farced.
Christmas and Epiphany, add Hulala 15.
First Sunday 'before,' Hulali 5, 6, 7; and Ps. lxxxi., sung.
Second Sunday 'before,' Hulali 9, 10, 11; Ps. lxxxi. is sung.
First Sunday 'after,' Hulali 12, 13, 14; and Ps. cxxx., sung.
Second Sunday 'after,' Hulali 16, 17, 18; Ps. cxxx. is sung.
In consequence of these simplifications, the whole of the first part of the office is somewhat altered in R. C., especially on feasts, to the end of the Motwa.

[2] The Gloria is always said after each Marmitha.

[3] In practice the farcing is sometimes only said after each second, or fourth, or even each sixth clause.

[4] Printed in U.

strength, deliverance, preservation, and healing for the pains of our bodies and souls. Grant this to us in thy lovingkindness and mercies, as thou art wont, at all times, Lord of all, etc.

Another. Blessed and adorable, high and exalted and incomprehensible, are the eternal mercies of thy glorious Trinity, which freely have compassion on sinners, O our good Hope and Refuge full of mercies, who forgivest trespasses and sins, Lord of all, etc.

MADRASHA [1] *for the day.*

They say six Hulali (Ps. lxxxii. to cxix. 88 incl.) *in the same manner as before.*

Prayer. O thou who openest thy door, etc.

Another. O thou who hearest the voice, etc., *both as at the Evening Service,* page 83.

SECOND MOTWA *and* CANONS *from the Gez̤a.*

In the THIRD MOTWA *of* The Company of the Catholici *they say the rest of the Psalter, but* Deut. xxxii. 21a-44 *is said with proper farcings from the Khudhra.*

QALI D'SHAHRA.[3]

They say another Hulala, with the following prayers:—

Prayer of the First Qala. May the sounds of our Hallelujahs please thee, O our Lord and our God, and the melodies of our songs; and accept from us in thy lovingkindness the spoken[4] fruits of our lips, which with praise we offer to thy glorious Trinity, night and day, Lord of all, etc.

Prayer of the Second Qala. Make us worthy, O our Lord and our God, with the watchful ones and the companies of angels, with voices full of confession to sing praise to thy glorious Trinity, night and day, Lord of all, etc.

Prayer of the Third Qala. Continual glory, O my Lord, and unceasing Hallelujahs and endless praises, and voices full of

---

[1] A doctrinal hymn.   [2] Including the twenty-first Hulala.
[3] An additional Hulala sung to a chant. Lit. *Voices of the Vigil.*
[4] Or *reasonable.*

confession, every nature of rational beings whom thou hast created is bound to raise to thy glorious Trinity, night and day, Lord of all, etc.

The Qali d'Shahra for Feasts are found in the Geza. Two clauses are said at a time by each side, and Hallelujah *between the clauses of each pair; some say* Hallelujah *twice, some thrice. They say the Gloria in the same way. If the Feast does not fall on a Sunday, they kneel down between the Qali.*

Night Anthems.

Prayer of the first Night Anthem. By the speaking mouths, O my Lord, which thou hast created, and by the glorifying tongues which thou hast appointed, and by all the companies on high and below, may the Name of thy Godhead and of thy majesty be worshipped, glorified, honoured, exalted, confessed, and blessed in heaven and earth, Lord of all, etc.

Prayer[1] of the second Anthem. May thy Godhead, O my Lord, be pleased with our service, and may our prayers be received before thee, and may thy mercies greatly intercede for our wickedness, and from thy great treasury may our petitions be answered in our need, at all times, Lord of all, etc.

Prayer[1] of the third Anthem. Come, O my Lord, to the help of thy worshippers, who keep vigil on the festival of N; and reveal thyself to us in thy mercy, and hearken to the words of our prayers, which on thy holy festival we offer to thee, Lord of all.

Prayer[1] after the Night Anthem. Make us worthy, O our Lord and our God, by pure thoughts and sweet and holy melodies, with the heavenly hosts and the Wise Men and the Shepherds, to celebrate the holy festival of the Nativity of Christ our Lord and Saviour, in thy lovingkindness and mercy, Lord of all, etc.

Or[1] this. Answer, O my Lord, them that keep vigil in thy

---

[1] Om. T., R. C.

holy festival of N, in thy compassion. And wash the filth of our sins by thy gift; multiply like water the flocks of them that believe in thy salvation, and make firm thy Church, the faithful vine which thou hast planted, Lord of all, etc.

They say the proper CANON[1] *and its Continuation, and the* TISHBUKHTA, *Praise to him who is good, as below* (page 161). *Then the proper* KARUZUTHA.[2]

SUNDAYS

THE HULALI.[3]

On Sundays 'before' they say Hulali 5 to 11 inclusive (Ps. xxxvii. to lxxxi. incl.), *without farcings or prayers of the Marmyatha. But the prayers of the Hulali are said, as on ferias. Between each Hulala they sing slowly,* Hallelujah, Hallelujah, yea, Hallelujah. Glory be to thee, O God, *twice.* Hallelujah, Hallelujah, yea Hallelujah. O Lord, have mercy upon us. Let us pray, Peace be with us. Ps. lxxviii. and lxxxi. *are farced with* Hallelujah *between each clause; these are sung slowly.*

On Sundays 'after' they say Hulali 12 to 18 inclusive (Ps. lxxxii. to cxxxi. incl.), *as before, farcing* Ps. cxix. v. 89 to the end [4] *and* Ps. cxxx., *with* Hallelujah *between each clause. These are sung slowly.*

QALTHA.[5]

Prayer[6] *of the Qaltha.* For thy nature, etc., page 95.

They sing the Qaltha of the day, as in the Khudhra, and the Psalms that follow.

---

[1] According to T., preceded by the prayer *Glory to thee from al mouths,* as on Sundays (below, page 161); according to R. C., by *To thy wonderful and unspeakable dispensation,* etc. (page 80).

[2] From the Khudhra or Geza. Printed in U.

[3] For R. C., see note on Feasts.   [4] Or vv. 89-97?

[5] These rules are also given in R. C., A.

[6] Not mentioned in U. on Sundays.

Sundays throughout the year 'before.' Ps. lxxxvi. *farced after the first clause, and then after every second clause, with* Hallelujah. Then Ps. cxxi.; *then* lxxxviii. 10, 11; *then* cxxxviii. 7, 8, *from* Stretch forth thy hand and save me; *each psalm farced as above, and so all that follow.* Then Glory be, etc. Hallelujah, Hallelujah, yea, Hallelujah. From everlasting, etc. *Repeat the first two clauses of* Ps. lxxxvi., *with* Hallelujah, Hallelujah, yea, Hallelujah *between them. So on all Sundays.*

Sundays throughout the year 'after.' Ps. xci., cxxiii. 1-4 (omitting the last clause of v. 3), cii. 26, 27, cxxxviii. part of 7, 8, as above (ending as above).

Sundays of Advent[1] *'before.'* Substitute Ps. xl. 1-15 for Ps. lxxxvi. above.

Sundays of Advent[1] *'after.'* Substitute Ps. xlviii. 1-11 for Ps. xci. above.

Sundays of the Hallowing of the Church 'before.' Substitute Ps. xlv. for Ps. lxxxvi. above.

Sundays of the Hallowing of the Church 'after.' Substitute Ps. lxxxiv. for Ps. xci. above.

Palm[2] *Sunday.* Ps. xcvi., xcvii., xcviii., then cxxi., etc., as on Sundays 'before.'

On Feasts and Memorials there is no Qaltha.

Motwa.

Prayer before the Motwa for Sundays. May our prayer, O my Lord, please thee, and may our request come before thee, and from the great treasury of thy compassion may our petitions be answered in our need, at all seasons and times, Lord of all, etc.

They say the proper Motwa as given in the Khudhra; then the prayer for the season as at the Evening Prayer. (Prayers after the Royal Anthem, page 80.)

Tishbukhta[3] of the Night Service *by Mar Babai the Great, on Sundays from Advent*[1] *to Epiphany.* Blessed is the Compas-

---

[1] Syr.: *Annunciation.*   [2] So A.; om. U., R. C.   [3] Om. A., R. C.

sionate one, who in his lovingkindness. Hath supplied our life in prophecy.* With the eye of the Spirit Isaiah saw. The wondrous Child of the Virgin.¹ * For Mary without union bore. Emmanuel, the son of God.* From her the Holy Ghost fashioned. The body which was united (with him), as it is written.* That it might be an adorable habitation and temple. For the Brightness of the Father in one Sonship.* And at the beginning of his marvellous conception. United it with him in one honour.* That he might fulfil in him all things that were his. For the salvation of the world, as seemed good to him.* In the day of his Annunciation² [or Nativity] the watchful ones glorified him. With their hallelujahs in the heights above.* And also the earthly ones offered him worship. With their offerings in one honour.* One is Christ the Son of God. Worshipped by all in two natures.* In his Godhead begotten of the Father. Without beginning, before all time.* In his manhood born³ of Mary. In the end of times, in the body which was united (with him).* His Godhead was not of the nature of (his) mother. And his manhood not of the nature of the Father. The natures are preserved in their qnumi.⁴ In one person⁵ of one Sonship.* And as the Godhead is. Three qnumi⁴ (but) one essence.* So the sonship of the Son. Is in one person⁵ two natures.* So the holy Church hath learnt. To confess the Son who is Christ.* We worship, O my Lord, thy Godhead. And thy manhood without division. *Say this verse thrice.** One is the power, one the majesty. One the will, and one the glory.* Of Father, Son, and Holy Ghost. For ever and ever. Amen and Amen.

*Another,*⁶ *for all Sundays of the year, by Mar Babai of Nisibis.* Glory to thy mercies, which sent thee to us. O Christ the Sun of righteousness.* The brightness which shone from the house of David. And called the nations to repentance.*

---

¹ Syr.: *virginity.* ² Advent. ³ Syr.: *begotten.*
⁴ For this term see *The Catholicos of the East and his People,* p. 308.
⁵ Parsopa. See also as above. ⁶ Om. A., R. C.

Come near, ye penitent, and ask for mercies. While there is time[1] for repentance.* Let every man leave that which is in his heart. And ask for mercies with openness of face.[2]* Hear our request and grant our petitions. O Christ, who lovest the voice of the penitent.* Neglect not, O my Lord, our entreaty. Which we offer to thee in penitence of soul.* Thou knowest, O my Lord, that our iniquity is great. Stretch out to us the hand which is full of mercies.* We are like unto the younger son in thy sight. Who scattered the goods of the house of his fathers.* We have sinned and provoked thee, pity and have mercy. O good and merciful Lord.* Let thy mercies pity our trespasses. For by thy living blood thou hast bought us.* With the widow we beseech. Thee, the Judge, who aboundest in mercies.* Pardon our trespasses and wipe out our sins. O thou who art good, and bearest the burden of our sin.* May thy cross be a house of refuge to us. And drive away from us the power of the Evil one.* And in that day when the children of Adam. Are shaken together from the dust.* And every man is awakened from the sleep. Of mortality for the Questioning.* In that judgment when good and bad. Are repaid according to their deeds.* May thy compassion intercede for us. And may we not be condemned in thy just judgment.* And in that hour when thy mercies shine forth. May we go forth to meet thee according to thy will.* And with the saints and just men who loved thee. May we sing glory to thy Godhead.* And may we all together lift up glory. To Father, Son, and Holy Ghost.* To whom be praise from his worshippers. For ever and ever. Amen and Amen.

Another,[3] *for the Hallowing of the Church, by Mar George, Metropolitan of Nisibis.* Glory to thy mercies, O Christ our King. O Son of God, worshipped by all.* For thou art our Lord, and thou art our God. And the head of our life and our blessed hope.* And thee the companies on high glorify. And the assemblies below with one accord.* Confessing thee

---

[1] Syr.: *place*.   [2] *i.e.* confidence.   [3] Om. A., R. C.

that thou art hidden. And wast revealed in our flesh[1] in the latter times.* When thy mercies pitied (us), thou wast well pleased in thy love. To come to save us and make free our race. Thou didst heal our pains and didst pardon our trespasses. Thou didst quicken our deadness in thy mercies.* And didst raise up on earth a holy Church. After the type of that which is above, in heaven.*. By a type thou didst foreordain her, in love thou didst espouse her. In mercies thou didst receive her, by suffering thou didst perfect her.* And lo, the Enemy of man troubleth her. With his arrogant pertinacity through his ministers.* O my Lord, neglect not the holy Church. And let not the promise of thy word[2] be made false.* Let not her desirable beauty be disfigured. And her great wealth be made poor.* Remember thy promise to Peter. Fulfil in deed that which thou hast spoken.* Make firm her gates and make strong her bars. Exalt her horn and lift up her walls.* Bless her sons and preserve her children. And give peace to her priests and confound them that hate her.* And make thy peace to dwell in her. And bring to nought divisions and schisms in her.* And grant us to be a peaceful habitation. Without controversy in the faith. While we keep our faith. In a good hope and perfect love.* May our actions also be approved before thee. And may we find mercies in the day of recompense.* That without ceasing we may lift up glory. To thy Father, and to the Holy Ghost, through thee.* To whom be praise in all generations. For ever and ever, Amen and Amen.

They say the KARUZUTHA[3] *appointed in the Khudhra.*

Prayers of the Madrasha. Of thee who art full of mercies, *and* Blessed and adorable, *as above,* page 152.

MADRASHA *for the day, from the Khudhra.*

Prayer of the first Suyakha. Thee who art hidden from all in thy being, and who art revealed and who shinest forth by the wonderful deeds of thy dispensation, the power of whose might heaven and earth proclaim, we are bound to confess, worship, and glorify, at all times, Lord of all, etc.

---

[1] Syr.: *body.*   [2] Syr.: *words.*   [3] Printed in U.

FIRST[1] SUYAKHA: *on Sundays 'before,'* Hulala 12 (Ps. lxxxii. to lxxxviii. incl.); *on Sundays 'after,'* Hulala 19 (Ps. cxxxii. to cxli. incl.).

Prayer of the second Suyakha. Thee who art hidden in thy being, and secret in thy Godhead, and unspeakable in thy glory, great King of glory, Being who art from everlasting, we confess, worship, and glorify, at all times, Lord of all, etc.

SECOND[1] SUYAKHA: *on Sundays 'before,'* Hulala 13 (Ps. lxxxix. to xcii. incl.); *on Sundays 'after,'* Hulala 20 (Ps. cxlii. to cl. incl.).

QALI D'SHAHRA.[2] *Prayer.* May the sounds of our Hallelujahs, *as above*, page 153.

On Sundays 'before' they sing Hulala 14, Marmitha 1 (Ps. xciii., xciv., xcv.); *on Sundays 'after,'* Hulala 21, Marmitha 1 (Ex. xv. 1-22; Is. xlii. 10-14, and xlv. 8). *After each Marmitha*, Glory be. From everlasting. Hallelujah, Hallelujah, yea Hallelujah. Let us pray, Peace be with us.

Second Prayer. Make us worthy, *as above*, page 153.

On Sundays 'before,' Hulala 14, Marmitha 2 (Ps. xcvi., xcvii., xcviii.); *on Sundays 'after,'* Hulala 21, Marmitha 2 (Deut. xxxii. 1-21a); *the Gloria, etc., as before.*

Third Prayer. Continual glory, *as above*, page 153.

On Sundays 'before,' Hulala 14, Marmitha 3 (Ps. xcix., c., ci.); *on Sundays 'after,'* Hulala 21, Marmitha 3 (Deut. xxxii. 21a-44); *with Gloria. They repeat the first clause of the Hulala, and say,* Let us pray, Peace be with us.

Prayer of the Night Anthem. By the speaking mouths, *as above*, page 154.

NIGHT ANTHEM *for the day, as in the Khudhra.*

On Sundays the two last verses are always as follows:—

From everlasting to everlasting. O Christ, neglect us not. And be not far from thy worshippers. For in thee, O my Lord, we have taken refuge. Guide us in thy way of life, that we may all sing praise to thee, O Lord God.

---

[1] Given only in U. [2] These are sung slowly, to a chant.

And let all the people say Amen and Amen. O Mary, the holy Virgin. Mother of Jesus our Saviour. Beseech with us of Christ, that he make his peace to dwell among us. And keep us from all harm by night and by day.   Ps. cvi. 46.

From the Fast to Pentecost, these verses are not said. In the Annunciation (Advent), the verse And let all the people *is not said.*

They say,[1] Let us pray, Peace be with us.

Prayer of the Shubakha on Sundays. Glory to thee from all mouths, and confession from all tongues, and worship and honour[2] and exaltation from all creatures, O secret and glorious Being, who dwellest in the exalted heights, Lord of all, etc.

They say the proper SHUBAKHA, *two verses at a time, farced with* Glory, ingah,[3] ahingah, ahingah, to thee, O Lord.

They say the proper Continuation from the Khudhra.

TISHBUKHTA[4] *by Mar Narsai.* Praise to him who in his goodness hath made our race free. From the slavery of the Evil one and of death.* And[5] hath made peace between us and the companies of those on high. Who were angry, because of our iniquity.* Blessed is the Compassionate one, who, when we sought him not. Came forth to seek us, and rejoiced in (giving) us life.* And showed a type of our being lost. And returning again, in the sheep that went astray.* The heir, the Son, hath called our nature. Which went astray and returned, and was dead and is quickened again.* And hath made glad the spiritual companies. With our repentance and quickening.* Unspeakable is the great love. Which the Friend of our race hath showed to us.[6]* Who of our race hath made a Mediator. And reconciled the world with his greatness.* It is a thing too great for us and for all creatures. It is a new thing which he hath done to our humanity.* That he hath made our body a holy temple. That he might perfect in it the adoration of

---

[1] Om. U.   [2] T. om. *and honour.*
[3] These additions have no meaning.   [4] A., R. C. om. name of author.
[5] R. C., U., om. *And.*   [6] A. *me.*

all.* Come, ye earthly and heavenly ones. Wonder and be astonished at the greatness of the step.* By which our race hath come to the great heights. Of the incomprehensible Godhead.* Let heaven and earth, and all that is in them. Confess with us, him who exalteth our race.* Who hath renewed our image, and wiped out our iniquity. And hath called us by his Name, and hath made all things subject to us.* He is worthy of glory from all mouths. Who hath lifted us up above all.* And let us all give praise to him. For ever and ever, Amen and Amen.

KARUZUTHA, *as appointed in the Khudhra; or say,*[1] Father of mercies (*the first part*) *as above,* page 6; or [2] *the following.*

Let us all stand up, etc. (page 6).

O thou who didst teach us to pray and not to be slothful, we make request. *Answer.* O our Lord, have mercy upon us. *And so after each clause.*

O thou who didst spend the night in prayer to[3] God for the salvation of our race, we, etc.

O thou who didst give us a proof of thy mercy through our earthly fathers, we, etc.

O thou who didst save us from mighty Death,[4] and in whom we trust to save us, we, etc.

O thou who didst save us from the power of darkness, and hast brought us to the kingdom of thy well-beloved Son, we, etc.

O thou who saidst, Ask and it shall be given you, Seek and ye shall find, Knock and the treasure of mercies shall be opened to you, we, etc.

For the welfare of our holy fathers NN,[5] and all those who serve under them, we, etc.

O merciful God, who in mercy governest all, we, etc.

O thou who art glorified in heaven and worshipped on earth, we, etc.

---

[1] So U.   [2] So R. C.
[3] Syr.: *of.*   [4] Syr.: *deaths.*
[5] Patriarch, Metropolitan, and Bishop of the Diocese.

Give us the victory, O Christ our Lord, in thy coming, and give peace to thy Church, saved by thy precious blood, and have mercy upon us.

MEMORIALS

HULALI [1] 12, 13, 14 (Psalms lxxxii. to ci. inclusive), *with farcings and prayers both of the Hulali and Marmyatha* (page 86).

There is no Qaltha on Memorials.

Prayer before the Motwa. We beseech thee, etc., *as above on Feasts*, page 152 ; *and they say the proper Motwa from the Khudhra, and a proper collect, Canon, and Tishbukhta,*[2] *and the proper Karuzutha and Madrasha with its prayers.*

The Qali d'Shahra are as noted in the Khudhra, with prayers as above (page 153); *then the proper Night Anthem with its prayer* (page 154), *and Canon instead of the Shubakha with the proper prayer of the season*[2] (page 80).

TISHBUKHTA. Glory to him who in his goodness, *as on Fridays in the ferial service*, page 100.

They say the Karuzutha appointed in the Khudhra, or one of those given above for Sundays (page 162).

---

[1] For R. C., see note on Feasts, page 152.   [2] So R. C.; om. U.

MORNING SERVICE

FOR

SUNDAYS, FEASTS OF OUR LORD, AND MEMORIALS OF SAINTS [1]

Prayer before the Morning Psalms. Make us worthy, O our Lord and our God, according to the will of thy Godhead and thy glorious Majesty, to serve before thee purely and diligently, wakefully and earnestly, justly and uprightly, honestly and in holiness, and without blame. And may our service, O my Lord, please thee, and our prayer and vigil persuade thee, and our request propitiate thee, our beseeching honour thee, and our entreaty appease thee. And may the mercies and compassion of thy Godhead be for the pardon of the trespasses of thy people, and for the forgiveness of the sins of all the sheep of thy pasture, whom thou hast chosen for thyself in thy lovingkindness and mercies, O thou good Friend of the sons of men, Lord of all, etc.

They answer, Amen. Bless, O my Lord.

Another. Enlighten us, O my Lord, with thy light, and gladden us by thy coming; cause us to rejoice in thy salvation, and make us partakers of thy mysteries. And grant and vouchsafe [2] that, together with the heavenly companies clothed in light, and the bands of angels, with voices full of confession, we may sing praise to thy glorious Trinity, O Creator who rulest all, O Creator who needest not the service of creatures,

---

[1] This follows the Night Service without a break. For Sundays in the Fast, see page 207.   [2] Syr.: *make us worthy.*

who didst create light in thy lovingkindness, and didst order darkness in thy mercy, and gavest light to creation in thy wisdom and knowledge and Godhead which cannot be comprehended by spiritual or earthly beings, Lord of all, etc.

Or they use two prayers in the book Abukhalim.[1]
They say[2] *In the beginning,*[3] *as in the Khudhra.*

THE PSALMS. Ps. c. *farced with* In the beginning, *if noted in the Khudhra.*[4] *If not, as on ferias, but the farcing is said after the second as well as after the first clause.*[4]

Prayer on Sundays and Feasts.[5] To thee, O my Lord, all creatures whom thou hast created lift up glory and praise. For thou alone art their true light, and dost enlighten the worlds and (all) creatures in thy lovingkindness and mercy, Lord of all, etc.

Ps. xci. [*If*[6] *it be a day on which* In the beginning *is not said, the psalm is sung in the order of the ferial service; otherwise thus.*] Whoso dwelleth under the defence of the Most High. And is made glorious in the shadow of God. *When the Creator established the light the angels wondered at it. And when it shineth forth each morning let them and us give him glory.* Whoso dwelleth . . . and show him my salvation. *When the Creator established, etc.** Glory be.* From everlasting.* *When thou didst create the light which is poured forth, the spiritual ones glorified thee. And it was made known to them that he who created the light, created them also.** Whoso dwelleth under the defence of the Most High. And is made glorious in the shadow of God.* *By angels thou art glorified, and by the sons of men thou art praised. And all together with one accord cry and say,* Blessed is thy Annunciation[7] [or *Nativity,* or *Baptism,* or *Resurrection,*

---

[1] So U.; R. C.: *in the Khudhra or Geza.*   [2] So U.

[3] Syr.: *Brashith.* This is a verse sung on some Sundays, Festivals, and Memorials, proper to each, but always dealing with the creation of the world, and commencing with the words *In the beginning.*

[4] So R. C., not U.

[5] R. C. also on Memorials (by implication). T. does not mention these. U. mentions Sundays only.

[6] So. R. C.; U. does not mention this first provision. Each choir takes two clauses at a time in this psalm.   [7] Advent.

or *Ascension*, or *Descent of thy Holy Spirit*], O Christ our Saviour. Let[1] us pray, Peace be with us.

Prayer. Glorious, O my Lord, page 104.

Ps. civ. vv. 1-16a. Bless the Lord, O my soul. *Glory becometh thee, O God.* Bless the Lord, O my soul . . . full of sap. *No Gloria. Add,* Glory becometh, etc.

Ps. cxiii.[2] Praise the Lord ye his servants.[3] O praise the Name of the Lord. *Glory becometh thee, O God, for thou art the Creator of the light.* Praise the Lord ye his servants . . . mother of children.* Glory be.* From everlasting.* Praise the Lord ye his servants.[4] *Glory becometh,*[5] *etc.* Praise the Lord ye his servants.[3]* O praise the Name of the Lord.* *Glory becometh,*[6] *etc.*

Prayer on Sundays and Memorials.[7] Thou, O my Lord, art the Creator of light in thy lovingkindness, and thou orderest the darkness in thy wisdom, and enlightenest creation with thy glorious light. And thee, O my Lord, continual praise without ceasing becometh. And to thy Name is due confession and worship in heaven and earth, Lord of all, etc.

Prayer on Feasts of our Lord. Thou, O my Lord, art alone the Creator of light, and thou orderest the darkness in thy wisdom and by thy judgments, and enlightenest creation with thy glorious light, by the instrumentality of the sun and moon, thy luminaries. And from thy bright light resplendent with rays shine all lights by night and by day, the work of thy hands. And to thee is due worship, for thee is praise fitting, for there is none other God but thee, Lord of all, etc.

Ps. xciii. The Lord is King and hath put on glorious apparel. *We worship thee, O everlasting Being.* The Lord is King . . . becometh thine house, O Lord for ever. *We worship thee, O everlasting Being. No Gloria.*

---

[1] Om. R. C.
[2] Each choir takes two clauses at a time in this Psalm.
[3] R. C. repeats this clause.
[4] R. C. om. this clause.
[5] R. C. om. the farcing.
[6] R. C. adds *Let us pray, peace be with us.*
[7] U. om. *Memorials.*

Ps. cxlviii., cxlix.,[1] cl., cxvii., *without farcing and all under one Gloria. Add,* Glorify the Lord, all the whole earth.* O Giver of light, O Lord, even to thee do we lift up glory. Let us pray, Peace be with us.

Prayer of the Morning Anthem. To thee, O Christ, the true Light, the glorious Brightness who art of the Father, who wast revealed and didst shine forth in the world, for the renewal and salvation of our nature, in the firstfruits which are of us, we lift up praise, and honour, and confession, and worship, at all times, Lord of all, etc.

MORNING ANTHEM *for the day, as in the Khudhra or Geza. They*[2] *repeat it, and say the verse,* Glory be, etc. *The last verses are invariable, and are as follows:—*

From everlasting to everlasting. At the early dawn . . . sons of men *(three verses), as at the ferial service,* page 106.

They[2] *add,* Let us pray, Peace be with us.

Prayer. In the glorious light, O my Lord, of thy revelation, and in the joyful Epiphany[3] of thy coming, which all creatures whom thou hast created look for, and hope for, and expect, make us all in thy lovingkindness and mercies worthy to be glad and have joy, with the true sons of thy mysteries in Jerusalem above, Lord of all, etc.

TISHBUKHTA [4] *by Mar Ephraim the Syrian doctor.* A light hath shone forth to the righteous. And gladness to them that are true of heart.* *Yudh.* Jesus our Lord the Christ. Hath shone forth to us from the bosom of his Father. He hath come and taken us out of darkness. And hath enlightened us with his excellent light.* *Alap.* The day hath shone forth on the sons of men. And the power of darkness hath fled. A light hath shone forth for us from his light. And hath enlightened our eyes which were darkened.* *Shin.* He hath caused his glory to shine forth in the world. And hath enlightened the lowest depths. Death is extinguished and darkness hath

---

[1] R. C.: *Memorials only.*   [2] So U.   [3] Syr.: *Shining forth.*
[4] This Tishbukhta is acrostic, the initial letters giving *Ishu Mshikha (Jesus Christ).* But *Ishu* is not now spelt with an Alap. R. C., A., om. name of author.

fled. And the gates of Sheol are broken.* *Wau.* And he hath enlightened all creatures. Who of old were in darkness. And [1] the dead who lay in the dust arose. And glorified (him) because salvation had come to them.* '*E.* He gave salvation and granted us life. And was exalted to his Father on high. And furthermore he cometh in his great glory. And enlighteneth the eyes of all who have waited for him.* *Mim.* Our King cometh in his great glory. Let us light our lamps and go forth to meet him. And let us be glad in him as he hath been glad in us. And maketh us glad by his excellent light.* *Shin.* Let us lift up glory to his Majesty. And let us all confess his high Father. Whose mercies are many, and [2] who sent him to us. And hath given us hope and salvation.* *Yudh.* His day suddenly shineth forth. And his saints go forth to meet him. And light their torches. All who have laboured and been wearied and have made themselves ready.* *Kheith.* The angels and watchful ones of heaven are glad. in the glory of the just and righteous. And place crowns on their heads. And with one accord sing praises and hallelujahs.* *Alap.* My brethren arise and prepare yourselves. That we may confess our King and our Saviour. Who cometh in his glory and maketh us glad. In his excellent light in the kingdom.

If there be a Sugitha [3] *it is here added.*

Another, by Mar Narsai. [4] The light of Christ's Epiphany. [5] Hath made glad earth and heaven.* Error, like darkness. Had spread over (all) created things. And the light of Christ hath shone forth. And the world hath gotten comfort.* The night is like. Unto the time from Adam till now. And the day of Christ's revelation. Unto the course of hours of the day time.* Our Lord also hath named the morning. The beginning of his preaching. And the evening time, the end. Which giveth the world rest from its labour.* For this

---

[1] U., R. C. om. *And.*   [2] A. om. *And.*
[3] U. only; a special anthem is meant (from the Khudhra or Geza).
[4] R. C. om. name of author.   [5] Syr.: *Shining forth.*

hope were looking. Priests and kings and prophets. And the Creator hath given them rest. In the haven of the day of his revelation.* In his revelation (all) created things rested. Which were troubled by sin. And the world began to meditate. On the consideration of things to come.* He delivered a new Testament. To them that received his teaching. And impressed it with his own blood. That his promises should not lie.* With promises of the kingdom on high. He fixed the course of reasoning beings. And lo, they wait for his revelation. Earthly and heavenly ones.* Now the revelation hath drawn nigh. Of the king who reigneth (and is) of our race. Come let us be ready to see him. With the companies of heavenly beings.* Let us take to ourselves love as oil. For that day which is full of fear. Lest we hear that voice. I know not your deeds.* With the talent of the word of doctrine. May we be paid while we live. That we may be worthy to hear that voice. Come, receive the things promised you.* In the hope of life to come. Let us make fast the ship of our mind. And in love and faith. May we reach the haven of joys.* *They say,* A light hath shone forth to the righteous. And gladness to them that are true of heart.

Another, of the Company of Ananias.[1] O all ye works of the Lord, bless ye the Lord. O ye heavens of the Lord, bless ye the Lord. *Say the first proper farcing from the Khudhra; then*[2] *repeat the above; or,*[3] Praise him and magnify him for ever.* O ye angels of the Lord, bless ye the Lord. O ye waters that be above the heavens, bless, etc.* O all ye powers of the Lord, bless, etc. O ye sun and moon, bless, etc.* O ye stars in heaven, bless, etc. O ye rain and dew, bless, etc.* O all ye winds, bless, etc. O ye fire and heat, bless, etc.* O ye night and day, bless, etc. O ye light and darkness, bless, etc,* O ye cold and heat, bless, etc. O ye snow and ice, bless, etc.*

---

[1] R. C., A. om. these words.   [2] So R. C.
[3] So A., U. Perhaps these words are meant to be said after each couplet.

O ye lightnings and clouds, bless, etc. O all the earth, bless, etc.* O ye mountains and hills, bless, etc. O all that bring forth upon the earth, bless, etc.* O ye seas and rivers, bless, etc. O ye springs of water, bless, etc.* O ye fishes and all that moveth in the waters, bless, etc. O all ye fowls of heaven, bless, etc.* O all ye beasts and cattle, bless, etc. O ye sons of men, bless, etc.* O ye sons of men, bless, etc.[1] O ye house of Israel, bless, etc.* O ye priests of the Lord, bless, etc. O ye servants of the Lord, bless, etc.* O all ye spirits and souls of the righteous, bless, etc. O ye perfect and humble men of heart, bless, etc.* O Ananias, Azarias, and Misael, bless, etc. O ye apostles and prophets, bless, etc.* O ye martyrs of the Lord, bless, etc. O all that stand in the house of the Lord, bless, etc.[1]* We praise and exalt (him) for ever and ever.[2] *Or,* We bless Father, Son, and Holy Ghost, for ever and ever, Amen and Amen.[3] *Repeat the first farcing. Then,*[4] Glory be, etc., *and* From everlasting, *with the second farcing. Repeat* O all ye works, etc. O ye heavens, etc., *and say the third farcing.*

Prayer of the Gloria in excelsis, on Sundays and Feasts of our Lord.[5] We glorify, and exalt, and sing hallelujahs and praises to the hidden and sacred Nature, blessed and incomprehensible, of thy glorious Trinity,[6] and thy lovingkindness to our race we are bound to confess, worship, and glorify at all times, Lord of all, etc.

Tishbukhta.[7] Glory to God in the highest, *thrice.*[8] * And on earth peace.* And a good hope to men.* We worship thee.* We glorify thee.* We exalt thee.* Being who art from eternity.* Hidden and incomprehensible Nature.* Father, Son, and Holy Ghost.* King of kings.*

---

[1] A. om. this clause; but so U., R. C.   [2] So A.; om. R. C.
[3] So U.; om. R. C.   [4] A. om. all the rest.
[5] So R. C.; T. has merely *Prayer of the Gloria in excelsis*; U. merely *Then they pray.*
[6] So T.; U., R. C. om. *and thy loving . . . all times.*
[7] U. ins. rubrick directing that on feasts one clause is to be said in the sanctuary, the next in the nave.   [8] A., R. C. om. *thrice.*

And Lord of lords.* Who dwellest in the excellent light.* Whom no son of man hath seen.* Nor can see.* Who alone art holy.* (And) alone mighty.* (And) alone immortal.* We confess thee.* Through the Mediator of our blessings.* Jesus Christ.* The Saviour of the world.* And the Son of the Highest.* O Lamb of the living God.* Who takest away the sins of the world.* Have mercy upon us.* Thou who sittest at the right hand of thy Father.* Receive our request.* For thou art our God.* And thou art our Lord.* And thou art our King.* And thou art our Saviour.* And thou art the forgiver of our [1] sins.* The eyes of all men hang on thee.* Jesus Christ.* Glory to God thy Father.* And to thee and to the Holy Ghost, for ever, Amen.

On Memorials is said a proper Tishbukhta from the Khudhra, and the prayer before it is that of the season, as at evening service, page 80.

Prayer of HOLY GOD *on Sundays and Feasts.* To thee, O my Lord, and to thy Christ, and to thy living holy, lifegiving and divine Spirit, we lift up praise, honour, confession, and worship, at all times, Lord of all, etc.

On Memorials. Praise to thy Name, and worship to thy Majesty, and continual giving of thanks, are we bound to lift up to thy glorious Trinity, at all times, Lord of all, etc.

The deacon sings, Lift up your voices, etc. *And they reply,* Holy God, etc., *as on ferias,* page 106, *but sung slowly. Then,* Let us pray, Peace be with us. Our Father *farced* (page 1). *They give the kiss of peace.*[2]

Prayer, on Sundays and feasts. O Compassionate one, whose Name is holy, and whose dwelling-place is holy, the place of whose tabernacle is holy; and holy are the exalted hosts who praise thee with holy hallelujahs; who art called holy by spiritual and by earthly beings, with holy voices which cease not; Make holy, O our Lord and our God, the temple of our souls, and purify our thoughts; pardon our trespasses, make white our defilements; and make us, O my Lord, pure

---

[1] A. om. *our.*

[2] So U.; om. R. C.

sanctuaries for thine exalted Godhead, and temples adorned and befitting the honour of the service of thy love, O thou who makest all holy by the power of thy Word, and of thy Spirit, Lord of all, etc.

Another. Holy art thou, O my Lord, continually, and everlastingly glorious. Thou art high and exalted above all, incomprehensibly; thou art worshipped by the watchful ones and men, as Three in One, O great King of glory. O Being who art from everlasting, we confess, worship, and glorify (thee) at all times, Lord of all, etc.

On Memorials. O Compassionate one, *and* Bless, O my Lord, *as on ferias,* page 106.

If the Martyrs' Anthem is said, this prayer is added on Sundays.[1] By the prayer, O my Lord, of the martyrs who desired thee, and the confessors who loved thy Name, and the just who kept thy commandments, and the prophets who announced thy mysteries, and the apostles who preached thy gospel, and the martyrs who suffered for thee, and offered not incense to idols, but to thy holy Name, may the beloved flock of thy pasture be kept from all harm, hidden and open, Lord of all, etc.

Then follow the Martyrs' Anthem and prayers, the prayers for help, and the rest as at the ferial service, pages 107, 108, 16.[2]

Martyrs' Anthem.[3]

Sunday Morning 'Before.'

And ye are all the children of the most Highest. Or,[4] *Ye are the martyrs of the Son and his chosen ones.* The martyrs of the holy Son. In a good course were crowned. By the preaching of the truth. And with

Ps. lxxxii. 6.

---

[1] So T.; om. R. C., U. In practice the Martyrs' Anthem is seldom said on Sundays and festivals. Neither R. C. nor A. give these Anthems for Sundays, but in a few of the fuller manuscripts of the 'Before and after' they are to be found, and they are therefore given here.

[2] But U. says the blessing on Feasts is to be found in the book called Abukhalim (see Glossary).

[3] This and the following anthem are from U.; om. R. C., A.

[4] These alternative headings are not from the Psalter. They are

the angels in heaven. Rejoice and glorify God. Being made intercessors on our behalf.

And praise becometh well the just. Famed and holy martyrs. Athletes of the faith. Beg for mercies from God. That he may send us help. And strengthen our weakness. By the overflowing mercies of his lovingkindness. Ps. xxxiii. 1.

And sing[1] *lustily with the voice.* Tell me, martyrs, for whom. Ye endure torments and stripes. And have reckoned death but as sleep? We heard that our Saviour said. He who shall love his life[2] for my sake. Hath everlasting life. Ps. xxxiii. 3.

Let thy merciful kindness, O Lord, be upon us. May that loving-kindness which preserved. The boy David from Saul. Keep the Church and its children. May priests have concord. Among kings may reconciliation prevail. And may martyrs have the crown of (their) confession. Ps. xxxiii. 21.

He divided[3] *the rock and the water gushed out.* Moses the Captain of the Hebrews. Caused water to gush out from the stone. And gave the rebellious people to drink. How much (more) then shall the bones. Of the martyrs which are placed in the Churches. Cause help to gush out to the sons of men? Ps. lxxviii. 21.

Open me the gates of righteousness. Open is the gate of Paradise. And the righteous enter in and dwell. By the fountain of help. And the Right hand receiveth them. Which planted Paradise. And placeth crowns on their heads. Ps. cxviii. 19.

---

headed *Of the text*, i.e. from the Bible (outside the Psalter), but many are not from the Bible at all. The style of these two anthems is very different from the other Martyrs' Anthems, and they seem to be of a later date.

[1] Syr.: *tell*.

[2] Syr.: *soul*—paraphrased from St. Matthew x. 39, and St. John xii. 25. The second *life* is a different word, as in St. John.

[3] Psalter: *struck*.

Unto the godly hath shone forth light in the darkness. With light which shone from the sun. As with a garment brighter than snow. Are the righteous clothed in Eden. And are glad and rejoice and exult. Among the trees of Paradise. When they hear the voice of the Son.

Ps. cxii. 4.

The light which shone forth for the righteous. Lamps of resplendent light. The martyrs hold in their hands. And wait for the Bridegroom of the Highest. That they may go in with him to the bridechamber. And their lamps go not out. On which their necks sprinkle blood.

Ps. xcvii. 11.

Look unto him and trust in him. Ye martyrs saw Christ. Bearing his cross[1] on his shoulder. And ye bore your crosses.[1] (And) went out to the four quarters (of the world). And made disciples of (all) creation. In the name of the Trinity.

Ps. xxxiv. 5.

They are not in the labours of other folk. The just who lay down in thy hope. Sleep and are in peace, and at rest. And the watchful ones keep their bodies. And power descendeth from on high. And ever visiteth their bones. Until the day of resurrection.

Ps. lxxiii. 5.

For at the head of the book it is written of me. The company of Ananias in the furnace. Wrote an epistle to Daniel. Come, arise with us in prayer. Daniel wrote its answer. Fear ye not the fire. Which the persecutors have kindled for you.

Ps. xl. 10.

O come, hearken, and I will tell you. Tell us, O Daniel, Child beloved of God. How thou didst see the Son. I saw him flying on the clouds. And like unto the Ancient of days. And his dominion is heaven and earth.

Ps. lxvi. 14.

His tongue talketh of judgment. Tell us, O Robber. Of the brightness of Paradise. And show us the tree of life. That we may pluck a benefit from it. Love, and hope, and salvation. An offering to the King of kings.

Ps. xxxvii. 31.

---

[1] These are two different words in the Syriac.

The king's daughter stood in glory. The Church is like unto Paradise. And the martyrs within her to trees. And their deaths to precious buds. And blessed is he who hath drawn near. To the bones of the saints. And hath received help from them. _{Ps. xlv. 10.}

And the queen on her right hand. The Church went forth with hosannas. To meet the heavenly Bridegroom. And spake with him and said unto him. Come to me, for I have loved thee. And cast off Sion which hath hated thee. And I and my children will worship thee. _{Ib.}

How good and beautiful. How seemly it is to sing praises. In this holy house. In which are prophets and apostles. And martyrs, and priests, and teachers. And in which is set up the Holy Table. For the pardon of the children of Adam. _{Ps. cxxxiii. 1.}

As an eagle that flieth over his nest. Ye martyrs are like eagles. And more harmless than doves. And lighter than air. When on the sea he calleth, ye answer. And when on dry land, ye neglect (him) not. May your prayer be a wall to us. _{Deut. xxxii. 11.}

Stretch forth thy hand and save me. O our Lord, O our Lord, was the cry. Of Simon Peter in the waves. Deliver me, O my Lord, for lo, I sink. Our Saviour stretched forth his right hand. And held him by the hand, and said unto him. Be strong, and be not in doubt. _{Ps. cxxxviii. 7.}

In the days of old. A cherub with a sword and spear. Went around Paradise. Lest Adam, who had sinned, should enter in. And our Lord opened it by his cross. And prophets and apostles entered in. And Adam entered in as the son of the King. _{Ps. xliv. 1.}

Give ear, Lord, unto my prayer. On the mount of Horeb, Elijah. Prayed before God. For the people who had trodden down the law. And he bound the doors of heaven. That rain should not come down in its season. On a people who had offended and done wickedly. _{Ps. lxxxvi. 6.}

He spread on them a cloud, and overshadowed them. A cloud of fire went. Before the rebellious people. When they went out of Egypt. And while they rejected Christ. The holy martyrs received him. And lo, their memorial is in creation.

Ps. cv. 38.

How good and beautiful. How beautiful are the companies. And how sweet the voices of the choirs. Of the martyrs who are laid in the churches. And who ask for mercies and compassion. And forgiveness of trespasses and sins. For the children of Adam (who was) of dust.

Ps. cxxxiii. 1.

For he hath done a marvellous thing. That which was wrought, etc., *as above*, page 111.

Ps. xcviii. 1.

O hear ye this, all ye people. In the morning faithful Shmuni, etc., *as above*, page 111.

Ps. xlix. 1.

And your prayers be on all of us. Gadai and Maccabæus, etc., *as above*, page 111.

Like as the arrow in the hand of the giant. How hard was the arrow, etc., *as above*, page 112.

Ps. cxxvii. 5.

There shall I make the horn to spring forth for David. From the house of David and Abraham. The Creator chose a Virgin. And caused his hidden power to dwell in her. And by the power of the Holy Ghost. She conceived and bore Christ. The Judge of the heights and the depths.

Ps. cxxxii. 18.

Glory be, etc. Glory be to thee, O my Lord, for that thou wast pleased. With the fragrance of the death of thy saints. The martyrs who suffered for thee. And because they loved thee on the earth. Thou didst exalt them in heaven. Glory be to thee, who exaltest thy servants.

From everlasting to everlasting. Above in the heights among the watchful ones. Is appointed thy memorial, O our father.[1] With the just who prevailed and conquered. And also with the martyrs who were crowned. Christ the King, whom thou didst love. Maketh thee an heir of the bride-chamber on high.

---

[1] Or *Awa.*

And let all the people say Amen and Amen. O our Lord may thy kingdom come. And may thy will be done on earth. As it is in heaven. And give us the bread of our need. And lead us not into temptation. But deliver us from the Evil one.* On the first day¹ there is no affliction. Nor torments for the wicked. The fire of Gehenna is extinguished. And every one remaineth at ease. And all cry with one voice. Great is the first day of the week.* Great is the first day of the week. And great is it in heaven. For on it our Lord rose from the grave. And on it the departed are quickened. And put off mortality. And put on the vesture of the resurrection.

Ps. cvi. 46.

Martyrs' Anthem.

Sunday Morning 'After.'

He executeth judgment for them that are despised. Or,² *Verily, verily I say unto you, He that heareth you, heareth me; and he that despiseth you, despiseth me; and he that despiseth me, despiseth him that sent me.* Your labours are not despised, O martyrs. And Christ the King, whom ye loved, passeth not away. On the earth are laid your bones, for ye have conquered. And in the book of life are your names, O friends of the Son.

Ps. cxlvi. 6.
St. Luke x. 16.

For the glory of thy name. Or, *Because they saw that the world passeth away and is destroyed, and that its desirable things are as vanity, and are destroyed and come to nought and are lost, they all said to one another, Provide neither gold, nor silver, nor brass in your purses.* Not for the wealth of the world have we loved thee. Say the martyrs to Christ with openness of face.³ But because we have truly learnt. That thy kingdom and Godhead may not be fathomed.

Ps. lxxix. 9.
St. Matt. x. 9.

---

¹ Sunday.   ² See note, p. 172.   ³ Confidence.

And sing lustily with the voice. Or, *Because we have a God who helpeth us, and in the name of his authority we work mighty deeds and signs, and in his Name we throw down high walls.* Ps. xxxiii. 3. The martyrs say one to another, Come, let us go forth. And bring to nought the error which hath waxed strong in the four quarters (of the world). And in the Name of Jesus we will reprove Satan. And like the walls of Jericho he will fall before us.

They sing among the mountains. Or, *A report went forth and a decree was heard, Whoso is a Christian, and secretly worshippeth God, shall have his limbs cut off one by one, and shall be cast out to the mountains and hills and seas and islands.* Ps. civ. 12. Among the mountains and hills the king commanded. That the limbs of the blessed martyrs should be cut off. And the Holy Ghost entered with them to the contest. And gave them the victory in the judgment before the persecutors.

The land shall give her increase. Or, *In the beginning the Lord blessed the earth, which was cursed by the blood of Abel; and when the blood of the saints was shed, it was drunken therewith, and was blessed that it might give good fruits to God.* Ps. lxxxv. 12. The earth which was drunken with the blood of the martyrs. Shall give fruits thirtyfold, and sixtyfold, and an hundredfold. And in the Church, which hath carried their bones in processions with honour. May the peace of our Lord reign for ever.

The righteous cried, and the Lord heard them and delivered them. Or, *And they fixed their gaze above, and worshipped the living Father, and lifted up praise to the Son, and entreated the Holy Ghost to weave a crown and place it on their heads.* Ps. xxxiv. 17. The martyrs cried from the fire to God. For thy sake we die, come thou and help us. And send a watcher from on high to us. The fire saw the spiritual one, and sprinkled dew.

Look unto him and trust in him. Or, *They cease not from fighting with us, and give no sleep to our eyes; and we put not our armour off from us, and deny not Christ the Son, who suffered for us, and we fear not the fire nor the sword, until the evening of death come.* Ps. xxxiv. 5. The martyrs saw the terrible swords glittering, and the slayers threatening them, and thus they spoke. By the power which came down and abode on Mount Sinai, and the staff that divided the sea in the hands of Moses. And by him who said, Eli, Eli, lama sabachthani. We will not deny Christ, who suffered for us.

For thy sake we have been killed daily. Or, *Who shall tell your victories, and relate your deeds, O famous martyrs who stood mightily in the contest, and conquered the Evil one valiantly, and endured bitter torments?*   Ps. xliv. 22.   O martyrs killed for the hope of innocence. May your prayer be a wall to us at all times. And by that power by which ye conquered in the contest. May we conquer the Enemy who fighteth with us.

His salvation is nigh them that fear him. Or, *The saints heard that voice, and the martyrs hearkened: Whoso confesseth me before the judges of this world, and beareth his cross, and followeth me uprightly, I (will) confess him before God and them that minister to him.*   Ps. lxxxv. 9.   The martyrs drew near to entreat God, and this entreaty the just offered to him who is good. By the right hand which divided the sea before the people, and made firm the waves under the feet of Simon Peter. By the majesty which was buffeted in the judgment-hall. Send not the rod of wrath on the inhabited (world).

I will speak peace of thee. Or, *Thine is the sword, and dire sufferings and torments for a season, and ours are our necks,[1] and the blood of our lives[2] until the evening of death come.*   Ps. cxxii. 8.   Peace to the Company that was crowned. In the days of Sapor, the king of the city of Lidan. In tens they came in (to be slain) by the sword. And their mouth ceased not (to sing) praise.

Peace be in thy strength. Or, *The heathen king deceived himself, and trusted that by shedding the conquering blood of the famous martyrs the power of Christ the King would be conquered, and his (own) name magnified;*   Ps. cxxii. 7.   and he began to put to death the famous martyrs for the Name of their

---

[1] Syr.: *neck.*   [2] Syr.: *soul.*

Lord. Peace to the Company that was crowned. In the days of Chosroes, the king in the country of Persia.[1] And the blessed ones were led as lambs to the slaughter. For their Lord, whose love they desired and whose Name they confessed.

And I spake of peace. Or, *My peace I give unto you, my peace I leave with you.* Peace to the Company that was crowned. In the days of Mar Tahmazgard, in the city of Seleucia.[2] One hundred and fifty thousand were they in number. Who received the testimony and were given the crown.

<small>Ps. cxx. 6.
St. John xiv. 27.</small>

He sent a man before them. Or, *Behold, I send you forth as lambs in the midst of wolves; be ye therefore wise as serpents and harmless as doves.* As the herald who is sent before a king. His Lord sent Mar Adai to the country of Persia.[1] And like ravening wolves they went out to meet him. And became harmless lambs at his prayers.

<small>Ps. cv. 17.
St. Matt. x. 16.</small>

For thou art my hope from the womb. Or, *My soul is exceeding sorrowful, even unto death; tarry ye here, and watch with me. And give me peace, and go ye in peace.* How sad was holy Mar Shimun.[3] When he said farewell to his city. By God I adjure you, my beloved. Gain ye your lives by fasting and prayers.

<small>Ps. lxxi. 4, 5.
St. Matt. xxvi. 38.</small>

And from the deep of his heart. Or, *The light of his countenance was darkened, and he was disfigured by sadness,* for that he was scarcely delivered from the snares of the Evil one, and his eyes were fixed on high, as he asked for salvation in his prayer. How sad was the firstborn Christopher. When the prison-house detained him amidst the harlots. And he fixed his eyes on heaven, saying. Grant me, O my Lord, a terrible appearance, that they look not on me.

<small>Ps. lxiv. 6.</small>

He shall be like a tree planted by the streams of water. Or, *This is he who was chosen from the belly, and sanctified from the womb, and was filled with the grace of the Holy Ghost.* Cyriac is like a sweet cluster of

<small>Ps. i. 3.</small>

---

[1] Syr.: *Paris*. [2] Syr.: *Slukh*. [3] Mar Shimun (Simon) Bar Ṣabaʻi?

grapes. And his mother is like the vine which bare it. Whose root is in earth and whose branches are in heaven. And its fruit giveth help to the sons of men.

How good and beautiful. Or, *How fitting and beautiful it is when the golden mouth reproveth the heathen king.* Ps. cxxxiii. 1. *Thy kingdom and thy dominion abide not, but pass away, and thy diadem and thy crown are destroyed, and thy authority cometh to nought.* How fitting it was when the faithful Julitta. Bare her beloved Mar Cyriac. When he reproved the heathen king, and said unto him. Thy diadem and thy dominion come to nought, and thy hope is destroyed.

When brethren dwell together in unity. Or, *Behold me and the sons which thou hast given me; I offer them as propitiatory sacrifices to thy honour, and as sweet clusters of the vine to thy glory.* Ib. How fitting was it when faithful Shmuni. Took the seven clusters, the sons of the kingdom. And encouraged them one by one, saying. Draw near and accept the terrible sword, and take to thyself a crown.

Let them rejoice in his joy. Or, *Lay up for yourselves a treasure in heaven, where moth doth not corrupt, and where thieves do not break through and steal.* Ps. lxviii. 3. St. Matt. vi. 20. Lo, everlasting joy is laid up on high. For the just who have served and have wrought well in the vineyard of the Son. Come, my brethren, let us walk in love towards them. And reach their habitations by faith.

Out of the hand of the ungodly and evil man. Or, *He was brought as a lamb to the slaughter, and as a sheep before her shearer he was dumb, and opened not his mouth in his humiliation.* Ps. lxxi. 3. Isa. liii. 7. Killed through envy by his wicked brother, was Abel, the firstborn of old of the martyrs. And his blood crieth out on the earth with groaning. And cried like thunder when he was slain. And lo, his Lord, who saw his open oppression, giveth him joy alway in his kingdom.

He rode upon the cherubims, and did fly. Or, *They are laid in the earth, and their eyes are fixed on high, and they wait for Jesus their Lord coming on the clouds of heaven, that he may give a resurrection to the departed.* Ps. xviii. 10. Above the splendour of the clouds, is borne in procession. The Son of the King, who cometh to make the dead alive again. And the just hear the sound of the trumpet[1] that (goeth) before him. And they are clothed with a vesture of glory, and go forth to meet him.

The Lord upholdeth the righteous. Or, *As the fragrance of sweet incense and spices the savour of their deeds is wafted on, and help welleth forth from the bones of the saints who loved their Lord.* A pillar full of compassion was Mar Augin. And a tree whose smell was pleasant was Mar Kudhahwai. And an olive tree with beauteous branches was Mar Babai. May their prayer be a wall to us at all times.

Ps. xxxvii. 17.

He flew upon the wings of the wind. Or, *Hail to the athlete of righteousness, for that he endured, and was not made careless by the snares of the Evil one, who thirsteth for blood. Like a swift deer ran.* St. George the illustrious before the persecutors. And the blessed one walked on nails of iron. That by his prayers he might give peace to the world which was in confusion.

Ps. xviii. 10.

For that he is thy Lord, worship thou him. Or, *Heaven and earth rejoice in him, and Bethlehem, and the Wise men and the shepherds, and Mary his mother, and St. John who preached his Epiphany from one end of the world to the other.* O Mary, mother, etc., page 36.

Ps. xlv. 12.

The hope of all the ends of the earth. Or, *And O thou Hope of all creatures, of the nations far and near, bless thy servants, and keep them from harm, and pour forth on them from thy gift the dew of thy mercies.* O Christ, the hope and boast of our nature. Turn to us by the prayer of Mary who bare thee. And by the prayer of the prophets, and apostles, and teachers. Make to pass away from us the destruction which threateneth us.

Ps. lxv. 5.

From the rising up of the sun unto the going down thereof. Or, *As the fragrance, etc.*[2] As a pure pearl without spot. Shone the beauty of Mar Saurishu

Ps. l. 1.

---

[1] Syr.: *horn.*   [2] As above.

in the four quarters (of the world). And as the fragrance of sweet incense and spices. The savour of Raban[1] Hurmizd is wafted through all countries.

Let thy servants praise thee, O Lord. Or, *How good and beautiful and becoming it is when brethren dwell in unity, and order their wills in concord before God.* Ps. cxlv. 10. Cf. Ps. cxxxiii. 1. Let both the brothers praise thee, O Lord. Mar Akha[2] and Mar Yukhanan,[3] the blessed pair. Who in one yoke wrought well and served. May their prayer be a wall for us at all seasons.

And we were counted as sheep appointed to be slain. First with the sword the proud men killed him. And secondly he was fried in the fire by the wicked. And thirdly the impious ones ground him in the mill. And fourthly he was boiled in oil by the oppressors.* And fifthly the blood-shedders fried him in the pan. And sixthly he was stoned with stones by the accursed ones. And seventhly they crushed his bones and cast him out. May our Lord make us worthy to have joy among their companies. Ps. xliv. 22.

Righteous and upright. ' The king Constantine went forth to war. And spake thus in his prayer before God. When I return in conquest and victory. I will reverence[4] the cross of Christ the King. Deut. xxxii. 4.

As a city surrounded by a wall. As a merchant our Lord entered creation. And bought therein a holy Church, and dwelt within it. And raised up in it four wondrous scribes. The altar, and the priesthood,[5] and the cross, and baptism. Ps. cxxii. 3.

In the seas and in all deep places. I passed through the seas and trode on the waves. Yet my eyes have seen nought like the ship of Mar Anthony. Which bare prophets and guided apostles. Which bare martyrs and confessors, and went to Eden. Ps. cxxxv. 6.

---

[1] *i.e.* Monk.   [2] *i.e.* Brother.   [3] John.
[4] Syr.: *I worship.*   [5] Syr. : *priest.*

From the mouth of young men and boys. Peace to thee, O martyr Mar Pithiun. Who wast a father to many in the faith. Peace to thee, who didst love Christ. With a pure and true heart and perfect love.

<small>Ps. viii. 2.</small>

My spirit hath rejoiced in God my Saviour. Mary, who bare Christ, rejoiced. And John when he baptized him in the river Jordan. Heaven and earth and all that is in them rejoice. In the Star which shone forth out of Jacob for the salvation of all.

<small>St. Luke i. 47.</small>

Glory be, etc. Peace to your camp, O blessed ones. Merchants bearing life to the sons of men. Open the treasure of your prayers to the needy. And preserve the country where ye dwell from harm.

From everlasting to everlasting. Beg for us all of thy Lord. O our famous and holy father,[1] the friend of the Son. That by thy prayers may be helped and saved. All who are afflicted and distressed, and who take refuge in thee.

And let all the people say Amen and Amen. O God, who didst have pity on Nineveh, have pity on us. And cease not to look on our evil generation. For if thou shuttest thy door in the face of us sinners. To whose door shall we go and knock, O thou Friend of men?* Let the voice of our prayer, O Lord, be. As the fragrance of sweet incense before thy greatness. And may our request be the key of the heavenly treasure. To open and bring forth help to the sons of men.* On the first day[2] there is no affliction or torment. For the wicked who have transgressed and wrought wickedness in their deeds. The fire and flame of Gehenna is extinguished. And every one remaineth at ease, and confesseth the Lord.* Blessed is the first and holy day.[2] For on it our Lord rose from the grave in great glory. And on it the departed arise in the quickening. And put off mortality and put on glory.

<small>Ps. cvi. 46.</small>

---

[1] Or *Awa*.   [2] Sunday.

COMPLINE

Hulala 3 (Ps. xxii. to xxx. inclusive).
Prayer. For thy nature, page 95.
Ps. lxxxviii. *No Gloria or farcing.*
Prayer. Thee, who art hidden in thy being, page 160.
Ps. xc. *No Gloria or farcing.*
Prayer. Thee, who art hidden from all, page 159.
Ps. cxxx. and cxliii. *No Gloria or farcing.*

Prayer. Thee, who dost form us in thy lovingkindness, and dost cause us to die in thy justice, and dost quicken us in the overflowing multitude of thy mercy, we confess, worship, and glorify, at all times, Lord of all, etc.

He says one of the Anthems of the departed (pp. 190 *sqq.*).

Prayer. May thy compassion, O my Lord, rise before us, and may thy lovingkindness pardon our sins, and may the everlasting mercies of thy glorious Trinity come to the assistance of thy worshippers who call (on thee) and beseech thee, at all times, Lord of all, etc.

Canon: *to the tune* God is worshipped.

Bow down thine ear, O Lord, and answer me. In that thy judgment, O Greatest of judges. When thy justice hath dominion over all. May thy compassion intercede for us. And thy lovingkindness stand before us.   s. lxxxv . .

---

[1] From U. This is extremely rare as a separate service, but it is found in some manuscripts of the *Before and After;* also as a separate book (Syr.: *Ṣuba'tha*). For its use as amalgamated with Evening Service on Memorials, see page 82 ; for its use in the Fast, see below, page 212. There is much confusion on the subject.

Glory be to the Father, and to the Son, and to the Holy Ghost. At the door of thy mercies, O our Lord Jesus. Thy servants knock, beseeching. And asking of thee compassion, and mercies, and forgiveness of trespasses. Return answer to them when they pray.* By the prayer of Mary the blessed mother, and John, who baptized his Lord. The apostles, who made disciples of all nations, and the teachers, who preached the truth. And the martyrs, who endured all afflictions, for the love of Christ the King. May thy worshippers be preserved.

TISHBUKHTA. At that hour when thy judgment-seat instituteth the searching. Enter not, O Lord, into judgment with thy servants.* At that hour when thy will visiteth them that have lain down. Cast us not out, O Lord, into outer darkness.* O Christ, who forsakest not any who cry to thee. In thy mercy reject not the request of thy worshippers.

The deacon says the KARUZUTHA. Let us all stand up, etc. (page 6).

O Living one, who didst descend among the dead, and didst preach a good hope to the souls that were held in Sheol, we, etc.

O thou by whose wounds our scars have been healed, and who by thy death didst slay the Slayer, we, etc.

O, thou at whose passion the lights (of heaven) were darkened, and all creatures clothed themselves with weeping and sorrow, we, etc.

O thou at whose crucifixion the spiritual beings groaned, when the will of thy Father restrained them, that they should not destroy them that crucified thee, we, etc.

O thou who by thy death didst burst the graves, and didst quicken the dead, to reprove them that crucified thee, we, etc.

O thou who didst mingle thy blood with our blood, and didst redeem our trespasses with the sacrifice of thyself on Golgotha, we, etc.

For the welfare of our holy fathers NN,[1] and all those who serve under them, we, etc.

---

[1] Patriarch, Metropolitan, and Bishop of the diocese.

O merciful God, who in mercy governest all, we, etc.

O thou whom the angels of light glorified in heaven at thy death, and at whose slaying the earth was sad, and in whose resurrection it rejoiced, we, etc.

O thou good Shepherd, who didst give up thy life[1] for thy sheep, and didst save them from death by thy blood, save, O my Lord, our life from the Evil one, and have mercy upon us.

Prayer. Forgive, O my Lord, our trespasses in thy compassion, wipe out our offences and make them to pass away in the overflowing multitude of thy mercy, O thou who forgivest trespasses and sins, Lord of all, etc.

Another. Blessed and adorable, page 153.

He says the MADRASHA (pp. 192 *sqq.*).

Prayer. Thee, the Quickener of the dead, and the good Hope of them that are buried, we confess, and worship, and glorify, at all times, Lord of all, etc.

Ps. xci., *farced alternately, after each clause, with* Protect me, O God, *and* From the Evil one and his hosts. *No Gloria.*

Ps. cl. and cxvii., *both farced after each clause with* Glory be to thee, O God. *They say,* Glory be to the Father, etc.* *Glory be to thee, O God.* From everlasting to everlasting, Amen.* *Glory be to thee, O God.*

TISHBUKHTA. Glory to thee, O my Lord, page 221.

Prayer. Thee, O Giver of our life, and good Hope of our souls, we confess, and worship, and glorify, at all seasons and times, Lord of all, etc.

Ps. cxxi., *farced after each clause with* Preserve me, O God. *No Gloria.*

TISHBUKHTA. Glory be to thee, O God, page 215.

Prayer. May the mercies, O my Lord, which formed me without entreaty, beg and beseech for me of thy justice in the great and glorious day when thy greatness is revealed from heaven, O just Judge, who art full of mercy, and who forgivest trespasses and sins, Lord of our death and of our life, Father, Son, and Holy Ghost, for ever. *Amen.*

---

[1] Syr.: *soul.*

Ps. li., *farced alternately, after each clause, with* O Christ the King, have mercy upon us, *and* O Christ the King, glory to thy Name. (*In the last clause substitute* offerings *for* young bullocks.[1]) Then, O be favourable and gracious unto my miserable soul. *O Christ the King, have, etc.** And build thou its walls, which have been thrown down and have fallen by wickedness and sin. *O Christ the King, glory, etc.** Then shalt thou be pleased with the sacrifices of righteousness, and with perfect burnt-offerings. *O Christ the King, have, etc.** And then shall they lift up to thee the fruits of glory and praise. *O Christ the King, glory, etc.** Glory be, etc. *O Christ the King, have, etc.** From everlasting, etc. *O Christ the King, glory, etc.** Have mercy upon me, O God, after thy lovingkindness. *O Christ the King, have, etc.** And according to the multitude of thy mercies do away mine offences. *O Christ the King, glory, etc.*

TISHBUKHTA. O Christ, who in thy mercies hast compassion on sinners. Turn to the prayer of thy weak servants.* And as thou hast kept us in the day which is past. May thy lovingkindness keep us in the night which is full of terror.* And drive away from us the Evil one, our Enemy. And may thy cross be a wall to our souls.* And waken us when we sleep in the multitude of thy compassion. That we may stand and glorify thee, who in thy goodness dost preserve us.* Let us kneel and worship thee. For ever and ever, Amen.

They proceed. In thy cross I have taken refuge, O our Saviour. Under its wings protect me from the Evil one and his host.* With the publican we ask mercy. Have compassion on us, and have mercy upon us.* O our Lord, with thy right hand overthrow Satan. Who maketh (men) drunken without wine, and causeth them to slip without mud.* At thy hands, O God, whose mercies are manifold. May our correction be, and not at the hands of man.* O Christ, who forsakest not any who call to thee. In thy mercies reject not the request of thy worshippers.

---

[1] So some copies of the Syriac Psalter.

TISHBUKHTA *by the holy Mar Ephraim.* Grant me, O my Lord, that if I wake. I may stand watchfully before thee. And that if I lie down. My sleep may be without sin.* And if I grow slothful in watching. May I be pardoned by thy lovingkindness. And if I sin in lying down. May thy compassion forgive me.* And by the cross of thy humiliation. Grant me restful sleep. And deliver me from evil dreams. And from abominable phantoms.[1]* And in peaceful sleep. Lead me all the night. And let not the Evil ones have dominion over me. And thoughts full of wickedness.* And from hateful desires. May I be delivered by thy body with which thou hast fed me. And may I lie down and rest in quietness. And may sleep be my preserver.* And make the wall of thy mercies to surround. The soul which is thy image. And may thy right hand overshadow. The body which thy hands have fashioned.* And surround me with the wall of thy mercies. As with a mighty shield. That when (my) body is at rest and in quiet. Thy power may be its preserver.* And as the fragrance of incense. May my sleep be before thy greatness. And let not the Evil one approach my bed. By the supplication of her who bare thee.* And by thy sacrifice for us. Stay Satan, that he harm us not. And fulfil in me thy promise. And by thy cross preserve my life.* That when I wake I may confess thee. For that thou hast shown thy love to my feebleness. And that I may lift up glory to thee and to thy Father. And to the Holy Ghost who sanctifieth.* Both now and always. For ever and ever.

They say, Holy God (p. 10), *and* Our Father.

Prayer. May thy living and life-giving voice, O my Lord, which called and raised Lazarus unto a resurrection for a season, call and raise thy servants (to be) on thy right hand, in the great and glorious day when thy justice is revealed from heaven, O just Judge, who art full of mercy, and who forgivest trespasses and sins, Lord of all, etc.

---

[1] Syr.: *similitudes.*

Another. Quicken them that have fallen asleep, in thy compassion, and preserve them that are alive, in the overflowing abundance of thy mercy; and grant a good resurrection to the departed who have fallen asleep in the hope of the quickening, that they may lift up to thee praise, and honour, and confession, and worship, at all times, Lord of all, etc.

Or this. Be with us, O my Lord, continually, in thy mercies, and lead us according to the goodwill of thy Godhead, and protect and help our life under the wings of thy care; and save and rescue our bodies and our souls from the Evil one and his hosts, at all seasons and times, Lord of all, etc.

Then follow the prayers for help, and the rest, page 16.

ANTHEMS OF THE DEPARTED AND MADRASHI AT COMPLINE

SUNDAY

Bow down thine ear, O Lord, and answer me. O Christ the Son, who didst come for our salvation. That thou mightest renew the image of Adam which was destroyed. And didst put on our flesh,[1] and in it didst save our race. And didst give us a good expectation of the resurrection of the dead. In thy lovingkindness pardon thy servants in the day of thy coming.

Ps. lxxxvi. 1.

For thy lovingkindness, O God. In thy lovingkindness thou didst create our race in the beginning. And didst clothe it with excellent glory in Paradise. And because it did foolishly, and sinned and fell from glory. Thou didst send thy beloved Son to us. And he gave us in his compassion the promised life which hath no end.

Ps. xxv. 6.

For I put my trust in thee. In the abundance of thy mercy I put my trust, O God, and beseech thy lovingkindness. Give me in thy mercies forgiveness of (my) trespasses. By which I offend before thee. And (may) peace and tranquillity lead me all (my) days.

Ps. xxxi. 16.

---

[1] Syr.: *body.*

Give ear, Lord, unto my prayer. At the time when thou callest the dead from the graves. That thou mayest pay to every man according to his deeds. The books are opened to bear witness to (men's) works. And he that openeth (his) mouth[1] fleeth, and is hidden. Let thy mercies pity thy servant, that he may not utterly perish. Ps. lxxxvi. 6.

Until thou have mercy upon us. At the door of thy mercy I knocked. That I might enter, but thy justice answereth me not. In thy mercies have pity on me, for as the prophet I cry. That if thou judgest justly, O my God. Our humanity cannot be justified in the terrible judgment. Ps. cxxiii. 2.

Let us go before him with praise. Let us all offer praise to God. In the memorial of Mary, the mother of Christ. And in her name let us take refuge, that we may receive help. And by her prayers may our congregation be preserved from the harm (wrought by) the Apostate. Who hateth our nature. Ps. xcv. 2.

Seek the Lord and be strong. O saints, prophets, apostles, and teachers. And confessors, and martyrs, and priests, and monks. Beseech for us all of Christ, who gave you the victory. That by your prayers we may receive from his treasury. An answer to all our petitions in the way that may best help us. Ps. cv. 4.

Glory be, etc. Glory to thee, Jesus, our victorious King. Who by thy cross hast saved our race from error. May thy great power renew our nature.[2] And may death be brought to naught, and the quickening reign. And may we be worthy of mercies by thy will, O King the Quickener.

From everlasting, etc. O Compassionate one, whose door is open to the penitent. And who careth that sinners should repent. Pardon my trespasses and make my offences to pass away. And grant and vouchsafe that I may inherit the kingdom. In the great day when thou comest with all thy saints.

---

[1] To make excuses for himself?   [2] Syr.: *form.*

MADRASHA. *Antiphon.* O just Judge, who hast no respect of persons. Make me worthy in thy mercies to see thee in the day of judgment. *Verses.* O thou who helpest me, and art full of mercies, have compassion on me when I am lost. And grant me to have a share among the companies of the saints.* In lovingkindness thou hast fashioned our dust, and hast called us thine image. In thy mercies mingle our lives with the life which endeth not.

MONDAY

Praise the Lord, O ye righteous. The souls of the righteous are in the hands of the Lord. For they loved him, and believed him, and kept his commandments.
Ps. xxxiii. 1.

O glorify him with a new song of praise. Because thou didst please Christ, he hath taken thee from the world. That thou mightest go and have joy in the bridechamber of the kingdom.
Ps. xcvi. 1.

God is my hope, even from my youth. My hope from my youth is he who quickeneth me. That in the day of thy coming I may stand and confess thee.
Ps. lxxi. 4.

These pass away, but thou endurest. This world now passeth away. Come, let us beg for mercies and forgiveness of trespasses.
Ps. cli. 26.

Both behind and before. All generations and families of the house of Adam. Look to, and wait for the Epiphany of thy coming.
Ps. cxxxix. 4.

Both small and great. Lo, all the departed [1] have lain down in thy hope. That by thy glorious resurrection thou mayest raise them in glory.
Ps. cxv. 13.

O hear ye this, all ye peoples. Adam among the dead was made subject to death. For eating of the tree took away his independence of it.[2]
Ps. xlix. 1.

---

[1] This word is only used of the faithful departed.
[2] Syr.: *its power* or *his power.*

He lifted up his voice, and the earth was moved. Adam among the dead heard a voice saying. Be of good courage, for the penalty is taken away by the Son.   Ps. xlvi. 6.

Blessed is he in whom thou art well pleased. Blessed is he whose countenance shineth.[1] In the hour when the judgment seat of the kingdom is set.   Ps. lxv. 4.

All ye servants of God. Famous priests and holy nation. Pray for me, that I may go (hence) and be accepted.   Ps. lxvi. 14.

Turn thee unto me and have mercy upon me. At that hour when thy judgment seat is set for the searching. Enter not into judgment, O Lord, with thy servants.   Ps. xxv. 15.

And show some token upon me for good. In that hour when thy will visiteth them that have lain down. Cast us not out, O Lord, into outer darkness.   Ps. lxxxvi. 17.

Open me the gates of righteousness. O Gate of truth, which art open to them that are lost. Call us to enter into thy treasury above.   Ps. cxviii. 19.

Unto the godly hath shone forth a light in the darkness. Make thy light, O our Lord, to dwell in our souls. And bring to nought among us the wars of the Crafty one.   Ps. cxii. 4.

By day and by night. May the prayer of the Virgin be a wall to us. And drive away from us the wars of the Crafty one.   Ps. xlii. 3.

Seek the Lord and be strengthened. Prophets and apostles and martyrs and teachers. Seek of God mercies for the world.   Ps. cv. 4.

At all seasons and times. O our holy father,[2] beseech Christ. That he may make his peace to dwell in the four quarters (of the world).

Beg of the Lord, and pray before him. Ask of thy Lord for us, O martyr George. Compassion and mercies and forgiveness of trespasses.   Ps. xxxvii. 7.

---

[1] Syr.: *shone*.   [2] Or *Awa*.

Glory be to the Father, and to the Son, and to the Holy Ghost. Praise to thee, Jesus our Saviour. For death is in thy hands, and life at thy will.

MADRASHA. *Antiphon.* May our Lord, whose cross thou didst confess. Give rest to thy spirit, O our brother. And when he cometh in great glory. May he give thee joy with him in the kingdom. *Verses.* O our brother, go thou in peace. May our Lord be with thee. May the cherub who keepeth Paradise. Open the door before thee.* In the service wherein I have served with you. Let not my love be forgotten by your love. And when ye stand in the sanctuary. Remember me in prayer.

TUESDAY

O Lord God of my salvation. O Lord God, the Lord of death and mortality. May thy sweet Spirit lead me. In the way of life. When thou comest in thy kingdom.
Ps. lxxxviii. 1.

I will alway bless the Lord. Blessed is Christ, who condescended and tasted death. And gave us his body and his blood. And gave life to Adam. And saved his children by his cross.
Ps. xxxiv. 1.

Ascribe ye praise unto God. The children of Adam lauded the Son with hosannas. And with voices of praise. Glorified him and sang to him. For he is the Quickener of our departed.
Ps. lxviii. 34.

And I have stretched forth my hands unto thee. Grant and vouchsafe to me that in the day when thy mercies shine forth. I may go forth to meet thee with hosannas. And with all thy saints. Make me worthy to inherit the kingdom.
Ps. lxxxviii. 9.

He lifted up his voice, and the earth was moved. O Voice, which saidst to the sinful woman, Thy trespasses are forgiven. Forgive me my trespasses in thy
Ps. xlvi. 6.

judgment. That I may stand and confess thee. With the just who were approved before thee.

How good and beautiful. The Voice, which called Lazarus from the grave. Calleth thee and quickeneth thee. And placeth thee at his right hand. In the day when his greatness shineth forth. Ps. cxxxiii. 1.

Thou hast brought me down to the lowest pit. Death hath brought me and cast me into devouring Sheol. And hath caused me to tremble exceedingly. And hath terrified my mind. And hath separated (my) soul from (my) body. Ps. lxxxviii. 5.

As the embers of an oak tree. Bitter is death, and dire is the day of departure. Which divideth brother from brother. And parents also. From speech with their loved ones.

Both small and great. Pray for me, all ye my friends and beloved ones. That I may be worthy of Abraham's bosom. And with Lazarus. Have joy there in the kingdom. Ps. cxv. 13.

VERSE OF PRAYER. *And sinners shall be converted unto thee.* Pardon and save all sinners. For thou art merciful and canst forgive trespasses. And takest away the offences of the sons of men. Who come to thee in repentance. Ps. li. 13.

Glory be, etc. O Mary, the holy Virgin, mother of Jesus our Saviour. Beseech and beg for mercies for sinners that they perish not. For they take refuge in thy prayers. May thy prayer be a wall to us in this world and in that which is to come.

From everlasting, etc. By the prayer of the just, who propitiated thee, and the righteous, who were approved before thee. The prophets, and apostles, and teachers, and martyrs, and priests and monks. Keep the congregation of thy worshippers, that they may lift up to thee a new (song of) glory. Father, Son, and Holy Ghost.

MADRASHA. *Antiphon.* Blessed is he, who, in (his) loving-kindness, created our nature in the beginning. And in his love accomplished our renewal in the end of times. *Verses.*

Remain in peace, O habitation which is but for a season, (and is) full of distresses. For lo, the weight of my trespasses hindereth me from the kingdom.* In the morning when all creatures rise for the searching of the judgment. Let me not be confounded, O my Lord, (but let me stand) among the congregations that are clothed with light.

WEDNESDAY

From this time forth for evermore. Remain in peace, O habitation which is but for a season. Which cannot save them that possess it. For I will depart and see the country of light. Where the just who have laboured, do dwell.
Ps. cxv. 18.

For there is no salvation in his hand. Remain in peace, O transitory world. Whose pride cometh to nought, and whose glory vanisheth away. For I will depart and see the city of the just. Jerusalem which is above.
Ps. cxlvi. 2.

And all my bones shall say. Blessed is thy day, O Son of the Lord of all. Who comest and rendest the bosom of Sheol. Glorious is thy quickening, which is looked for. By the generations who have passed away, and (by those) which remain.
Ps. xxxv. 10.

They pass away, but thou abidest. Lo, this world passeth away. And all its desires come to nought. And blessed is he who hath prepared for himself. Provision for the world which passeth not away.
Ps. cii. 26.

Praise him with the voice and with crying. At the sound [1] of the horn and of the trumpet. All the departed rise. And lift up glory to the Father, and to the Son. And to the Holy Ghost, for he quickeneth us.
Ps. cl. 5.

Both small and great. All men tread the way of death. And not even the just remain behind. And each of them runneth that he may obtain. According to his deeds in this world.
Ps. cxv. 13.

---

[1] Syr. : *voice.*

My lovers and my neighbours did stand looking upon my trouble. My lovers have left me, and have gone far from me. And also my possessions have remained for others. And my trespasses alone surround me. And (their) penalty maketh me tremble. **Ps. xxxviii. 11.**

The hope of all the ends of the earth. We have no hope in which we can boast. But thy cross which pardoneth our trespasses. For it is a high wall to us. And delivereth us from harm. **Ps. lxv. 5.**

Excellency and glory are before him. In the day when Christ the King shineth forth. He giveth life to the dead and changeth the living. And the just fly to meet him in the air. Pray for me that I may be with them. **Ps. xcvi. 6.**

And I sought him, but I found him not. I saw that the world faded away and perished. Through this wickedness which reigned in it. And I ran and took refuge. In the living cross of the Son of the Lord of all. **Cant. iii. 1.**

From this time forth for evermore. Remain in peace, my brethren and my companions. Our Lord recompense (you) with a reward for your love. And when ye stand in the sanctuary. Remember me in your prayers. **Ps. cxv. 18.**

Glory be, etc. The archangel flew and came down. To the holy one, the daughter of David. And gave her the message by which was typified. Peace and tranquillity to the race of man.

From everlasting, etc. May the prayers of the apostles, who were blessed fountains. In the thirsty and distressed world. And who gave the world to drink of a spiritual drink. Be a wall to our race.

MADRASHA. *Antiphon.* Glory to the voice which cried on the tree. And took away the penalty of the transgression of the commandment. *Verses.* May that voice which called Lazarus call thee. And make thee to dwell in the country where the just dwell.* May the voice of the horn call thee,

May the trumpet waken thee. May the Holy Ghost join thee to the ranks of the Saints.

THURSDAY

Unto thee, O Lord, I lifted up my soul. O Christ the King, our Saviour. In the day of thy coming quicken us. And raise us to thy right hand. In the day when thy greatness shineth forth.

Ps. xxv. 1.

O God, in thee have I trusted, let me not be confounded. We venerate[1] thy cross, O my Lord. By which we are raised and quickened. And by which our departed are quickened. And their bodies are clothed with glory.

Ib.

Such as are gentle, them doth he learn his way. Lo, in the prophets is our quickening. And in the apostles our recompense. And in the gospel of our Lord is the way. Which leadeth to the kingdom.

Ps. xxv. 8.

He lifted up his voice, and the earth was moved. The voice of the Son quickeneth. Adam, who lay in sorrow. And instead of the promised land. Giveth him a bride-chamber on high for an inheritance.

Ps. xlvi. 6.

How good and beautiful. The voice, which called Lazarus. And the maiden, the daughter of Jairus. Calleth and quickeneth thee. And placeth thee at his right hand.

Ps. cxxxiii. 1.

Mine eyes have looked for thy salvation, and for the word of thy righteousness. Mine eyes have looked for thy salvation. And the word of thy righteousness. Leave thou me not in Sheol. O thou good Hope of them that are in the graves.

Ps. cxix. 123.

And let my soul be joyful in God. And let my soul be joyful in God. And have pleasure in his salvation. And all my bones shall say. Lord, in thy lovingkindness give me life.

Ps. xxxv. 9.

Because I am in trouble answer me speedily. Because I am in

---

[1] Syr. : *worship.*

trouble answer me speedily. Bring my soul near to thy salvation. When I have lain down, may thy voice awaken me. From the grave (to enter) the kingdom. *Ps. lxix. 18.*

They shall rejoice and sing. May the bodies of the departed, who have clothed themselves with thee, O our Lord. In the waters of baptism. Be made clean by thee. From the stains of sin. *Ps. lxv. 14.*

Let them be glad in his joy. To the departed, who have eaten thy body. And have had joy in thy living blood. Grant, O our Lord, memorials. In the land where the just dwell. *Ps. lxviii. 3.*

The heavens are thine, the earth also is thine. Both worlds are thine, O my Lord. This world and that hereafter[1] alike. Preserve the living in thy compassion. And grant a quickening to the dead. *Ps. lxxxix. 12.*

The Lord is faithful in his words. May our departed, O my Lord. Who have confessed thy Trinity. Receive the promise which the robber. Received from thee on Golgotha. *Ps. cxlv. 13, Syr.*

Fear hath fallen upon me. It is not an (earthly) judgment that I fear. Nor am I troubled that I have fallen asleep. But I fear thy judgment, O my Lord. For God judgeth by fire. *Ps. lv. 5.*

VERSES OF PRAYER. *O Lord, heal me, for my bones are vexed.* In dire sickness of body. Am I tormented, O Lord. Heal my pain in thy compassion. As (thou didst heal) just Hezekiah. On whom the prophet placed a cake of figs and he was healed. So place on me, O my Lord, the medicine of thy mercies. *Ps. vi. 2.*

Give ear to my words and receive (them). As the censer which Aaron offered. May the savour of our assembly please thee. And as the request of the Ninevites. Receive the prayer of thy servants, O my Lord. And as thou didst answer Daniel in the pit. Answer, O my Lord, and help thy worshippers. *Ps. cxli. 1.*

---

[1] Syr.: *Here and there.*

Glory be, etc. Blessed art thou, O holy Virgin. Blessed art thou, Mother of Christ. Blessed art thou, whom all generations. And peoples call blessed. And because of thy Child thy name is exalted in creation. As the prophet said.

From everlasting, etc. By the prayer of the just, who propitiated thee. O Christ our King and our Lifegiver. Rescue thy Church from the evil ones. And preserve her children by thy cross. And bring to nought in her wars, and strifes, and divisions. For she hath been bought by thy living blood.

MADRASHA: *to the tune* Blessed is he who in lovingkindness. *Antiphon.* Flee from the world, flee from its riches, and also from its wickedness. And look and find out how bitter is the way of death. *Verses.* Look on me, my brethren (and see), that though I have run my course and have worked. Yet lo, I depart, and none of my possessions have accompanied me.* The wealth of the world saveth not the race of men. And not even that which clotheth him entereth with him into the kingdom.

FRIDAY

Tune: *Thou hast named thy vineyard.*

He that is before the worlds. The Father, who formed Adam. Called him also his image. And because he rebelled and transgressed the commandment. He brought him in his turn under death. Over which he had had dominion.

Ps. lv. 20.

In the days of old. In the beginning thou didst fashion our image, O Creator. And because (man) sinned and broke¹ thy law. Thou didst dissolve his form. And he turned again to his earth.

Ps. xliv. 1.

Thou hast fashioned me, and laid thine hand upon me. Thy command hath fashioned us and brought us into being. And thou hast set us in Eden, in

Ps. cxxxix. 4

---

¹ Syr.: *dissolved.*

Paradise. And because we have transgressed thy word. We have inherited a land of thorns.

Thou hast brought me down to the lowest pit. Lo, death hath taken me and hidden me in his clefts. Bring thou my soul out of the house of bondage. That I may confess and praise thee. O Quickener of the dead. Ps. lxxxviii. 5.

We have sinned with our fathers and have done amiss and dealt wickedly. We have trodden down thy commandment, and have transgressed thy word. And have been condemned because we sinned and dealt wickedly. And now we beseech (thee). In thy mercies forgive our trespasses. Ps. cvi. 6.

Thou art merciful, O Lord, and righteous. O just Judge, Creator of the world. Quickener of all the departed. Quicken us who are dead. In thy great mercies. Ps. cxvi. 5.

O come, let us praise the Lord. Life that is not destroyed and blessings that fade not. And joy that lasteth for all generations. Do the righteous inherit. In the day of thy coming. Ps. xcv. 1.

VERSES OF PRAYER. *Our God is our strong refuge.* O Christ, the true refuge and hope. Neglect us not at any time. And pardon our trespasses. And cleanse our stains. Ps. xlvi. 1.

Hear my voice, O God, when I beseech thee. O thou that hearest, and neglectest not, and savest, and rescuest. Hear, O my Lord, the request of thy worshippers. And return answer to our requests. From the treasure of thy mercies. Ps. lxiv. 1.

In the evening, and morning, and at noonday. Thou hast called us to the vineyard of thy Gospel, O Lord of all. Strengthen us, that we may do thy will. And may thy mercies preserve us. By night and by day. Ps. lv. 18.

Glory be, etc. By the prayer of her who bare thee, O Christ our Saviour. Pardon our trespasses in thy lovingkindness.

And forgive our offences. According to the multitude of thy mercies.

From everlasting, etc. O prophets and apostles and martyrs and teachers. Beseech and make requests for us all. That we may be worthy of forgiveness of trespasses. In the judgment.

And let all the people say Amen and Amen. A blessing which passeth not away is kept for thee in heaven. O our holy father,[1] the dwelling-place of the Holy Ghost. Pray for our assembly. That we may be worthy of forgiveness.

Ps. cvi. 46.

MADRASHA: *to the tune* At the door of thy mercies. *Antiphon.* O El, O God, hear our request, which is audible to thee. And in thy mercies return answer to the petition of our soul by which thou art persuaded. *Verses.* At the door of thy mercies thy servants knock, O thou who willest that we should live. Open to us that we may enter and receive an alms as poor men.* O thou who art overflowing with compassion, show thy love as thou art wont. Lest the hater of man mock the work of thy hands.* O thou who art mighty in the worlds, support that which thou hast fashioned by the force of thy power. For lo, it is disturbed by evil sufferings and by demons.

SATURDAY

I was glad when they said unto me. Our Lord cometh and quickeneth the dead. And giveth hope to all the departed.

Ps. cxxii. 1.

I will alway bless the Lord. Blessed is he who made death to come but once. Which taketh both good and bad alike.

Ps. xxxiv. 1.

And let my soul be joyful in God. Let my soul, which hath taken refuge in thy cross. See thy compassion in the day of thy coming.

Ps. xxxv. 9.

---

[1] Or *Awa.*

Thou hast fashioned me, and laid thine hand upon me. When I was not thou didst fashion me from the dust. And, now that I have lain down, give me life that I may confess thee. *Ps. cxxxix. 4.*

I will magnify thee, O my Lord the King. Christ our King shineth forth from on high. And giveth life to the dead, and raiseth them that are in the graves. *Ps. cxlv. 1.*

Turn thee unto me and have mercy upon me. O Son of God, quicken our departed. And clothe them with glory in thy kingdom. *Ps. xxv. 15.*

He lifted up his voice, and the earth was moved. At the voice of the Son the graves are rent. And the dead rise and give glory. *Ps. xlvi. 6.*

Unto the godly hath shone forth light in the darkness. A new sun shineth forth on them that are in the graves. And from their graves they shall confess thy majesty. *Ps. cxii. 4.*

Turn thee unto me and have mercy upon me. Have compassion on me and give me life, and forgive me my trespasses. That I may see thy compassion in the day of thy coming. *Ps. xxv. 15.*

And show a token upon me for good. Thy will is accomplished, and thy commandment hath led me. In thy mercies give me life, that I may stand and confess thee. *Ps. lxxxvi. 17.*

Both small and great. At the mouth of the graves stand the souls. And look on the Son, who shineth forth from on high. *Ps. cxv. 13.*

Blessed be the Name of the Lord. Blessed is Christ, who quickened us when we were dead. And hath promised hope and life to the departed. *Ps. cxiii. 2.*

From this time forth for ever more. Remain in peace, O Church with thy children. May our Lord be a wall to thy flock. *Ps. cxxxi. 4.*

And they shall bear thee in their arms. Moses and Elijah go forth to meet thee. And receive thee in tabernacles of fire. *Ps. xci. 12.*

For ever and ever. Remain in peace, O habitation, and ye that dwell therein. May peace increase in thee from whom I have gone out.

Ps. xlviii. 13.

There shall be thy habitation and thy rest. Among the desirable trees of Paradise. Shall be thy habitation and thy rest.

Glory be, etc. Glory to the Father, and confession to the Son. And to the Holy Ghost who quickeneth us.

From everlasting, etc. Praise to thee, Jesu our Saviour. In whose hands is death, and at whose will is life.

MADRASHA : *to the tune* Blessed is he who in lovingkindness. *Antiphon.* Where is Adam, whom the Lord formed from dust. And called him his image, and made heaven and earth subject to him ? *Verses.* Where is Moses, who on the Mount of Sinai saw his Maker. And the power of the Lord spake with him face to face.* Where is David, the prophet and king, the heart of the Lord. Of whom the Lord who chose him bore witness, that there was none like him.

THE SERVICES OF THE GREAT FAST[1]

ON SUNDAYS

AT THE NIGHT SERVICE

All the services as on other Sundays of the year (pp. 151, 155), *except as is here provided; and except that the Qali d'Shahra are said in inverted order, those for weeks 'after' being said on weeks 'before,' and those for weeks 'before' on weeks 'after.'*

On the five Sundays of the Fast[2] *the priest, after* Glory be to God (p. 151), *puts incense in the censer and vests himself in the ma'apra,[3] and holding the censer in his hand, stands before the shkhinta[4] and says this Canon. The people repeat it, and it is said five times, and the priest says the prayer that follows it.[5]*

CANON. In the middle of the night I have arisen to confess thee for thy judgments, O Righteous one.* In the night with the watchful ones. Let us sing glory to him. To him who watcheth and sleepeth not. Whom the watchful ones serve. In the night when are silent. The voices of all conditions

---

[1] These are all taken from U.; they are not in A., R. C. They are from the Khudhra.

[2] The first Sunday ('across the fast'), which is not properly in the Fast, and Palm Sunday, which is a Feast of our Lord, are not included. Some copies of the Khudhra say *all Sundays of the fast*.

[3] The outer vestment used at the Eucharist.

[4] A quasi-altar in front of the Sanctuary doors, or on one side of them. See Glossary.

[5] The Canon and prayer are given also in T., and are found in the manuscripts of the Takhsa.

(of men). May our prayer please thee. O Lord, who hast goodwill to the penitent. Who hearest and neglectest not. Who answerest, and savest, and rescuest. Hear, O my Lord, our request. And return answer in thy mercies to our petitions. For thou alone. Art full of mercy and forgivest trespasses.

He proceeds. In [1] the middle of the night I have arisen to confess thee for thy judgments, O righteous one. *They answer*,[2] I am the friend of all that fear thee and keep thy commandments. By night with the watchful ones.[3]* The earth, O Lord, is full of thy mercies, O teach me thy commandments. By night with the watchful ones.[3]* Glory be to the Father, etc. By night, etc.[3]* From everlasting to everlasting. By night, etc.[3]

Prayer. In the middle of the night we arise, O my Lord, wakefully to serve thee. *Repeat.* When the voices of all conditions (of men) are alike silent, let us sing praise to thy glorious Trinity without ceasing, O thou Watchful one, who art continually served by the watchful ones, O thou Holy one, who dwellest in thy holy ones, and art willingly propitiated. Pardon, O my Lord, our trespasses in thy compassion, and enlighten the eyes of our hearts with the light of thy knowledge. That we may know how to offer to thee in pureness of thought pure sacrifices of our minds, with the spoken [4] fruits of our lips, with praises which befit thy holy Name, Lord of all, etc.

He proceeds. Our Father, etc. (page 151).

On all Sundays of the Fast they say after the Motwa this TISHBUKHTA *by Mar Saurishu Catholicos.* Our Father which art in heaven. Holy in thy nature. Make thy worshippers worthy. To sing Holy to thy Name.* May thy kingdom come. In a mystery before the times. As though already.

---

[1] U. om. this clause.
[2] T. makes the answer begin at *The earth*.
[3] T. om. this line. [4] Or *reasonable*.

We lived in it.* Let us fulfil thy will. On earth without fear. As in heaven. There is none that (can) harm us.* The bread of our need. Give us all the days. Of the nature of mortals. For it is ever needy.* Before we are fashioned. Thou knowest our wickedness. In thy love thou hast fashioned us. In thy mercies wipe out our trespasses.* We have trespassed against thy being. And have offended against one another. May we forgive each other. And do thou, O Lord, (forgive) us all.* That we stand not in temptations. Of demons and lusts. Which chastise us. For we are weak.* In thy pity, O Compassionate one. Save us from the Evil one. For thou alone art able. To overcome his cruelty.* Thine is the kingdom. And the power, and the glory. Grant that we may be. Heirs of thy Beloved.* And with thy saints. May we pay to thy majesty. The glory which is meet for thee. For ever and ever, Amen.

AT THE MORNING SERVICE

All as on other Sundays (page 164), *except the following.*
Prayer before the Morning Psalms. Grant us, O our Lord and our God, although we are not worthy. *Repeat.* And make us worthy, although we deserve it not, to bear the yoke of the holy fast, with a meek heart boiling over with true love towards thee. And take away from us slothfulness, which is a barren mother, and forbidden to virtuous sons; and sow in us diligence, and energy, and watchfulness, lest one of our senses break the fast while another keepeth it, and confusion reign over that which we have begun. But when the body fasteth from food, may the soul also fast from evil and hateful (deeds), that our fast may be perfect and complete; and when we are watchful and cautious, and when we sing Holy, purely and circumspectly and in holiness, may we serve before thee with Moses, and Joshua, and Elijah, and Daniel, and the company of Ananias, and all other just men who have striven in this contest. And may our service

please thee, O my Lord, and our prayer persuade thee; may our beseeching honour thee, and our entreating propitiate thee. And may the mercies and compassion of thy Godhead pardon the trespasses of thy people, and forgive the sins of all the sheep of thy pasture, which thou hast chosen to thyself in thy lovingkindness and mercies, Lord of all, etc.

Another. Receive, O our Lord and our God, the pure fast of thy servants, in thy lovingkindness, and be propitiated by them in the greatness of thy mercy, as thou wast propitiated by the just, who kept the fast purely and circumspectly, and strove therein in watchfulness and holiness. And may their prayers by night and by day be heard before the terrible judgment-seat of thy greatness, and may their alms, which they pour forth for the poor, obtain a good memorial before the high throne of thy majesty, and be unto them as armour and a shield to drive away from them tribulations which take hold on them; and as (their gifts) are openly made use of in abundance, so may they be heard secretly in pureness and righteousness, that thou mayest shed forth on them (that gave them) thy mercies and compassion, and continually sprinkle their hearts (therewith), O thou who didst create the light in thy lovingkindness, and didst order the darkness in thy wisdom, and in the knowledge of thy Godhead, which cannot be fathomed by spiritual beings, or by those that are in the body, Lord of all, etc.

THE PSALMS *are said thus on Sundays and week-days:*—

Ps. c., *as on ferias*, page 103.

Prayer. To thee, O my Lord, all creatures, page 165.

Ps. xci., Whoso dwelleth under the defence of the Most High. And is made glorious in the shadow of God. *Thou art my confident hope: O Christ, may I never be confounded.* Whoso dwelleth . . . and show him my salvation (two clauses by each side). *Thou art my confident hope, etc.** Glory be.* From everlasting.* *When thou didst create the light which is poured forth, the spiritual ones glorified thee. And it was made known to them that he who created the light, created them also.** Whoso dwelleth under the defence of the Most High. And is made glorious in the shadow of God. *By angels thou art glorified. And by the sons of men thou art praised.* And all together with one accord cry and say, Blessed is thy fast, O Christ our Saviour. Let us pray, Peace be with us.

Prayer. Glorious, O my Lord, page 104.

Ps. civ. 1-15a. Bless the Lord, O my soul. O Lord my God, thou art become exceeding great. *The glory of the Lord shall be for ever.* Bless the Lord, O my soul . . . out of the earth (two clauses at a time). *The glory, etc.** Glory be.* From everlasting.* *The glory of the Lord shall be for ever.*

Prayer. To thee, O Creator of all natures, and Maker of all beings, Fashioner of the height and depth in thy loving-kindness and mercies, we lift up praise, and honour, and confession, and worship, at all times, Lord of all, etc.

The following psalms are said, two clauses at a time, with farcings at the beginning and end, in the weeks of the mysteries.[1] *In other weeks they are said as on* [*ordinary Sundays*[2] *and*] *ferias* (pages 166, 104).

Ps. cxiii. Praise the Lord, ye his servants. O praise the Name of the Lord. *Glory to him who created the light.* Praise the Lord, ye his servants . . . joyful mother of children. (No Gloria.) *Glory to him who created the light.*

Ps. xciii. The Lord is King, and hath put on glorious apparel. The Lord hath put on strength and hath waxed strong. *We worship thy Godhead, O my Lord.* The Lord is King . . . becometh thine house. O Lord, for ever. (No Gloria.) *We worship, etc.*

Ps. cxlviii. 1-7. O praise the Lord of heaven. Praise him in the height. *Let them praise God.* O praise the Lord of heaven . . . shall not be broken. (No Gloria.) *Let them praise God.*

Ps. cxlviii. 7—end. Praise the Lord upon earth. Ye dragons and all deeps. *Give praise to God.* Praise the Lord

---

[1] See Glossary.

[2] But on Sundays Psalm cxiii. is apparently said as above, and is not followed by a prayer. The rubrick is very ambiguous.

upon earth . . . even the people that draweth near to him. (No Gloria.) *Give praise to God.*

Ps. cxlix. O praise the Lord with a new song of praise. His song of praise in the congregation of the saints. *For him praise is meet.* O praise the Lord with a new song of praise . . . all his saints. (No Gloria.) *O Son of God, have pity on us.*

Ps. cl. O praise the Lord in his holiness. Praise him in the firmament of his power. *Father, Son, and Holy Ghost.* O praise the Lord in his holiness . . . praise the Lord. (No Gloria.) *Father, Son, and Holy Ghost.*

Ps. cxvii. O praise the Lord, all ye heathen. Praise him, all ye nations. *O Christ the Light, we praise thee.* O praise the Lord, all ye heathen. Praise him, all ye nations.* For his merciful kindness is strong upon us. Truly he is the Lord for ever. *O Christ the Light, we praise thee.* Glory be, etc. From everlasting, etc. *O Christ the Light, we praise thee.*

They add, Glorify the Lord, all the whole earth.* O Giver of light, O Lord, even to thee do we lift up glory.

Deacon. Let us pray, Peace be with us.

For the rest, see above, page 167.

WEEKS OF THE MYSTERIES IN THE FAST

[On Week Days]

EVENING SERVICE

Glory be to God in the highest, etc. Our Father, etc., *as on ferias*, page 1.

Evening Prayer. Let us confess, O my Lord, page 2.

They say the proper Hulala, with its prayer (pp. 86 to 95).

They proceed. Glorious art thou, O our Lord, and it is meet that we should lift up glory to thee. Every day, for ever and ever, Amen.* Glory to Christ, and confession to him who hath opened our mouth. And hath granted us to chant hallelujahs in his praises.* Glory to Christ, and confession to him who hath opened our mouth. And granted us to sing in his praises.* Glory to Christ and confession to him who hath opened our mouth. And granted us to glorify (him) in his praises.* To Father, Son, and Holy Ghost. Let us lift up glory, for ever, Amen. *Repeat thrice.*

Our mouth is not sufficient to confess thee, O our Lord. All the days of our life, for thy lovingkindness.* Our mouth is not sufficient to praise thee, O our Lord. All the days of our life, for thy lovingkindness.* Our mouth is not sufficient to glorify thee, O our Lord. All the days of our life, for thy lovingkindness.

O Lord, who art merciful to mortals. Have compassion on us in thy lovingkindness, and have mercy on us.* For none that liveth among (thy) creatures is justified before thee.

Thou, O my Lord, hast turned us from all error, for thou art God, and for thee glory is fitting, for ever and ever, Amen.

They say the LAKHUMARA, *with its collects before and after, as on ferias,* page 3.

They say the FIRST SHURAYA *for the day*[1] (page 3, etc.).

Prayer. Thy mercy, O our Lord, page 5.

PSALMS cxli., cxlii., cxix. 105-113, cxvii., *as above,* page 5.

Prayer. Hear, O our Lord, page 5.

They say the SECOND SHURAYA *and the* KARUZUTHA, *as above,* page 6.

Prayer. To thee, O Lord, mighty God, page 10.

Deacon.[2] Lift up your voices, etc. *They say,* Holy God, page 10.

Prayer. Holy and glorious, page 10.

Deacon.[2] Bless, O my Lord.[3] Bow your heads, etc., page 11.

Priest.[4] May Christ make, etc.

Prayer. May our souls be perfected, page 11.

They say the EVENING ANTHEM (page 11, etc.).

Prayer. Pity us, O thou Compassionate one, page 11.

THIRD SHURAYA *from the Khudhra, and the* SUBA'A[5] (*if it is said here*), *with its proper collect, but without* Our Father, *and its collects,* May thy Name, *and* In heaven and on earth (*as on Memorials in the Festival Service,* page 82);[6] *the Martyrs' Anthem is not said in the Fast.*

Prayer. Make us worthy, page 82.

They say the verses appointed in the Khudhra; then the prayer of the Shuraya and the CANON *and* TISHBUKHTA *in the Khudhra.*

---

[1] The First and Second Anthems are not said in the Fast.

[2] U.: *They answer.*

[3] Om. U., but it is inserted in the ordinary ferial office. This is ascribed rightly to the deacon in U. in that place.

[4] U. om. these words here.   [5] Compline.

[6] U. has a rubrick saying that custom differs in this matter. The practice is usually to say Compline, as here, in the middle of Evening Service; but some say it directly after Evening Service, in which case U. directs Our Father and the rest, as on pages 12, 16, to be said directly after the Shuraya. The former custom was to separate the services by an interval, and to say Compline at bedtime (see page 185).

Karuzutha. O mighty Lord, Almighty, page 82.

They say, Holy God (page 10) *and* Our Father.

Prayer. Of thee who art full of mercies, *as at the Festival Night Service,* page 152.

Another. Blessed and adorable (page 153).

Then follow the prayers for help, and the rest as before (page 16).

NIGHT SERVICE

Priest. Glory be to God in the highest, etc. (page 85).

Canon.[1] Psalm iii. 5—*end.* I laid me down and slept, and rose up again. For the Lord sustained me. *It is meet and right that we should sing Holy to thee and glorify thee, O our Saviour, and that we should chant with the angels, with voices full of praise, Glory be to thee, O God.* I laid me down . . . upon thy people. *It is meet and right, etc.*

Ps. cxxxiv. Bless the Lord, all ye servants of the Lord. Ye that by night stand in the house of the Lord. *The saints sing Glory by night with the watchful ones, and tens of thousands of the companies on high repeat the glory of the greatness of Jesus our victorious King.* Bless the Lord, all ye servants . . . out of Sion. *The saints sing, etc.*

Glory be to the Father, and to the Son, and to the Holy Ghost. To him whom the Cherubim surround. To whose honour Seraphim sing Holy. The glory of whose greatness angels and the sons of men repeat. Jesus our victorious King.* Who came and saved us by his cross. And promised us the kingdom, which passeth not away, and is not destroyed. And joy without end. To him be glory, and on us be his mercies.

They proceed. I laid me down and slept and rose up again.* For the Lord sustained me.* As those that are on high are watchful. And cease not from praising thee. Make us also

---

[1] To be also said on all Fridays of the year, U.

that are below to be watchful. That we may glorify thee with the angels.* Glory and honour are fitting. For Father, Son, and Holy Ghost. From those that are on high and those that are below. From spiritual ones and them that are in the body. And especially from the sons of the Church. Whom he hath made worthy to praise him. That they may glorify him in threefold wise. With a threefold song of his holiness. To him be glory from all and in all.* And I laid me down in my sins. And slept the sleep of wickedness. And now I have risen up again by thy will. And have obtained a portion with them that glorify thee. Forgive me all my sins and offences. And make me worthy to glorify thee. Whom I have loved. Glory to thee who dost waken us. Glory to thee who dost raise us. Glory to thee who dost quicken us. Glory to thee who dost renew us.

When this is done the priest prays before the Sanctuary doors as follows, uncovering his head,[1] and holding the censer in his hand.

Of thee, who wakenest them that sleep, and raisest the fallen, who comfortest the afflicted and pardonest sinners, who art the great refuge of the repentant, we beseech and ask, Waken us who sleep, O my Lord, in thy compassion, and lighten the weight of our sloth in thy pity. And grant that we may be made worthy to arise and serve before thee, purely and circumspectly, watchfully and diligently. O Watchful one, whom[2] the watchful ones serve with their hallelujahs, and Seraphim with their crying of Holy, and those that are below[3] with their songs, and all nations with their adorations, Lord of all, etc.

They answer, Our Father, *farced* (page 1).

Deacon. Let us arise to prayer. Let us pray, Peace be with us.

Prayer. Let us arise, *as on ordinary ferias*, page 85.

---

[1] These words are thus in the Khudhra. The meaning is (apparently) *letting the ma'apra fall on to his shoulders.* The East Syrians take off their turbans or hats for all prayers, though not necessarily on entering a church out of service time. This prayer is also in T.

[2] T.: *and* (error).   [3] Or *the lower orders (of angels).*

They say, Hallelujah, etc.
Prayer. Strengthen, O our Lord (page 85).
They say, Hallelujah, etc.
Prayer. May the secret strength (page 86).
They say the HULALI *according to the directions of the Khudhra, and between them they say*, Hallelujah, Hallelujah, yea Hallelujah, Glory be to thee, O God; *repeat thrice.* O Lord, have mercy upon us. Let us arise to prayer. Let us pray, Peace be with us.
They say the MOTWA *as directed in the Khudhra.*
Prayer of the Shubakha. To thee be glory, page 97.
They say the SHUBAKHA (page 97) *to a sad*[1] *tone. Between each clause they say*, Glory be to thee, O God. *They add the Gloria.*
TISHBUKHTA, *by Mar Abraham of Izla.* Glory be to thee, O God. *Repeat.* By day and by night. Glory be to thee, O God.* At all seasons and times. In thy mercy have compassion on us, O God. We ask mercy of thee. And forgiveness of sins.* Remove from us the Evil one. Who alway layeth snares for us. Keep us by thy living sign. That the Evil one may see (it) and depart.* Make thy right hand which is full of mercies. O Lord, to overshadow us. O Lord, thy mercies are everlasting. Forsake not the work of thy hands.* May thy cross be a wall to us. O Christ, who by it[2] hast saved us. Glory to thee, O our Lord Jesus. And praise to the Father who sent thee.* And to the Holy Ghost be sung hallelujahs. For ever and ever. For ever and ever. And for evermore. Amen.
KARUZUTHA. O mighty Lord, eternal Being, page 101.
Prayers. Of thee who art full of mercies, *and* Blessed and adorable, *as in the Festival Night Service*, page 152.
They say the Verses [*of the* MADRASHA] *from the Khudhra.*
Prayers of the Suyakhi. *Before the first Psalm*, For thy nature, page 95.
Prayer of the second psalm. Thee who art hidden from all, page 159.

---

[1] Syr.: *groaning*.   [2] Syr.: *by thy cross*.

Prayer of the third psalm. Thee who art hidden in thy being, page 160.

The prayers of the Qali d'Shahra are as on Feasts (page 153), *and the Qali d'Shahra are as in the Khudhra.*

Prayer of the Night Anthem. By the speaking mouths, page 154.

They say the NIGHT ANTHEM; *then the prayer,* Pity us, O thou Compassionate one, page 11.

They say the proper CANON, *and* TISHBUKHTA *for the day, and the* KARUZUTHA, O thou who didst teach us, *as on* page 162.

MORNING SERVICE

Prayer before the Morning Psalms. Vouchsafe,[1] O our Lord and our God, that our services and prayers may be joined with those of the monks who pleased thee in their fasts, and of the Nazarites who propitiated thee by their life, and caused[2] the will of thy majesty to be well pleased with their services, and prayers, and supplications. Receive our little fast, and our scanty prayers and weak requests; and return answer to our petitions in thy mercies from thy rich and overflowing treasury. And may the service of our weakness, O my Lord, please thee, and the prayer of our poverty persuade thee, and the fast of our sinfulness propitiate thee; and may the mercies and compassion of thy Godhead grant the pardon of the trespasses of thy people, and the forgiveness of the sins of all the sheep of thy pasture, which thou hast chosen to thyself, in thy lovingkindness and mercies, Lord of all, etc.

Another. Thee, O Christ, the true Light of all lights, who feedest lights from thy light, and dwellest in the excellent light, which no son of man hath seen nor can approach unto, we beseech and ask thee, even we who are weak and sinful, to enlighten the darkness of our minds by the brightness of

---

[1] Syr.: *Make us worthy*; cf. ἀξιόω.
[2] U.: *cause thou* (misprint).

thine unspeakable light; so that the lamps of our souls being enlightened with the oil of mercy and pity, we may also be enlightened with the light of thy light which enlighteneth all, and may rejoice in the joy of thy countenance which delighteth all, and may desire to meet (thee at) thy manifestation which reneweth all, O thou who didst create the light in thy loving-kindness, and dost order the darkness in thy wisdom, and in the knowledge of thy Godhead,[1] which cannot be fathomed by spiritual ones or by those that are in the body, Lord of all, etc.

Prayer before the Morning Psalms on Fridays of the Fast. Blessed art thou who art worshipped in thy Church on earth by earthly worshippers; and glorious art thou who art to be worshipped in thy Church in heaven by heavenly worshippers; and adorable is the nature of thy Being, one in essence, and three in attributes, by all intelligences and minds of beings of fire and spirit, who around the appointed place of the Shechinah[2] of thy greatness, in noiseless cries, sing Holy and Hallelujah with mouths of fire, and in the mountains where they meditate[3] on thy glory, kneel and worship continually without inclining, O thou who art worshipped by true worshippers, who worship thy majesty in spirit and in truth. And may the service of our weakness, etc., *as in the former of the above prayers.*

Another for the same. Hear, O our Lord and our God, the prayer of thy people who wait for thee; and receive the supplication of (the sheep of) thy pasture which knock at the door of thy majesty, and pity and have mercy on thine offending servants. Bring back, O my Lord, the erring and the lost, save the captives and the persecuted; have mercy on the oppressed and tormented; turn to the miserable and poor, and pity the strangers and exiles; provide for the orphans and give sustenance to the widows; loosen (the bonds of) those that are bound and are held in the grasp of iniquity;

---

[1] Syr.: *in thy knowledge and Godhead.*
[2] Syr.: Shkhinta. See Glossary.
[3] Syr.: *mountains of meditations,* ti'uriyas (θεωρίας).

and protect those that journey by sea or by land; for thou art our God who helpest (from) above in thy mercy, O thou who didst create the light, etc., *as in the latter of the above prayers.*

The Psalms *follow as noted under Sundays in the Fast. See above,* page 208.

Prayer of the Lakhumara. Thee, O my Lord, we are bound, page 104.

They say the Lakhumara *antiphonally; when the one side says it the other side makes a prostration*[1]*; the farcing is,* To show thy lovingkindness in the morning, and thy faith in the night season.

Prayer. Thee who quickenest, page 104.

Psalm li., *with the proper farcings, from the Khudhra.*

Prayer. Sprinkle us, O our Lord and our God, with the refreshing dew of the kindness of thy love, and wash us with it from the defilements of sin, O good Shepherd who camest forth to seek us, and didst find us when we were lost: who willest that we should return, in thy lovingkindness and mercies, Lord of all, etc.

The officiant[2] *says,* My voice shalt thou hear in the morning, O Lord: and in the morning I will be prepared, and will appear before thee. *The people answer the same.*

And they go on to the Verses [*of the* Morning Anthem] *in the Khudhra.*

The deacon says the Karuzutha. He that openeth the gate of repentance, *and that which follows it.* [*From the Khudhra.*]

At the end of the Karuzutha the deacon says. Let us commit our own souls and one another's souls to the Father, Son, and Holy Ghost.

Prayer. To thee, O Lord, mighty God, page 10.

Tishbukhta. To thee be glory, O our God, page 105.

Prayer. O Christ the good Hope, *and* Holy God, *as on* page 106.

Prayer. Holy and glorious, page 10.

---

[1] Syr.: *worships.*   [2] Syr.: *He who says.*

Deacon. Bless, O my Lord.[1] Bow your heads, etc., page 11.
Prayer. May our souls be perfected, page 11.
They then say an extra Hulala, called Quṭa'a.[2]
Prayer. Thy glorious Godhead, full of mercies and compassion, the hope and life and salvation of all creatures, are we bound to confess, worship, and glorify, at all seasons and times, Lord of all, etc.

They proceed. Glorious art thou, O our Lord . . . glory for ever, Amen. *Repeat thrice.* (*As at the Evening Service in the Fast,* page 211.)

TISHBUKHTA, *as in the Khudhra.*

They say, Holy God (page 10) *and* Our Father, *farced* (page 1).

Prayers. O Compassionate one, whose Name, *and* Bless, O my Lord, thy servants, page 106.

They say the prayers for help, and the rest as on ordinary ferias, pages 16, 108.

---

[1] Om. U. here.

[2] Formerly that which follows was said as a separate service three hours after the Morning Service.

ORDINARY WEEKS OF THE FAST

[ON WEEK DAYS.]

EVENING SERVICE

This is as in the weeks of the mysteries (page 211), except that before the Suba‘a they always say the Lord's Prayer and its collects (page 212).

NIGHT SERVICE

Priest. Glory to God in the highest, etc. (page 85).

CANON. Ps. cxix. 57-65. In the portion of the Lord I have resolved to keep thy statutes. And I have looked for thy presence with my whole heart, O save me, according to thy word. *At this time I have risen to confess thee, O our Lord, for thy judgments, and I wonder at the deeds of thy wisdom, and confess thy Name.* In the portion . . . O teach me thy statutes. *At this time, etc.*

Ps. xcii. 1, 2. It is a good thing to confess the Lord. And to sing unto thy Name, O most Highest. *In the night, with the watchful ones, let us sing praise to him that watcheth and sleepeth not; and in the night, when all is*[1] *silent, let us chant a song of glory to him.* It is a good thing to confess the Lord. And to sing unto thy Name, O most Highest. To show forth thy lovingkindness in the morning. And thy faith in the night season. *In the night, etc.*

Glory be to the Father, and to the Son, and to the Holy Ghost. Glory to thee, O our Saviour. Who didst give us rest in the night, and didst preserve us. And in the morning didst awaken us, that with the watchful ones we might sing to thee a song of glory.* In the portion of the Lord I have

---

[1] Syr.: *all divisions are.*

resolved to keep thy statutes.* And I have looked for thy presence with my whole heart. O save me, according to thy word.* Not by us are our ways determined, O Christ our Saviour. But thou art the Fashioner of our deeds in thy power and wisdom.* Send us from thy presence help and healing, O Christ our Saviour. That by the power of thy grace we may please thee in words and in deeds.* At the door of thy lovingkindness we knock, O Christ our Saviour. And we ask for forgiveness for our offences, have pity on us in thy mercies.* To thee, O our Lord, we call, and ask for compassion and mercies from thy treasury. For we know that thou art compassionate and merciful, and forgivest (our) trespasses.* O feeble soul, how long hast thou lain in thy bed in the sleep of ease[1]? Arise, put oil in thy lamp, for lo, the bridegroom is come.* Lo, the virgins, thy fellows, are ready to enter with the bridegroom. And thou, why art thou careless, and remainest in the filth of thine (ill) deeds?* Come, my brethren, let us take refuge in prayer, for it is a strong armour. And by it we will conquer Satan, our enemy, who hateth our nature.

Then Our Father, *farced, and the rest in order* (page 85).

The HULALI *are as marked in the Khudhra.*

Some say the MOTWA; *but some omit it, and say the Night Anthem only.*

SHUBAKHA, *as in Ferial Service* (page 97).

TISHBUKHTA, *by Mar Shimun Bar Ṣaba'i, Patriarch; or, as some say, by Mar Ephraim.* Glory to thee, O my Lord, who didst create us. Though not moved thereto by any from the beginning.* Glory to thee, O my Lord, who didst call us. Thy living image and likeness.* Glory to thee, O my Lord, who didst nurture us. In freedom and as reasonable beings.* Glory to thee, O just Father. Whose love was pleased to fashion us.* Glory to thee, O holy Son. Who didst put on our flesh,[2] and didst save us.* Glory to thee, O living Spirit. Who didst enrich us with thy gifts.*

---

[1] Syr.: *thine ease.* [2] Syr.: *body.*

Glory to thee, O hidden Nature. Who didst reveal thy qnumi[1] in our manhood.* Glory to thee, O my Lord, who didst draw us. From the error of idols.* Glory to thee, O my Lord, who didst bring us. To the knowledge of thy Godhead.* Glory to thee, O my Lord, who didst make us. Reasonable[2] instruments for thy service.* Glory to thee, O my Lord, who didst invite us. To the exalted habitation of heaven.* Glory to thee, O my Lord, who didst teach us. The orders of the heavenly beings.* Glory to thee, O my Lord, who didst make us worthy. To glorify thee with the angels.* Glory to thee from all mouths. Father, Son, and Holy Ghost.* From those that are above and those that are below. Glory to thy Trinity.* In both worlds glory to thee. From the spiritual beings and from them that are in the body.* From everlasting to everlasting. And for ever and ever, Amen.

KARUZUTHA. O mighty Lord, eternal Being, page 101.

Prayers. Of thee who art full of mercies *and* Blessed and adorable, *as in the Festival Night Service*, page 152.

They say the MADRASHA, *and the* SUYAKHI, *as in the Khudhra.*

Prayer of the first Suyakha. Grant us, O my Lord, in thy compassion, and vouchsafe[3] in thy mercy, that with the watchful ones and the companies of the angels we may sing praise, with voices full of confession, to thy glorious Trinity, at all times, Lord of all, etc.

Of the second. Thee, who art hidden from all in thy being, page 159.

Of the third. May thy Godhead, O my Lord, be pleased with our service, and may our prayers be received before thee, and may our petitions be answered from the treasury of thy compassion, at all seasons and times, Lord of all, etc.

Prayer of the Night Anthem. By the speaking mouths, page 154.

Or this.[4] By every mouth mayest thou be glorified, and by

---

[1] See above, page 157.
[2] Or *speaking*.
[3] Syr.: *make us worthy*.
[4] So T.; om. U.

every tongue confessed, and in the heart mayest thou be believed. And with lips of glory may those in heaven and those on earth glorify thee, O thou Cause of our life and good Hope of our souls, Lord of all, etc.

They say the NIGHT ANTHEM *and the prayer* Pity us, O thou Compassionate one, page 11, *then the proper* CANON, *and* TISHBUKHTA *for the day.*

KARUZUTHA. O thou who didst teach us, page 162.

MORNING SERVICE

The prayers before the Psalms as in the ordinary Ferial Service (page 103), *and the Psalms as noted under Sundays in the Fast* (page 208); *and the Lakhumara and* Ps. li. *are said as on ordinary ferias* (page 104).

KARUZUTHA. O Father, who in thy mercy *from the Khudhra.*

Prayer. To thee, O Lord, mighty God, page 10.

TISHBUKHTA. To thee be glory, O our God, page 105.

Prayer. O Christ, the good Hope; *and* Holy God, *as on* page 106.

[*Prayer* Holy and glorious, *deacon's interjection, and prayer* May our souls, *as on* page 218.[1]]

They say an extra Hulala, called Quṭa'a.

And they conclude as on page 219.

---

[1] Om. U. here.

PRAYER AT NOON IN THE FAST

They begin in the usual manner (pages 1, 2), *and say three Hulali as noted in the Khudhra.*

They proceed. Glorious art thou, etc., *as at Evening Service of the Fast,* page 211; *then the* NIGHT ANTHEM *with its Prayer and* CANON, *and the proper* TISHBUKHTA.

KARUZUTHA. O thou who didst teach us, page 162.

They say, Holy God (page 10), *and* Our Father, *farced* (page 1).

Prayers. O thou who openest thy door *and* O thou who hearest, page 83.

Prayers for help, and the rest as at Evening Service throughout the year (page 16).

AN OCCASIONAL KARUZUTHA [1]

Let us all stand up, etc., page 6.

O our God, abounding in mercies, who justifiest sinners without recompense, we, etc.

O good Shepherd, who wentest forth to seek our race, and didst give thyself for us, we, etc.

O Physician of our nature, who didst come, and wast revealed in the flesh, and didst pardon our trespasses and heal our wounds, we, etc.

O true Judge, who art not alway angry, but art long-suffering with us, in the hope that we may repent, we, etc.

O Lord, who didst grant to the penitent hope and comfort, by (the example of) the publicans and harlots whom thou didst receive and pardon.

For the welfare of our holy fathers NN,[2] and all those who serve under them, we, etc.

O merciful God, who in mercy governest all, we, etc.

O thou who art glorified in heaven and worshipped on earth, we, etc.

For sinners, that they may repent, and for the penitent, that they may be made righteous, and for the righteous, that they may be perfected, we, etc.

Have compassion on us, and pardon our trespasses in thy lovingkindness, and pour out thy compassion on our souls, and be reconciled to us all, and have mercy upon us.

---

[1] From U.   [2] Patriarch, Metropolitan, and Bishop.

ROGATION OF THE NINEVITES[1]

Tishbukhta for Monday of the Rogation, and also for Fridays of the Great Fast, by Mar John, or as some say by Mar Bar Soma. In suffering, and with tears and entreaty. We call to thee, good Lord.* Be to us Physician and Guide. For bitter is our suffering, and our pain is hard (to bear).* There are not among us just men who may propitiate thee. For our iniquity hath waxed strong and our trespasses have increased.* They have stirred up and disturbed the sea and the dry land. And all that is in them, with our evil deeds.* In our time that which is written is come to pass. For the end of the worlds hath come upon us.* Save us in thy mercies from storms. Which have confused and shaken the heights and the depths.* O good Shepherd, feed thy flock. For whose sake thou hast borne suffering.* Vouchsafe to priests and kings alike. To[2] dwell in peace and quietness.* And may we be thine according to thy will. Father, Son, and Holy Ghost.* Father, Son, and Holy Ghost. For ever and ever, Amen and Amen.

Another, by Mar Khnana of Khdhaiwa. In suffering and with tears, come, let us draw near. Come, let us draw near to penitence.* For our iniquity hath waxed strong, and without number. Without number are our offences.* The crafty foe hath found a place. Hath found a place, and lo, he spoileth us.* Blessed be he that hath fought and conquered him. Hath fought and conquered him by diligence.* The Lord of our race by the Son of our race. By the Son of our race hath honoured our race.* And through our slackness the evil demons. The evil demons have laughed at our

---

[1] From U.; see Kalendar.   [2] Syr.: *That we may dwell.*

weakness.* Our wounds are corrupted and putrid. And putrid to those that pass on the way.* Come, let us draw near to that Physician. To that Physician who healeth without price.* In penitence of soul let us come to him. Let us come to him, to Jesus our King.* For he in his lovingkindness will cleanse us. Will cleanse us from the stains of our soul.* And let us all give him praise. For ever and ever, Amen and Amen.

Another for Wednesday of the Rogation. In suffering and with tears it is meet that all men. Should weep and lament for their infirmity.* And more than all it is meet that I. Should weep and lament without ceasing.* For the watchful ones and men recoil from my wickedness. And I cannot show my wounds.* Body and soul are corrupted and defiled. With the scars of lusts.* For I desired the world with its hateful deeds. And the prince of the world hath gotten domination over me.* He hath overthrown me and cast me out without pity. Like a lion ready for (his) prey.* He hath robbed me and humbled me and mocked me. Like Adam among the trees.* He saw that I was careless like Eve. And he had no pity on me, for he slayeth men.* To thee I cry, who in thy goodness didst form me. Cover my nakedness and heal my wounds.* Seek me when I am lost, and take hold of my life. For thou alone hast compassion without reward.* In the day of thy revelation make me glad, O our Lord. That I may see thy face without shame.* Pity me both here and hereafter.[1] For thou alone art the Friend of men.* Blessed is the Compassionate one, who aboundeth in mercies. For in (his) lovingkindness he hath compassion on those who are not worthy.* And let us all give him praise. For ever and ever, Amen and Amen.

In the Rogation of the Ninevites, Hallelujah is thus said between the Hulali:—

Hallelujah. Halle-ingih-lujah.[2] Yea Hallelujah. Glory be

---

[1] Syr.: *there.*

[2] The additional syllable has no meaning. This curious method of saying Hallelujah is also often used at other times.

to thee, O God. Halle-ingih-lujah, yea Hallelujah. In thy mercies have compassion on us, O God. Halle-ingih-lujah, yea Hallelujah. O thou who art full of mercies, have mercy upon us. *The other side answers*, O our Lord, have mercy upon us. O our Lord, receive our request. O our Lord, be reconciled to thy servants.

The Qaltha at the Night Service is the same as on ordinary Sundays 'after' [1] *(page 156).*

The Suba'a (Compline) is said at the Evening Service as in the Fast [2] *(page 212).*

---

[1] So A. in the list of Qalyatha; om. U. and R. C.

[2] In addition to the usual services, a long series of anthems, etc., ascribed to St. Ephraim, are sung in the forenoon of the three days of the Rogation. These, which are printed in R. C., are usually found in a book by themselves, called *Mimra d'Ba'utha* (Discourse of the Rogation).

BLESSING OF THE MONTHS [1]

The Lord of the whole earth.[2] Order the month, and bless it. To be the crown of the year, in thy lovingkindness. And make the month blessed. Even ———[3] joyful in thy compassion. May our request enter before thee. O Lord of months and of years. Prayer is the key of creation. May it open for us the door of mercies.* Bless, O my Lord, this month. And order it with all fruits. And give in it mercy and compassion. And increase in it peace and tranquillity. And keep, O my Lord, in thy compassion. This country and its inhabiters. From the harm and opposition. Of the Devil, the Apostate.* Bless, O my Lord, this year. And its crown likewise. And let there not be in it fear. Neither commotion nor terror. Let ———[3] come in joy. And be accepted like the request. Of Elijah and the son of Amram. May their prayer be a wall to us.* Bless, O my Lord, the months of the year. The seasons and weeks and days. Bless the vineyards and things planted. Bless the crops and fields. Bless, O my Lord, ———,[3] which hath come. And may it be enriched with all blessings. And let there not be in it punishments. Nor sufferings nor distresses.* Bless, O my Lord, this year. And the months and the days. And priests and the children of the Church. And this country and city.

Ps. xcvii. 5.

---

[1] These anthems are said at the Evening Service of the first day of each month, February excepted—*i.e.* on what in the West we should call the evening of the last day of the preceding month. They are not given in A.

[2] R. C. om. the words, *The Lord of the whole earth.*

[3] The name of the month.

And make distresses to pass away from us. And give us times of joy. By the prayer of the fathers. Until the end of days.* Bless, O my Lord, this month. By the prayer of them that keep thy commandments. And make the plague to pass away from us. And grant us mercy and compassion. By the prayer of the blessed one. Mar N[1] the confessor. May we be delivered from Gehenna. And enter with thee into the bridechamber.

The following three verses are by Mar Abraham of Slukh.[2]

Bless the crown of the year with thy lovingkindness. O God,[3] make the year to be blessed. May spring burst forth[4] with fruits. May abundance be multiplied in every year. Be it leap year or an ordinary year. Raise up, O Ahiyah,[5] in the Church. Men to keep vigil by night in (thy) service. May times of quietness come to us. May Augustus[6] arise with victory. May Theologus,[7] head of the priesthood. Put on healing and grace. May the threshing-floors be filled, O my Lord, with blessing. Pour forth thy mercies on creation.

<small>Ps. lxv. 12.</small>

Hear my voice, O God, when I beseech thee.[8] *Shin.* Hear the voice of the crying of mankind. *Mim.* O Christ, thou Sea of mercy. *Shin.* Send the rain of blessings. *Alap.* Make the herbs of the fields to sprout forth. *Simkath.* Satisfy the orphans and widows. *He.* Give peace in all quarters (of the world). *Resh.* Appease tumults and contentions. *Alap.* Give concord to all kingdoms.

<small>Ps. lxiv. 1.</small>

Merciful art thou, O Lord, and righteous. O Compassionate one, overflowing with goodness. O Depth full of kindness. May our prayer be heard before thee. As the request of Nineveh. Have compassion on us

<small>Ps. cxvi. 5.</small>

---

[1] The patron saint.
[2] Seleucia (by Ctesiphon). R. C. om. name of author.
[3] Ti'un = Θεόν.   [4] Or *make it prosperous*.
[5] I AM. Exodus iii. 14.   [6] *i.e.* the king.
[7] Syr.: *Tiulugh*. The patriarch is meant.
[8] This acrostic spells *Shimsha-sahra* (sun-moon).

as thou hadst on the sinful woman. Answer us speedily as thou answeredst the Canaanitish woman. Show us thy glory in the day of the resurrection. [1] Make us glad with thine elect in the kingdom.

The following three verses were written by Mar Gabriel in the year 1910 of the Greeks.[2]

And shall glorify thy name, for thou art great. O our Lord, bless this year. And its crown with perfection. And grant a moderate climate. Temperate, quiet in goodness.* Bless also with abundance. The months and weeks and days. Bless October with the wine-press. And the ingathering of all fruits.* In November grant a blessing. And fill it with benefits and good things. In December, by thy lovingkindness. Satisfy the lands with rain.* In January continually. Sow thou peace and concord. That (men) may sow in security. The seeds that are needed.* In February, the month of distresses. Let there not be chastisement. And bless March with a blessing. That it may bring gentle rain as it is wont.* And may April come with joy. And fill the earth with rejoicing. In May preserve the fields. From hail and injurious drought.* In June give plenty. To orphans as well as to widows. A store without end. To all the year alike.* In July bestow an overflowing. Of all good things and blessings. In August decree for mankind. Great rejoicing and joy.* In September all creatures. Lift up praise to thy name. And thanksgiving and confession. Yea and Amen, with rejoicing.

Ps. lxxxvi. 9, 10.

El, El, haste thee to help me. Alap. El, compassionate God. *Beith.* Bless this month. *Gamal.* O mighty and pitiful one. *Dalath.* Guide us as is best for us. *He.* Grant us health in thy mercies. *Wau.* And pour forth a supply on us, O my Lord. *Zain.* Provide us with temporal blessings. *Kheith.* Have compassion on us, O merciful Lord. *Teith.* Give us grace in thy compassion.

Ps. xxii. 19.

---

[1] U. ins. *And.* [2] A.D. 1599; R. C. om. date and name of author.

Yudh. Give us this day such a store. *Kap.* Abundant and unfailing. *Lamadh.* That it take away from us want of corn. *Mim.* O our Lord, bless this day. *Nun.* The sheep and the cattle alike. *Simkath.* Increase among us plenty and peace. *'E.* And riches without loss. *Pe.* Save us from the hand of the calumniator. *Ṣadhi.* May thy cross rescue us. *Qop.* Make us holy at all times. *Resh.* O High and Boundless one. *Shin.* Increase among us[1] every kind of food. *Tau.* O Depth that cannot be filled. Glory which cannot be diminished. Will we lift up to thee with (every) breath that we breathe.

Have mercy upon us, O Lord, have mercy upon us. O our Lord, we stand before thee. And ask mercy of thee. And make request of thy lovingkindness. That food may be multiplied to us with blessings.* And give us the bread of our need. As thou didst promise us, O my Lord. And give us a supply of all good things. Continually, at all times.* Bless with thy mercies the crown of the year. And grant in it rain[2] for our sustenance. The former (rains) that we may sow our corn. The latter that it may grow and ripen.* And let not locust and young locust spread over us.[3] And make the caterpillar[4] to pass away from us. Let not the corn-worm be seen in our land. And cast out the white locust from our country.* Let not the blight hurt our crops. And deliver us, O El, from burning winds. And let there be no palmer-worm in our time. And let not the plague[5] overcome us.* For thou knowest well that our nature. Is weak, and cannot bear. Famine and distress and affliction. Do thou in thy mercies visit our race.* Give[6] us bread that faileth not. Wheat and herbs for our sustenance. With all good gifts of food. In abundance, for in thee is our hope.* And purify us from our defilements. And cleanse that in us which is blameworthy and hateful. And wash us from our foulness. And make

Ps. cxxiii. 3.

---

[1] R. C. om. *among us.* [2] R. C.: *rains.* [3] Lit. *tread us down.*
[4] Or *cricket.* [5] Cholera. [6] R. C.: *And give.*

clean our bodies and our souls.* [1] Have compassion on us, and pardon our trespasses. Remember not our offences against us. In (thy) lovingkindness make us worthy of forgiveness. That we may confess thee both here and above.[2]

The following verses are by Mar Audishu.[3]

He that is before the worlds. Alap. O Creator of created things. *Wau.* Who dost grant all petitions. *Dalath.* Drive away from us all chastisements. *Beith.* Bless[4] us with all blessings. *Zain.* Feed[4] the hungry and the widows. *He.* Give peace in all quarters (of the world). *Gamal.* Rebuke the enemies that provoke strife. *Gamal.* Perfect us in all knowledge.   Ps. lv. 20.

Hear my prayer, O God. Alap. O El, the compassionate God. *Beith.* Bless this month. *Gamal.* Perfect our assembly in all victory. *Dalath.* That we may conquer the Evil one, the slanderer. *He.* Give plenty in every dominion. *Wau.* And quiet peace and tranquillity. *Zain.* Give us food continually. *Kheith.* Have compassion on us in the day of searching. *Teith.* Grant us the grace of compassion. *Yudh.* O Sea of mercies and pity. And set us on the right hand. Of thy greatness, O Merciful one.   Ps. lxi. 1.

As[5] *a city surrounded with a wall.* From this city of wrath.[6] May the hidden Being cause to pass away. Every wrathful enemy. And robbery, with the rod of wrath. And may its king be strong. And enter into treaties[7] with (other) kings. And gain a storehouse and treasure. Abiding and not wasting. May his city be preserved by the will. Of the Lord from every robber. And when this creation is consumed. And destroyed, as is fore-determined. May it be worthy to behold and see. The blessing which man hath not seen.   Ps. cxxii. 3.

---

[1] R. C. ins. *And.*
[2] Lit. *there.*
[3] R. C. om. name of author.
[4] U. om. this line.
[5] Om. R. C. Every line of this verse ends with the syllable *za.*
[6] Syr.: *Arguza*; the meaning is doubtful.
[7] Syr.: *a mystery.*

Thou hast formed the earth and set it fast. In the thought of the mind of thy greatness. On the first day of the week thou didst form to thyself. Creatures in countless numbers. On the seventh (day) thou didst complete thy work. Bless our month with thy blessings. And enrich our year with thy good things. And give us joy here with thy gladness. And above[1] number us among thy companies.

Ps. cxix. 90.

We shall confess thee for ever. Let us confess thy Unity. And worship thy Trinity. And ask mercy of thee. And lasting[2] peace for thy Churches. Bless our month in thy compassion. And fill our year with thy store. And give us rest in this thy world. And in that which is to come show us thine Image.

Ps. lxxix. 14.

Let[3] thy merciful kindness, O Lord, be upon us. By the holy angels. And by mortal sons of men. May this village be blessed. And may this country and its inhabiters. Be blessed with all blessings. And made rich with all good things. And may blessed times come to them. And may all lands be made prosperous.

Ps. xxxiii. 21.

The Lord shall give his people the blessing of peace. Bless our assembly, O our Saviour. And make thy lovingkindness to dwell in it. And grant us the power to glorify thee. The assemblies above and those below. And all to love one another. And to gain love and concord. As the spiritual ones have gained. One will, that they may be approved by thee.* Thou art compassionate from all eternity. And merciful for ever. What is the wickedness of creation. Compared with the overflowing mercies of thy lovingkindness?[4] Sprinkle the face of our nature. With the dew of mercy and pity. And rescue us from the hand of the Evil one. And from the tares, the sons of error.* May Adam and the camp of the just. And Moses and the chain of the prophets. And Peter and the company of the apostles. Stephen and all the martyrs. And

Ps. xxix. 10.

---

[1] Lit. *there.*   [2] Syr.: *great.*   [3] Om. R. C.   [4] See p. 47.

Ephraim and the assembly of teachers. And Antony and the hermits. Beseech thee, O our Lord Jesus. That thou have mercy on the world.* The departed, who clothed themselves with thee, O our Lord. In the water of baptism. By thee may their bodies be cleansed. From the defilements of sin. To the departed who have eaten of thy body. And have had joy in thy living blood. Grant, O our Lord, a memorial. In the country where the just abide.

FARCINGS OF THE PSALMS[1]

Psalm 1. Blessed is he who hath borne thy yoke, and hath meditated in thy law, O Lord, by day and by night.

2. Like a horse without understanding, the arrogant men raged, and crucified Christ.

3. When I spake of thy truth, O our Lord, the wicked rose against me; deliver me from their attack.

4. There is none like the Lord, in whom I have trusted; who rescueth me from the snares and wiles of the evil ones.

5. Thou hast corrected me, O Lord, that thou mightest make me wise; reject not my request.

6. Have compassion on my weakness, O thou who didst fashion me, and correct me in thy love.

7. Blessed be God, who directeth and comforteth his servants.

8. O Son, whom the children praised in Jerusalem with their hosannas, save thy worshippers by (thy) request.

9. We will confess thee for that thou hast turned us back from error[2] to the knowledge of thee; may thine adversaries be judged.[3]

10. Because the ungodly have laid wait for the righteous with their wiles, and have blasphemed thy Name, let them be judged without mercy.[4]

11. The sinners have dealt craftily with me; in thee, O Lord, have I trusted.

---

[1] From P. and R. C.   [2] R. C.: *by thy mercies.*
[3] R. C. : *put to confusion.*
[4] R.C.: *bring their counsel to nought, O my Lord.*

12. Deceit hath increased and love waxed cold; O Christ, neglect (us) not.

13. Be propitiated by me and save me, O Lord, for I will confess thee.

14. Rescue thy Church from evil ones, O Lord of created things.

15. With purity of thoughts, O our Lord, make me to stand before thine altar.

16. Glorious is (our) confident hope in thee, who didst fashion us; in thee my weakness rejoiceth.

17. O my Lord and my God, have mercy on me, for I am persecuted unjustly.

18. Heaven and earth and all that is in them, those who are above and those who are below, kneel and worship and glorify[1] God their Creator.

19. Adorable is God who is from everlasting, who created reasonable beings to understand his other works and to know his praise.

20. In God we will place our confident hope, for he can save the humble from[2] the arrogance and pride of them that trust in themselves.

21. The Lord causeth the distresses of his servants to pass away, and maketh them glad with the salvation of the greatness of his power, and bringeth low the proud.

22. O my God, my God, let me not fall into the hands of men who have not esteemed thee.

23. We will cast our care on the Lord, who tendeth them of his household.

24. Let us be diligent in (our) duty, for he saveth us, the Almighty.

25. To thee, O my Lord, I lift up mine eyes, for thou art my true hope.

26. O Judge, the greatest of judges, cast not down my head in thy judgment.

---

[1] R. C. om. *and glorify.*   [2] R. C. om. *from . . . themselves.*

27. Cast me not out before thy face, O Searcher of secret things.

28. To thee our souls cry, Come to help us and save us.[1]

29. O thou who art good, and whose mercies are overflowing, to thee praise is due.

30. We will confess thy Name, for thou hast saved us, and hast destroyed them that wrathfully hate us.[2]

31. As a dead man they forgat me in my trouble, (but) the Lord comforted me.

32. Our Maker is the friend of men; let us propitiate him, that he may have compassion upon us.

33. Praise becometh the just, and confession befitteth them.

34. Blessed is the Lord,[3] who gave victory to his athletes in their contests.

35. They who boil over in zeal for thee are persecuted; O Christ, neglect (them) not.

36. Thou art good and just and wise, O mighty Lord.

37. Suddenly shineth forth justice and burneth up[4] the ungodly.

38. Let our correction be seasoned with thy mercies, O Compassionate one.

39. The ungodly have afflicted me, O our Lord; in thee is my true hope.

40. There is no number to thy benefits (given) to us, O Compassionate one.

41. Blessed is he on whom Mercy hath had compassion[5] in the judgment of thy justice.

42. To thee, O God, I pray for compassion; by thy mercies I will turn (to thee).

43. Judge me, O Lord, with my adversaries, and let thy help accompany me.

---

[1] P.: *me* (error?).
[2] R. C.: *and hast broken them that hate us by thy power.*
[3] R. C.: *the King.*   [4] R. C.: *destroyeth.*
[5] R. C.: *who hath found mercy.*

44. O Creator, who didst rescue our first fathers by thy strength, save thy worshippers when (they) make request (to thee).

45. Glory to thee, O our Saviour, who didst honour thy Church which thou didst choose, and didst adorn her with all beauties.

46. O God, our invincible helper, destroy the proud, and make us glad with thy salvation.

47. Blessed is he who bowed down and gave us his body for food; and by his blood wiped out the trespasses of his flock.

48. Exult and rejoice, O race of Adam, and be exalted, in Jesus, who rose, and by his death conquered death.

49. Hear ye now, O rulers of the people; with fear serve God, the Lord of all.

50. Blessed is he who by the sacrifice of his beloved made all sacrifices to end and cease.

51. With the hyssop of thy mercies may our defilements be cleansed, O Compassionate one.

52. Blessed is he who exalteth the humble and bringeth low the proud.

53. Save thy Church, O thou who knowest all.

54. Thou art my true hope.

55. To thee, O my God, is committed my judgment.

56. Cast me not, O Lord, into the wile of the crafty.

57. From the tumult of men protect me, O my Lord and my God.

58. God keepeth the just and rejecteth the wicked.

59. The ungodly have oppressed and afflicted me; deliver me, O my Lord and my God.

60. Save thy worshippers, O Christ, as thou didst promise.

61. In every place art thou, O God; receive our petition.

62. To God am I in subjection, for he is my true hope.

63. In thy mercies, which are better than life, have pity on me, O Compassionate one.

64. From the wickedness of the crafty protect me, O my Lord and my God.

65. It is not our hands that make our ways prosperous, O Christ our Saviour; for thou art the orderer of our works by thy power and wisdom.

66. Glory to thee, our Creator, who gavest us rest by night and didst keep us, and in the morning didst wake us, that in the light we might see thy wonders.

67. O Christ, who gavest talents of spiritual silver to thy servants, grant help to thy worshippers, who have received thy gift.

68. The time hath come[1] that idols be rooted out, and the one God be worshipped, the Lord of all.

69. O Christ, have pity on me.

70. Help me, O my Lord and my God.

71. Come, my brethren, let us take refuge in prayer, which is a strong weapon; and by it we will conquer Satan, our enemy, who hateth our nature.

72. Long[2] ages ago the Lord promised to Abram and David the birth of Christ, who should shine forth from Mary.

Or,[3] The lovingkindness of God hath been poured forth from on high on all, by the coming of Christ, the Saviour of all creatures.

73. Thy spirit is longsuffering, O our Lord, and thy punishment is sharp.

74. O Lord of all, who didst reveal all, cast not out thy worshippers.

75. Let us honour the feast of thy baptism, O Christ our Saviour.

76. Exalted art thou for ever, O King of all kings.[4]

77. O Lord of all, who didst reveal all, keep thou thy worshippers.

78. The sons of Israel, a perverse people.

79. Because we have sinned, the[5] oppressors have subdued us, and have polluted thy holy place; O Compassionate one, have pity on us.

---

[1] R. C.: *come near.* [2] So P. [3] So R. C.
[4] R. C.: *of all creatures.* [5] R. C.: *our.*

80. Thou didst keep in their generations our fathers, who were approved before thee; O thou who seest all, save thy Church.

81. Blessed is the Lord, who aideth his saints who keep his words, and destroyeth quickly them that hate him.

82. O judges, judge justly, and be ye far from iniquity.

Or, on feasts and memorials.[1] The watchful Intelligence called me as from sleep, and wakened me: Arise, thou that art sunk in sleep, and cast off the weight of thy sloth.

83. There is none like thee among things that are made, O God Almighty.

84. How glorious and excellent is the house of thy holiness, O God, who hallowest all.

85. Send, O our Lord, help and salvation to thy worshippers by the great power of the cross.

Or, He who would picture the sun erreth greatly, for he hath not the mind to comprehend its glorious things. He who would be an inheritor of the kingdom on high, let him free his soul from the slavery of this world.

86. O Christ, the friend of the penitent, open the door to our prayer, and receive our request.

87. Adorable is God the Creator, who careth for all generations.

Or, We are (made) poor and weak by our deeds; there are not among us just or righteous men to propitiate thee. We know not either how to pray or how to glorify (thee), and we fear to speak words that are not worthy of thee. Therefore the Lord built him a house upon earth, that whoso would see the Lord should come to his house.

88. Thou art merciful who didst fashion us; in thy lovingkindness have pity on us.

89. The good things which God had [2] promised to Abram and to David, in our days he fulfilled by deeds in Christ; glory to him.

---

[1] So the alternatives that follow. On memorials, Ps. lxxxii. to ci. incl. only are said. In Kurdistan these alternatives (to Ps. xc. incl.) are not used on memorials.   [2] R. C. om. *had.*

Or, May that lovingkindness and that gift which descended and dwelt on the disciples overshadow, O my Lord, and dwell upon thy worshippers for ever.

90. O thou who carest for us, O Almighty, have compassion on our sinfulness.

Or, O Lovingkindness, full of all mercy; O Humility, which liftedst up the weakness of the earthly.

91. Thou art my confident hope, O Christ; let me never be confounded.

92. O Mighty and All-powerful one, keep thou thy worshippers.

93. We worship thy being, which is without beginning, O thou who art glorious on high; keep thy Church and rescue her.

94. Thou who knowest all and art all-powerful, who judgest all and art our Lord, save thy servants who call to thee.

95. From error and trespasses and death hath our Lord saved us in his compassion; let us worship him and glorify him.

96. Glorious[1] is thy coming, O Christ the Saviour of all; for thou hast made us worthy with the spiritual ones to glorify thee.

Canon for Christmas.[2] For this salvation, which hath (come) to us this day, by Jesus, the son of our race, who was born [*or* baptized] this day.

97. O Church, sing glory to the Lord who renewed thee, and exalted thy weakness by his ascension, and made thee to rejoice.

Canon for Christmas, etc. Exult, O people, who are saved; and give glory, and keep not silence, in the birth [*or* baptism] of the Saviour, who hath made glad the heights and the depths.

98. Blessed is he who bowed down and was baptized by John in Jordan, and by his baptism gave pardon to all.

---

[1] R. C.: *Blessed.*

[2] And the Epiphany. These are said also to be used on all feasts of our Lord, the necessary alteration being made; perhaps also on memorials of saints (see farcing to Psalm ci.).

Canon for Christmas, etc. Give glory, O sons of the Church, O sons of the faithful Church, to him who was born of the Virgin [*or*, baptized by the son of the barren woman] for the salvation of the world.—*At the end of the Psalm.*[1] What is this, that the nations have left their gods, and swear in the name of a man who is not as thou sayest?[2] What is this, that the nations have cast away their images, and have believed and confessed the Father, Son, and Holy Ghost?

99. There is no power like thine, O our Saviour, who didst fill the[3] apostles in the upper chamber[4] with the Holy Ghost.

Canon for Christmas, etc. Glory and hallelujah, worship and hallelujah in the birth [*or* baptism] of Christ.

100. The righteous clothe themselves with glory, and above in the clouds fly to meet our Lord when he cometh.

Canon for Christmas, etc. Let us confess and glorify the Child who was born unto us [*or* baptized for us], and the Son who was given unto us.

101. The Lord in whom I have trusted, by his mercies rescueth me from the evil ones[5] who have hated me.

Canon for Christmas, etc. Let us praise and glorify the bright Light of righteousness which hath burst forth from the house of David.—*At the end of the Psalm,*[1] Come, my beloved, let us sing glory in the day of the memorial of famous N [*or* on the festival of N], and shout and cry with the hallelujah of the watchful ones, who have come down in companies and celebrated it with processions.

102. Have compassion on our error, O unchangeable Being.

Or,[6] O Compassionate one, hear our request and our prayers.

103. Blessed is the compassionate Lord, whose lovingkindness overfloweth.

---

[1] P. omits this verse.
[2] See page 95.
[3] R. C. ins. *holy.*
[4] R. C. om. *in the upper chamber.*
[5] R. C.: *the enemies.*
[6] This and the following alternatives are for the Rogation of the Ninevites.

Or, Give peace and tranquillity to the earth as thou art wont.

104. Adorable is the Creator, for ever and ever.

Or, Glory becometh thy great Name at all times.

At verse 19. We worship thee, Father, Son, and Holy Ghost.

105. Let us confess the Lord for his benefits to us, and ask of him that he supply that which we lack, for his love overfloweth for ever.

Or, Yea, confess the hidden Being who is without beginning.

At verse 23. For in Egypt he wrought wonders, and[1] saved his people.

At verse 37. Away from Egypt he wrought wonders, and saved his Church.[2]

106. O Lord, pardon the sins of thy servants who have sinned, and offended, and provoked thy Name with their deeds; in thy lovingkindness have compassion on them.

107. Blessed is our Saviour.

108. O my God, I will confess thee.

109. Save us,[3] O Lord, from the ungodly among the people, and from the peoples who with one accord have gathered themselves together against us[3] to destroy us[3] unjustly.

110. We confess thee, O our Lord Jesus, who in thy manhood art of David and of Abraham, and in thy being from thy Father.

111. Let all the upright confess with us the Being who created us, and[4] the Almighty who governeth all in his wisdom and justice and goodness.

112. Blessed are they who tread without fear the way of Christ, and walk in his holy laws and keep his commandments.

113. Glorious is the Being who by his servants called the nations to know his wonderful things, so that by his power

---

[1] R. C. : *and they did not believe in him.*
[2] R. C. : *his people.*
[3] R. C. : *me.*
[4] R. C. om. rest of this farcing.

they conquered in the world, and who investeth them in heaven with glory.

114. In the middle of the night I have risen up to confess thee, O our Lord, for thy judgments; and I wonder at the deeds of thy wisdom and confess thy Name.

115, 116.[1] The Lord of our death and our life is God alone.

117. O nation and nations, one Church, glorify Christ.

118. There is none strong and full of mercies like the Lord, my refuge.

119. *Alap.*[2] Help thou my weakness, O Christ, to fulfil thy will.

Beith. In thy love, O our Lord, thou hast established me, and by thy gospel hast given wisdom to my childishness.

Gamal. Thy doctrine, O our Saviour, is sought out and honoured above all things and good.

Dalath. The haters of the truth hath trodden me down; O Lord of all, help thou me.

He. All error is vanity; O Christ, guide me in thy truth.

Wau. May the right have victory, O Lord, in thy servants before all kings.

Zain. This time is like a dream; comfort me, O our Lord, with thy hope.

Khêith. I look alway to thy love; O Christ, save me from oppression.

Têith. Better than all honour I have loved thy word; O Lord, comfort me.

Yudh. More than all thou, O Lord, knowest what helpeth us.

Kap. O Just one, O Lord to whom all is revealed, save the afflicted who cry to thee.

Lamadh. They that fear the Lord, who passeth not away, are in no danger from mortals.

---

[1] These are one psalm in the Syriac. All after this to Psalm cxlvii. 12 are numbered one behind the English Prayer Book.

[2] In the Syriac the first letters of the farcings (but not of the sections of the psalm as in the Hebrew) follow the order of the alphabet.

Mim. O Lord, who didst raise the meek and didst strike down the proud, glory to thee.

Nun. Thy word is light and life and truth, O our Saviour.

Simkath. Confirm me in thy hope,[1] O our Lord, that I[2] may stand firm in thy teaching.

'E. Help thy Church, O our Saviour; cast not away her who hath loved thee.

Pe. Save, O our Lord, them that call on thy Name, who groan because thy[3] truth is despised.

Sadhi. Be pleased with me, O Lord, and save me, that they who err may know thy glory.

Qop. May the voice of thy praise not cease, O God, in the mouth of thy servants.

Resh. Thy fear is above all things; O Lord, judge me.

Shin. Thy glory, O our Lord, is better than all, and hath alway helped me when I was persecuted.

Tau. Receive our petition, O our Lord, and fill our mouth with praise.

120. The ungodly have driven me far away; O thou who art boundless, comfort me.

121. I looked for thee, who art more watchful than all; alway keep my weakness.

122. Make us glad, O our Lord, with thy salvation, and with the joy of thy Churches.

123. O Compassionate one, receive my petition, and may they that despise me be laughed to scorn.

124. Blessed is our Maker, who rescueth his worshippers from the evil ones.

125. Created things, whose confident trust is in the Lord, can in no wise be moved.

126. In thy hope have I gone, O our Lord, and have fled to thee; help thou me.

127. Beneath the wings of thy kindness protect me, O my Lord and my God.

128. Pour forth thy gift, O our Lord, in thy lovingkindness on thy servants.

---

[1] R. C.: *Confirm in us thy hope.*   [2] R. C.: *we.*   [3] R. C.: *the.*

129. Hear, O our Lord, the voice of our petition, and keep us from the Evil one.

130. O thou who art good and just and compassionate, in thy lovingkindness have mercy on us.[1]

131. Raise me, O my Lord, from the dust, that I may glorify thee and confess thy Name.

132. O Christ, keep the priesthood, and make thy peace to dwell in the Churches.

133. A bridechamber and blessing which passeth not away, hath our Lord promised to his saints.

134. At all seasons it becometh the saints to glorify thee, O our Saviour.

135. The people glorified thee when they went forth, for thou didst give victory by their hands.

136. Let us confess our God, who in the multitude of his lovingkindnesses hath saved his servants from the evil ones and oppressors who hate (us) without cause, and [2] from the hand of the ungodly.

137. Because that Jerusalem sinned, and received not the prophets and apostles who came to her, she became a reproach among the people.

138. We venerate [3] thine honourable cross, O our Lord Jesus, for by it thou didst save our nature.

139. O thou who knowest all before thou createst all, save us, O Almighty.

140. From the will and attack of the evil ones protect me, O my Lord and my God.

141. Blessed art thou, O Lord, who rejectest not the request of thy worshippers.

142. Thou art the help of the desolate, O Almighty.

143. I am oppressed by them that hate the truth; O God, save thy servant.

144. Blessed is the Lord, who maketh the evil ones to sink, and giveth victory to them of his household.

145. We will confess thee, O our Maker, for thou hast guided us with the light of day, and hast brought us to the

---

[1] R. C.: *me*. [2] P. om. *and*. [3] Syr.: *worship*.

evening that thou mayest give us rest by night, and that thou mayest preserve us.

146. Let the heavenly ones and the earthly ones confess thee, O everlasting Being, who in thy great mercy didst condescend and didst put on [1] our manhood.

147. When thou didst create this light, O our Maker,[2] the angels marvelled at it; and when each day[3] it shineth forth, both they and we will[4] glorify thee.

147, *verse* 12.[5] Blessed is he who, in the place of Mount Zion, formed Jerusalem above.

148. The heaven of heavens glorify thee, for thou didst bring them into being.

149. The nations sang praises to the God who saved them.

150. The Son of God hath sanctified you and bidden you to his kingdom.

Exodus xv. 1-22. Blessed is the Creator Being, who by all (his) wonders delivered his servants,[6] and by his Christ saved his Church.

Or, Gloriously will I glorify thee.

Isaiah xlii. 10-14 *and* xlv. 8. Glory to the Lord, who by his strength destroyed the proud and saved his servants in [7] his mercies, for he created all and formed all.

Or, Being who art from everlasting.

Deuteronomy xxxii. 1-21*a*. Incline, O Lord, to my prayer, and neglect not my request.

Canon for Christmas.[8] Sing praises, sing praises, sing praises, O Watchful ones, at the birth [*or* baptism] of Christ the King.

Deuteronomy xxxii. 21*a*-44. Blessed is he who hath lifted up a hard people and hath revealed to them things to come.

---

[1] R. C.: *take.*
[2] R. C.: *God.*
[3] R. C.: *morning.*
[4] R. C. om. *will.*
[5] This is the Syriac Ps. 147.
[6] R. C.: *people.*
[7] R. C. om. rest of this farcing.
[8] And Epiphany, etc.

PRAYERS ON VARIOUS OCCASIONS[1]

When there is a scarcity of rain.[2] In thy goodness spread thy lovingkindness on our wickedness. *Repeat.* And pour forth thy mercies, O Merciful one, on us who are exiled from thee, and make thy compassion, O Compassionate one, to flow forth on our unrighteousness, and overshadow our confusion with thy pitiful wings; have compassion in thy pitiful pity on our sinfulness; and enrich our poverty with thy gift, O good Giver; and answer our afflicted state in times of affliction; and satisfy our hunger from thy table, O thou who feedest the worlds; and sprinkle the dew of thy kindness on our fields; and inebriate our ploughed fields and our lands with the rain of thy good pleasure; and bring our souls out of the prison house of distresses, and fill our hearts with thy true hope and strong trust, for thou dost care for our life, and suppliest all things that may help us in thy lovingkindness and mercies, Lord of all, etc.

Another. Have pity, O my Lord, and mercy on our evil generation, for its sighs have waxed strong, and its good things have become small; and let the right hand of thy Majesty rest over the world and its inhabiters; and let them that dwell therein abide in quietness beneath the shadow of thy wings; and let wars cease and contentions come to an end; and let variances be brought to nought and chastisements be withheld, and may peace be assured and tranquillity reign in every place continually, that thereby we may propitiate

---

[1] From T.

[2] See also a special verse of the Wednesday Motwa, above, page 149.

thy Godhead, and be approved by the good pleasure of thy Majesty, and abstaining from evil things confess and worship and glorify thy glorious Trinity, at all times, Lord of all, etc.

Prayer for the crops. Glory to thee, who dost plant all trees that they may bear pleasant fruits for the joy of thy servants; bless, O my Lord, these crops of thy servants, and may the fruits which propitiate thy Majesty be increased twofold therefrom, and may we lift up to thee glory for the things which thou suppliest, for ever. *Amen.*

Prayer for the sick. O thou who givest life to all in thy compassion, and raisest all in thy good pleasure, and drivest away all pains and sicknesses in thy mercy; heal, O my Lord, this thy servant in thy compassion, and raise him up from his sickness in the abundance of thy lovingkindness, that he[1] may confess thee for thy salvation (shown) to him, now and at all times, Lord of all, etc.

Prayer for one tempted by a devil. O Healer of all pains, and Assuager of all plagues, heal, O my Lord, this thy servant, of the plague of the Enemy; and as thy lovingkindness drave out Legion from him who dwelt among the graves, and didst cast him into the sea and overthrow him, and didst give ease to thy servant, so, O my Lord, also from this thy servant let thy power drive him away, and thy good pleasure root him out; and may (thy servant) be to thee a dwelling-place, and may he be signed with the living sign of thy cross, and bear thy pleasant yoke, and be joined to thy flock, O our compassionate Maker, Father, Son, and Holy Ghost, for ever. *Amen.*

Prayer for infants. May he who blessed the childhood of Isaak, so that there welled forth from him the promise of life in this world, and they saw within him the sign of salvation, bless thee and exalt thy parents, and make them glad with thy growth and the welling forth of thy wisdom; and may the right hand and lovingkindness of the Highest keep thee now and at all times, Lord of all, etc.

---

[1] Or *we.*

Prayer over wine. O heavenly Beverage, flowing from the blessed Grape,[1] bless, O my Lord, this wine, and mingle with it the compassion of thy lovingkindness, that it may make glad the heart of them that drink it, and cause the mind of them that give to drink of it to rejoice; that when they rejoice at the taste of the wine of thy grapes,[1] they may confess and glorify thee for thy lovingkindnesses towards them, now and at all times, Lord of all, etc.

Prayer over the oil of healing. O true Healer, whose word is full of all salves and helps and healing medicines, do thou, O my Lord, make thy lovingkindness to dwell in this oil, that it may help and cure all our sicknesses, and relieve our afflictions, and give ease in our distresses, and remedy our pains, and cleanse our wounds, and take away our fevers; and may it be found (effectual) for all salves and helps by the salve which thou hast given us in it, and may we lift up to thy Trinity, which is full of all good things, praise and honour and confession, now and at all times, Lord of all, etc.

Prayer for a reader. May God, the Lord of all, in his lovingkindness and mercies, bless the reader, that he may give wisdom to the hearers by his holy teaching, for ever. *Amen.*

Prayer for the faithful. May our Lord Jesus Christ bless this assembly of the faithful in his lovingkindness and mercies for ever. *Amen.*

Prayer for a house. May the Trinity, by whom the houses of the just and righteous fathers were blessed and hallowed, keep this house and protect them that dwell in it from all harm, hidden and open. *Amen.*

Prayer when a man kisses[2] *the cross.*[3] May the power which is hidden in the cross make me to gain power and courage for the war with the demon, the enemy, by the mercies of our good God. Amen.

Prayer when a man kisses the book of the Gospel. May the power which is hidden in the Gospel, full of life and grace,

---

[1] These are different words in the Syriac.
[2] Syr.: *gives the peace to.*
[3] This and the following six prayers may be said by a layman.

fill my mind with wisdom, that I may know the meaning of the word. Amen.

Prayer when a man kisses the tomb[1] *of the saints.* May our Lord and our God make us partakers of thy virtue, O our holy father, and may we be worthy of mercies and compassion by thy prayers. Amen.

Prayer[2] *when a man goes on a journey.* O God of Abraham, and of Isaak, and of Jacob, God of the just fathers and the prophets, God the Father of our Lord Jesus Christ, I make request to thee and entreat thy greatness, at this time when I set forward on this journey, that thy help may accompany me, and that thy lovingkindness may help me, for thou keepest my soul with my body from all adversities, and rescuest me from all harm. As thou wast with Joseph in the land of Egypt, and with Daniel in the lions' den, and with the company of Ananias in the fiery furnace, and with Jeremiah in the miry pit,[3] so also be with me, O Compassionate one, lightening the burden of this my journey, and overthrowing the enemies and evil ones before me, and be thou my Sustainer and Saviour, that the cause for which I set forth may receive a good fulfilment; and pour forth on me all good things. At my request to thee, O Compassionate one, grant me to meet with kindness (in) the land whither I go, and cause me to return, O my Lord, with my mouth filled with gratitude, and my tongue with praise, that I may return to my dwelling and my house with joy and gladness, to lift up praise and honour and confession and worship to thy living and holy Name, now and at all times, Lord of all, etc.

Prayer when a man enters a boat or ship. In the confident hope of thy mercy, O Lord, we pray and make request of thy overflowing mercies, make the sea peaceful before all who make a voyage in this ship of thy worshippers, and open the full and overflowing treasure of thy helps in their voyage; and may they go in peace and return in tranquillity, their hearts rejoicing, and their minds glad in the prosperity which they

---

[1] Shkhinta (Shechinah).   [2] See also above, page 149.   [3] Lit. *den.*

gain from thy rich treasure, O Lord, full of mercies; and be thou to them, O Lord, a guide and a way, and an overseer by day and by night, and vouchsafe that they in soul and body may be perfect, and deliver them from the harm of the enemy in thy lovingkindness and mercies, that they may lift up to thee praise and honour and confession and worship, now and at all times, Lord of all, etc.

Prayer of a man for himself. Lord, thou knowest how I should call to thee; I am only a brute beast, and know nothing. Thou hast brought me to this age of life; save me for thy mercies sake; I am thy servant, and the son of thy handmaid. O Lord, give me life in thy good pleasure. Amen.

Another. O Lord, as thou knowest and willest and pleasest, grant to me even those things which help my poverty and weakness and infirmity; for mercies and compassion and lovingkindness are thine for ever. Amen.

Prayer when a priest washes his hands at the time of the Creed.[1] May God, the Lord of all, wash the filth of our trespasses and sins with the hyssop of his compassion, and cleanse the defilements of our iniquities with the overflowing sea of his mercy for ever. Amen.

When he wipes his hands. May the Lord wipe away the contamination of our sins in his lovingkindness and mercies for ever. Amen.

Prayer in fevers. In thy Name, O good Father, and in the Name of the Only-begotten, our Lord Jesus Christ, and in the Name of the Spirit of holiness, living and holy, I drive out the fever from thy servant N, son of M;[2] and I destroy thee, O shivering fever, by that Power who called to Simon Peter's[3] wife's mother, who was held of a fever, so that she stood up and was made whole, and began to minister to our Lord. Now also, O Lord the mighty God, make firm the knees of this thy servant N, son of M,[2] and may he rise up and be made whole of this sickness by the power of the God of Gods and Lord of Lords; and by thy help heal this thy

---

[1] At the liturgy, in the Place of the deacon.
[2] The *mother's* name.
[3] Syr.: *Kipa* (Cephas).

servant, and make him whole, by the prayer of St. Mary the blessed, the mother of the Light, and by the prayer of all the saints of our Lord, now and at all times, Lord of all, etc.

Grace before meat.[1] Stretch forth, O our Lord and our God, the right hand of thy mercy from the height of thy holiness, and bless and hallow this food of thy worshippers, in the name of thy glorious Trinity; and enrich it with the benefits and blessings which come from thee, Father, Son, and Holy Ghost, for ever.[2] Our Father, etc. (*without farcings*).

Grace after meat.[3] A thousand thousand and ten thousand times ten thousand thanksgivings to God the Lord of all. May this food be multiplied and increased, and remain stedfast and never fail, by the prayers of the twelve apostles, and the just and righteous fathers who were and are approved by their Lord in every generation. May this table be as the table of our father Abraham, and not fail or fall short of heavenly blessings in every age while this world remaineth; may the houses of the faithful be blessed, and their offerings[4] be accepted, may their departed be quickened, may their trespasses and sins be pardoned, and may they be worthy of the good things of the kingdom, O thou who art glorious, and feedest all in thy lovingkindness and mercies, now and at all times, Lord of all, etc. Our Father, etc.

Or this. O thou who didst satisfy thousands in the desert, so that they ate from a few loaves, bless, O my Lord, this table, that it may be full and rich; that the poor may eat and be satisfied, and that the orphans may be supplied from it, and all classes be supported by it, and have joy from its good things; as the table of chosen Abram, and David the king and prophet, and Solomon and Hezekiah, and Constantine the victorious. So, O my Lord, may this table of thy servant be blessed and enriched with good things, by the overflowing mercies of thy lovingkindness. Bless, O our Lord, the husbandmen (who sowed the corn) for it; bless, O my Lord,

---

[1] Lit. *Prayer on the table.*
[2] Here he crosses himself and the food.
[3] Lit. *Prayer of the satisfaction of the table.*
[4] Eucharists.

them that prepared it; bless, O my Lord, them that eat of it; bless the house and them that dwell in it. Make, O my Lord, thy blessing to overshadow the house and abide in it; and may they that dwell in it ever be kept from evil things. Bless beasts and men; bless vineyards and orchards; bless crops and fruits, and all of us together, now and at all times, and for ever and ever. Our Father, etc.

Prayer for hallowing unclean water.[1] *This only.* Thee, O mighty, holy, and glorious God, we confess and worship, and with the boldness which thou hast given us we ask of thy kindness to stretch forth the right hand of thy mercy, and bless and hallow this water; and to make thy help to abide in it; that wherever it is placed or poured out, or floweth forth or is thrown, it may cast thence all defilement and uncleanness from a dead man, and from things[2] strangled[3]; and that all who drink of it, or who use it, may gain from it cleanliness and comeliness and purity of soul and body; and may it give, by thy pure gift, help and salvation to souls which desire and rejoice in the holiness and order of the household of thy Majesty; and for all thy helps and graces towards us we will lift up to thee praise and honour and confession and worship, now and at all times, and for ever and ever. Amen. *He makes the sign of the cross on the water.*

Prayer said over a bride when she enters the church after forty days. O compassionate and merciful Christ, our God, whose lovingkindness is poured forth on all, pour forth thy lovingkindness and help on this bride, and sanctify her by thy mercies, and make her worthy to love the good and hate the

---

[1] A Syrian correspondent writes :—' After a funeral, things that have become ceremonially unclean are sprinkled with water. Some of the water used in washing the body is mixed with other water, and blessed and sprinkled over the house, bedding, and relatives. A man who skins or plucks off the hair of an unclean animal, that is, one which has died without its throat being cut, or of a dead ass or horse, or the like, need not be sprinkled thus.' Also after a funeral all the worshippers in many places wash in a stream, the water of which has been blessed.

[2] Syr.: *a thing* or *a man*.   [3] Or *drowned*.

evil, and to do deeds that are approved by thee; and may fruits of gladness come from her bosom, and grow up in the faith of thy holy Church; and may she walk before her bridegroom according to thy good pleasure, and look to him with her eyes as is right, and hear with her ears his commands and confess them; and may her mouth speak fitly about him; and with her heart may she truly love him, and with her hands do his will; and may her feet walk circumspectly in holiness. And may bride and bridegroom and groom's man and bride's maid be kept from all harm by the prayers of her who bare thee, the second heaven, St. Mary the blessed, and of all thy saints, now and at all times, and for ever and ever. *Amen.* *He makes the sign of the cross on her head.*

Blessing said over a boy and his mother, forty days after his birth, when the mother brings him into Church. O Lord the mighty God, the Creator of heaven and of earth, and of all that is in them, who gave the law to the first fathers, and didst command therein that every male when forty days old should come to thy holy temple, and make an offering to the priest, and that he should pray over him, and that he should be purified, and didst fulfil this command, even thou, O my Lord, by the entrance of thy beloved Son into the temple when forty days old, when the aged Simeon took him in his arms, and confessed, and asked of him a release from his life; now also, O Lord God, bless and sanctify this child N, who hath come to thy holy Church, which is the dwelling-place of holiness, to ask of thee to grant him that the milk which he draweth in may be increased, and that he may be kept from the Evil one and his hosts, and may grow in holiness and the true faith all the days of his life. *Amen.*

For the boy's mother. And mayest thou, the mother of the boy, be moved in the hidden man which is in the heart, to good works, and may there come forth from thy loins sons and daughters who may propitiate God by their goodly deeds; and mayest thou have joy in the blessings of the Lord; and thou and thy son, may ye be kept from all harm by the prayers of the Virgin clothed in light, the second heaven, St. Mary, who bare Christ our God,[1] and by the prayer of all the saints, now and at all times, and for ever and ever. *Amen.* *He makes the sign of the cross over their heads.*

Prayer for a woman who asks for the prayers of the Church. O our Lord Jesus Christ, the secret Son[2] of the hidden Father, who didst make thy mercies to bow down to our weak and feeble race, and didst come down from heaven to earth, and didst take man's body from the Virgin Mary, the daughter of David, and didst fulfil the law of Moses thy servant, when on the eighth day thou madest an offering of circumcision; and by a bodily growth didst offer purification for purification[3] as it is written; for thou art the acceptable offering, and sweet odour, and by thee thy Father is reconciled to our weak and feeble race; do thou, O Lord, the mighty God, now give pardon and forgiveness and purification to this thy handmaid N, who hath presented herself this day in thy holy temple, and hath come to (me) thy weak and sinful servant, and asketh blessings and prayers, and gifts of grace from heaven, given though the priesthood from thy mercy, O Creator of us all. Yea, when (we) make request to thee, O Lord Almighty, return answer, O Lord, in thy mercies to this thy handmaid at this time, and send on her the grace of the Holy Ghost; that she may be sanctified and cleansed from all uncleanness of flesh and spirit, and be adorned with purity and holiness, that she may please thy will and keep thy commandments, now and at all times, and for ever and ever. *Amen.*

Prayer over new cloths and vessels[4] offered to the Altar. O Lord God of our fathers, who in the first ages didst mystically typify beforehand the mysteries of the faithful Church by the hands of the head of the high[5] priest, Moses the prophet, when thou didst command him with holy oil to sanctify the tabernacle and all its cloths and vessels,[4] that they might be set apart in grace and holiness, because thou art holy; we

---

[1] We may notice this close approach to the term Theotokos.
[2] *Lit.* Child.
[3] *i.e.* didst give baptism instead of the cleansing of the old law.
[4] One Syriac word includes all these.   [5] Syr.: *head.*

also, O merciful Lord, Friend of man, make request to thee and beseech thee, according to thy promise to thy holy apostles, to send thy grace which worketh all blessings, and purify and sanctify this cloth,[1] and bless it, that it may be for priestly use as becometh the ministration thereby of thy divine and pardoning mysteries; and anoint it with thyself, who art the oil of complete perfection; and may we be to thee pure and holy temples in which thy Godhead dwelleth, Father, Son, and Holy Ghost. *Amen.*

Or this. O Lord the God of hosts, Almighty, holy, and glorious, who art eternally holy, and dwellest in light that man cannot attain unto, whose glory and holiness hath filled all things, and who hast not left thyself without those who shall glorify thee, and hast created the companies on high to glorify and to sing Holy to thy Majesty, not that thou needest praise, but that they who glorify thee may be magnified in thee, and hast created the worlds in thy lovingkindness, and hast raised up high priests to thy honour, and hast set firm a tabernacle for thy dwelling-place,[2] and hast decked it with glorious cloths and vessels,[3] and censers and chalices, and candlesticks and cups, and whatever else is (used) in the Mosaic service which thou hast commanded; now also, O Lord, we thy servants, saved by the cross of thine Only-begotten, beseech thy mercies to hallow these cloths and vessels[3] on which our hands have been laid, and which have been offered for the service of thy altar, to be for the honour of thy habitation,[2] and the praise of thy holy Name, Father, Son, and Holy Ghost. And receive, O my Lord, as an oblation the will of these persons who have offered them, and of whosoever have been partakers with them, for thou art a Sea who pourest forth blessings in thy lovingkindness and mercies, and to thee is due confession from the mouth of all speaking beings whom thou hast created, now and at all times, and for ever and ever. Yea, and Amen. *He makes the sign of the cross on the cloths and vessels.*[3]

---

[1] *Or* vessel.   [2] Shkhinta (Shechinah).   [3] See Note 4, p. 257.

INDEX I

TABLE OF THE DIVISIONS OF THE PSALTER

(Each *Hulala* is divided into two, three, or four *Marmyatha*, which are marked by the dashes.)

Hulali.   *Psalms.*
1. i. ii. iii. iv.—v. vi. vii.—viii. ix. x.
2. xi. xii. xiii. xiv.—xv. xvi. xvii.—xviii.—xix. xx. xxi.
3. xxii. xxiii. xxiv.—xxv. xxvi. xxvii.—xxviii. xxix. xxx.
4. xxxi. xxxii.—xxxiii. xxxiv.—xxxv. xxxvi.
5. xxxvii.—xxxviii. xxxix. xl.
6. xli. xlii. xliii.—xliv. xlv. xlvi.—xlvii. xlviii. xlix.
7. l. li. lii.—liii. liv. lv.—lvi. lvii. lviii.
8. lix. lx. lxi.—lxii. lxiii. lxiv.—lxv. lxvi. lxvii.
9. lxviii.—lxix. lxx.
10. lxxi. lxxii.—lxxiii. lxxiv.—lxv. lxxvi. lxxvii.
11. lxxviii.—lxxix. lxxx. lxxxi.
12. lxxxii. lxxxiii. lxxxiv.—lxxxv. lxxxvi.—lxxxvii. lxxxviii.
13. lxxxix.—xc. xci. xcii.
14. xciii. xciv. xcv.—xcvi. xcvii. xcviii.—xcix. c. ci.
15. cii. ciii.—civ.—cv.
16. cvi.—cvii. cviii.—cix. cx. cxi.
17. cxii. cxiii. cxiv. cxv.—cxvi. cxvii. cxviii.—cxix. 1-89.
18. cxix. 89-end—cxx. cxxi. cxxii. cxxiii. cxxiv. cxxv.—cxxvi. cxxvii. cxxviii. cxxix. cxxx. cxxxi.
19. cxxxii. cxxxiii. cxxxiv. cxxxv.—cxxxvi. cxxxvii. cxxxviii.—cxxxix. cxl. cxli.
20. cxlii. cxliii. cxliv.—cxlv. cxlvi. cxlvii. 1-12—cxlvii. 12, cxlviii. cxlix. cl.
21. Exodus xv. 1-22, Isaiah xlii. 10-14, xlv. 8—Deuteronomy xxxii. 1-21a—Deuteronomy xxxii. 21a-44.

INDEX II

TABLE OF THE PSALMS, SHOWING WHEN THEY ARE SAID IN THE DAILY OFFICES

A.—*Regular Course.*

Hulali 1-7 incl.	Monday and Thursday, Night Service.
,, 8-14 incl.	Tuesday and Friday, Night Service.
,, 15-21 incl.	Wednesday and Saturday, Night Service.
,, 5-11 incl.	Sundays 'before,' Night Service.
,, 12, 13, 14	{ Sundays 'before,' Suyakhi and Qali d'Shahra, Night Service.
,, 12-18 incl.	Sundays 'after,' Night Service.
,, 19, 20, 21	{ Sundays 'after,' Suyakhi and Qali d'Shahra, Night Service.
,, 12, 13, 14	Saints' Days, Night Service.
The whole Psalter.	Festivals of our Lord, Night Service.
Hulala 3	Compline, daily (if said; see page 185).

B.—*At other times.*

[M., Morning Service; E., Evening Service; N., Night Service; C., Compline.]

Psalm.	
iii. 5-end	N. Canon in the Fast (weeks of the mysteries).
xi.	E. Monday, First Marmitha.
xii.	Do. do.
xii. 1-7	E. First Monday, First Shuraya.
xiii.	E. Mon., First Marmitha; N. Mon., Shubakha.
xiv.	E. Monday, First Marmitha.
xv.	{ E. Monday, Second Marmitha; and Memorials not falling on Fridays, Marmitha; N. Monday, Qaltha.
xv. 1-5	E. First Monday, Second Shuraya.

Psalm.

xvi.	⎫ As xv.
xvii.	⎭
xvii. 1-6a	E. First Tuesday, First Shuraya.
xxi. 1-5	E. First Tuesday, Second Shuraya.
xxiii. 1-5	E. First Wednesday, First Shuraya.
xxiv. 1-6	E. First Wednesday, Second Shuraya.
xxv. 1-5	E. First Thursday, First Shuraya.
xxv.	E. Tuesday, First Marmitha; and N. Tuesday, Qaltha.
xxvi.	Do. do.
xxvii.	Do. do.
xxviii. 1-8	E. First Thursday, Second Shuraya.
xxviii.	E. Tues., Second Marmitha; N. Tues., Shubakha.
xxix.	E. Tuesday, Second Marmitha.
xxx.	Do. do.
xxx. 1-5	E. First Saturday, First Shuraya.
xxxi. 21-24	E. Last Friday, Third Shuraya.
xl. 1-15	N. Sundays 'before' of Advent, Qaltha.
xl. 7-10a	E. Middle Friday, Third Shuraya.
xl. 16-20	E. Second Tuesday, Second Shuraya.
xlii. 1-5	E. Second Monday, First Shuraya.
xlv.	⎧ N. Sundays 'before' of the Hallowing of the Church, ⎨ and all Wednesdays, Qaltha.
xlv. 14-17	E. First Wednesday, Third Shuraya.
xlvii. 1-5	⎧ E. First Sunday of each Shawu'a, First Shuraya, ⎨ (from Ascension to Advent, add vv. 5-9).
xlviii. 1-3	E. First Sunday of each Shawu'a, Second Shuraya.
xlviii. 1-11	N. Sundays 'after' of Advent, Qaltha.
xlix. 1-5	E. Sixth Sunday of each Shawu'a, First Shuraya.
li.	C. daily.
li. 1-18	M. daily (ferias only).
liv. 1-5	E. First Saturday, Second Shuraya.
liv.	N. Thursday, Shubakha.
lxii.	E. Wednesday, First Marmitha.
lxiii.	Do. do.
lxiv.	Do. do.
lxv. 1-5a	E. Second Sunday of each Shawu'a, First Shuraya.
lxv.	⎧ E. Wednesday, Second Marmitha; and Sunday and ⎨ Feasts, Marmitha (exc. Advent to Epiphany).
lxvi.	Do. do. do.
lxvi. 1-4 (or 1-5)	E. Second Sunday of each Shawu'a, Second Shuraya.
lxvii.	As lxv.; and N. Wednesday, Shubakha.
lxvii. 1-6	E. Second Tuesday, First Shuraya.
lxxii. 1-5	E. Second Wednesday, First Shuraya.
lxxv. 1-5	E. First Friday, First Shuraya.

INDEX II

Psalm.

lxxxii. 1-5 (*or* 1-5a)	E. First Friday, Second Shuraya.
lxxxiv.	N. Sundays 'after' of the Hallowing of the Church, Qaltha.
lxxxv.	E. Friday, First Marmitha; and Memorials falling on Fridays, Marmitha.
lxxxvi.	As lxxxv.; and N. Sun. 'before,' Qaltha (except Advent, Hallowing of the Church, and Palm Sunday).
lxxxvii.	E. Friday, Second Marmitha; and Sundays and Feasts, Marmitha (Advent to Epiphany).
lxxxviii.	As lxxxvii.; and N. Friday, Qaltha; and C. daily.
lxxxviii. 10, 11	N. Sundays 'before' and Palm Sunday, Qaltha.
lxxxix. 1-5	E. Third Sunday of each Shawu'a, First Shuraya.
lxxxix. 5-9a	E. Third Sunday of each Shawu'a, Second Shuraya.
xc.	C. daily.
xci.	M. daily, and N. Sundays 'after' (except Advent, Hallowing of the Church, and Palm Sunday); and Rogation of Ninevites, Qaltha; and C. daily.
xcii. 1, 2	N. Canon in the Fast (ordinary weeks).
xciii.	M. daily, and E. Fourth Sunday of each Shawu'a, First Shuraya.
xcv. 1-8	E. Middle Fri., First Shuraya; N. Fri., Shubakha.
xcvi.	E. Thursday, First Marmitha; and N. Palm Sunday and all Thursdays, Qaltha.
xcvii.	Do. do. do.
xcviii.	Do. do. do.
xcix.	E. Thursday, Second Marmitha.
c.	E. Thursday, Second Marmitha; and M. daily.
ci.	E. Thursday, Second Marmitha.
ci. 1-10	E. Second Wednesday, Second Shuraya.
cii. 26, 27	N. Sundays 'after' (except Palm Sunday), and Rogation of the Ninevites, Qaltha.
civ. 1-16a	M. daily. (In the Fast, 1-15a.)
cxiii.	Do.
cxvi. 11-13a	E. First Friday, Third Shuraya.
cxvii.	M. and E. and C. daily.
cxix. 1-17	E. First Monday, Letter Psalm.
,, 17-33	E. First Tuesday, Letter Psalm.
,, 41-49	E. Second Thursday, First Shuraya.
,, 49-65	E. First Thursday, Letter Psalm.
,. 57-65	N. Canon in the Fast (ordinary weeks).
,, 65-89	E. First Saturday, Letter Psalm.
,, 89-105	E. Second Monday, Letter Psalm.
,, 105-113	E. daily.

INDEX II

Psalm.

cxix. 113-129	.	E. Second Tuesday, Letter Psalm.
,, 121-129	.	E. Second Thursday, Second Shuraya.
,, 145-161	.	E. Second Thursday, Letter Psalm.
,, 161-end	.	E. Second Saturday, Letter Psalm.
cxxi.		{ N. all Sundays 'before,' and Palm Sunday, Qaltha; and C. daily.
cxxiii. 1-3a . .		{ E. Second Monday, Second Shuraya; and N. all Sundays 'after' (exc. Palm Sunday) and Rogation of the Ninevites, Qaltha.
cxxiv. 1-6 . .		E. Second Saturday, First Shuraya.
cxxv. 1-3 . .		E. Second Saturday, Second Shuraya.
cxxvi. 1-7 (or 1-6). . . .		E. Fifth Sunday of each Shawu'a, First Shuraya.
cxxvii. 1-5 . .		E. Fifth Sunday of each Shawu'a, Second Shuraya.
cxxx. (or 1-8) .		E. Sixth Sunday of each Shawu'a, Second Shuraya.
cxxx. . . .		C. daily.
cxxxiv. . . .		N. Canon in the Fast (weeks of the mysteries).
cxxxvii. 1-4		E. Seventh Sunday of each Shawu'a, First Shuraya.
cxxxviii. 1-4a (or 1-3a) . .		E. Seventh Sunday of each Shawu'a, Second Shuraya.
cxxxviii. 7a-8 .		N. all Sundays and Rogation of the Ninevites, Qaltha.
cxxxix. 1-5 . .		E. Middle Friday, Second Shuraya.
cxli.		E. daily.
cxlii.		Do.
cxliii. . . .		C. daily.
cxlv. 1-7a . .		E. Last Friday, First Shuraya.
cxlv. 18-end		E. Last Friday, Second Shuraya.
cxlv.		E. Saturday, First Marmitha.
cxlvi.		Do. do.
cxlvii. 1-12 . .		Do. do.
cxlvii. 12-end .		E. Sat., Second Marmitha; N. Sat., Qaltha.
cxlviii. . . .		As cxlvii. 12-end, and M. daily.
cxlviii. 1-7a		E. Fourth Sunday of each Shawu'a, Second Shuraya.
cxlix. . . .		{ E. Saturday, Second Marmitha; and N. Saturday, Qaltha; and M. daily.
cl.		{ E. Saturday, Second Marmitha; and N. Saturday, Qaltha; and M. daily and N. Saturday, Shubakha; and C. daily.
Ex. xv. 20-21a.		E. Second Wednesday, Third Shuraya.

This table does not include the proper psalms noted in the Khudhra for feasts of our Lord, Sundays, memorials, etc.; or the psalms used at the Liturgy, at Baptism, or in similar offices.

APPEN

THE KALENDAR [1]

First Sunday of 'Annunciation' or Advent,[4]

Second Sunday of 'Annunciation,'

Third Sunday of 'Annunciation,'

Fourth Sunday of 'Annunciation,'

The Nativity, December 25th,[5]

Friday. Mar Yaqu (James),[6] the Lord's Brother,*[7]

First Sunday of the Nativity,

Friday. Mart Máriam (St. Mary),

Second Sunday of the Nativity,

Monday, Tuesday, and Wednesday; Rogation of Mar Zaya (very rarely observed),[8]

---

[1] All the dates are in old style. For the sources of this Kalendar see Introduction.

[2] The lessons are those used in the Liturgy; there are none in the daily offices, except on Easter Day. The 'lections' (in the more limited sense) are arranged in three divisions at the suggestion of the Rev. W. C. Bishop, M.A., to whom the writer is also indebted for the index to the Lectionary which follows.   [3] St. Paul.

DIX

AND LECTIONARY [2]

	The Lections.			
Law.	Prophecy.	Acts.	The Apostle.[3]	The Gospel.
Gen. xvii.	Isa. xlii. 18—xliii. 14	...	Eph. v. 21—vi. 10.	Luke i. 5-26
Num. xxii. 9-21	,, xliii. 14—xliv. 6		Col. iv. 2-end	,, i. 26-57
Gen. xviii. 1-20	Judg. xiii. 2-25	...	Eph. iii.	,, i. 57-end
,, xxiv. 50-end, & xxv. 12-29	1 Sam. i. 1-19	...	,, v. 5-21	Matt. i. 18-end
...	Isa. vii. 10-16, & ix. 1-4 & 6-8, & Micah iv. 1—v. 6, & v. 7-10	...	Gal. iii. 15—iv. 7	Luke ii. 1-21
...	...	...	...	...
,, xxi. 9-22	1 Sam. i. 19-end	...	,, iv. 18—v. 2	Matt. ii.
Exod. xv. 11-22	Mic. vi. 1-6	i. 1-15	Rom. xvi.	Luke i. 26-57
,, ii. 1-11	Isa. xlix. 1-7		2 Tim. ii. 16-end	,, ii. 21-end
...		...	...	...

[4] The year is divided into periods of about seven weeks each, called *Shawu'i*. These are: Advent, Epiphany, the Fast, Resurrection, the Apostles, Summer, Elijah and the Cross, Moses, Hallowing of the Church. The two last are only four weeks each
[5] Popularly called in the plain of Urmi 'The little feast' (in contrast to Easter).
[6] In the present Greek Kalendar, Sunday after Christmas.
[7] The days marked with an asterisk are now obsolete.
[8] Kashkul MS. (see Introduction).

Epiphany. ['The Shining forth'] Jan. 6th,[1]

Friday. Mar Yukhánan (John) the Baptist,

First Sunday of the Epiphany, . . .

Monday, Tuesday, and Wednesday. Rogation of the Virgins.[2]
Friday. Paṭrus-Polus (St. Peter and St. Paul), .

Second Sunday of the Epiphany, ...

Friday. The four Evangelists. [Also[3] 'the memorial of the one hundred and fifty Bishops who excommunicated Macedonius'[*]], .

Third Sunday of the Epiphany, . . .

Friday. Mar Isṭapánus (St. Stephen), ...

Fourth Sunday of the Epiphany, .

Friday. The Greek Doctors[4] . . . . .

Fifth Sunday of the Epiphany, ...

---

[1] In Urmi, 'The new waters.' On this day only our Lord's baptism is commemorated; not, as in the West, the coming of the Magi.
[2] Observed in some places by girls.

The Lections.

Law.	Prophecy.	Acts.	The Apostle.	The Gospel.
Numb. xxiv. 2-end	Isa. iv. 2-6, & xi. 1-6 & 9-11, & xii	...	Tit. ii. 11—iii. 8	Matt. iii.
...	,, xxxv. 3-end, & xl. 1-9	xiii. 13-34	Eph. ii. 19—end of iii.	Mar. vi. 14-30
Exod. iii. 1-16	,, xliv. 21—xlv. 5	...	2 Tim. iii. 1-16	Luke iv. 14-31
...	...	...	...	...
...	2 Ki. iv. 8-38	ix. 32-43 & xiv. 8-16, & xx. 7-13	2 Cor. x. 1-8, & xi. 21-end	Matt. xvi. 13-20, & Jo. xxi. 15-25
Numb. x. 29—xi. 11	Isa. xlv. 11-18	...	Heb. iii. 1-14	Jo. i. 1-29
...	1 Ki. xviii. 30-40	v. 12-33	2 Cor. i. 8-15	Matt. x. 1-16
,, xi. 11-21	Isa. xlv. 18—xlvi. 5	...	Heb. iii. 14—iv. 11	Jo. i. 29-43
...	1 Ki. xxi. 1-22	vi. 8—vii. 2, & vii. 51—viii. 3	2 Cor. iii. 18—end of iv.	Matt. xi. 20-end, & xxiii. 29-end
,, xi. 23—end of xii.	Isa. xlvi. 5-end	...	Heb. vii. 18-end	Jo. i. 43—ii. 12
...	1 Sam. xxii. 6-18	xxi. 27-35, & xxii. 30—xxiii. 17	2 Tim. ii. 8-20, & iv. 1-9, & 14-19	Matt. iv. 23—v. 20
Deut. xviii. 9-end	Isa. xlviii. 12-21	...	Heb. vi. 9—vii. 4	Jo. iii. 1-22

[3] Kashkul MS. Also Raban Pithiun.
[4] Especially Diodorus of Tarsus, Nestorius, and Theodore the Interpreter.

Monday of the Rogation of the Ninevites,[1]

Tuesday of the Rogation of the Ninevites, .

Wednesday of the Rogation of the Ninevites,

Thursday of the Rogation of the Ninevites,[2]

Friday. The Syrian Doctors.[3] [Also, Memorial of Mar Saurishu of Bith Garmai[4]], ...

Sixth Sunday of the Epiphany, . .

Friday. Mar Awa, Catholicos,[5] or 'One Person' (the Patron Saint), ...

Seventh Sunday of the Epiphany, .

Friday. The forty Martyrs [of Sebaste] who were frozen to death,[6]

Eighth Sunday of the Epiphany. [Also, Memorial of all the Eastern (Syrian) Catholici][4], ...

Friday of the Departed, .

---

[1] In commemoration of the preaching of Jonah. This Rogation always holds its position relative to the Fast, and is seventy days before Easter. It was instituted by Mar Saurishu of Beith Garmai on account of a great plague (Kashkul MS.).

[2] The Fast lasts only until the Liturgy on this day has been celebrated.

Law.	Prophecy.	Acts.	The Apostle.	The Gospel.
...	Isa. lxiii. 17—end of lxiv., & Amos v. 3-16 & Hab. iii.	...	1 Tim. ii. 1—iii. 11	Matt. v. 17-38
...	,, lix. 1-19, & Lam. v.	...	Rom. xii.	,, v. 17-38
Gen. xviii. 20-end	,, lxiii. 7-17	...	Col. iii. 1—iv. 2	,, vi. 1-19
...	,, lxv. 16—lxvi. 3, & Jer. xvii. 21-27	...	,, iii. 1-18	Jo. xvi. 23-end
...	2 Ki. xiii. 14-22	xii. 25—xiii. 13	Heb. xiii. 1-10, & 16-22	Matt. xvi. 24—xvii. 10
Deut. xxiv. 9-end	Isa. lxiii. 7-17	...	,, viii. 1—ix. 11	Jo. iii. 22—iv. 4
...	,, xli. 8-17	xviii. 19—xix. 21	2 Cor. x. 4-end	Matt. xxiv. 45—xxv. 24
,, xiv. 2—xv. 5	,, xlii. 5-10, & 14-18	...	1 Tim. vi. 9-end	,, vii. 28—viii. 14
As on the Confessors' day (below)		...	...	...
Exod. xv. 22-26, & xvi. 4-8, & 9-11	Isa. xliv. 23—xlv. 8, & lxv. 17-25, & lxvi. 1-3	...	Eph. i. 15—ii. 8	Mar. i. 1-12
...	Ezek. xxxvii. 1-15, & Ecclus.[7] xliv. 1-23	...	1 Cor. xv. 34-57	Jo. v. 19-30

[3] *i.e.* East Syrian. Mar Ephraim and Mar Narsai (*cir.* 520 A.D.) are especially commemorated. [4] Kashkul MS. [5] A.D. 536-552.

[6] Byzantine Kalendar, Mar. 9; Armenian, Mar. 16; others Mar. 10 or 11; in the Kashkul MS., Thursday in the week after the Rogation of the Ninevites.

[7] In the Syriac, Son of Sira.

APPENDIX

Sunday before [*lit.* entering] the Great Fast,[1]   .   .   .

First Monday of the Fast,[2]   .   .   .   .   .   .

   This and the two following days are the Rogation[3] of the Angel Gauriel (Gabriel).

First Tuesday of the Fast, ...

First Wednesday of the Fast, ...

First Thursday of the Fast,   .   .   .

First Friday of the Fast, ...

Second Sunday of the Fast, ...

Second Friday of the Fast, ...

Third Sunday of the Fast, .   .   .

Third Friday of the Fast, .   .   .

Fourth Sunday of the Fast,   .

Middle (Fourth) Monday of the Fast, .   .   .

Middle Tuesday of the Fast,   .   .

Middle Wednesday of the Fast, or the Division of the Fast,

Middle Thursday of the Fast, ...

---

[1] *Rule in the Khudhra.*—This Sunday is always fifty days before Easter. If there are eight Sundays after Epiphany, the above order is followed; if seven, the Memorial of the Forty Martyrs is dropped; if six, the Evangelists and St. Peter and St. Paul are joined together; if five, also the Greek and Syrian Doctors; if four, also St. Stephen and Mar Awa; the service being

THE KALENDAR AND LECTIONARY

The Lections.

Law.	*Prophecy.*	*Acts.*	*The Apostle.*	*The Gospel.*
Exod. xxxiv. 1-8, & 27-end	Isa. lviii. 1-13, & v. 14	...	Eph. iv. 17—v. 5, & 15-22	Matt. iii. 16—iv. 12
Gen. i. 1-20	Josh. i. 1-12	...	Rom. i. 1-26	,, v. 17-38
,, i. 20—ii. 8	,, i. 12—ii. 12	...	,, i. 26—ii. 6	,, v. 38-end
,, ii. 8-end	,, ii. 8-end	...	,, ii. 6-28	,, vi. 1-19
,, iii. 1-20	,, iii. 1-14	...	,, ii. 28—iii. 27	,, vi. 19-end
,, iii. 20-end	,, iii. 14—iv. 10		,, iii. 27—end of iv.	,, vii. 1-15
,, v. 18-32	,, iv. 15-end	...	,, v.	,, vii. 15-28
,, v. 32—end of vi.	,, v. 1-13		,, vii. 1-14	Mar. xi. 27—xii. 12
,, vii.	,, v. 13—vi. 6	...	,, vii. 14-end	Matt. xx. 17-29
,, ix. 8-end	,, vi. 6-end	...	,, vii. 25—viii. 12	Mar. xii. 13-35
,, xi.	,. vii. 10-16	...	,, viii. 12-28	Matt. xxi. 23-end
,, xii. 1-10	,, vii. 16-end	...	,, ix. 1-14	Jo. v. 1-19
,, xii. 10—xiii. 8	,, viii. 1-18	...	,. ix. 14-30	,, v. 19-end
,, xiii. 8-end	,, viii. 18-30		,, ix. 30—x. 18	,, vi. 51-70
,, xiv. 1-18	,, viii. 30-end	...	,, x. 17—xi. 13	,, vii. 1-14

partly of the one and partly of the other. The Sundays are joined in the same way.

² The first, fourth, and seventh weeks of the Fast are called the 'Weeks of the Mysteries' (sacrament).

³ Very rarely observed.

Middle Friday of the Fast,

Fifth Sunday of the Fast,

Fifth Friday of the Fast,
Sixth Sunday of the Fast,

Sixth Friday of the Fast,

Feast (or Sunday) of Hosannas,[1]

Last (Seventh) Monday of the Fast,

Last Tuesday of the Fast,

Last Wednesday of the Fast,

The Passover,[2]

Friday of the Passion,[3]

---

[1] Palm Sunday. The red willow used on this day is called the Hosanna tree.
[2] Maundy Thursday.

	The Lections.			
Law.	Prophecy.	Acts.	The Apostle.	The Gospel.
Gen. xiv. 18—xv. 16	Josh. ix. 1-15	...	Rom. xi. 25-end	Jo. vii. 14-37
,, xvi. & xvii.	,, ix. 15-end	...	,, xii.	,, vii. 37—viii. 21
,, xviii. 1-20	,, xiv. 6-end	...	,, xiii.	,, viii. 31-end
,, xix. 1-27	,, xxi. 43—xxii. 10	...	,, xiv. 10-end	,, ix. 39—x. 22
,, xix. 27-end	,, xxii. 10-21	...	,, xv. 1-14	,, xi. 1-45
,, xlix. 1-13 & 22-27	Zech. iii. 7—iv. 7, & 11-end, & vii. 9-11, & viii. 4-6 & v. 12, & 16-20, & ix. 9-13	...	,, xi. 13-25	Matt. xx. 29—xxi. 23
,, xxxvii. 1-23	Josh. xxii. 21-30	...	Heb. i. & ii.	Jo. xi. 47—xii. 12
,, xxxvii. 23-end	,, xxii. 30-xxiii. 2	...	,, iv. 14—vi. 9	,, xii. 12-44
,, xxxix. 7 end of xl.	,, xxiii.	...	,, ix. 11-end	,, xiii. 1-18
Exod. xii. 1-21	Zech. ix. 9-13, & xi. 4-6 & 12-14, & xii. 9-end, & xiii. 7-end	...	1 Cor. v. 7-9, & x. 15-18, & xi. 23-end	Matt. xxvi. 17-25, & Jo. xiii. 22-28, & Matt. xxvi. v. 25, & Jo. xiii. 3-16, & Matt. xxvi. 26-31
...	Isa. lii. 13—end of liii., & Dan. ix. 21-end	...	Gal. ii. 17—iii. 15	Matt. xxvii. 1-33, & Lu. xxiii. 27-31, & Matt. xxvii. 33-44, & Lu. xxiii. 39-44, & Matt. xxvii. 45-55, & Jo. xix. 31-38, & Matt. xxvii. 57-62

[3] Good Friday. On this day the liturgy may not be celebrated (Rubrick at end of Order of Consecration of Churches in Ṭakhsa, Part ii.)

Baptism,[1]

The Great Sabbath, or Saturday of Light,

Feast of the Resurrection.[2] Evening,[3]

   ,,   ,,   Morning,

   ,,   ,,   Liturgy,

Monday of the Week of Weeks,

Tuesday of the Week of Weeks,

Wednesday of the Week of Weeks,

Thursday of the Week of Weeks,

Friday of the Week of Weeks. The Confessors,[4]

New Sunday,[5]

Mar Giwárgis (George), April 24th,[7]

Saturday. Mar Khanáuya (Ananias) 'of the wolves,'[8]

Third Sunday of the Resurrection,

Monday. Raban Hurmizd of Shiraz,

Friday. Sons of Shmuni (Salamone),[9]

---

[1] These are the lections in the Baptismal office.

[2] In Urmi, 'The great feast.' Easter is determined by the Greek method.

[3] That is, the Evening before.   [4] Under King Sapor.

[5] In the Syriac, Prayer of the Companions of Khananya.

[6] Also called Red Sunday. Locally observed in many places as Mar Audishu's day.

	The Lections.			
Law.	*Prophecy.*	*Acts.*	*The Apostle.*	*The Gospel.*
...	...	...	1 Cor. x. 1-14	Jo. ii. 23—iii. 9
Gen. xxii. 1-20	Jonah i. & ii.	...	,, i. 18-end	Matt. xxvii. 62-end
...	...	...	,, xv. 20-29	,, xxviii.
...	...	...	...	Lu. xxiv. 1-13
...	Isa. lx. 1-8, & 1 Sam. ii. 1-11	...	Rom. v. 20—end of vi., & Heb. xiii. 20-end	Jo. xx. 1-19
...	Isa. lx. 9-end	ii. 14-37	Eph. vi. 10-end	,, xiv. 18—xv. 15
...	,, lxi. 1-10	ii. 37-end	1 Cor. xv. 1-20	Lu. xxiv. 13-36
...	,, lxi. 10—lxii. 6	iv. 23-32	Eph. iv. 1-17	Jo. xv. 1-26
...	,, liv. 1-16	vi. 1-8	Col. ii. 8—iii. 4	Matt. x. 1-16
...	Song of the Three Children,[5] vv. 2-35	vi. 8—viii. 3	Heb. xi. 3-11, & 32—xii. 3	,, x. 16-34
...	Isa. lv. 4-end	iv. 32—v. 6	Col. i. 1-21	Jo. xx. 19-end
...	Dan. vi. 6-end	xii. 1-25	Phil. i. 12-27	Matt. x. 37-end, & xix. 27-end
...	...	...	...	...
...	Isa. lvi. 1-8	v. 34-end	Eph. i. 1-15	Jo. xiv. 1-15
As on Mar Awa's day		...	...	...
As on the Confessors' day		...	...	...

[7] This day, being fixed, does not always fall in this place, but it is inserted here in the Khudhra. [Elsewhere, in East and West, April 23rd.]

[8] Kashkul MS. In the old Roman martyrology, on April 21st is Ananias, martyr in Persia (Smith and Cheetham, *Dict. Chr. Ant.*).

[9] The martyrs of 2 Maccabees vii. Usually observed on the first Tuesday of May.

Fourth Sunday of the Resurrection,
Fifth Sunday of the Resurrection,
Sixth Sunday of the Resurrection. Mar Adai (Adæus),

Ascension Day,

Sunday after the Ascension,
Pentecost, the first day of the Shawu'a of the Apostles,

    'Order of Worship,'[1]
Wednesday.[2] Memorial of the first Eucharist,*
Friday of Gold,[3]

Second Sunday of the Apostles,

Third Sunday of the Apostles,
Fourth Sunday of the Apostles,
Fifth Sunday of the Apostles,
Sixth Sunday of the Apostles,

Seventh Sunday of the Apostles,

Wednesday.[2] The Seventy Apostles,*
Friday. The Seventy Apostles,

Sunday of the Twelve Apostles,[4] or Nusardéil,

Friday. Mar Sargis (Sergius),[5] and Mar Yaqu (James) of Ṣuwa,[2]

---

[1] Special service after the Pentecost liturgy.   [2] Kashkul MS.
[3] In allusion to A

THE KALENDAR AND LECTIONARY

The Lections.

Law.	Prophecy.	Acts.	The Apostle.	The Gospel.
...	Isa. xlix. 13-24	viii. 14-26	Eph. i. 15—ii. 2	Jo. xvi. 16-end
...	,, xlix. 7-14	ix. 1-20	Heb. x. 19-37	,, xxi. 1-15
...	,, li. 9-12 & lii. 7-13	x. 1-17	Eph. ii. 4-end	,, xvii.
...	2 Ki. ii. 1-16	i. 1-15	1 Tim. i. 18—end of ii., & iii. 14-end	Lu. xxiv. 36-end
...	Isa. vi.	i. 15-end	Phil. i. 27—ii. 12	Mar. xvi. 2-end
Exod. xix. 1-10 & xx. 18-22	...	ii. 1-22	1 Cor. xii. 1-28	Jo. xiv. 15-18 & 25-27, & xv. 26—xvi. 16
		...	...	,, iv. 4-31
...	...	...	...	...
...	,, xxxv. 3-end	iii.	,, xii. 28—end of xiii.	Lu. vii. 1-23
...	Joel ii. 15-27	iv. 5-23	,, v. 6—vi. 12	,, vii. 31-end
Deut. i. 3-18	Isa. i. 1-11	...	,, vii. 1-8	,, x. 23-end
,, i. 16-34	,, i. 11-21	...	,, ix. 13-end	,, vi. 12-47
,, i. 33—ii. 2	,, i. 21-end	...	,, xiv. 1-20	,, xii. 16-35
,, iv. 1-10	,, ii. 1-22	...	,, x. 14-33	,, xii. 57—xiii. 18
,, iv. 10-24	,, v. 8-26	...	,, xv. 58—end of xvi.	,, xiii. 22-end
	...	...	...	...
	,, xli. 8-21	xiii. 13-24 & xiv. 20-24	Rom. viii. 28—ix. 6.	Matt. x. 37—xi. 15
...	1 Ki. xviii. 30-40	v. 12-33	2 Cor. i. 8-15	Lu. xiv. 1-15
...	...	...	...	...

[4] The first day of the Shawu'a of Summer.
[5] In some places observed on the preceding Sunday (see page 282).

278   APPENDIX

Second Sunday of Summer,

Friday.[1] Mar Mari, disciple of Mar Adai,
Third Sunday of Summer,
Fourth Sunday of Summer,

Mar Tuma,[2] July 3,

Transfiguration [*lit.* Revelation], August 6,[3]

Fifth Sunday of Summer,

Sixth Sunday of Summer,
Friday. Mar Shimun Bar Ṣaba'i, [Ninth] Catholicos and Martyr,
   A.D. 314-330 or 326-344,

Seventh Sunday of Summer,

First Sunday of Eliya (Elijah),

Second Sunday of Eliya,

Third Sunday of Eliya,

Friday.[1] Eliya the Tishbite, and Mar Ishuyaw (Jesuadedit),
Feast of the Cross, September 13,[4]

---

[1] Kashkul MS.   [2] St. Thomas the Apostle. Fixed day.
[3] Fixed day. Armenian Kalendar, July 14.
[4] Fixed day. *Rule in the Khudhra :*—The fourth Sunday of Elijah must be the first after the Cross, and if necessary the other Sundays of this Shawu'a must be changed. Excepting only that if Holy Cross Day fall in the week before the first Sunday of Elijah, then the first Sunday keeps its place, and

	The Lections.			
Law.	Prophecy.	Acts.	The Apostle.	The Gospel.
Deut. iv. 3-41	Isa. iii. 16—end of iv.	...	2 Cor. iii. 4-end	Lu. xv. 4-end
...	...	...	...	...
,, v. 1-17	,, v. 1-8	...	,, vii. 1-12	Jo. ix. 1-39
,, v. 16—vi. 4	,, ix. 8-end	...	,, x.	Mar. vii. 1-24
	Isa. lv. 4—lvii. 12, or as Mar Awa	...	Eph. iii., or as Mar Awa	Jo. xx. 19-end
...	Isa. vi.	i. 15-end	1 Tim. i. 18—end of ii., & iii. 14-end	Matt. xvi. 24—xvii. 10
Lev. xxii. 26—xxiii. 23	,, xxviii. 14-23	...	2 Cor. xii. 14—xiii. end	Lu. xvi. 19—xvii. 11
,, xix. 1-15	,, xxix. 13-end	...	1 Thess. ii. 1-13	,, xvii. 5-20
...	,, xli. 8-17	xviii. 19—xix. 21	2 Cor. x. 4-end	Jo. xv. 1-26
,, xix. 15-end, & xx. 9-15	,, xxx. 1-16	...	1 Thess. ii. 14-20	Lu. xviii. 2-15
Deut. vi. 20—vii. 7.	,, xxxi. 4-end	...	2 Thess. i.	,, xviii. 35—xix. 11
,, vii. 7-12	,, xxx. 15-27	...	,, ii. 15—end of iii.	Matt. xiii. 1-9
,, vii. 12-end	,, xxxii. 1—xxxiii. 7		Phil. i. 12-26	,, xiii. 24-44
...	...	...	...	...
...	,, lii. 13—end of liii.	ii. 14-37	1 Cor. i. 18-end	Lu. xxiv. 13-36

on the following Sunday the service of the fourth Sunday of Elijah is used. There is only one Festival of the Cross, but in the district of Ṭal in Kurdistan a separate memorial of St. Helena is kept in September. On Sept. 13 (not 14 as elsewhere) the Invention of the Cross is chiefly commemorated, not the Exaltation. The Holy Eastern Church also combines the two.

Fourth Sunday of Eliya, First of the Cross,

Fifth Sunday of Eliya, Second of the Cross,

Sixth Sunday of Eliya, Third of the Cross,

Seventh Sunday of Eliya, Fourth of the Cross,

First Sunday of Mar Mushi (Moses),[1]

Second Sunday of Mar Mushi,

Third Sunday of Mar Mushi,
Fourth Sunday of Mar Mushi,

First Sunday of the Hallowing of the Church, or Ma'alta,[2]

Second Sunday of the Hallowing of the Church. [Also Mar Yukhánan the Arab],

Third Sunday of the Hallowing of the Church,
Friday. Mar Augin,[3]
Fourth Sunday of the Hallowing of the Church,

---

[1] If Easter fall late, all or some of the Sundays of Mar Mushi are omitted; and (apparently) if it fall as late as possible, the last Sunday of Elijah also. If Easter fall on the earliest possible day, the fifth and fourth Sundays of Elijah will have to be interchanged so as to follow the rule given above (page 278). But this arrangement is not explicitly ordered.

[2] *i.e.* 'Entrance.' On this day the people move from the summer chapel to the nave of the church for their daily prayers.

[3] Kashkul MS.

The Lections.

Law.	Prophecy.	Acts.	The Apostle.	The Gospel.
Deut. viii. 11-end	Isa. xxxiii. 13-end	..	Phil. i. 27—ii. 12	Matt. iv. 12—v. 17
,, ix. 1-9	,, xxv. 1-9	...	,, iii. 1-15	,, xvii. 14-end
,, ix. 13-23	,, xxv. 9—xxvi. 20	...	,, iv. 4-end	,, xv. 21-39
,, x. 12-end	,, xxviii. 23—xxix. 13	...	1 Cor. xiv. 26-end	,, xviii. 1-19
,, xi. 1-13	,, xl. 1-18		2 Cor. i. 23—ii. 17	,, xx. 1-17
,, xi. 26—xii. 2	,, xl. 18—xli. 8	...	Gal. v. 16-end	,, xii. 46-end
,, xii. 1-29	,, xli. 8-21	...	,, vi.	Jo. v. 1-19
,, xii. 29—xiv. 3	,, xli. 21—xlii. 5	...	1 Tim. v. 1-17	Matt. viii. 23—ix. 10
Exod. xl.	,, vi.		1 Cor. xii. 28—end of xiii.	,, xvi. 13-20 & xxi. 12-14
,, xxxix. 32-end	1 Ki. viii. 10-30	...	Heb. viii. 1—ix. 6	,, xii. 1-14
Num. vii. 1-11	Isa. liv. 1-16		,, ix. 6-16	Jo. ii. 12-23
...	...	...	...	...
...	1 Ki. vi. 1-20, & Ezek. xlii. 1-8		,, ix. 16-end	Matt. xxii. 41—xxiii. 13

Additional Note.—Every eventuality with regard to Easter seems to be provided for in the above rules. In the first part of the Kalendar the following modifications are said to be usually observed. If the Nativity fall on a Sunday, St. Mary is the following Friday, there is only one Sunday of the Nativity, Epiphany is on Friday, and the Saints' days come after instead of before the Sundays given in the table; if on a Monday, there is only one Sunday of the Nativity, Epiphany is on Saturday, and the Saints' days similarly come after the Sundays; if on a Tuesday, there is only one Sunday of the Nativity, and Epiphany is on Sunday.

DAYS FOR WHICH NO SPECIAL LESSONS ARE APPOINTED IN THE LECTIONARY[1]

January	1.	Mar Shalíṭa of the village of Aníṭus.*
,,	24.	Companions of Mar Giwárgis (George), martyrs.*
March.		First Wednesday. Mar Giwárgis.
April	15.	Mar Shimun (Simon) Bar Ṣabá'i, martyr.[2]
,,	27.	Mar Crisṭapárus[3]* (Christopher) and Mar Giwárgis, martyrs.
May	15.	Mart Máriam.[4]
July	15.	Mar Quriáqus (Cyriac) and Yulíti (Julitta) his mother.[5]
,,	29.	Paṭrus-Polus (St. Peter and St. Paul).**[6]
August	1.	Fast of Mart Mariam begins.[4] [August is the month of the Sons of Shmuni (Salamone).[7]*]
,,	10.	Mar Shalíṭa,[8] disciple of Mar Augin.*
,,	15.	Mart Mariam.[4]
September	1.	Raban Hurmizd of Shiraz.[9]*
,,	8.	Nativity of Mart Mariam, and Yunákhir and Khana her parents.[10]
,,	19.	Mar Shalíṭa,[8] disciple of Mar Augin.
October.		First Monday. Mar Giwárgis.
		First Wednesday. Mar Tiadúrus the Interpreter, Mar Yukhánan (John) of Kashkar, Mar Sargis (Sergius), and Bakus (Bacchus), martyrs[11] (cir. 300 A.D.).*

---

[1] From the Kashkul MS., unless otherwise noted. The MS. begins with October. Days marked with an asterisk are obsolete.

[2] Byzantine Kalendar, May 9.

[3] Byz. Kal. Ap. 17; otherwise Ap. 14 or 21.

[4] From the Khudhra. The service is in almost all respects the same as on the other Festivals of St. Mary.   [5] So Byzantine Kalendar.

[6] Perhaps the same as St. Peter ad Vincula of the West (August 1).

[7] Aug. 1 in present Greek Kalendar.

[8] Patron saint of the patriarchal church at Qudshanis.

[9] 'On this day, long after his death, he opened the eyes of a blind man.'

[10] Joachim and Anna (Byz. Kal. Sept. 9; Armenian Kal. Aug. 27).

[11] Byz. Kal. Oct. 7.

October   1. Khanánya[1] (Ananias), who baptized Paul; first Metropolitan of Damascus.*
 ,,   2. Mar Papa, [Eighth] Catholicos (died *cir.* 326 A.D.).*
 ,,   4. The eight boys of Ephesus.[2] *
 ,,   12. Three hundred martyrs at Shigar.*
 ,,   13. Mar Yukhánan (John) the Evangelist.*
 ,,   25. Raban Píthiun, martyr, opponent of the Magi.
November 1. Mar Qupriánus (Cyprian), martyr.[3]
 ,,   15. Mar Audíshu.[4]
 ,,   17. Mar Agnátis[5] (Ignatius), disciple of the sons of thunder.* Mar Giwárgis.* Mar Basilíyus.[6] *
 ,,   19. Mar Yaqu[4] (James) the mutilated.[7] *
 ,,   22. Mar Diyudúrus (Diodorus), Bishop of Tarsus,* and twelve thousand martyrs.*
December 22. Mar Quriaqus (Cyriac), 'killed by Halinus in Persia.' Mar Auráham (Abraham), Doctor.[8]

If any of these days are observed, and the Liturgy is celebrated, the most suitable lessons from the former table are read: thus, those for the January Festival of St. Mary are read on all her festivals; those for the Confessors or Mar Awa are generally used for the other days.

---

[1] So Byzantine Kalendar.

[2] The Seven Sleepers (Byz. Kal. Aug. 4; also Oct. 22 in present Greek Kalendar).

[3] Probably the Bishop of Carthage (Byz. Kal. Oct. 2; otherwise Sept. 14).

[4] Traditional.

[5] Byz. and Ethiopian Kal. Dec. 20; Armenian, Dec. 16; otherwise Dec. 17, Feb. 1, Jan. 29, or July 1.

[6] Armen. Kal. Nov. 12; Byz. and Ethiopian Kal. Jan. 1; otherwise May 23 or June 14.

[7] His limbs were cut off one by one (Byz. Kal. Nov. 27).

[8] In addition to these names, the Kashkul MS. contains a long list of obsolete commemorations of purely local saints, which seem to be scarcely important enough to be inserted in this place.

INDEX TO THE LECTIONARY

The Law.

Gen. i. 1-20	. .	1 M. Fast.
i. 20—ii. 8	.	1 Tu. Fast.
ii. 8-end	. .	1 W. Fast.
iii. 1-20	. .	1 Th. Fast.
iii. 20-end	.	1 F. Fast.
v. 18-32	. .	2 Su. Fast.
v. 32—end of vi.		2 F. Fast.
vii.	. . .	3 Su. Fast.
ix. 8-end	. .	3 F. Fast.
xi.	. . .	4 Su. Fast.
xii. 1-10	. .	4 M. Fast.
xii. 10—xiii. 8		4 Tu. Fast.
xiii. 8-end	.	4 W. Fast.
xiv. 1-18	. .	4 Th. Fast.
xiv. 18—xv. 16		4 F. Fast.
xvi., xvii.	. .	5 Su. Fast.
xvii.	. . .	1 Su. Advent.
xviii. 1-20	.	{ 5 F. Fast and 3 Su. Advent.
xviii. 20-end		W. Ninevites.
xix. 1-27	.	6 Su. Fast.
xix. 27-end	.	6 F. Fast.
xxi. 9-22	. .	1 Su. Nativity.
xxii. 1-20	.	Great Sabbath.
xxiv. 50-end		4 Su. Advent.
xxv. 12-29	,	4 Su. Advent.
xxxvii. 1-23	.	7 M. Fast.
xxxvii. 23-end		} 7 Tu. Fast.
xxxix. 7—end of xl.		} 7 W. Fast.
xlix. 1-13, 22-27		} Su. Hosannas
Ex. ii. 1-11	. .	2 Su. Nativity.
iii. 1-16	. .	1 Su. Epiphany.
xii. 1-21	. .	Passover.
xv. 11-22	.	St. Mary.
xv. 22-26	.	8 Su. Epiphany.
Ex. xvi. 4-8, 9-11		8 Su. Epiphany.
xix. 1-10	.	Pentecost.
xx. 18-22	.	Pentecost.
xxxiv. 1-8, 27-end		} Su. before Fast.
xxxix. 32-end		} 2 Su. Church.
xl.	. . .	1 Su. Church.
Lev. xix. 1-15	.	6 Su. Summer.
xix. 15-end	.	7 Su. Summer.
xx. 9-15	. .	7 Su. Summer.
xxii. 26—xxiii. 23		} 5 Su. Summer.
Num. vii. 1-11	.	3 Su. Church.
x. 29—xi. 11		2 Su. Epiphany.
xi. 11-21	. .	3 Su. Epiphany.
xi. 23—end of xii.		} 4 Su. Epiphany.
xxii. 9-21	.	2 Su. Advent.
xxiv. 2-end	.	Epiphany.
Deut. i. 3-18	. .	3 Su. Apostles.
i. 16-34	. .	4 Su. Apostles.
i. 33—ii. 2	.	5 Su. Apostles.
iv. 1-10	. .	6 Su. Apostles.
iv. 10-24	. .	7 Su. Apostles.
iv. 3-41	. .	2 Su. Summer.
v. 1-17	. .	3 Su. Summer.
v. 16—vi. 4	.	4 Su. Summer.
vi. 20—vii. 7	.	1 Su. Elijah.
vii. 7-12	. .	2 Su. Elijah.
vii. 12-end	.	3 Su. Elijah.
viii. 11-end	.	4 Su. Elijah.
ix. 1-9	. .	5 Su. Elijah.
ix. 13-23	. .	6 Su. Elijah.
x. 12-end	.	7 Su. Elijah.
xi. 1-13	. .	1 Su. Moses.
xi. 26—xii. 2		2 Su. Moses.
xii. 1-29	. .	3 Su. Moses.
xii. 29—xiv. 3		4 Su. Moses.
xiv. 2—xv. 5		7 Su. Epiphany.

INDEX TO THE LECTIONARY   285

Deut. xviii. 9-end	5 Su. Epiphany.	Isa. vi. . . .	Su. aft. Ascension and Transfiguration and 1 Su. Church.
xxiv. 9-end	6 Su. Epiphany.		

Prophecy.

Josh. i. 1-12 . .	1 M. Fast.	vii. 10-16 .	Nativity.
i. 12—ii. 12	1 Tu. Fast.	ix. 1-4, 6-8 .	Nativity.
ii. 8-end .	1 W. Fast.	ix. 8-end .	4 Su. Summer.
iii. 1-14 . .	1 Th. Fast.	xi. 1-6, 9-11	Epiphany.
iii. 14—iv. 10	1 F. Fast.	xii.	Epiphany.
iv. 15-end .	2 Su. Fast.	xxv. 1-9 . .	5 Su. Elijah.
v. 1-13 . .	2 F. Fast.	xxv. 9—xxvi. 20 . . .	6 Su. Elijah.
v. 13—vi. 6	3 Su. Fast.		
vi. 6-end .	3 F. Fast.	xxviii. 14-23	5 Su. Summer.
vii. 10-16 .	4 Su. Fast.	xxviii. 23—xxix. 13 .	7 Su. Elijah.
vii. 16-end .	4 M. Fast.		
viii. 1-18 .	4 Tu. Fast.	xxix. 13-end	6 Su. Summer.
viii. 18-30 .	4 W. Fast.	xxx. 1-16 .	7 Su. Summer.
viii. 30-end	4 Th. Fast.	xxx. 15-27 .	2 Su. Elijah.
ix. 1-15 . .	4 F. Fast.	xxxi. 4-end	1 Su. Elijah.
ix. 15-end .	5 Su. Fast.	xxxii. 1—xxxiii. 7 .	3 Su. Elijah.
xiv. 6-end .	5 F. Fast.		
xxi. 43—xxii. 10	6 Su. Fast.	xxxiii. 13-end . .	4 Su. Elijah.
xxii. 10-21 .	6 F. Fast.		
xxii. 21-30 .	7 M. Fast.	xxxv. 3-end	Friday of Gold and St. John Baptist.
xxii. 30—xxiii. 2 .	7 Tu. Fast.		
xxiii. . .	7 W. Fast.	xl. 1-9 . .	St. John Baptist.
Jud. xiii. 2-25 .	3 Su. Advent.		
1 Sam. i. 1-19 .	4 Su. Advent.	xl. 1-18 . .	1 Su. Moses.
i. 19-end .	1 Su. Nativity.	xl. 18—xli. 8	2 Su. Moses.
ii. 1-11 . .	Resurrection (liturgy).	xli. 8-17 . .	Mar Awa and Mar Shimun Bar Saba'i.
xxii. 6-18 .	Greek Doctors.		
1 Ki. vi. 1-20 .	4 Su. Church.	xli. 8-21 . .	Seventy Apostles and 3 Su. Moses.
viii. 10-30 .	2 Su. Church.		
xviii. 30-40 .	Four Evangelists & Twelve Apostles.	xli. 21—xlii. 5	4 Su. Moses.
		xlii. 5-10, 14-18	7 Su. Epiphany.
xxi. 1-22 .	St. Stephen.	xlii. 18—xliii. 14 .	1 Su. Advent.
2 Ki. ii. 1-16 .	Ascension.		
iv. 8-38 . .	St. Peter and St. Paul.	xliii. 14—xliv. 6 . .	2 Su. Advent.
xiii. 14-22 .	Syrian Doctors.	xliv. 21—xlv. 5 .	1 Su. Epiphany.
Isa. i. 1-11 . .	3 Su. Apostles.		
i. 11-21 . .	4 Su. Apostles.	xliv. 23—xlv. 8 .	8 Su. Epiphany.
i. 21-end .	5 Su. Apostles.		
ii. 1-22 . .	6 Su. Apostles.	xlv. 11-18 .	2 Su. Epiphany.
iii. 16—end of iv. . .	2 Su. Summer.	xlv. 18—xlvi. 5 .	3 Su. Epiphany.
iv. 2-6 . .	Epiphany.	xlvi. 5-end .	4 Su. Epiphany.
v. 1-8 . .	3 Su. Summer.	xlviii. 12-21	5 Su. Epiphany.
v. 8-26 . .	7 Su. Apostles.	xlix. 1-7 .	2 Su. Nativity.

INDEX TO THE LECTIONARY

Isa. xlix. 7-14	5 Su. Resurrection.	Zech. iii. 7—iv. 7	Su. of Hosannas.
xlix. 13-24	4 Su. Resurrection.	iv. 11-end	Su. of Hosannas.
li. 9-12	6 Su. Resurrection.	vii. 9-11	Su. of Hosannas.
lii. 7-13	6 Su. Resurrection.	viii. 4-6, 12, 16-20	Su. of Hosannas.
lii. 13—end of liii.	F. of the Passion and Feast of the Cross.	ix. 9-13	Su. of Hosannas and Passover.
liv. 1-16	Th. Week of Weeks and 3 Su. Church.	xi. 4-6, 12-14	Passover.
		xii. 9-end	Passover.
		xiii. 7-end	Passover.
lv. 4-end	New Sunday.	Ecclus. xliv. 1-23	The Departed.
lv. 4—lvii. 12	St. Thomas.	Song of Three Children, 2-35	Confessors.
lvi. 1-8	3 Su. Resurrection.		
lviii. 1-13, 14	Su. before Fast.	*The Gospel.*	
lix. 1-19	Tu. Ninevites.	Matt. i. 18-end	4 Su. Advent.
lx. 1-8	Resurrection (liturgy).	ii.	1 Su. Nativity.
		iii.	Epiphany.
lx. 9-end	M. Week of Weeks.	iii. 16—iv. 12	Su. before Fast.
lxi. 1-10	Tu. Week of Weeks.	iv. 12—v. 17	4 Su. Elijah.
lxi. 10—lxii. 6	W. Week of Weeks.	iv. 23—v. 20	Greek Doctors.
lxiii. 7-17	6 Su. Epiphany and W. Ninevites.	v. 17-38	M. and Tu. Ninevites and 1 M. Fast.
		v. 38-end	1 Tu. Fast.
lxiii. 17—end of lxiv.	M. Ninevites.	vi. 1-19	1 W. Fast and W. Ninevites.
lxv. 16—lxvi. 3	Th. Ninevites.	vi. 19-end	1 Th. Fast.
		vii. 1-15	1 F. Fast.
lxv. 17-25	8 Su. Epiphany.	vii. 15-28	2 Su Fast.
lxvi. 1-3	8 Su. Epiphany.	vii. 28—viii. 14	7 Su. Epiphany.
Jer. xvii. 21-27	Th. Ninevites.		
Lam. v.	Tu. Ninevites.	viii. 23—ix. 10	4 Su. Moses.
Ezek. xxxvii. 1-15	The Departed.	x. 1-16	Four Evangelists and Th. Week of Weeks.
xlii. 1-8	4 Su. Church.		
Dan. vi. 6-end	St. George.	x. 16-34	Confessors.
ix. 21-end	F. of the Passion.	x. 37-end	St. George.
		x. 37—xi. 15	Seventy Apostles.
Joel ii. 15-27	2 Su. Apostles.	xi. 20-end	St. Stephen.
Amos v. 3-16	M. Ninevites.	xii. 1-14	2 Su. Church.
Jonah i., ii.	Great Sabbath.	xii. 46-end	2 Su. Moses.
Micah iv. 1—v. 6	Nativity.	xiii. 1-9	2 Su. Elijah.
v. 7-10	Nativity.	xiii. 24-44	3 Su. Elijah.
vi. 1-6	St. Mary.		
Habak. iii.	M. Ninevites.		

INDEX TO THE LECTIONARY 287

Matt. xv. 21-39	6 Su. Elijah.	Lu. xii. 16-35	5 Su. Apostles.
xvi. 13-20	St. Peter and St. Paul and 1 Su. Church.	xii. 57—xiii. 18	6 Su. Apostles.
		xiii. 22-end	7 Su. Apostles.
xvi. 24— xvii. 10	Syrian Doctors and Transfiguration.	xiv. 1-15	Twelve Apostles.
		xv. 4-end	2 Su. Summer.
		xvi. 19— xvii. 11	5 Su. Summer.
xvii. 14-end	5 Su. Elijah.	xvii. 5-20	6 Su. Summer.
xviii. 1-19	7 Su. Elijah.	xviii. 2-15	7 Su. Summer.
xix. 27-end	St. George.	xviii. 35— xix. 11	1 Su. Elijah.
xx. 1-17	1 Su. Moses.	xxiii. 27-31, 39-44	F. of the Passion.
xx. 17-29	3 Su. Fast.		
xx. 29— xxi. 23	Su. of Hosannas.	xxiv. 1-13	Resurrection, morning.
xxi. 12-14	1 Su. Church.	xxiv. 13-36	T. Week of Weeks, and Feast of Cross.
xxi. 23-end	4 Su. Fast.		
xxii. 41— xxiii. 13	4 Su. Church.	xxiv. 36-end	Ascension.
		John i. 1-29	2 Su. Epiphany.
xxiii. 29-end	St. Stephen.	i. 29-43	3 Su. Epiphany.
		i. 43—ii. 12	4 Su. Epiphany.
xxiv. 45— xxv. 24	Mar Awa.	ii. 12-23	3 Su. Church.
		ii. 23—iii. 9	Baptism.
xxvi. 17-31	Passover.	iii. 1-22	5 Su. Epiphany.
xxvii. 1-44, 45-55, 57-62	F. of the Passion.	iii. 22—iv. 4	6 Su. Epiphany.
		iv. 4-31	Pentecost ('Order of Worship')
xxvii. 62-end	Great Sabbath.		
xxviii.	Resurrection, evening.	v. 1-19	4 M. Fast and 3 Su. Moses.
		v. 19-30	The Departed.
Mar. i. 1-12	8 Su. Epiphany.	v. 19-end	4 Tu. Fast.
vi. 14-30	St. John Baptist.	vi. 51-70	4 W. Fast.
		vii. 1-14	4 Th. Fast.
vii. 1-24	4 Su. Summer.	vii. 14-37	4 F. Fast.
xi. 27—xii. 12	2 F. Fast.	vii. 37— viii. 21	5 Su. Fast.
xii. 13-35	3 F. Fast.	viii. 31-end	5 F. Fast.
xvi. 2-end	Su. after Ascension.	ix. 1-39	3 Su. Summer.
		ix. 39—x. 22	6 Su. Fast.
Lu. i. 5-26	1 Su. Advent.	xi. 1-45	6 F. Fast.
i. 26-57	2 Su. Advent, and St. Mary.	xi. 47—xii. 12	7 M. Fast.
i. 57-end	3 Su. Advent.	xii. 12-44	7 T. Fast.
ii. 1-21	Nativity.	xiii. 1-18	7 W. Fast.
ii. 21-end	2 Su. Nativity.	xiii. 3-16, 22-28	Passover.
iv. 14-31	1 Su. Epiphany.		
vi. 12-47	4 Su. Apostles.	xiv. 1-15	3 Su. Resurrection.
vii. 1-23	F. of Gold.		
vii. 31-end	2 Su. Apostles.	xiv. 15-18, 25-27	Pentecost.
x. 23-end	3 Su. Apostles.		

INDEX TO THE LECTIONARY

John xiv. 18—xv. 15	M. Week of Weeks.	Acts vii. 51— viii. 3	St. Stephen.	
xv. 1-26	W. Week of Weeks and Mar Shimun Bar Ṣaba'i.	viii. 14-26	4 Su. Resurrection.	
		ix. 1-20	5 Su. Resurrection.	
xv. 26—xvi. 16	Pentecost.	ix. 32-43	St. Peter and St. Paul.	
xvi. 16-end	4 Su. Resurrection.	x. 1-17	6 Su. Resurrection.	
xvi. 23-end	Th. Ninevites.	xii. 1-25	St. George.	
xvii.	6 Su. Resurrection.	xii. 25—xiii. 13	Syrian Doctors.	
xix. 31-38	F. of the Passion.	xiii. 13-24	Seventy Apostles.	
xx. 1-19	Resurrection (liturgy).	xiii. 13-34	St. John Baptist.	
xx. 19-end	New Sunday and St. Thomas.	xiv. 8-16	St. Peter and St. Paul.	
xxi. 1-15	5 Su. Resurrection.	xiv. 20-24	Seventy Apostles.	
xxi. 15-25	St. Peter and St. Paul.	xviii. 19— xix. 21	Mar Shimun Bar Ṣaba'i and Mar Awa.	
		xx. 7-13	St. Peter and St. Paul.	
		xxi. 27-35	Greek Doctors.	
		xxii. 30— xxiii. 17	Greek Doctors.	

Acts of the Apostles.

Acts i. 1-15	St. Mary and Ascension.
i. 15-end	Su. aft. Ascension and Transfiguration.
ii. 1-22	Pentecost.
ii. 14-37	M. Week of Weeks and Feast of Cross.
ii. 37-end	Tu. Week of Weeks.
iii.	Friday of Gold.
iv. 5-23	2 Su. Apostles.
iv. 23-32	W. Week of Weeks.
iv. 32—v. 6	New Sunday.
v. 12-33	Twelve Apostles and Four Evangelists.
v. 34-end	3 Su. Resurrection.
vi. 1-8	Th. Week of Weeks.
vi. 8—vii. 2	St. Stephen.
vi. 8—viii. 3	Confessors.

The Apostle.

Rom. i. 1-26	1 M. Fast.
i. 26—ii. 6	1 Tu. Fast.
ii. 6-28	1 W. Fast.
ii. 28—iii. 27	1 Th. Fast.
iii. 27—end of iv.	1 F. Fast.
v.	2 Su. Fast.
v. 20—end of vi.	Resurrection.
vii. 1-14	2 F. Fast.
vii. 14-end	3 Su. Fast.
vii. 25—viii. 12	3 F. Fast.
viii. 12-28	4 Su. Fast.
viii. 28— ix. 6	Seventy Apostles.
ix. 1-14	4 M. Fast.
ix. 14-30	4 Tu. Fast.
ix. 30—x. 18	4 W. Fast.

INDEX TO THE LECTIONARY

Rom. x. 17—xi. 13	4 Th. Fast.
xi. 13-25	Su. of Hosannas.
xi. 25-end	4 F. Fast.
xii.	Tu. Ninevites and 5 Su. Fast.
xiii.	5 F. Fast.
xiv. 10-end	6 Su. Fast.
xv. 1-14	6 F. Fast.
xvi.	St. Mary.
1 Cor. i. 18-end	Great Sabbath and Feast of Cross.
v. 7-9	Passover.
v. 6—vi. 12	2 Su. Apostles.
vii. 1-8	3 Su. Apostles.
ix. 13-end	4 Su. Apostles.
x. 1-14	Baptism.
x. 15-18	Passover.
x. 14-33	6 Su. Apostles.
xi. 23-end	Passover.
xii. 1-28	Pentecost.
xii. 28—end of xiii.	F. of Gold and 1 Su. Church.
xiv. 1-20	5 Su. Apostles.
xiv. 26-end	7 Su. Elijah.
xv. 1-20	Tu. Week of Weeks.
xv. 20-29	Resurrection, evening.
xv. 34-57	The Departed.
xv. 58—end of xvi.	7 Su. Apostles.
2 Cor. i. 8-15	Four Evangelists & Twelve Apostles.
i. 23—ii. 17	1 Su. Moses.
iii. 4-end	2 Su. Summer.
iii. 18—end of iv.	St. Stephen.
vii. 1-12	3 Su. Summer.
x. 1-8	St. Peter and St. Paul.
x.	4 Su. Summer.
x. 4-end	Mar Shimun Bar Ṣaba‘i and Mar Awa.
xi. 21-end	St. Peter and St. Paul.
xii. 14—end of xiii.	5 Su. Summer.
Gal. ii. 17—iii. 15	F. of the Passion.
Gal. iii. 15—iv. 7	Nativity.
iv. 18—v. 2	1 Su. Nativity.
v. 16-end	2 Su. Moses.
vi.	3 Su. Moses.
Eph. i. 1-15	3 Su. Resurrection.
i. 15—ii. 2	4 Su. Resurrection.
i. 15—ii. 8	8 Su. Epiphany.
ii. 4-end	6 Su. Resurrection.
ii. 19—end of iii.	St. John Baptist.
iii.	3 Su. Advent and St. Thomas.
iv. 1-17	W. Week of Weeks.
iv. 17—v. 5	Su. before Fast.
v. 5-21	4 Su. Advent.
v. 15-22	Su. before Fast.
v. 21—vi. 10	1 Su. Advent.
vi. 10-end	M. Week of Weeks.
Phil. i. 12-26	3 Su. Elijah.
i. 12-27	St. George.
i. 27—ii. 12	Su. after Ascension and 4 Su. Elijah.
iii. 1-15	5 Su. Elijah.
iv. 4-end	6 Su. Elijah.
Col. i. 1-21	New Sunday.
ii. 8—iii. 4	Th. Week of Weeks.
iii. 1—iv. 2	W. Ninevites.
iii. 1-18	Th. Ninevites.
iv. 2-end	2 Su. Advent.
1 Thess. ii. 1-13	6 Su. Summer.
ii. 14-20	7 Su. Summer.
2 Thess. i.	1 Su. Elijah.
ii. 15 — end of iii.	2 Su. Elijah.
1 Tim. i. 18— end of ii.	Ascension and Transfiguration.
ii. 1—iii. 11	M. Ninevites.
iii. 14-end	Ascension and Transfiguration.
v. 1-17	4 Su. Moses.
vi. 9-end	7 Su. Epiphany.
2 Tim. ii. 8-20	Greek Doctors.
ii. 16-end	2 Su. Nativity.

2 Tim. iii. 1-16 .	1 Su. Epiphany.
iv. 1-9, 14-19	Greek Doctors.
Tit. ii. 11—iii. 8	Epiphany.
Heb. i., ii. . .	7 M. Fast.
iii. 1-14 . .	2 Su. Epiphany.
iii. 14—iv. 11	3 Su. Epiphany.
iv. 14—vi. 9	7 Tu. Fast.
vi. 9—vii. 4	5 Su. Epiphany.
vii. 18-end .	4 Su. Epiphany.
viii. 1—ix. 11	6 Su. Epiphany.
viii. 1—ix. 6	2 Su. Church.
Heb. ix. 6-16 .	3 Su. Church.
ix. 11-end .	7 W. Fast.
ix. 16-end .	4 Su. Church.
x. 19-37 .	5 Su. Resurrection.
xi. 3-11, 32—xii. 3 .	Confessors.
xiii. 1-10, 16-22 . . .	Syrian Doctors.
xiii. 20-end	Resurrection.

GLOSSARY OF TECHNICAL ECCLESIASTICAL TERMS

Abukhálim(ă), a book containing collects and some occasional offices, such as the office for the preparation of the elements.

After, see *Qdhamuwathar*.

Aghúna, martyrdom (ἀγών). So *Aghunista* (ἀγωνιστής), a martyr.

'*Anídha*, (1) a departed Christian; (2) the book of the burial services for laymen, women, and children.

Annunciation, Syr. *Subára*, Advent, 25 days.

Antidoron (or rather *Antidhoron*), Syr. *mkapríina*, a portion of the holy loaf not consecrated, given to communicants after their communion (Greek ἀντίδωρον).[1] The Greeks give it to non-communicants. Also called *eulogiae*.

Apisqúpa, a bishop (ἐπίσκοπος). The Episcopate is divided into three divisions: (1) Patriarchs, (2) Metropolitans, (3) Bishops. The last are also called *simple bishops*.

Apitrúpa (ἐπίτροπος), a steward or churchwarden. Also *rab baita* (pl. *rabai bati*).

Apostle, Syr. *Shlíkha*, (1) the Epistle for the day, always taken from St. Paul. So the Greek ἀπόστολος. (2) Any apostle or missionary, especially the Twelve and the Seventy.

Arkidhyáqun or *Arkidhyaqúna*, an archdeacon (ἀρχιδιάκονος). The presbyterate is divided into three divisions: (1) Archdeacons, (2) Chorepiscopi, (3) Priests. According to some, the first two are interchanged. In the vernacular often contracted to *arkan*.

Athlíta, a martyr. So the Greek ἀθλητής.

Athwátha, see *Letter psalm*.

Basaliqi, see *Royal Anthem*.

---

[1] The writer is indebted to the Glossary in Dr. Littledale's *Offices of the Holy Eastern Church* for much of the information given here about Greek technical terms.

Bathqyama (daughter of the promise), a nun.
Bati, see *Verses*.
Ba'úlha, see *Rogation*.
Before, see *Qdhamuwathar*.
Bím or *bema*, (1) usually the raised space between the sanctuary doors and the dwarf wall in the nave parallel to them (= σολέα, σολέας, σολείον, or σολία nearly); (2) rarely the sanctuary = Greek βῆμα.
Birúna, an episcopal mitre, head-dress, or hood. Perhaps = Greek βῆρος, Lat. *birrus*, a priestly garment.
Bráshith, a verse from Genesis i., said on some festivals; lit. *In the beginning* (page 165).
Bukhra, see *Firstborn*.
Burákha, lit. *blessing*. The marriage-service book.

Canon, Syr. *Qanúna*, Gk. κανών, (1) any ecclesiastical law, also any rule or regulation in grammar, etc.; (2) in the liturgy, the ending of several long prayers which are said in a low voice, marked by the raising of the voice, and in most cases by the use of cymbals; (3) an antiphonal chant or part of a psalm introduced into some of the services, especially in the fast.
Carshúnic, Arabic written in Syriac characters, as in the case of the liturgical Gospels in the town of Mosul.
Cathólicos, Syr. *Qathuliqa*, a name of the Patriarch (καθολικός). Said by the East Syrians to be so called because he has all the divisions of the priesthood in himself, and all jurisdiction.
Chaldeans, Syr. *Kaldáyi*, the later Magi or Astrologers. In modern times, the Uniats, or East Syrians who acknowledge the Pope.
Chorepiscopus, Syr. *Kurapisqúpa* (χωρεπίσκοπος). The second division of the second order, the Presbyterate. See *Arkidhyáqun*. These officers were never bishops among the East Syrians.
Conclusion, Syr. *Khuthámá*, or Sealing. The Blessing.
Continuation, Syr. *H'pakhtha*, the second part of certain anthems.
Crowning, see *Kulala*.

Dapa, an altar slab.
Dawidha, the psalter, from *Dáwidh*, *David*. This book contains the psalms with prayers and farcings, the canticles of Moses and Isaiah, and the psalter prayers; and usually also the litanies.
Dinkha or *Beith Dinkha*, the Epiphany.
Diupátkhin, 'the book of the living and the dead' (Rubrick in Takhsa). The diptychs, δίπτυχα, or list of persons to be prayed for in the liturgy.
Dukhrána, see *Memorial*.

GLOSSARY OF TECHNICAL ECCLESIASTICAL TERMS 293

Evening Anthem, the third anthem sung at the evening service on ferias. A collection of these anthems proper to the various seasons is found in the Kashkul (*q.v.*); but as this book is rare, many copies of the Qdhamuwathar have alternative anthems, one for each week-day.

Farcing, Syr. *Giyûra*, a clause interpolated in the Psalms, Lakhumara, and Holy God, in the manner shown in the preceding translation. The Greek στιχηρόν is somewhat similar.

Feast, Syr. *'Idha*. This name is usually confined to feasts of our Lord, saints' days being called memorials.

Firstborn, Syr. *Bukhra*, an eucharistic loaf.

Firstfruits, Syr. *Rishitha*, (1) the offerings given to a bishop, metropolitan, or patriarch ; (2) human nature ; (3) our Lord.

Geza or *Gaza*, lit. *the treasury* (*q.v.*), a large volume containing hymns and anthems proper to festivals.

Ghantha, lit. *inclining*. Some of the long prayers in the liturgy, said with bowed head and in a low voice, are so called.

Giyûra, see *Farcing*.

Gospel, Syr. *Iwangaliyun* (εὐαγγέλιον), (1) the four Gospels, which are only counted as one; (2) the portion appointed for the Gospel for each day ; (3) the book of the liturgical Gospels.

Great Feast, in the Urmi vernacular, Easter day.

Gudha, one of the two choirs, 'before' or 'after.'

Gultha, (1) an ecclesiastical vestment now obsolete (shape unknown); (2) an altar cloth.

Haikla, see *Temple*.

Hallowing of the Church, Syr. *Qûdash 'idta*, the last four weeks before Advent.

High priest, Syr. *Rab kahni* or *Rab kumri*, a bishop. So the Greek ἀρχιερεύς.

Hiuparkíya, an ecclesiastical province, under a metropolitan (ὑπαρχία = ἐπαρχία of the Greeks. Plural, usually *hiuparkíyas*.

Hiupathiáqna (ὑποδιάκονος), a sub-deacon (now obsolete). The diaconate is divided into deacons, sub-deacons, and readers. We notice that the Greek rough breathing becomes *h* in Syriac, unlike the modern Greek pronunciation, and the upsilon has the sound of an English *u*.

Holy God, the prayer beginning with these words, recited by all (p. 10).

Holy of holies, Syr. *Qdhush qudhshi*, (1) the space under the canopy in front of the altar ;(2) all the sanctuary.

Holy thing, Syr. *Qudhsha*, the eucharistic species.
Horn, see *Qarna*.
Hosannas, Sunday (or Festival) of, Palm Sunday.
House of Absolution, the south side of the sanctuary.
House of the Altar, the east side of the sanctuary.
House of the Deacon, the baptistery, on the south of the sanctuary, used also as a vestry, etc.
House of the Door, the west side of the sanctuary.
House of the Holy thing, or of the Treasury (q.v.), the north side of the sanctuary.
H'pakhtha, see *Continuation*.
Hulála (pl. *Huláli*), one of the twenty-one divisions of the psalter, corresponding to the Greek κάθισμα.

'*Idha*, see *Feast*.
Ikhidháya, a monk ; lit. a hermit.
'*Iri*, see *Watchful ones*.
Iṣṭaṭyúna, the same as Madrásha, q.v. (apparently from *statio*).
Iwangaliyun, see *Gospel*.

Jordan, Syr. *Yúrdnan*, the font. See *Wazna* (the usual word).

Kahna, a priest in his ministerial aspect (*sacerdos*), as opposed to *qashísha* (vernacular *qasha*), which is used with reference to his rank. The word *lahnútha* (priesthood) includes all three orders, even the diaconate.
Kaldayi, see *Chaldeans*.
Karuzútha (pl. *Karuzcátha*), the litany-bidding prayer, said by the deacon. Greek ἐκτενή.
Kasa, the chalice.
Káshkul (lit. *containing all*), a large book containing the evening anthems and the Motwas at the night service for ferias in the different seasons.
Khadh parsupa, see *One Person*.
Khnana, earth from the tombs of the martyrs, used at weddings, etc.
Khudhra, lit. *Cycle*, a large volume, containing the parts of the liturgy and daily offices proper to Sundays, Feasts of our Lord, and the principal saints' days. The lections are not written at length.
Khuthama, see *Conclusion*.
Kiruṭaníya (χειροτονία), ordination (not other layings-on of hands).
Knitting of the bridechamber, a part of the marriage ceremony, in which the bridechamber is blessed. So called because it was

the custom to make an osier screen in the large family room to fence it off.

Kuláia, or *Crowning*, (1) a ceremony at baptism and marriage. So in Greek στέφανος = the nuptial crown, στεφανοῦν or στεφανοῦσθαι is to marry, or be wedded ; (2) martyrdom.

Kurapisqúpa, see *Chorepiscopus*.

Kurásta, the book of the Burial Service for the clergy.

Kushápa, lit. *Beseeching*. Some of the long prayers in the liturgy, said by the priest kneeling and in a low voice, are so called.

Kwantha, a hood, now obsolete.

Lakhumára, an ascription of praise, said by all (page 3). So called from its first words, *To thee, Lord*.

Laqna, a vessel containing oil, used at baptism. Gk. λάγηνος, Lat. *lagena*. See *Qarna*.

Lections, Syr. *Qiryáni*, (1) all the portions of Scripture read at the Liturgy, including Epistle and Gospel ; (2) those from the Old Testament and Acts only.

Letter psalm, Syr. *Letters* (*Athwátha*), a portion of the cxix. Psalm, which is acrostic.

Liturgy, (1) Syr. *Qurbána* or *Offering* (*q.v.*), the Eucharist ; (2) Syr. *Qudásha* or *Hallowing*, one of the three services for the Eucharist, ascribed to Mar Adai and Mar Mari, to Nestorius, and to Theodore the Interpreter.

Little feast. In the Urmi vernacular, Christmas day.

Ma'álta, lit. *Entrance*, the first day of the Hallowing of the Church, the fourth Sunday before Advent. So called because on this day the East Syrians go into the church for their daily prayers, having during the summer said them in the outer chapel.

Ma'apra, (1) a long vestment worn outside the albe and stole by bishops and priests at the Eucharist. Among the West Syrians it is a mitre or a woman's head-dress ; (2) a veil put on a child's head at baptism.

Madrásha, a doctrinal hymn.

Mádhbkha, lit. *the sacrificing place*, (1) the altar ; (2) the sanctuary. So θυσιαστήριον, which has both meanings.

Malka, (1) the priest's loaf in the Liturgy; (2) the holy leaven, said to be descended from the Apostles. Ordinary leaven is *khmíra*.

Mandíla, the chrisom or white baptismal robe. Gk. μανδύλιον, Lat. *mantele*, a napkin ; also in Arabic.

Mar, lit. *My lord*. Title of honour given to all bishops, alive and dead, and to certain other saints, as St. John Baptist, St. Ephraim, St. Stephen, St. Cyriac. The feminine is *Mart* (*q.v.*).

Marmítha (pl. *Marmyátha*), a subdivision of a hulala (*q.v.*). Gk. στάσις, but the Greek divisions are not the same as the East Syrian.

Mart, lit. *My lady*. Seldom applied to any one but the Blessed Virgin (Mart Mariam).

Martuta, the pallium worn by patriarchs (obsolete),

Martyrs' Anthem, sung at the end of Evening and Morning Prayer. There is one for each morning and each evening.

Mastabtha, a raised pace in front of the altar.

Matunīya, a genuflexion. So μετανοία.

Memorial, Syr. *Dukhrána*, (1) a saint's day; (2) a commemoration of the faithful departed.

Mitrapuldita, a metropolitan (μητροπολίτης), see *Apisqúpa*. Also called *Mitran* or *Matran*.

Mkaprana, (1) see *Antidoron*; (2) a small veil or napkin.

Momyána, an exorcist (obsolete).

Morning Anthem, an anthem from the Khudhra or Geza, said after the psalms at Morning Service on Sundays and Festivals.

Motwa, (1) an anthem at the night service, sung sitting, whence its name. Gk. κάθισμα. These vary with the season, and are found in the Kashkul for ferias, and in the Khudhra and Geza for other days; (2) the anthems at the burial service.

Mqablána, see *Veil*.

Mshamshána, see *Shamasha*.

Mysteries, Syr. 'Razi, (1) the Eucharist (rarely also in the singular 'raza); (2) any other sacrament (chiefly in the singular).

Nahíra, a candlestick.

Napqa, a monk, lit. one who has left the world, or who is exercised in warfare. (So Sunhadus, Book vii., Preface.)

Naqúsha, an oblong board and mallet of wood, struck together to call people to church. Gk. σήμαντρον. (The Greeks also make them of iron or brass.)

Night Anthem, an anthem from the Khudhra or Geza, said after the Qali d'Shahra on Sundays; also on festivals and on ferias in Lent.

Nithi Mar, lit. Let him come, O my Lord: the Invocation in the Liturgy and baptismal office.

Nuqáya, the mixed chalice.

Nusárdéil, the Sunday of the Twelve Apostles.

GLOSSARY OF TECHNICAL ECCLESIASTICAL TERMS 297

Offering, Syr. *Qurbána*, (1) the Eucharist; (2) any gift.
One Person, Syr. *Khadh Parsúpa*, the Patron Saint.
Ordering of the Mysteries, Syr. *Ṭukas 'razi*. The consumption of the eucharistic species at the end of the Liturgy by the priest and sacristan. At this time, in practice, the officiating priest and assistants make their Communion.
Palu, in the Urmi vernacular, the fourth or middle Wednesday of the Great Fast; lit. *division* (for *palgu*).
Pathúra, (1) a table; (2) the paten; (3) occasionally both chalice and paten.
Paṭaryarka or *Paṭaryarkis*, πατριάρχης, a Patriarch. See *Cathólicos*.
Peace, Syr. *Shlama*, the kiss of peace. So Gk. εἰρήνη.
Pilása, the paten.
Piryaduṭa, originally the deputy of a Chorepiscopus (*q.v.*), then the Chorepiscopus himself. Also called Sa'ura or Visitor. The authorities often confuse these names and Archdeacon.
Piṣkha (the Passover), Maundy Thursday.
Priestly prayer, a collect. (These may only be said by priests.)
Purshana malkaya, lit. *the portion of the malka* (*q.v.*), the priest's loaf in the Eucharist. The general name for the holy loaves is *bukhra*, firstborn, *q.v.*
Qala d'gawa (pl. *Qali*), lit. *Song of the congregation*. The anthems on the two Wednesdays at the night service in place of a Motwa are so called (page 130).
Qala d'shahra (pl. *Qali*), lit. *Vigil song*. The extra hulala sung at the night service on Sundays and festivals after the Motwa are so called.
Qaltha (pl. *Qalyátha*), lit. *Little song*, or according to others, *A short (portion)*. Anthem and psalms said after the hulali at the night service before the Motwa (as a preparation for the liturgy). These are found in the Khudhra, and are said to date from the time of Mar Narsai, *circ.* 520 A.D.
Qandára, an episcopal vestment worn above the martuṭa (pallium) and beneath the kwantha (hood). Said in the book of *Heavenly Intelligences*[1] to be the sign of honour given by the Arab power to the patriarchs.
Qandéila, a lamp. Gk. κανδήλα (*sic*), Lat. *Candela*. Especially the lamp in the sanctuary, which is ordered always to be kept burning, though this is not done in practice.

---

[1] Attributed, erroneously, to Mar Shimun Bar Ṣaba'i.

GLOSSARY OF TECHNICAL ECCLESIASTICAL TERMS

Qankáya, a Sacristan, who must be a priest or deacon (according to the books), helps in the preparation of the elements, administers the cup, cares for the sanctuary, etc.

Qanki (a plural noun), the sanctuary; so the books, and now in some districts; in others the baptistery. Probably = *cancelli*.

Qánun dkhilat, a form of *Qanúna* (see *Canon*, No. 3), beginning with the word *Dkhilat* = Terrible art thou, sung solemnly in the Liturgy on the greatest festivals.

Qanúna, *Qánun*, see *Canon*.

Qariwa, *Qaryuta*, see *Shoshwina*, *Shoshwinta*.'

Qarna, a horn, Lat. *cornu*, (1) the altar being divided into three parts, the north and south parts are so named; (2) a vessel for containing the holy oil for baptism. The *laqna* contains ordinary oil, with which a little of the holy oil is mixed.

Qarúya, (1) a reader, whose office is the third of the three subdivisions of the diaconate (now obsolete). See *Hiupathiaqna*. His office was to read the *Qiryáni* or lections from the Old Testament and Acts; (2) any reader.

Qashísha (vernacular *Qásha*), a priest. See *Kahna*, *Arkidhyaqun*.

Qathuliqa, see *Catholicos*.

Qathuliqi or *Qathuliqáita*, Catholick (epithet of the Church only).

Qdhámuwáthar, lit. *Before and after*. More fully, *Kthawa daqdhám wadhwáthar*, lit. *Book of before and of after*. The book containing the anthems, etc., for ferias and festivals as far as they do not vary with the season; so called because the weeks are called 'before' or 'after' according as the first or second choir begins the service. See Introduction.

Qdhush qudhshi, see *Holy of holies*.

Qilítha, a monastery or cell; now used for the Patriarch's house; Lat. *cella*; Gk. κέλλα, κέλλη, or κέλλιον.

Qiryána (pl. *Qiryáni*), see *Lections*.

Qléiríqi, the clergy. Gk. κληρικοί.

Qṣatha, lit. *that which is broken*, the eucharistic loaf, before or after baking.

Qudash 'ídta, see *Hallowing of the Church*.

Qudasha, see *Liturgy*, No. 2.

Qudhsha, see *Holy thing*.

Qulása (derived from Greek κλέος), the deacon's interjections in the Liturgy.

Qurbana, see *Offering*, and *Liturgy*, No. 1.

Quṭa'a, an extra Hulala said at morning service in the fast.

Rab baita, see *Apitrupa*.
Rab kahni, see *High priest*.
Rab kumri, see *High priest*.
Raban, a monk; lit. *our great one*.
'Raza (pl. *'razi*), see *Mysteries*.
Rishitha, see *Firstfruits*.
Rogation, Syr. *Ba'utha*, a fast of three days. The principal rogation is that of the Ninevites, twenty days before the beginning of the Great Fast; a special service is appointed for each day.
Royal Anthem, Syr. *Basaliqi* (βασιλικοί), an anthem said in the festival service in place of the evening anthem, *q.v.* (page 78).

Sa'ura, (1) see *Piryaduta*; (2) in the vernacular, a sexton.
Sealing, see *Conclusion*.
Semantron, see *Naqusha*.
Shamasha (in the vernacular often *Shâmasha*), a deacon. See *Hiupathiaqna*.
Shamashutha, (1) a deacon's office; (2) in the vernacular, a book containing the deacon's part in the Liturgy.
Shawu'a, one of the periods into which the ecclesiastical year is divided, most of which are *seven* weeks, whence the name.
Shkhinta (a feminine form of *Shechinah*), (1) a dwelling-place of God, as a church; (2) a saint's tomb in a church; (3) a *quasi* altar at the east end of the nave, on which the cross, books, censers, etc., are placed. There are two or three of these in each church.
Shlama, see *Peace*.
Shlikha, see *Apostle*.
Shoshwina, (1) a godfather at baptism; (2) the groomsman at marriage. In the vernacular and occasionally in the books, *Qarîwa*, lit. *neighbour*.
Shoshwinta(?), (1) a godmother; (2) a bridesmaid. In the vernacular and occasionally in the books, *Qaryuta*.
Shubakha (pl. *Shubakhi*), lit. *praise*, a psalm said at the night service before the Tishbukhta (*q.v.*). So in Greek the last three psalms (sung at daily mattins, see page xxiii) are called αἶνοι (Lat. *laudes*, hence the name Lauds).
Shumlaya, confirmation of a bishop by the Patriarch after he has been consecrated by the Metropolitan.
Shuraya (pl. *Shurayi*), a psalm, or portion of a psalm, usually introducing an anthem. Cf. the Greek προκείμενον, which is a verse preceding lections.

Shushipa (t), (1) a chalice veil ; (2) a veil for covering the font, etc.

Siamidha, lit. *Laying on of hands*, (1) an ordination or consecration of any ecclesiastical order ; (2) the book containing the service for the same ; (3) the consecration of a church, also called *Qudash madhbkha*, the hallowing of the sanctuary ; (4) confirmation, in which there s the laying on of hands, immediately after and as part of baptism ; (5) any prayer said at the laying on of hands on things or persons.

Skhakha, one of the ancient sections into which the Syriac Bible was divided.

Soma, (1) any fast ; (2) also called *Soma raba*, the great fast, Lent (fifty days) ; (3) in the vernacular a personification of Lent.

Subá'a, lit. *satisfaction*, (1) Compline ; (2) grace after meat. In the first sense also called *Suba'tha* (distinguish *Subatha*).

Subára, see *Annunciation*.

Subátha, the preparation of the elements.

Sudára, a veil, Lat. *sudarium*.

Sudhra, (1) an albe ; (2) any shirt.

Sugitha, an anthem at morning service on some festivals, etc., found in the Khudhra or Geza.

Suláqa, the Ascension.

Sunhádus, the book of Canon Law (σύνοδος). We notice that the aspirate of ὁδός is retained. The adjective *sunhadiqáya* (συνοδικός) is also used = *synodic*.

Supára, a tonsure. Gk. στεφανή.

Suyákha (pl. *Suyákhi*), lit. *Conclusion*. Extra psalms, said on some days at the evening service before the Royal Anthem, and at the night service.

Takhsa, lit. *Order*. Gk. τάξις. (1) Any arrangement or order, especially ecclesiastical ; (2) the book containing the liturgies and several other priestly offices (see Introduction).

Temple, Syr. *Haikla*, (1) any of the parts of a church, all of which are walled off from one another ; (2) especially the nave. The Greek ναός is the nave of a parochial church, the choir of a monastic one.

Throne, Syr. *trúnus* (θρόνος), the altar.

Tishbúkhta (pl. *Tishbukhyátha*), a hymn of praise ; *e.g.* the Benedicite or Gloria in excelsis.

Treasury, (1) Syr. *Geza*, *q.v.* ; (2) Syr. *Beithgeza*. A recess in the north wall of the sanctuary for the sacred vessels.

Tukas 'razi, see *Ordering of the Mysteries*.

Turgama, lit. *Interpretation*, explanatory hymns sung before the Epistle and Gospel, not very ancient in date.

Twiláita, a movable altar slab (*tabella*).

'*Udhrána*, one of the numerous collects 'for help' in the daily offices distributed among all the priests present (page 16).

'*Unáya*, the first verse of some anthems; an antiphon.

'*Unitha* (pl. '*unyátha*), (1) an anthem; (2) a subdivision of the same (see *Verses*).

'*Unitha d'bim*, anthem of the bema, sung during the communion of the people, by those who are outside the sanctuary.

'*Unitha d'iwangaliyun*, anthem of the Gospel, sung in the liturgy directly after the Gospel.

'*Unitha d'qanki*, anthem of the sanctuary, sung in the liturgy in the first part of the service.

'*Unitha d'razi*, anthem of the mysteries, sung in the liturgy after the offertory.

Urára, a stole. These for all orders are in shape like Western stoles, not like that of a Greek priest. (Greek ὡράριον, the deacon's stole, which is of this shape.)

Veil, (1) Syr. *Wíla*, the veil closing the open space between sanctuary and nave, called the 'sanctuary door' (there is often also a door here); (2) Syr. *mqablána*, a humeral veil, worn by the deacon who holds the paten while the priest communicates the people; (3) see also *Shushipa* and *Mkaprana*.

Verses, Syr. *bati*, houses: the subdivisions of the anthems.

Verses of prayer, a subdivision of some of the long anthems, as at the Wednesday Night Service, the verses of which are especially prayerful.

Wazna, the Font.

Watchful ones, Syr. '*Iri*, the angels. From Dan. iv. 13, LXX. εἴρ (v. 10).

Weaving of the bridechamber, see *Knitting*.

Weeks of the mysteries. The first, middle, and last weeks of the Great Fast; lections are appointed for each day except Saturday (see the Table of Lections above).

Warda, lit. *Rose*, a book of hymns for festivals.

Wíla, see *Veil*.

Yalda or *Beith Yalda*, (1) the Nativity (of Christ); (2) any birthday.

Zumára, lit. *Song*, a few verses of the Psalms, sung before the Gospel.

Zunára, the girdle, worn by all the clergy.

SYRIAC WORKS PUBLISHED AT THE MISSION PRESS, URMI.

To be had at the Office of the 'Archbishop of Canterbury's Assyrian Mission,' 7 Dean's Yard, Westminster.

1. *The Takhsa, or Order*, part i., containing the three liturgies, baptismal service, etc., in red and black; large 4to. Price 21s. in sheets.
2. *The Takhsa*, part ii., containing the collects, occasional prayers, offices of the Prothesis, for the consecration of Churches, of Absolution, for the Renewal of the leaven, Benedictions, etc., in red and black; large 4to. Price 21s. in sheets.
3. *The Marriage Service*, in red and black; small 4to, limp cloth. Price 5s.
4. *The Lectionary*, giving a table of all the proper lections from the Khudhra; 8vo, limp cloth. Price 5s.
5. *A Grammar of Classical Syriac* (Eastern Syriac form); explanations in vernacular Syriac; 8vo. Price 10s. 6d.
6. *A Grammar of Vernacular Syriac*, with spelling book; explanations in the vernacular; 8vo. Price 10s. 6d.
7. *The Qdham-u-wathar*, or 'Before and After,' with additions, giving the daily offices; small 4to, in red and black. *Nearly ready.*
8. *The Psalter*, as divided by the Eastern Syrians, with the proper prayers and farcings, and the Old Testament canticles; small 4to. Price 5s.
9. *Catechisms*, in the vernacular; 8vo. Price 3s. 6d. and 2s. 6d.
10. *Vocabulary of Verbs* of vernacular Syriac, with English translations; with a short *English Grammar* prefixed (the explanations in vernacular Syriac); small 4to. Price 5s.
11. *An Easy Ecclesiastical History* of the first four centuries, in the vernacular; 8vo. Price 2s. 6d.

The Service Books mentioned above are all in classical Syriac.

Also to be had at the same Office.

A Translation of the Takhsa, Part I., into English; large 4to.
The Catholicos of the East and his People, by Arthur John Maclean, M.A., and William Henry Browne, LL.M., being an Account of the East Syrian people; with map and illustrations; crown 8vo. 5s.
Christians under the Crescent in Asia, by E. L. Cutts, D.D.; with map and illustrations; crown 8vo. 5s.
Amina, a Tale of the Nestorians, by the Same. 1s.
And many pamphlets descriptive of the East Syrians, and of the Archbishop of Canterbury's Mission.

Eastern Church Association.

OBJECTS OF THE ASSOCIATION.

(1) To give information as to the state and position of the Eastern Christians, in order gradually to better their condition through the influence of public opinion.

(2) To make known to the Christians of the East the doctrine and principles of the Anglican Church.

(3) To take advantage of all opportunities which the Providence of God shall afford for intercommunion with the Orthodox Church, and also for friendly intercourse with the other ancient Churches of the East.

(4) To assist, as far as possible, the Bishops of the Orthodox Church in their efforts to promote the spiritual welfare and the education of their flocks.

STANDING COMMITTEE.

The Right Rev. the LORD BISHOP of READING (*Chairman*).
The Very Rev. the DEAN of ST. PAUL'S.
The WARDEN of KEBLE COLLEGE, Oxford.
Rev. W. BRIGHT, D.D., Canon of Christ Church, Regius Professor of Ecclesiastical History in the University of Oxford.
Rev. W. R. CHURTON, B.D., Fellow of King's College, Cambridge.
Rev. N. T. GARRY, Hon. Canon of Christ Church, Oxford.
Rev. W. C. E. NEWBOLT, Canon of St. Paul's.
Rev. T. A. LACEY.
Rev. S. T. M. PRICE.
Rev. R. MILBURN BLAKISTON.
Sir THEODORE C. HOPE, K.C.S.I., C.I.E.
Sir JOHN CONROY, Bart., Fellow of Balliol College, Oxford.
G. W. E. RUSSELL, Esq., M.P.
W. J. BIRKBECK, Esq.
C. R. FREEMAN, Esq.
EDWIN FRESHFIELD, Esq., LL.D., V.P.S.A.
ATHELSTAN RILEY, Esq.
C. KNIGHT WATSON, Esq., F.S.A.
H. O. WAKEMAN, Esq., Fellow of All Souls College, Oxford.

[OVER.

Treasurer—
G. T. BIDDULPH, Esq., 43 Charing Cross.

Secretary—
Rev. A. C. HEADLAM, All Souls College, Oxford.

Assistant Secretary—
Miss GOODWIN, 4 Rawlinson Road, Oxford.

The Association hopes to carry out, as far as it is able, two practical objects :—

(1.) To publish books bearing on the History and Services of the Eastern Churches.

(2.) To send two or more clergymen who, besides discharging any clerical duty they may find to do, should promote the study of Oriental Church Life, and cultivate friendly relations with Eastern Christians.

Any one desirous of becoming a Member of the Association is requested to communicate with the Secretary or Assistant Secretary.

MESSRS.

RIVINGTON, PERCIVAL & Co.'S

LIST OF

Recent Publications

34 *KING STREET, COVENT GARDEN*
LONDON

34 KING STREET, COVENT GARDEN,
LONDON, W.C.

February 1894.

Crown 8*vo.* 7*s.* 6*d.*

Arts and Crafts Essays

By Members of the Arts and Crafts Exhibition Society.

Edited with a Preface by WILLIAM MORRIS.

LIST OF CONTRIBUTORS.

William Morris, Walter Crane, G. T. Robinson, W. A. S. Benson, Somers Clarke, Stephen Webb, Emery Walker, T. J. Cobden Sanderson, F. Madox Brown, Heywood Sumner, W. R. Lethaby, May Morris, Alan S. Cole, Reginald Blomfield, Lewis F. Day, Edward S. Prior, Halsey Ricardo, J. H. Pollen, T. G. Jackson, Mary E. Turner, John D. Sedding, Selwyn Image.

'We recommend to all who are interested in a most pressing problem of the age to see what it is that they (the members of the Arts and Crafts Exhibition Society) have to say for themselves.'—**Saturday Review.**

'Valuable and interesting essays.'—**Glasgow Herald.**

'The value of its sensible utterances as a handy book of reference to the industrial arts is not easily overrated.'—**Studio.**

'There is much practical pursuit of beauty in the essays, and very little affectation of mere archaism.'—**Times.**

'We hope these essays will enjoy a wide circulation; they must inevitably exercise a healthy influence wherever read.'—**Yorkshire Post.**

'The essays differ considerably in value, but are all distinguished by earnest purpose, and may be perused with pleasure even by those who are not wholly discontented with the present standards of taste.' —**Standard.**

'The book is worthy of the attention of all who desire to see more of the artistic element introduced into common things.'— **Aberdeen Journal.**

'Contains expositions of the various arts and crafts of great merit and originality of thought and treatment.'— **Art Journal.**

London: 34 King Street, Covent Garden.

Crown Quarto. With Numerous Illustrations. 16s.

Inigo Jones and Wren

Or the Rise and Decline of Modern Architecture in England.

By W. J. LOFTIE,

Author of 'A History of London,' etc.

CONTENTS.—Introduction—The Decay of Gothic-Elizabethan Architecture—The Beginnings of Palladian—Inigo Jones—Wren—Wren's Churches—The Successors of Wren.

In this volume an attempt is made to unravel the history of Inigo Jones's two great designs for Whitehall, and to elucidate the different schemes made by Wren for St. Paul's. The illustrations are from published plates, largely supplemented by photographs, especially of those charming buildings of the Transitional Period which are to be found in the West country, where the Bath stone forms such a ready vehicle for the expression of poetry in stone.

'We have no hesitation in saying that it ought to be read at once by every man who cares about the architectural appearance of our towns. . . . Mr. Loftie's fascinating book.'—Daily Chronicle.

'This new book of Mr. Loftie's is one which possesses an amount of general interest concerning modern architects and architecture in general, and Inigo Jones and Wren and their works in particular, as should make it very widely attractive. . . . It is but seldom one comes across a book so thoroughly architectural written so specially for non-architectural readers, and for so difficult a task it could not, we think, have been more competently fulfilled in every way.'—British Architect.

'It is cleverly and intelligently written, and evidences large and painstaking research. It contains much interesting biographical information of the career of Inigo Jones and Wren, and in every sense is a thoroughly readable volume, splendidly printed and admirably illustrated.'—Birmingham Daily Gazette.

Crown 8vo. With Portraits and Illustrations. 6s.

Recollections of Dr. John Brown

Author of 'Rab and His Friends.'

With Selections from Correspondence.

By ALEXANDER PEDDIE, M.D., F.R.C.P.E., F.R.S.E., ETC.

London: 34 King Street, Covent Garden.

In March. Demy 8vo. With Map and numerous Illustrations.

Diary of a Journey Across Tibet

By Captain HAMILTON BOWER, 17th Bengal Cavalry.

CONTENTS.

From Simla to the Frontier—Commencement of Exploration—Deserted by our Guides—Meeting with Nomads—In the Neighbourhood of Lhasa—Negotiations with Lhasa Officials—Marching Northwards—Entering Inhabited Country—Country with Stone Houses—The Guides supplied by the Lhasa Officials Desert—In the Neighbourhood of Chiamdo—Chiamdo to Garthok—Garthok to Lithang—Lithang to Ta Chen Lu—Through China back to India—Religion, Country, People, etc.—Flora and Fauna.

This work is the account of the journey across Tibet from East to West of the daring explorer, Captain Bower, during which he went over some 800 miles of new country, having to spend about three months at altitudes of from 14,000 to 16,000 feet above the level of the sea, and in temperatures generally ranging from freezing-point to below zero. For five months Captain Bower never camped below the level of the summit of Mont Blanc. The illustrations are taken from special photographs and sketches, and there are also reproductions from drawings of the extremely rare birds procured, and a list of the botanical species found, some of which latter are absolutely new to science.

London: 34 King Street, Covent Garden.

Crown 8vo.   8s. 6d.

East Syrian Daily Offices

Translated from the Syriac, with Introduction, Notes and
Indices, and an Appendix containing the
Lections and Glossary

By ARTHUR J. MACLEAN, M.A.,
Dean of Argyle and the Isles,
Joint-Author of the Catholicos of the East and his People.

Published for the Eastern Church Association.

*Royal Quarto.   Printed in Large Type on paper specially made
for the Work.   £2. 2s. net, in sheets only.*

An Altar Book

Containing the Order for
the Administration of the Holy Communion, according to
the Book of Common Prayer,
together with additional matter translated from the English Missals
of the earlier part of the Sixteenth Century.

Edited by a Committee of Priests.

Special care has been taken to render the Book in all respects serviceable for practical use at the Altar, the Editors believing that there is room for improvement upon the attempts which have hitherto been made to meet what has for years been an admitted need.

CONTENTS.—1. Kalendar (Rubricated)—2. Temporale—3. Ordinary and Canon (Rubricated), with musical notation—4. Tones for singing Epistle and Gospel—5. Sanctorale—6. Commune Sanctorum—7. Missæ Votivæ—8. Missæ Defunctorum—9. Appendix containing divers Benedictions and Services of Holy Week.

London: 34 King Street, Covent Garden.

Crown 8vo. 2s.

A Social Policy for the Church

And other Papers on Social Subjects

By the Rev. T. C. FRY, D.D.,
Head Master of Berkhamsted School.

CONTENTS.—A Social Policy for the Church—What can the Clergy do?—Some Causes of Social Apathy—To Working-men—The Social Issues of Divorce—The Ethics of Wills.

Post Free to Subscribers, Ten Shillings a year, paid in advance; or Three Shillings a Number.

The Economic Review

CONTENTS OF THE JANUARY NUMBER, 1894.

Economists as Mischief-Makers. Rev. PROF. W. CUNNINGHAM, D.D.
Some of the Christian Socialists of 1848 and the following Years (II.). J. M. LUDLOW.
The Stress of Competition from the Workman's point of View. ROBERT HALSTEAD.
Workingmen's Clubs. J. WELLS, M.A.
The Coal War.
   I. CANNOCK CHASE. Rev. PREB. R. M. GRIER, M.A.
   II. LANCASHIRE. JAMES CHADBURN.
European Militarism and an Alternative. CHARLES ROBERTS, M.A.
Notes and Memoranda.
Legislation, Parliamentary Inquiries and Official Returns.
   EDWIN CANNAN, M.A.
Reviews and Short Notices.

*Royal 32mo. 2s.
Or in 2 vols. (the 'Hours' and 'Mirror' separately). 2s. 6d.
[Copies may also be had in sheets, complete. 1s. 6d.]*

The Hours of the Blessed Virgin Mary

According to the Sarum Breviary, together with
a brief Commentary from 'The Mirror of our Lady.'

This book is printed in red and black on toned paper, with a fine reproduction of an old engraving.

London: 34 King Street, Covent Garden.

Crown 8vo. 3s. 6d.

Faith

Eleven Sermons, with a Preface.

By the Rev. H. C. BEECHING, M.A.,
Rector of Yattendon, Berks.

In Two Volumes. Large Post 8vo. 21s. net.

A Paradise of English Poetry

Arranged by the Rev. H. C. BEECHING, M.A.,
Rector of Yattendon, Berks.

This work is printed on hand-made paper, bound in buckram, and published in a limited edition, which will not, under any circumstances, be reprinted. The publishers reserve the right to issue at a future date, should they think fit, a smaller and cheaper edition.

'Mr. Beeching's anthology of English poetry has one great and unusual merit: the pieces selected are selected purely and simply for their poetical merit, and for no other reason whatever. . . . Type and paper are extremely pleasant, and this "Paradise of English Poetry" is a very garden of Armida—so alluring is it to enter, so choice and varied in entertainment, so tempting to linger in, so hard to leave.'—**Athenæum.**

'That those who walk in the rose-scented avenues of Mr. Beeching's garden will say that the planting has been well done, we cannot doubt for a moment. He has not only a knowledge of English literature which is as sympathetic as it is profound, but he has the critical faculty, without which a knowledge of, and even a love for, literature is wasted. He does more than know what is good in literature,—that is comparatively easy. He knows what is bad, and with him base metal is never offered us for gold. There are not many men who can stand this test, but Mr. Beeching comes through it triumphantly. . . . Before we leave this book, we must commend Mr. Beeching's excellent notes. They are interesting, to the point, not too long, and often enable one to get an additional touch of pleasure from the verse they annotate.'—**Spectator.**

'A very skilful selection, and eminently worthy of its name. . . . Will commend itself to all true lovers of English poetry.' —**Times.**

London: 34 King Street, Covent Garden.

Crown 8vo.   6s.

From Advent to Advent

Sermons preached at the Chapel Royal, Whitehall.

By the late AUBREY L. MOORE, M.A.

Third Edition.   Crown 8vo.   3s. 6d.

Some Aspects of Sin

Three Courses of Sermons.

By the late AUBREY L. MOORE, M.A.

Crown 8vo.   3s. 6d.

The Message of the Gospel

Addresses to Candidates for Ordination,
and Sermons preached chiefly before the University of Oxford.

By the late AUBREY L. MOORE, M.A.

Crown 8vo.   7s. 6d.

The Fire upon the Altar

Sermons preached to Harrow Boys.   1887 to 1890.

By the Rev. J. E. C. WELLDON, M.A.,
Head Master of Harrow School, and Hon. Chaplain to the Queen.

Crown 8vo.   7s. 6d.

Old Truths in Modern Lights

The Boyle Lectures for 1890, with other Sermons.

By T. G. BONNEY, D.Sc., LL.D., F.R.S., F.S.A., F.G.S.,
Fellow of St. John's College, Cambridge, Honorary Canon of Manchester.

London: 34 King Street, Covent Garden.

Crown 8vo. 2s. 6d.

A Continuous Narrative of The Life of Christ

In the Words of the Four Gospels.

With Maps, Introduction, and Notes, arranged by the

REV. A. E. HILLARD, M.A.,
Assistant Master at Clifton College.

The main body of this book consists of passages from the four Gospels so arranged as to give a continuous chronological narrative of the Life of Christ. It is intended to give a clearer idea of the connection between the parts of Christ's ministry and the order of events in it than can be obtained by reading the Gospels in succession. Great care is taken by the system of division adopted, by the marginal analysis, and by inserting a separate map for each part of Christ's ministry, to make the sequence of events in the Life of Christ quite clear.

Crown 8vo. 5s.

Low Spirits and Other Sermons

By the late REV. WILLIAM RICHMOND HUTTON, M.A.,
Rector-Designate of Lower Hardres, Canterbury;
formerly Curate of St. Michael's, Helston,
and of St. Stephen's, Kirkstall.

'They certainly deserve publication on any ground, for they are of marked ability, and we cannot but feel that Mr. Hutton, had he lived, would have made his mark in the Church.'—**Church Review.**

London : 34 King Street, Covent Garden.

Crown 8vo.   2s. 6d.

Why we are Churchmen

Seven Plain Reasons.

By A. L. OLDHAM, M.A., Prebendary of Hereford,
Rector of St. Leonard, Bridgnorth,
and Rural Dean.

With a Preface by EDGAR C. S. GIBSON,
Principal of Wells Theological College,
and Prebendary of the Cathedral.

CONTENTS.

Summary—Churchmen put on their Defence—The Church, Christ's one visible Legacy to the World—Christendom in fragments—The National Church and Papal Claims—The Reformation and the Roman Mission—The Standpoint of the English Church—The Apostolic Ministry—The Church's Witness and Worship—The Church and the Message of Salvation—Helps to Holiness in the Church—Bad Reasons and Good for being Churchmen—Index.

Crown 8vo.

Lessons from the Old Testament

Selected and Arranged by the
Rev. M. G. GLAZEBROOK, M.A., Head Master of Clifton College.

Senior Course. *In Two Vols.*   2s. 6d. *net each vol.*
 Vol. I.—THE CREATION TO THE DEATH OF SAUL.
  Notes to Vol. I. in preparation.

 Vol. II.—THE DEATH OF SAUL TO NEHEMIAH.
  Notes to Vol. II. 1s. 6d. *net.*
  Text and Notes of Vol. II. together, 4s. *net.*

Junior Course. *In One Vol.* 2s 6d *net.*
  THE CREATION TO NEHEMIAH.

 Or in Three Parts, Cloth Limp, 1s. *net each.*
Part I.—THE CREATION TO THE SETTLEMENT OF THE TRIBES.
Part II.—OTHNIEL, EHUD, AND BARAK, TO REHOBOAM AND JEROBOAM.
Part III.—REHOBOAM AND JEROBOAM TO NEHEMIAH.

London: 34 King Street, Covent Garden.

Demy 8vo. With Maps and a Plan. 16s.

Venice
An Historical Sketch of the Republic

By HORATIO F. BROWN,

Author of 'Life on the Lagoons.'

'A bright, vigorous, and substantially accurate sketch of Venetian history has long been amongst the most necessary of our many historical desiderata. Mr. Horatio Brown has now to a large extent supplied this want in a work which seldom makes pretence to original treatment, but is drawn from the best sources.'—Prof. T. F. Tout in The English Historical Review.

'The reader can hardly fail to catch some of the enthusiasm of the writer as he follows this fascinating story of the rise and fall of a once rich and flourishing Republic.'—Manchester Examiner.

'At last we possess, in this excellent volume, a full and adequate history of Venice in English. It was a work worth doing, and Mr. Brown has performed it with care and judgment.—Daily Chronicle.

'Venice holds so high a place in the affections of all who are sensible to the charms of beauty and dignity that Mr. Horatio Brown's excellent sketch of its history is sure to receive a warm welcome.'—Saturday Review.

'Although, in general terms, this work may be described as a history of Venice, it has been carried out on so original a plan as to deserve a distinct and prominent place amongst the many volumes which have been devoted to a record of the rise, development, and decline of the Venetian Republic.'—Glasgow Herald.

'Mr. Brown has imprisoned the atmosphere of Venice into his pages, has for the most part made her heroes live again, and has brought out fully the poetry and pathos of her wonderful career.'—Westminster Gazette.

'Mr. Brown has performed his task with skill and taste; and a picture is presented of the process by which Venice was built up and fell from its high estate, which is at once brilliant and accurate.'—Scotsman.

'Mr. Brown's learned and yet thoroughly readable book is published in a fortunate hour, both for author and reader. When he writes about Venice we feel that his sympathy with his subject has given him the power both of comprehending things Venetian and of extending that comprehension to his readers.'—Manchester Guardian.

'This is in truth a chronicle which follows out with industry and accuracy the maze of Venetian history. . . . As an historical sketch it is admirable.'—Times.

'A valuable and fascinating work, evidently the result of research and study.'—Daily Telegraph.

London: 34 King Street, Covent Garden.

Second Edition, revised. With Illustrations. Crown 8vo. 6s.

Life on the Lagoons

By HORATIO F. BROWN,
Author of 'Venice: An Historical Sketch.'

Second Edition, revised. In two Volumes. Crown 8vo. 16s.
With numerous Illustrations,
including Pen and Pencil Drawings by JANE E. COOK.

Old Touraine

The Life and History of the Famous Châteaux of France.

By THEODORE ANDREA COOK, B.A.,
sometime Scholar of Wadham College, Oxford.

There is an itinerary for the tourist, and a map, genealogical tables, lists of pictures, manuscripts, etc., and an index, which will, it is hoped, save the necessity of purchasing guide-books for each of the Châteaux.

There are a few copies still left of the large-paper edition *de luxe* signed and numbered, with the illustrations hand printed upon Japanese paper and mounted, price £5, 5s. net each.

Crown 8vo. 4s. 6d.

Spain and Morocco

Studies in Local Colour.

By HENRY T. FINCK,
Author of 'Chopin, and other Musical Essays,' etc.

London: 34 King Street, Covent Garden.

Demy 8vo.   21s. net.]

Lectures and Essays on Fevers and Diphtheria
1849 to 1879
By SIR WILLIAM JENNER, BART., G.C.B.,

M.D. Lond. and F.R.C.P., D.C.L. Oxon., LL.D., Cantab. and Edin., F.R.S., President of the Royal College of Physicians from 1881 to 1888, Physician in Ordinary to H.M. the Queen and to H.R.H. the Prince of Wales, Consulting Physician to University College Hospital.

CONTENTS.

ON FEVERS: Tpyhus Fever—Typhoid Fever—Relapsing Fever—Febricula.

THREE LECTURES on the acute specific diseases, being the Gulstonian Lectures delivered at the Royal College of Physicians of London in 1853. An Address on the Treatment of Typhoid Fever, delivered before the Midland Medical Society, at Birmingham, November 4, 1879.

ON DIPHTHERIA: Its Symptoms and Treatment.

CLINICAL LECTURES on Croup and the Diseases that resemble it.

Several years since I collected from the journals to which I had originally sent them my papers on Fever. I now publish together all the papers I have written on Fever, because many of my medical friends have from time to time urged me to do it, and also because all the facts detailed and analysed were observed and recorded at the bedside and in the dead-house by *myself*. While collecting some of these facts in 1847 I caught typhus fever, and three or four years later typhoid fever. I mention this because it was said at the time, ' Before typhus and typhoid fevers can be said to be absolutely different diseases, some one must be found who has suffered from both,' and I was the first, so far as I know, who at that time could be proved to have suffered from both. Dr. E. A. Parkes attended me in both illnesses, and had no doubt about the diagnosis in each case. . . .—*Extract from the Preface.*

London : 34 King Street, Covent Garden.

Demy 8vo.   21s. net.

The Hygiene, Diseases, and Mortality of Occupations

By J. T. ARLIDGE, M.D., A.B. (LOND.), F.R.C.P. (LOND.);

Consulting Physician to the North Staffordshire Infirmary; late Milroy Lecturer at the Royal College of Physicians, etc. etc.

'Dr. Arlidge's work should be welcomed by legislators and philanthropists as well as by the members of the medical profession, whose duty it is to be specially acquainted with those causes which affect the health of the different sections of the industrial community. . . . It only remains for us to say that, having gone carefully through the book, we can confidently recommend it as a valuable work of reference to all who are interested in the welfare of the industrial classes.'—**Lancet.**

'A novel and important work dealing with a subject of great public as well as medical interest.'—**Times.**

'We have already briefly noticed Dr. Arlidge's interesting work; but the importance of the questions with which it deals is sufficient to justify a more complete account of the conclusions at which the author has arrived, and of the principal *data* upon which these conclusions have been founded.'—**Times.**

'From what we have quoted it will be seen that the researches undertaken by Dr. Arlidge, for his Milroy Lectures, and embodied in the volume before us, are, from a practical as well as a scientific point of view, of the most suggestive character to all who are concerned that wealth shall not increase while men decay.'—**Standard.**

'Will be considered the standard authority on the subject for many years to come.'—**Glasgow Herald.**

'This masterly work. . . . Dr. Arlidge in the preparation of this work has rendered a signal public service.'—**Aberdeen Journal.**

'This invaluable work.'—**Daily Telegraph.**

'Few, if any, British men have a better right than Dr. Arlidge to be heard on this particular subject. . . . (The volume is) crammed from cover to cover with most interesting and important information, given with a plainness of speech and a freedom from technical pretence that make it delightful reading for those without a smattering of medicine.'—**National Observer.**

'A book of great value and interest. **St. James' Gazette.**

'The valuable treatise.'—**Birmingham Daily Gazette.**

'Dr. Arlidge has given us a highly creditable and useful collection of material on this important subject.'—**Scottish Leader.**

'It should be quite invaluable. Perhaps, too, it may render a service to the community in its obvious moral—that special dangers on the part of workmen or workwomen should be met by special precautions.'—**Yorkshire Post.**

London: 34 King Street, Covent Garden.

With Maps. Crown 8vo.

Periods of European History

General Editor—ARTHUR HASSALL, M.A.
Student of Christ Church, Oxford.

The object of this series is to present in separate Volumes a comprehensive and trustworthy account of the general development of European History, and to deal fully and carefully with the more prominent events in each century.

The Volumes will embody the results of the latest investigations, and will contain references to and notes upon original and other sources of information.

It is believed that no such attempt to place the History of Europe in a comprehensive, detailed, and readable form before the English public has yet been made, and it is hoped that the Series will form a valuable continuous History of Mediæval and Modern Europe.

Period I. A.D. 476-918. By C. W. C. OMAN, M.A., Fellow of All Souls' College, Oxford. 7s. 6d. [*Now ready.*

,, II. A.D. 918-1272. By T. F. TOUT, M.A., Professor of History at Victoria University, Manchester.

,, III. A.D. 1272-1494. By R. LODGE, M.A., Fellow and Tutor of Brasenose College, Oxford.

,, IV. A.D. 1494-1598. By A. H. JOHNSON, M.A., sometime Fellow of All Soul's College, and Historial Lecturer to Merton, Trinity, and University Colleges, Oxford.

,, V. A.D. 1598-1715. By H. O. WAKEMAN, M.A., Fellow of All Souls' College, and Tutor of Keble College, Oxford. 6s. [*Nearly Ready.*

,, VI. A.D. 1715-1789. By A. HASSALL, M.A., Student of Christ Church, Oxford.

,, VII. A.D. 1789-1815. By H. MORSE STEPHENS, M.A., Balliol College, Oxford. 6s. [*Now ready.*

,, VIII. A.D. 1815-1893.

London: 34 King Street, Covent Garden.

RECENT PUBLICATIONS

Crown 8vo. With Maps. 7s. 6d.

European History, 476-918

By C. W. C. OMAN, M.A., Fellow of All Souls' College, Oxford.

Forming Volume I. of PERIODS OF EUROPEAN HISTORY.

'Notwithstanding its modest scale, this volume (Period I.) will be valued by all historical students as supplying a real want in our historical literature, and supplying it well. . . . He paints on a small scale, it is true, but his touch is sure and his insight keen. For the accuracy of his facts his historical reputation is a sufficient guarantee.'—**Times.**

'Though on a comparatively small scale, Mr. Oman's sketch is complete and vivid. His insight and acumen in appreciating the bearing of events and in estimating the influence of personal character are particularly striking, whilst his pleasing and picturesque style makes the perusal of his work as enjoyable from the literary as it is instructive from the historical point of view.'—**Glasgow Herald.**

'Mr. Oman seems to have, or to have acquired, the art of compression without sacrifice of interest, as we can testify from a somewhat careful reading of the volume. . . . We have only been able to indicate the main features of a most useful and well-executed work: we look forward with pleasure to the forthcoming volumes of the series, which promises to be a monument of utility and of interest to all students of European history. The volume, which is well printed and neatly bound, concludes with a full and well-constructed index.—**Birmingham Daily Gazette.**

Crown 8vo. With Coloured Maps. 6s.

European History, 1789-1815

By H. MORSE STEPHENS, M.A., Balliol College, Oxford.

Forming Volume VII. of PERIODS OF EUROPEAN HISTORY.

'The appearance of a text-book of this period of European history (Period VII.), such as the one before us, is an event which every genuine historian will heartily welcome. To say that Mr. Morse Stephens has compiled the best English text-book on the subject would be faint praise.'—**Journal of Education.**

'We are happy to extend a hearty welcome to this much-needed series, which, if it throughout keeps on the same high level of this volume (Period VII.), will fill up a painful gap in our accessible historical literature.'—**Educational Times.**

'Mr. Stephens has written a very valuable and meritorious book, which ought to be widely used. . . . We may conclude by warmly praising the very elaborate index, the extremely useful tables of rulers and ministers of the Napoleonic family, of Napoleon's marshals and ministers, and the concordance between the Republican and Gregorian calendars. All these are very elaborate, scholarly, full, and precise.'—**Manchester Guardian.**

'We have nothing but praise for Mr. Stephens' lucid, well-ordered narrative.'—**National Observer.**

London: 34 King Street, Covent Garden.

Crown 8vo. With Coloured Maps. 6s.

Outlines of Roman History

By H. F. PELHAM, M.A., F.S.A.,
Camden Professor of Ancient History in the University of Oxford.

'We know nothing in any language which can match his sketch for its ability, lucidity, and terseness.'—**Guardian.**

'But this is much more than a reprint, since the opportunity has been siezed to round off a lucid and scholarly narrative by many additions and alterations.' 'Its value as a popular manual of reference is heightened by an elaborate list of modern authorities, a copious index, and one or two excellent coloured maps.'—**Leeds Mercury.**

'Thus he has set himself to sketch the constitutional history of Rome, and he has performed his task with extraordinary ability. The result will be welcome to all students. We had good histories in abundance, and wars described in a fashion that would have satisfied Mr. Freeman; we had no constitutional sketch at once lucid, masterly, and brief.'—**Manchester Guardian.**

Demy 8vo. 16s.

A History of the Theories of Production and Distribution in English Political Economy, from 1776 to 1848

By EDWIN CANNAN, M.A., Balliol College, Oxford.

'It might well serve not merely as a text-book for students, but as a standard treatise on the particular branches of economics with which it deals.'—**Morning Post.**

'Apart from its interest as a history of the development of economic sciences in this country, as a clear summary of the views of the classical economists on the subjects with which it deals, Mr. Cannan's book will be of the greatest value to the student of economy.'—**Scotsman.**

'Mr. Cannan has produced a thoroughly good book, one that is indispensable to every student who desires to know under what conditions the great economists thought and wrote. He has filled an important gap in economic literature, and has turned the attention of economists to a long neglected field.'—**Annals of American Academy.**

London : 34 King Street, Covent Garden.

Demy 8vo. 5s.

Elements of Music, Harmony, and Musical Form

A Course of Study, Compiled expressly for the use of Students preparing for Examination.

By M. I. RICHARDSON.

Edited by GEORGE RISELEY, Organist of Bristol Cathedral, and Professor of the Organ at the Royal Academy of Music.

This work has been compiled with a special view to helping students who are preparing for examination. The desire has been felt to explain everything necessary to this purpose in as simple words as possible, and to avoid confusing the student by the introduction of any extraneous matter, or by a superabundance of technical terms.

The book is in three parts. The First Part treats of the elements of music, and assumes no previous knowledge of the subject on the part of the reader.

The Second Part is occupied with the consideration of the diatonic and chromatic concords and discords, suspensions, passing notes, pedals, etc., and, in fact, all that is generally placed under the head of 'Harmony.' It has been thought best to place all the diatonic chords first, and afterwards those which are chromatic.

The Third Part contains short explanations of the various musical forms, both instrumental and vocal.

Folio. 1s.

Technical Exercises for the Pianoforte

By BASIL JOHNSON,
Organist of Rugby School.

London: 34 King Street, Covent Garden.

Second Edition, Revised.   Crown 8vo.   7s. 6d.

Essays in English Literature
1780 to 1860.
By GEORGE SAINTSBURY.

Second Edition, Revised.   Crown 8vo.   7s. 6d.

Essays on French Novelists
By GEORGE SAINTSBURY.

Crown 8vo.   7s. 6d.

Miscellaneous Essays
By GEORGE SAINTSBURY.

CONTENTS.—English Prose Style—Chamfort and Rivarol—Modern English Prose (1876)—Ernest Renan—Thoughts on Republics—Saint-Evremond—Charles Baudelaire—The Young England Movement; its place in our History—A Paradox on Quinet—The Contrasts of English and French Literature—A Frame of Miniatures :—Parny, Dorat, Désaugiers, Vadé, Piron, Panard—The Present State of the English Novel (1892).

Demy 16mo.   3s. 6d. each.
Bound in paper boards, with parchment back.

The Pocket Library of English Literature
Edited by GEORGE SAINTSBURY.

VOL.   I.—TALES OF MYSTERY.
VOL. II.—POLITICAL VERSE.
VOL. III.—DEFOE'S MINOR NOVELS.
VOL. IV.—POLITICAL PAMPHLETS.

VOL. V.—SEVENTEENTH CENTURY LYRICS.
VOL. VI.—ELIZABETHAN AND JACOBEAN PAMPHLETS

The 'Seventeenth Century Lyrics' may also be had bound in Cloth, gilt lettered, 3s. 6d.

London : 34 King Street, Covent Garden.

Second Edition. Demy 16mo. 2s. 6d.

May also be had bound in Cloth extra, gilt lettered, and with gilt edges, 3s. 6d.

A Calendar of Verse

Being a Short Selection for every day in the year from Twelve Poets, one for each month.

With an Introduction by GEORGE SAINTSBURY.

'An admirable little book; perhaps the best of its kind in existence. . . . We can heartily commend this charming 'Calendar of Verse.' If we had not praised it as a string of pearls, we should have called it a book of gold.'—**Glasgow Herald.**

'Delightful to handle and to look at, delightful to read in. No extract exceeds twenty lines. The purpose of the volume is not that of introduction, much less of substitution, but rather to remind and refresh '—**Speaker.**

'A delightful volume of keynotes to English poetry by which we may strike a whole world of remembrance or discovery. It will be welcome to all those who, in these over-thoughtful days, are able, like common-sense Herrick, "to live merrily and trust in good verses."'—**Daily Chronicle.**

'The selections have been well made, and any who wish to store the mind day by day with high thoughts nobly expressed will find the book very much to their liking.'—**Yorkshire Post.**

'The dainty volume will be found a pleasant enough companion. It is prettily got up, and the inevitable introduction from the graceful pen of Mr. George Saintsbury.'—**Manchester Examiner.**

'Those in search of a very tasteful gift book could not do better than procure this "Calendar of Verse." The selections are very choice and varied, many of the best English poets having been laid under contribution from Shakespeare to William Morris.'—**Birmingham Daily Gazette.**

'The book will please poetry lovers.'—**Whitehall Review.**

Royal 16mo. 5s.

Love's Looking-Glass

A Volume of Poems.

By the Authors of 'Love in Idleness.'

'A little volume of poems entitled "Love in Idleness," was published a few years ago by three Oxford friends—Mr. J. W. Mackail, Mr. H. C. Beeching, and Mr. J. B. B. Nichols—and being speedily appreciated by all lovers of graceful and scholarly versification, it soon went out of print. The three writers now reappear in the same association in "Love's Looking-Glass," which contains the original poems, together with many additions. . . . The volume should prove as attractive as its predecessor, for the new poems it contains are not less scholarly, melodious, and graceful than the old.'—**Times.**

'This delightful volume of verse. . . . All the verse is full of an academic spirit, but it is that spirit in its happiest mood, without a touch of pedantry or artificiality.'—**Spectator.**

London : 34 King Street, Covent Garden.

Crown 8vo. With numerous Illustrations. 4s. 6d.

The Evolution of Decorative Art

An Essay upon its Origin and Development as Illustrated by the Art of Modern Races of Mankind.

By HENRY BALFOUR, M.A., F.Z.S.,

Curator of the Ethnographical Department (Pitt-Rivers Collection), University Museum, Oxford.

'Mr. Balfour, as curator of the ethnographical department of the University Museum at Oxford, which includes the wonderful collection formed by General Pitt-Rivers, should be a competent authority on the beginnings of decorative art and the evolution of the various forms which are now used in work of that nature. That he is so we can vouch after reading the extremely interesting and instructive book he has recently published. Using the specimens in the collection, he traces out and builds up a theory regarding the development of decorative art which extends from the flint implements of the prehistoric period up to the present. To those interested in the subject we can cordially recommend the book.'—**Surveyor**.

'A glance at the illustrations to Mr. Balfour's essay is enough to show that, short as it is, it is a real contribution towards the understanding of what he apologises for calling "Savage" Art. . . . Instead of inflicting upon us his ideas on Art, which might or might not have commended themselves to us, he confines himself to that which he knows, and the result is a most interesting and suggestive little book.'—**Art Journal**.

'A very suggestive essay upon the origin and development of decorative art as illustrated by the art of modern races of mankind, from the competent pen of the curator of the Pitt-Rivers collection at Oxford. It is in fact an introduction to the comparative and scientific study of æsthetics, based upon facts and not upon theory or sentiment. . . . No one has better opportunities for supplying the defect in the scientific treatment of æsthetics than the curator of the Pitt-Rivers collections.'—**Times**.

'Mr. Balfour's subject is an interesting one, and he has done it full justice. . . . The book is written in a bright style, and is eminently readable.'—**Aberdeen Journal**.

'A fascinating and scholarly monograph, which traces by a direct appeal to graduated examples—beginning with the prehistoric drawing of a reindeer found in the cave of Thayingen—the gradual development of beauty and skill in design.'—**Speaker**.

'He succeeds in making his hunt after the genealogies of various forms of decoration remarkably interesting to the general reader, and his deductions are doubtless of no little scientific value. All those who are interested in the subject should read the book for themselves.'—**Scottish Leader**.

London: 34 King Street, Covent Garden.

Crown 8vo. 7s. 6d.

The Art Teaching of John Ruskin
By W. G. COLLINGWOOD, M.A.

Crown 8vo. With Illustrations. *5s.*

The Dawn of Art in the Ancient World
An Archæological Sketch.

By WILLIAM MARTIN CONWAY.

Sometime Roscoe Professor of Art in University College, Liverpool, Victoria University.

Crown 8vo. 7s. 6d.

With Frontispiece and Thirty Illustrations in the Text.

Architecture, Mysticism, and Myth
An Essay in Comparative Architecture, being an Inquiry as to the Basis of certain Ideas common to the Sacred Buildings of many Lands.

By W. R. LETHABY.

Super Royal 4to, 324 pp. £3, 3s. net.

With One Hundred and Fifty Illustrations, of which Sixty are Full-Page, and Six Photogravure Plates.

English Pen Artists of To-day
Examples of their Work, with some Criticisms and Appreciations.

By CHARLES G. HARPER.

The English edition of this book is limited to 500 copies, and will not, under any circumstances, be reprinted in any form. Twenty-five numbered and signed copies only are issued in a special form, the illustrations hand printed upon Japanese paper and mounted. The binding of these copies is in half morocco, and the price Ten Guineas.

London: 34 King Street, Covent Garden.

Crown 8vo. 6s.

Outlines of British Colonisation

By the REV. WILLIAM PARR GRESWELL, M.A.

Author of 'Our South African Empire,' 'A History of the Dominion of Canada,' and 'Geography of Africa South of the Zambesi,' etc.

With an Introduction by the RIGHT HON. LORD BRASSEY, K.C.B.

CONTENTS.—The West Indies—Newfoundland—The Dominion of Canada—The West African Settlements—The South African Colonies—The Australasian Colonies—New Zealand—The Islands of the Pacific and Fiji—Ceylon and the Maldive Archipelago—Mauritius—Hong Kong—Appendices of Facts and Figures—Index.

Crown 8vo. 9s. net. With Illustrations.
Third Edition, Revised and Enlarged.

Health at School

Considered in its Mental, Moral, and Physical Aspects.

By CLEMENT DUKES, M.D., B.S.LOND.,
Member of the Royal College of Physicians of London;
Physician to Rugby School;
Senior Physician to the Hospital of St. Cross, Rugby;
Howard Medallist of the Royal Statistical Society of London.

London: 34 King Street, Covent Garden.

Crown 8vo. 5s.
With Maps and Illustrations.

Norway and the Norwegians
By C. F. KEARY, M.A., F.S.A.

CONTENTS.—The Land—The People—Seafaring—The Edda and its Mythology—The Sagas—History—Modern Norway—Norse Literature—The Wild Flowers of Norway—Genealogical Tables—Index.

Crown 8vo. 3s. 6d.
With a Map.

The Forest Cantons of Switzerland
Luzern, Schwyz, Uri, Unterwalden.
By J. SOWERBY, M.A.

CONTENTS.—Introduction—Topography and Characteristics—Political History—Constitutional History—Subject and Protected Lands—Ecclesiastical History—Economical Condition, Trade, etc.—Manners and Customs—Language and Dialects—Legends, Poetry, Literature, Art, etc.—Remarkable Men—Geology, Fauna, Flora, etc.—Canton and Town of Lucerne—Lake of Lucerne—Rigi and Pilatus—Schwyz: the Fortress of the Lands—Canton Uri—St. Gotthard—Canton Unterwalden—Alpine Exploration—Local Traditions—Index.

Royal 8vo. 21s. net.
With 73 Illustrations by the Author.

Rambles round Rugby
By ALFRED RIMMER.
With an Introductory Chapter on Rugby School by the REV. W. H. PAYNE SMITH.

London: 34 King Street, Covent Garden.

Two Volumes.   Crown 8vo.   7s. 6d. each.   Sold separately.

France of To-day
A Survey, Comparative and Retrospective.
By M. BETHAM EDWARDS,
Officier de L'Instruction Publique de France.
Editor of Arthur Young's 'Travels in France.'

'Your excellent work, "France of To-day," fulfils my highest expectations. It is in every way worthy of your high reputation as our first living authority on France.'—Mr. FREDERIC HARRISON.

'No living English writer, perhaps no living French writer, has a more intimate acquaintance than Miss Betham Edwards with France and the French. Like Arthur Young in the last century, she has wandered throughout the whole length and breadth of the country, and she adds to that writer's faculty of observation, broader sympathies and a greater range of intellectual cultivation. Her "France of To-day" is a delightful book, setting forth the French peasant and the French bourgeois as they are, naught extenuating nor aught setting down in malice.'—Daily News.

'The author is chiefly concerned with the France of the Republic; and within a short space she gives us a description which is undeniably interesting and readable, and can hardly fail, so far as it goes, to be instructive. A more elaborate work might convey more information, but not in a more attractive shape.'—St. James' Gazette.

'Undoubtedly a work inspired by a happy idea. Miss Betham Edwards styles her book "a survey, comparative and retrospective," and such it is, in the widest acceptation of the term.'—Saturday Review.

'Miss Betham Edwards knows more of rural life in France than probably does any other Englishwoman. The present volume describes the South-West, the South, and the East of France. No one interested in agriculture and industry will regret taking it as a companion there. We look forward eagerly to the volume which will complete the work.'—Academy.

'The characteristics of rural France, and the simplicity and strength which pervade the popular interpretation of life and duty, are charmingly indicated in these pages, and pessimists who profess to be in despair of human progress, will find not a little in this calm and philosophic survey of the social problem in modern France, to disarm their fears.'—Leeds Mercury.

'The tourist, the student of certain economical problems, and the general reader, will all find the book worth their attention.'—Yorkshire Post.

London : 34 King Street, Covent Garden.

Crown 8vo.   6s.

A Guide to Greek Tragedy

For English Readers.

By the Rev. L. CAMPBELL, LL.D.,
Emeritus Professor of Greek in the University of St. Andrews.

Crown 8vo.   4s. 6d.

The French Wars of Religion

Their Political Aspects.

By EDWARD ARMSTRONG, M.A.,
Fellow, Lecturer, and Senior Bursar of Queen's College, Oxford.

One Volume.   8vo.   18s. net.

The Iliad of Homer

Translated into English Prose by JOHN PURVES, M.A.,
Late Fellow of Balliol College, Oxford.
With an Introduction by EVELYN ABBOTT, LL.D.,
Fellow and Tutor of Balliol College, Oxford.

Crown 8vo.   6s.

A Short History of Greek Philosophy

For Students and General Readers.

By JOHN MARSHALL, M.A. Oxon., LL.D. Edin.,
Rector of the Royal High School, Edinburgh, formerly Professor of Classical Literature and Philosophy in the Yorkshire College, Leeds.

London : 34 King Street, Covent Garden.

Second Edition.   Demy 8vo.   2s. 6d.
High and Low Church
By LORD NORTON.

Being a Discussion relating to Differences of Views within the Church of England as to matters connected with its Doctrine and Practice.

Crown 8vo.   5s.
Things Old and New
Sermons and Papers.
By the Rev. G. H. FOWLER,
Late Principal of the Clergy School, Leeds.

With a Preface by the Rev. DR. TALBOT, Vicar of Leeds.

Crown 8vo.   6s.
The Religion of Humanity
And other Poems.
By ANNIE MATHESON.

Demy 16mo.   3s.
My Book of Songs and Sonnets
By MAUDE EGERTON KING.

Twelfth Thousand.   Fcap 8vo.   1s. 6d.
Popular Lessons on Cookery
By Mrs. BOYD CARPENTER.

London : 34 King Street, Covent Garden.

Crown 8vo. 3s. 6d.
With Illustrations by the Author, and Maps.

From Abraham to David

The Story of their Country and Times.

By HENRY A. HARPER,

Author of 'The Bible and Modern Discoveries,' and Member of the Executive Committee of the Palestine Exploration Fund.

'Young people, and elder ones also for the matter of that, will find great help from Mr. H. A. Harper's book, when they are studying the earlier portion of the Old Testament.'... 'Any parish priest who had got together a Bible-class of intelligent men—not boys—might, if he gave time and pains enough in preparation, utilise this little book effectively. The book, moreover, would be an excellent one for a parish religious library, and we are pleased to recommend it.'—**Church Times.**

With Maps. Crown 8vo. 7s. 6d.

History of English

A Sketch of the Origin and Development of the English Language, with Examples, down to the Present Day.

By A. C. CHAMPNEYS, M.A.,

Assistant Master at Marlborough College.

'We can cordially recommend this unpretending but useful book, which will doubtless find its way into the hands of, and be read by, many people who would be deterred by works of a more formidable appearance.'—**Oxford Magazine.**

'A scholarly and well-written introduction to the study of English philology.'—**Times.**

'It is pleasant to be able to say that this volume is very far above the ordinary level of its class.'—**Manchester Guardian.**

'A fresh and valuable book. ... A remarkably good condensation. ... The book is an exceedingly suggestive one.'—**Glasgow Herald.**

In two Volumes, sold separately. Crown 8vo, 6s. each.

The Victorian Age of English Literature

By MRS. OLIPHANT and F. R. OLIPHANT, B.A.

'These suggestive and highly interesting volumes appear to have been written with great care.'—**Spectator.**

'Mrs. Oliphant and her son have produced an interesting book. It omits few writers of any importance, and it at least endeavours to allot the *mot juste* to each of them.'—**Saturday Review.**

London: 34 King Street, Covent Garden.

Crown 8vo. 7s. 6d.

Studies in Secondary Education

Edited by ARTHUR H. D. ACLAND, M.P.,
Vice-President of the Council of Education;
and
H. LLEWELLYN SMITH, M.A., B.Sc.,

With an Introduction by the Right Hon. JAMES BRYCE, M.P.,
Chancellor of the Duchy of Lancaster.

Published under the Auspices of the National Association for the promotion of Technical and Secondary Education.

Crown 8vo. 5s.

Teachers' Guild Addresses, and the Registration of Teachers

By S. S. LAURIE, LL.D.
Professor of the Theory, History, and Art of Education in the University of Edinburgh.

CONTENTS.—The Philosophy of Mind, and the Training of Teachers—Theory, and the Curriculum of Secondary Schools—Method, and the Sunday School Teacher—Montaigne, the Rationalist—Roger Ascham, the Humanist—Comenius, the Encyclopædist and Founder of Method—The Schoolmaster and University (Day) Training Colleges—Selection from Evidence given before a Select Parliamentary Committee on a Teachers' Registration and Organisation Bill—Report of Select Committee of the House of Commons.

Crown 8vo. 7s. 6d.

Thirteen Essays on Education

Edited by the Hon. and Rev. E. LYTTELTON, M.A.,
Head Master of Haileybury College.

London: 34 King Street, Covent Garden.

Crown 8vo. With Illustrations. 1s.

Plain Handicrafts

Being Essays by Artists setting forth the Principles of Design and Established Methods of Workmanship.

A Guide to Elementary Practice.

Edited by A. H. MACKMURDO.

With a Preface by G. F. WATTS, R.A.

Demy 8vo. 1s.

Work and Overwork

In Relation to Health in Schools

An Address delivered before the Teachers' Guild, at its Fifth General Conference held in Oxford, April 1893.

By CLEMENT DUKES, M.D., B.S.LOND.

Physician to Rugby School ; Senior Physician to Rugby Hospital.

London : 34 King Street, Covent Garden.

Messrs. Rivington, Percival & Co. *issue the undermentioned Catalogues, which may be had on application:—*

Demy 8vo.

1. Complete Catalogue of all their Publications.

Crown 8vo.

2. A List of Recent Publications in General Literature.

Crown 8vo.

3. A Catalogue of Educational Works.

Demy 8vo.

4. A List of Medical Works.

RIVINGTON, PERCIVAL & CO.
34 *KING STREET, COVENT GARDEN, W.C.*
London

www.ingramcontent.com/pod-product-compliance
Lightning Source LLC
Chambersburg PA
CBHW020316240426
43673CB00039B/823